WAR AND THE LAW OF NATIONS

This book is a history of war, from the standpoint of international law, from the beginning of history to the present day. Its primary focus is on legal conceptions of war as such, rather than on the substantive or technical aspects of the law of war. It tells the story, in narrative form, of the interplay through the centuries between, on the one hand, legal ideas about war and, on the other hand, state practice in warfare. Neff covers the emergence, in various ancient societies, of an association between justice and warfare, which matured into the just-war doctrine of the Middle Ages. He then traces the decline of this conception of war in favour of a view of war as an instrument of statecraft, culminating in the evolution of what became known as the legal institution of war in the nineteenth century. There is also coverage of the much-neglected topic of measures short of war, most notably of reprisals, but also including the evolution of self-defence doctrines and practices over the years. International legal aspects of civil wars are also considered, notably the development of recognition of belligerency and of insurgency in the nineteenth century. The attempt by the League of Nations to restrict war is analysed, with an explanation of the deeper reasons for its failure and the way in which this paved the way for the substantial discarding, after the Second World War, of war as a legal institution, in favour of the alternate conception of aggression-and-self-defence. Treatment of new approaches to civil wars after 1945 and of the advent of war against terrorism brings the story to the present day.

STEPHEN C. NEFF is a Reader in Public International Law at the University of Edinburgh. He is the author of two previous books on international legal history: *Friends But No Allies: Economic Liberalism and the Law of Nations* (1990) and *The Rights and Duties of Neutrals: A General History* (2000).

WAR AND THE LAW OF NATIONS

NATIONS

A General History

by

STEPHEN C. NEFF

CAMBRIDGE
UNIVERSITY PRESS

CAMBRIDGE UNIVERSITY PRESS

Cambridge, New York, Melbourne, Madrid, Cape Town, Singapore, São Paulo

CAMBRIDGE UNIVERSITY PRESS

The Edinburgh Building, Cambridge, CB2 2RU, UK

Published in the United States of America by Cambridge University Press, New York

www.cambridge.org
Information on this title: www.cambridge.org/9780521662055

First published 2005

Printed in the United Kingdom at the University Press, Cambridge

A catalogue record for this book is available from the British Library

Library of Congress Cataloguing in Publication data

Neff, Stephen C.
War and the law of nations: a general history / by Stephen C. Neff.
p.   cm.
Includes bibliographical references and index.
ISBN 0-521-66205-2 (hardback)
1. War (International law) – History.   I. Title.

KZ6385.N44 2005
341.6–dc22   2004061769

ISBN-13 978-0-521-66205-5 hardback
ISBN-10 0-521-66205-2 hardback

To my nephews and nieces:

Eric	Delaney
John	Cameron
Alexander	Katherine Clark
Jocelyn	Thomas

War holds a great place in history, and it is not to be supposed that men will soon give it up – in spite of the protests which it arouses and the horror which it inspires – because it appears to be the only possible issue of disputes which threaten the existence of States, their liberty, their vital interests.

– Institute of International Law,
Preface to the Manual on the Laws of War on Land (1880)

CONTENTS

PREFACE

My great thanks go to my home institution, the University of Edinburgh School of Law, for sabbatical periods that were essential to the completion of this project – and also for intellectual stimulation in countless ways. The hospitality of two fine institutions was invaluable to me: the Max Planck Institute for Comparative Public and International Law, in Heidelberg, Germany (in 2000); and the George Washington University School of Law in Washington, DC (in 2003–4). For research and editorial assistance, I am grateful for the invaluable services of Dimitra Nassimpian, Ashley Theunissen, Kyle Sammin, Paul Margolis and Ozan Jaquette (and friends). In dealing with the perils of the New Technology, I have had the invaluable assistance of Roger Marlowe and of my brother Tom Neff. The following people (in prosaic alphabetical order) have assisted or inspired in manifold ways that were sometimes indirect but always much appreciated: Adnan Amkhan, Alan Boyle, Michael Byers, James Crawford, Yoram Dinstein, Thomas Giegerich, William Gilmore, Christine Gray, Susan Karamanian, Frederick Shiels, Ralph Steinhardt, Simonetta Stirling and Colin Warbrick. Only inspiration, and not errors, may be put to their charge. Finally, a most special thanks to the long-suffering staff at Cambridge University Press – to Leigh Mueller for heroic editing labours, and most specially to Finola O'Sullivan for her unique (and all too rare) combination of patience and vision.

LIST OF ABBREVIATIONS

AC	Appeal Cases (UK)
AFDI	*Annuaire Française de Droit International*
AJIL	*American Journal of International Law*
Annuaire	*Annuaire de l'Institut de Droit International*
BFSP	*British and Foreign State Papers* (UK)
Brit YB	*British Year Book of International Law*
C Rob	Admiralty Reports of Christopher Robinson (UK)
Columbia J Tr L	*Columbia Journal of Transnational Law*
CTS	*Consolidated Treaty Series*
Dods	John Dodson, Reports of Admiralty Cases (UK)
Dumont	Jean Dumont (ed.), *Corps universel diplomatique du droit des gens*
EHRR	European Human Rights Reports
F	Federal Reporter (USA)
Fed Cas	Federal Cases (USA)
FRUS	*Foreign Relations of the United States*
GAOR	General Assembly Official Records (UN)
GP	*Gazette du Palais* (France)
ICJ	International Court of Justice
ICLQ	*International and Comparative Law Quarterly*
ILM	*International Legal Materials*
ILR	International Law Reports
Inter-Am CHR	Inter-American Court of Human Rights
JDI	*Journal de Droit International*
Lieber Code	General Orders No. 100, 'Instructions for the Government of Armies of the United States in the Field' (1863), found in Hartigan, *Lieber's Code*, at 45–71
LNOJ	*League of Nations Official Journal*
LNTS	*League of Nations Treaty Series*
Moo NS	Edmund F. Moore, Reports of Cases of the Judicial Committee and the Lords of Privy Council, New Series (UK)
Op A-G	Opinions of the Attorneys-General (USA)
Parl Papers	Parliamentary Papers (UK)

PCIJ	Permanent Court of International Justice
RAI	*Recueil des arbitrages internationaux*
RDILC	*Revue de Droit International et de Législation Comparée*
Res and Dec	Resolutions and Decisions (UN)
RGDIP	*Revue Général de Droit International Public*
RIAA	Reports of International Arbitral Awards
SCOR	Security Council Official Records (UN)
Stat	Statutes at Large (USA)
UNTS	*United Nations Treaty Series*
US	United States Supreme Court Reports (USA)

INTRODUCTION

This is a history of the phenomenon of war, as viewed through the lens of international law. There is, to be sure, no such thing, strictly speaking, as *the* phenomenon of war, majestically constant throughout history and across the various human cultures. War, like other human practices, has always been a protean thing, incessantly changing its face throughout the course of recorded history in response to a dizzying array of factors – religious, technological, economic, psychological, political and so forth. And its history has been duly analysed from many of these standpoints. But the perspective of international law has been strangely neglected. Some attention (but surprisingly little) has been devoted to the history of the development of rules governing the *conduct* of war.[1] Our concern, however, is different: it is with the deeper ideas about the legal nature of war itself and how those have changed over the course of human history. This is, in short, a history of the way in which fundamental legal conceptions of war have evolved from the most distant retrievable past to the present day.

Much of our current picture of war is coloured by images of nineteenth-century conflicts between European states. This stereotype calls to mind solemnly proclaimed declarations and the summoning of ranks of uniformed troops (sometimes rather gaudily uniformed at that), in orderly arrays. These forces then engaged in combat on a field of battle against forces similarly decked out. The winning side imposed peace terms onto the other, at which point the contest was at an end; and the two nations resumed their interrupted course of friendship, though with the strategic balance between them now altered. International law provided the set of rules by which this type of contest was conducted. War of this type was seen to be so routine, so widely accepted, as to assume something of the character of a sporting contest or a ritual. In legal terms, it was said that war was an 'institution of international law'. It would be a great error to assume, however, that this view of war possessed some kind of universal validity. On the contrary, this nineteenth-century picture of war was the product of a very long historical process. Nor was it even very enduring, since many important changes lay ahead in the twentieth century (and beyond). Our task is

---

[1] For a notable example, see Best, *Humanity in Warfare.*

1

to trace the whole process of transformation of the legal nature of war, insofar as records enable us to do so, from the earliest periods of recorded history up to the present day, without falling into subservience to nineteenth-century stereotypes.

The focus of this history will not – or not exclusively – be on ideas in the abstract. It will also deal with the reciprocal impact of theory on practice and of practice on theory. We will see that, over the course of history, war has moulded law at least as surely as law has moulded war. Those who believe that ideas or doctrines have no impact on 'real life' are mistaken, though their error is an understandable one. But they are also mistaken who suppose that ideas or doctrines have a life entirely of their own, that they evolve through some kind of wholly innate dynamic in the manner of an embryo developing steadily along a predictable path into a person or an acorn into an oak tree. Indeed, even embryos must be nourished and acorns provided with soil and water. The interweaving of doctrine and practice in the area of war has been a complex and often untidy process through much (or rather all) of history – and never more than at the present day. Sometimes, as in the nineteenth century, the two have marched fairly closely in step. At other times, as in the Middle Ages, the divergence has been very wide. But never has the match been perfect. Our story therefore has always these two grand components, ever in wary (and sometimes jealous) partnership.

This story is not designed as a history of attempts to regulate the conduct of war – that is to say, it is not a history of how the rules governing warfare were drafted and agreed. Instead, it is a history of ideas about the legal nature and character of war as such. Specific rules about the waging of war have never existed in a vacuum. They have emerged from more deep-seated conceptions about the nature and role of war itself in international relations. It is those more deep-seated conceptions about war that are the subject of this narrative. For this reason, we will not immerse ourselves in the minutiae of, say, restrictions on particular weapons or categories of weapons, such as asphyxiating gases, or on the employment of certain tactics, such as assassination, ruses and perfidy, or the destruction of civilian infrastructure. Due notice will be taken of these developments, but not with the fastidious eye of the practising lawyer. Instead, our attention will be on the deeper – and more elusive – *general* conceptions of war that lawyers have entertained over the course of some twenty-five centuries. This history is therefore designed not exclusively – or indeed even primarily – for professional lawyers (although it is modestly hoped that they too will find much of interest in it). It is for those who wish to understand, in a general way, what war has meant to lawyers through the course of history, and what lawyers have made of war. Consequently, no prior knowledge of law is assumed on the part of persons embarking on this voyage.

If this history were to be truly comprehensive, it would have to be many times the length that it is. But constraining factors such as the stamina of authors, the patience of readers and the economics of the publishing industry conspire to keep this account at the level of grand theme or contour rather than of exacting detail. It is therefore sadly inevitable that certain aspects of the history of war must receive less attention here than their intrinsic interest might demand. For example, there will be comparatively little said about the material aspects of war, such as technology, logistics and strategy. Nor, sadly, will there be much about colonial warfare, which in many ways was quite distinct from conflict amongst developed (chiefly European) countries. Treatment of non-Western ideas of war will be more limited than is ideal, since they too exerted comparatively little impact on the main line of thought that produced modern international law. Nonetheless, an attempt will be made to give at least a modest insight into Islamic conceptions of war, which are of considerable intrinsic interest, as well as offering instructive comparative insights into Western ways. All too little attention will be given as well to the impact of socialist thought on war, on the ground that it made relatively little contribution to this area of law. Consideration of pacifist ideas will be largely confined to their contribution to medieval natural-law and just-war thought, with the peace movement of the nineteenth century and later left aside. In short, this account makes no claim to being an exhaustive treatment of the legal history of war. It should be considered as a pioneering exploration of the subject and not as the final word.

This pioneering expedition will take us through four historical eras. The first one runs from the misty beginnings up to about the year 1600. In that period, our focus will be on the development of an association between justice and war, culminating in the grand intellectual edifice of just-war doctrine in the European Middle Ages. In keeping with our broad-based approach, the concern will not be so much with the substance of just-war doctrine as with its general character – and particularly, of course, with the conception of war which both underpinned it and arose out of it. During this period, the dominant legal framework was that of natural law, with war seen primarily as a means of enforcing that law. Wars were fought on earth, but (at least in theory) for purposes made in heaven.

The second period, from about 1600 to 1815, was preeminently a time of transition, the great formative period of modern international law. The natural-law framework inherited from the Middle Ages continued to play an important role, but it was now supplemented in many important respects by what was sometimes called the law of *nations* or the 'voluntary law'. This period witnessed the gradual, and rather halting, metamorphosis of war from a tool of God into a tool of men. As a result, the law relating to war had a distinctly dualistic character at this time, smacking partly of nature and partly of culture. In its cultural guise, war took on many of the legal trappings that are familiar today, and which would reach their full maturity in the nineteenth century. It was a time when wars were considered to be 'perfect' if they were decked out in the fullest and most formal array, and otherwise 'imperfect'. This was a period of significant intellectual ferment, with dissident schools of legal thought concerning war arising to challenge the orthodox (or mainstream) tradition that descended from medieval just-war doctrine.

The third major period was the nineteenth century, the high tide of legal positivism. War was now seen unashamedly as a clash of rival national interests rather than as the pursuit of heavenly ideals or (more mundanely) of the rule of law. For war-makers, it was a *laissez-faire* era, with war so firmly ensconced as a routine feature of international life that it was unblushingly accorded the honourable status of an institution of international law. From this institutionalised conception of war, the natural-law or moral content was, for all practical purposes, entirely drained away. Earlier natural-law conceptions of war did not, however, perish altogether. Instead, they carried on in a sort of underground existence, outside the ornate legal framework of war properly speaking, under the sobriquet of 'measures short of war'. These comprised such actions as armed reprisals, interventions and emergency measures of various kinds. In addition, the nineteenth century brought civil wars, for the first time, into something like the mainstream of legal analysis, largely as a result of the crumbling of older conceptions of legitimacy and the rise of new aspirations for democracy and the self-determination of peoples. The result was the emergence of a body of law on the recognition of belligerency and also of something called 'insurgency'. This was one of the most striking examples of state practice taking the lead, with theory following meekly in its wake.

The fourth period, following the Great War of 1914–18, is the one in which we continue to live (if we are lucky). The outstanding feature of this era has been a reversion to the medieval just-war outlook. The process was tentative and halting at first, for the conceptual terrain had lost its familiarity to lawyers. In the interwar period, the League of Nations Covenant made (or revived) a distinction between lawful and unlawful resorts to war. But the League's approach was frustrated, in substantial part because the attempts to restrict the previously *laissez-faire* approach to war could not be made effective in the absence of similar constraints on the employment of coercive measures short of war. After the Second World War, an effort was made to correct this oversight by comprehensively prohibiting the resort to armed force – while also, at the same time, reinstating a full just-war system. The ambition was to harness war and justice more tightly together than ever before in the form of United Nations enforcement action. This led many lawyers to proclaim the death of war as a legal institution in the nineteenth-century sense. It gradually became apparent, however, that war was dispiritingly tenacious, even if it now marched under different banners than before – chiefly under the ever broader flag of self-defence (real or invented). This post-1945 period also provided ample evidence of the metamorphic power of war, as new kinds of conflict came to be 'welcomed' (if that is the right expression) into the institutional framework of war. First were wars of national liberation, as a result of anticolonial movements and Third-World pressure for racial equality. Then came the challenge of a new (or revived) scourge: international terrorism, against which the institutional weaponry of war was brought to bear. By the early twenty-first century, the practical exigencies of a coarse world showed every sign of continuing to press hard on the delicate constructions of legal theory.

To this broad story – with its dense combination of profound thought and brutal practice, of humanitarianism and savagery, of idealism and greed – we may now turn our full attention.

PART I

War as law enforcement (to 1600)

[J]ust as within a state some lawful power to punish crimes is necessary to the preservation of domestic peace; so in the world as a whole, there must exist, in order that the various states may dwell in concord, some power for the punishment of injuries inflicted by one state upon another; and this power is not to be found in any superior, for we assume that these states have no commonly acknowledged superior; therefore, the power in question must reside in the sovereign prince of the injured state . . . ; and consequently, war . . . has been instituted in place of a tribunal administering just punishment.

Francisco Suárez

The earliest instances of collective armed struggle predate recorded history and so remain the subject of speculation rather than of settled fact. Indeed, if the Christian story of the battle in heaven between the good and wicked angels be given credence, then war may be regarded as prehistoric in origin in the most thoroughgoing sense possible. Our concern, happily, is the more modest one – though difficult enough – of finding the origin not of war as such, but rather of the formation of coherent legal ideas about war. Here too, however, speculation occupies higher ground than established fact. But it seems likely that certain important, and long-lasting, distinctions were made very early on – between, for example, individual, interpersonal violence and collective, interstate conflict; or between wars against wholly foreign peoples, and conflicts against neighbouring polities which might be of the same, or very similar, language, religion and life-style. There is evidence that, between certain types of peoples, war was, for all practical purposes, a 'natural' occurrence, having something of the regularity and predictability of the seasons. The most obvious example was the eternal struggle around the great Asian steppe-lands between agricultural and nomadic ways of life, a conflict as ancient (in mythology at least) as the clash between Cain and Abel and as recent as (comparatively) the day before yesterday.[1]

A very decisive turning point must have come when war ceased to be regarded as natural or inevitable and came instead to be seen as a matter of conscious human choice. This is the point at which war may be said to have migrated from the realm of instinct or of divine command to the domain of reason. Stated in mythological terms, this was the point at which war ceased to be the domain of the impetuous and rambunctious god Ares and became instead the preserve of the cool and rational Athena. This change is unlikely to have occurred at any precisely identifiable point in the history of any civilisation, but its importance cannot be overestimated. From that time onward, it became necessary to think about war – about *offensive* war, that is – as a purposive activity. Why, in any given case, was it more important to embark upon war than to remain at peace? Various kinds of answers, from various points of view, could have been given to this question, in ancient times as today. The utilitarian, for example, may ponder whether the costs and risks were worth the expected gains. The ambitious ruler might estimate how much

---

[1] On prehistoric war, see generally Davie, *Evolution of War*; Turney-High, *Primitive War*; Keeley, *War Before Civilization*; Bohannan (ed.), *Law and Warfare*; Jonathan Haas (ed.), *The Anthropology of War* (Cambridge: Cambridge University Press, 1990); Dawson, *Origins*, at 13–33; and Ferrill, *Origins of War*.

wealth or glory or how many additional subjects a war was likely to produce. The priest may wonder whether a decision to make war would have the approval of the gods, without which there could be no possibility of success.

The real beginning of our story came when people began to think about war in terms of a general rationalistic framework that could be applied to *any* specific decision about war. Here, finally, we start to come upon something like solid historic ground for the first time. By about the middle of the first millennium BC, the Confucian tradition in China had devised a set of systematic ideas about government that was impressive not merely for the generality of its scope but also for the prominent role played in it by moral ideas. For the first time in history, a conception of war was integrated into a cohesive general structure of social, political and moral theory. War was seen as a means of last resort, to counteract antisocial conduct and reinforce the norms which integrated the society into a harmonious whole.

At about the same time, classical Greece and Rome were taking similar steps. This process began very haltingly with Plato and Aristotle. It became much more systematic in the hands of the stoics, whose views influenced Roman writers such as Cicero and Seneca in the first centuries BC and AD. The principal stoic achievement was the framework of thought known as natural law – the idea that the entire world was under the rule of a single universal, transcultural set of moral principles. This notion found some echo in later Roman law and was later clothed (though only very loosely) in a Christian garb, as one of classical antiquity's major legacies to the Middle Ages.

Our principal attention will be on this European intellectual adventure, since it was the one that gave birth, eventually and very gradually, to modern international law. The stoic-*cum*-natural-law picture of war was idealistic in the extreme. Stated with the greatest possible brevity, it was the belief that war, in its most proper and perfect sense, was a handmaiden of justice. Its purpose was not conquest or revenge or glory, but rather the vindication of the rule of law. This will be referred to as the just-war viewpoint in the broad or generic sense, although our initial focus will be on the specific form that this idea assumed under the auspices of medieval Christian society.[2] For intellectual coherence and detail of ideas about war, it is doubtful whether this achievement has ever been surpassed.

---

[2] On this generic conception of just war, see Kelsen, *Principles*, at 290.

It cannot be claimed that this idealism had much effect on the actual waging of war in the Middle Ages, when cynicism, greed and brutality had at least as wide a field of play as they ever have. Indeed, the radical contrasts of medieval times continue to amaze such distant observers as ourselves, not least in the area of war. It was an age that exalted chivalry, piety, self-discipline and altruism to the greatest heights, as evidenced in the great romances such as Amadis of Gaul, and which perhaps reached its highest pitch in the quest of the Arthurian knights for the holy grail. But the reality of medieval warfare was woefully different. It was an age of pillage, rapine, destruction and cruelty, best exemplified in the Hundred Years War between England and France in the fourteenth and fifteenth centuries. Perhaps the most apt picture of this combination of extremes was the conquest of Jerusalem in 1099, when the Christian knights indulged in a horrible massacre in liberating the tomb of their saviour, who had urged all men to turn the other cheek when smitten.[3]

If the pious theologians of the Middle Ages had little success in curbing the brutalities of contemporary warfare, it should not be thought that their ideas about the fundamental nature of war were without influence. On the contrary, the just-war framework laid down in the medieval period would endure and shape international legal conceptions of war for many centuries to come. It never entirely died out, although (as will be seen in due course) it underwent some remarkable transformations and changes of direction over time. Given that the general principles of just-war theory would be strongly revived after 1945, its first – and perhaps greatest – incarnation in the European Middle Ages is of more than 'merely' historical interest.

---

[3] On medieval warfare, see generally Contamine, *Middle Ages*; and Maurice Keen (ed.), *Medieval Warfare: A History* (Oxford: Oxford University Press, 1999).

1

Ares and Athena

There is no greater good than for a warrior to fight in a righteous war.

Bhagavad Gita[1]

Wars, then, ought not to be undertaken except for this purpose, that we may live in peace, without injustice; and once victory has been secured, those who were not cruel or savage in warfare should be spared.

Cicero[2]

Perhaps the single most obvious and widely agreed feature of war, throughout its long history, has been its character as a public and collective enterprise, arraying a whole people against a foreign foe. In the face of such an emergency, war has called typically for reserves of collective discipline and self-sacrifice beyond those required in ordinary times, thereby making it an exercise in social solidarity of the highest order. It is accordingly a great error to think of war primarily in terms of turbulence, confusion and anarchy. These factors are often present, to be sure, sometimes in very generous measure. But warfare, throughout recorded history at least, has also called for careful planning, meticulous preparation of many kinds – psychological, spiritual, logistical and so forth – as well as rational execution. That is to say, it has always been an activity that may be described, very loosely and with pardonable anachronism, as scientific. If the most obvious skills called for are those of the hardy and valiant warrior, it should not be forgotten that other, and quieter, activities also make important contributions to military victory. The arts of the priest, the tax-gatherer, the bureaucrat and the ruler are all required.

---

[1] *The Bhagavad Gita*, translated by Juan Mascaró (Harmondsworth: Penguin, 1962), at 51. (Original after 500 BC.)
[2] Cicero, *On Duties*, at 14–15.

Lawyers too have contributed to the art of war-making. But it would appear that their services were called to the colours (as it were) rather later than those others just mentioned. Systematic legal expositions of the nature and purpose of war arrived only relatively late in history. Moreover, such doctrinal writing as did emerge sometimes owed rather more to the fecund imaginations of pedants than to any close observation or analysis of state practice. This was notably the case in India, which, of the ancient civilisations, produced the largest body of writing on the subject of war. So extravagant was the Indian love of classification and definition that we find Kamandaka (the author of a treatise in the fourth century AD) meticulously identifying no fewer than sixteen different types of war, classified according to the results sought or achieved, the causes, the character of the parties engaged and so forth.[3] For the most part, though, we must look to an eclectic range of sources for evidence of the most ancient ideas about the legal character of warfare. Some of this may be gleaned from accounts of actual ancient wars. Other key indications may be extracted from religious and mythological sources.

From these various sources, supplemented by the exercise of some imagination, it is possible to discern, at least in broad outline, the ways in which warfare and justice – not, perhaps, the most obvious of intellectual soul-mates – came to be associated with one another in various ways. The most important conceptual step, or leap, occurred when war ceased to be viewed as a routine and 'natural' feature of international life, requiring no special explanation, and began instead to be seen as an exceptional and pathological state of affairs, calling for some kind of justification. In the later part of the first millennium BC, two societies, located at opposite ends of the Eurasian land mass – China in the east and the classical world of Greece and Rome in the west – took this step. It would prove to be one of the greatest intellectual leaps of human history, the reverberations from which are very much with us still.

Hallmarks of war

To articulate the essential legal features of war is, in brief terms, impossible. There is no capsule definition of war which can be said to be valid for all societies, in all conditions, through the whole of history.

---

[3] Bhatia (ed.), *International Law and Practice*, at 88. The editor comments that this classification 'does not seem to have a scientific basis at all'.

Nonetheless, it is possible to identify certain attributes of armed conflict that allowed for the growth of a body of legal ideas about war as such. We are therefore looking not so much for a definition of war as for a set of features which marked war off from other aspects of social life, so as to enable lawyers to consider it as a distinct legal phenomenon in the manner of, say, crime or succession or marriage or property. It appears that four such distinctive features of war are strong candidates in this regard. First, and perhaps most obviously, war has generally been seen as a violent conflict between collectivities or communities rather than between individuals, thereby being sharply distinguished from interpersonal violence. A second key feature is that war has been waged against foreign peoples rather than against domestic enemies. A third attribute is that war has been seen, in at least some circumstances, as being a rule-governed activity, at least to some extent and in various different senses. And finally, there has been the drawing of some kind of more or less definite boundary between times of war and times of peace. A few words on each of these points are necessary at the outset, since each has very important implications for the long-term development of the legal history of war.

Collective and public character

The single most striking feature of war is its collective nature. War is a struggle by a society as a whole, authorised and commanded by public authorities, and designed to further the over-all corporate interest of the community. As such, it is sharply contrasted with interpersonal violence such as feuding or duelling. Persons of a pacifistic temperament will be relieved to learn that some societies appear to have known only the one type of conflict and not the other. It has been contended, for example, that Eskimos and certain American Indian groups in California experienced person-to-person conflict but lacked any idea or practice of organised, collective combat.[4] War would therefore appear not – or at least not quite – to be a universal feature of the human condition. In all events, this distinction has sometimes found direct linguistic reflection. In ancient India, for example, the word *kalaha* referred to ordinary interpersonal quarrels; while the word *yuddha* was used for conflicts between societies conducted according to established rules.[5] Similarly, in ancient Rome, the term *inimicus* was applied to a personal enemy,

---

[4] Ruth Benedict, *Patterns of Culture* (London: Routledge and Kegan Paul, 1935), at 21–3.
[5] Viswanatha, *Ancient India*, at 109–11.

while *hostis* referred to the member of an enemy state, i.e., to what might be thought of as an 'official' enemy.[6]

The distinction between these two types of violence was aptly illustrated in Greek mythology, in the contrast between the two Olympian deities, Ares and Athena. Ares is often said to have been the god of war of ancient Greece, but this is not really correct. His actual sphere of activity was violence of the interpersonal sort such as the wreaking of vengeance. Homer had him denounced by Athena as a 'bloodthirsty marauder' and by Hera as a 'mindless bully who knows no law'. Zeus derided him as 'the most loathsome god on Olympus'.[7] One modern scholar, in this same vein, has dismissed him as a mere 'supernatural cut-throat'.[8] Warfare as an organised, disciplined, rationally conducted collective activity was the sphere of Athena, invariably portrayed with a helmet and breastplate. Her collective character was fittingly reflected in her role as a city-state patron *par excellence*. As Athena *Poulios*, she was the 'holder of the city'. As Athena *Pandemos* – goddess of 'all the people' – she embodied the collective ethos of the Greek city-state.

In ancient China, the Daoist war god, Guan Yü, exemplified some of these same points. He was of more humble origin than Athena, having begun his 'career' as a clearly historical mortal – as a general in the disorderly period accompanying the end of the Later Han Dynasty, in the late second and early third centuries AD. (His original vocation was the decidedly modest one of bean-curd seller.) His promotion to divine status was not specifically for valour or destructiveness alone but also for such worthy traits as mercy, wisdom, loyalty and discipline. He is therefore best seen as a sort of martial counterpart of Confucius rather than as an oriental Achilles. In fact, he was often worshipped alongside Confucius in Chinese temples as the embodiment of the wise man of action, to balance Confucius as the exemplar of contemplation and learning.

An important implication, if only an implicit one, of this first criterion for war is that, in time of war, individual concerns must be subordinated to the broader social interest. This implies an emphasis on solidarity, discipline and obedience within war-waging states. Plato voiced this concern when he lamented that one of the most serious threats to effective military strength in a state was a selfish tendency of

---

[6] Vattel, *Law of Nations*, at 259.
[7] Homer, *Iliad*, translated by Stanley Lombardo (Indianapolis: Hackett, 1997), at 5.38; 5.813; and 5.949. (Composed *c.* eighth century BC.)
[8] H. J. Rose, *Religion in Greece and Rome* (New York: Harper and Brothers, 1959), at 59.

some citizens to prefer their own private enrichment over submission to the discipline necessary to form an effective armed force.[9] Valour and bravado, he insisted, were not the principal traits sought in civilised warriors. What was needed instead was a cool-headed and disciplined devotion to the community interest. Plato was strongly of the view that soldiers must 'never do anything ... except by combined and united action as members of a group'.[10] Patriotism, in short, was less a matter of individual derring-do than of the extinction of the self in the community. The archetypal image of war in this sense was the Greek phalanx, with its forces marshalled into closely ordered ranks functioning as a single instrument of destruction. Achilles and his exploits may have been a suitable subject for stirring poetry; but he was clearly no model for a fighter in the serious business of real war.

Similar distinctions appear in other cultures. In Norse mythology, the older war god was Tiw, who was the counterpart of Athena in being associated with the collective, public-policy aspects of war. The contrasting deity, in this respect, was Odin, who was associated with fierceness, fanaticism and individual heroics. Warriors of an especially frenzied and fanatical disposition – known appropriately as *berserkers* – were particularly devoted to him. It was clear, however, that their fanaticism was valued in situations of individual, hand-to-hand combat. Grand strategy, on the other hand, remained the preserve of Tiw.[11] In India, too, much the same phenomenon was apparent in the role of Indra, the chief of the Vedic gods. He was a mighty warrior hero, vanquisher of monsters and the like. His heroism, however, was strictly individual. The true Indian war god was Skanda, who led organised hosts to victory. Skanda, incidentally, was also associated with yogic discipline and with chastity.[12] Chinese civilisation also made a similar distinction. A certain Chi You was the mythological counterpart of Ares, embodying anarchic violence, personal revenge and chaos. He was defeated by the Yellow Emperor, who exemplified the use of force on behalf of the community at large in the interest of law and order.[13]

[9] Plato, *Laws*, at 326.   [10] *Ibid.* at 489.

[11] H. R. Ellis Davidson, *Gods and Myths of Northern Europe* (Harmondsworth: Penguin, 1964), at 54–61, 66–9. Tiw, incidentally, gave his name to Tuesday – a day named for the god of war in Mediterranean as well as in Northern European cultures (as indicated by the French *mardi*, derived from Mars).

[12] Alain Daniélou, *The Gods of India: Hindu Polytheism* (New York: Inner Traditions International, 1985), at 297–300.

[13] M. E. Lewis, *Sanctioned Violence*, at 165–212.

Expressions such as 'military virtues' come readily, and rightly, to mind in this connection – obedience, patience, cooperation and discipline. These virtues of self-sacrifice, discipline and moderation were commonly seen as highly valued hallmarks of good citizenship in general – to the point that war was sometimes seen in positive terms as a means of promoting these traits, and sometimes even as the very best means of doing so. Aristotle, for example, regarded war as a force for nurturing the key virtues of justice and restraint. Times of peace and prosperity, he feared, might threaten the moral health of the body politic by tempting people to neglect these invaluable qualities.[14]

Against a foreign state

The second principal feature of war concerns the nature of the enemy side: that it be a foreign state or political entity of some kind. The Romans were very explicit on this point. The famous orator Cicero, for example, stressed that a true enemy must be a state, possessing 'a Commonwealth, a Senate-house, a treasury, a consensus of like-minded citizens'.[15] The immediate and obvious implication was sharply to distinguish war from domestic law enforcement. A criminal band, such as a pirate group, Cicero explained, 'is not counted as an enemy proper'. The distinction in his view was that an enemy state in wartime was the foe only of the particular country with which it was at war, whereas a pirate was 'the common foe of all'.[16] The later classical lawyer Ulpian, in the third century AD, was of a like mind. Enemies in a war (*hostes*), he pronounced, 'are those on whom the Roman people has publicly declared war, or who themselves [have declared war] on the Roman people'. Others were mere 'robbers or bandits'.[17]

This distinction was reflected in several concrete ways in Roman practice. For example, the formal process of declaring war was employed only against organised foreign states, not against barbarians, brigands, pirates or the like. Another distinction was that bandit groups, unlike states, did not acquire legal title to property that they captured; nor could they lawfully enslave persons whom they captured. In addition, there was no obligation to keep faith with brigands (i.e., to carry out promises, such as truce agreements, made to them), whereas faith was required to be kept with true foreign-state enemies.[18] Peace treaties were

---

[14] Aristotle, *Politics*, at 437.   [15] Cicero, *Philippics*, at 143.   [16] Cicero, *On Duties*, at 141.
[17] Justinian, *Digest*, 49.15.24.   [18] Cicero, *On Duties*, at 17–18, 141–5.

concluded only with enemy states and not with non-state groups. In reality, there has often been more flexibility in this area than theory would suggest. The Romans appear to have recognised, in practice, a kind of 'middle way' between, on the one hand, ordinary, day-to-day law enforcement and, on the other hand, war properly speaking, in order to deal with the problem of *latrociniae*, which were criminal bands that were so well organised and so powerful as to require enforcement operations on a military scale.[19] These operations, while falling short of true wars, were also legally distinct in several ways from ordinary law enforcement. Most obviously, military operations could be mounted against these enemies *en masse*, without any need for the scrupulous provision of proof of guilt in each individual case, as ordinary law enforcement required.[20]

Also excluded from the category of war by this criterion are civil conflicts. In Greece, there were two separate words used for the two types of strife: *stasis* for internal conflict, and *polemos* for war against foreigners.[21] It should be appreciated, however, that, in practice, ancient societies did not always draw the boundary between these two categories of conflict in ways that make sense to us. Foreignness was often seen in moral or cultural terms, rather than in a strictly political sense, as is now the case. That meant that foreignness could be, and often was, a matter of subtle gradation rather than of sharp distinction, with other societies being regarded as progressively more foreign with increasing distance (geographical, cultural, religious and so forth). Ancient Greece provides a ready illustration of this point. The Greek city-states saw the Hellenic world as a community with a large set of shared values and practices in the religious, linguistic and cultural spheres – with the result that fellow Greeks were not regarded as being altogether foreign. This distinction was reflected linguistically in the terms *xenoi*, referring to Greeks from other city-states, and *barbaroi*, who were fully foreign non-Greeks. A consequence of this outlook was that armed conflicts between Greek city-states were considered to be, to some extent, examples of civil strife.[22] In the words of Plato's Socrates, 'any quarrel with [fellow] Greeks they will regard as civil strife [*stasis*], because it is with their own people, and so won't call it war [*polemos*]'.[23]

---

[19] *Ibid.* at 78, n. 1.
[20] See O. F. Robinson, *The Criminal Law of Ancient Rome* (London: Duckworth, 1995), at 28–9.
[21] Plato, *Republic*, at 229. See also Price, *Thucydides*, at 67–72.
[22] See generally, to this effect, Price, *Thucydides*.
[23] Plato, *Republic*, at 227–30. On Greek attitudes to war, see Dawson, *Origins*, at 45–107.

This phenomenon was demonstrated in its most extreme form in the Chinese world, where the Confucian tradition adopted the radically cosmopolitan position that China represented the one true civilisation on earth. There was therefore, strictly speaking, no such thing as a truly 'foreign' society. There were barbarian kingdoms on the margin of Chinese society, to be sure. But these were seen as, so to speak, dark corners to which the light of Chinese civilisation had, as yet, penetrated only partially.[24] Military action against these neighbouring peoples was therefore perceived to be in the nature of law enforcement rather than of foreign war. As a consequence, China did not have – and indeed could not have had – a fully fledged conception of war in the sense identified here. The crucial conceptual divide in Chinese thought was not between domestic law enforcement and foreign war, but rather between different forms of law enforcement. Military actions carried out by subordinate officials on their own initiative were seen, in practice, as ordinary law enforcement. More serious operations, mounted by the central government, were regarded as an approximate counterpart of what other societies saw as foreign war. A notable illustration was the suppression of the large-scale and highly organised Yellow Turban Revolt of AD 184.[25]

War as a rule-governed enterprise

A third commonly supposed feature of war is that it is rule-governed. There are a number of senses in which this is so. One of these, noted above, was the requirement of subordination of individual prowess to the needs of the collectivity. War-making is commonly seen to involve chains of command, together with requirements of discipline and obedience on the part of the soldiers. More broadly, war may be seen as an enterprise calling for a high degree of rationality or understanding of the ways of the world, as an exercise more in skill and craftsmanship than in blind anger or emotion. The view of war as a skilled craft was reflected in Greek mythology in yet another of Athena's roles. In addition to being a warrior goddess and a patron of cities, she was a goddess of wisdom, and in addition a patron of craftsmen (particularly weavers). That she was a goddess of 'knowledge and skill' was attested by no less an

---

[24] Hsü, *China's Entrance*, at 8–9.
[25] Wolfram Eberhard, *A History of China* (3rd edn, Berkeley: University of California Press, 1969), at 82.

authority than Aristotle.[26] The Romans similarly were well aware of the nature of war as a skilled craft. The famous general Scipio Africanus was reported to have likened the talents of a good general to those of a surgeon, with both being careful to use force only with the utmost care.[27] Vegetius, the author of a famous and influential treatise on war of the late fourth century AD, attributed the Romans' martial success largely to their methodical and disciplined ways, which left as little as possible to chance.[28]

Much the same approach can be seen in non-Western traditions. In China, for example, we find evidence of the same outlook as early as the fifth to the third centuries BC (the exact date being highly uncertain), in the form of a famous discourse on *The Art of War* by a court official named Sun Tzu. This was a straightforward manual or handbook on how to go about winning wars, written from a wholly rationalistic viewpoint. In the Confucian classic, *The Book of Changes* (or *I Ching*), the section devoted to the army stressed the need for discipline and order in the conducting of military affairs.[29] Among the ancient Jews, similar attitudes were found, memorialised in their proverbs:

> Wisdom prevails over strength,
> knowledge over brute force;
> for wars are won by skilful strategy,
> and victory is the fruit of long planning.[30]

War has commonly been regarded as rule-governed in various other ways as well. For example, religious ritual played a prominent role in war-making in many ancient societies. Religious ceremonies of various sorts, such as sacrifices and the consulting of omens, were very common prior to important battles. Failure to observe the proper procedures meant courting defeat. In ancient China, campaigns began and ended at a temple. Religious insignia and spirit tablets accompanied the army on its travels, and 'travel sacrifices' were scrupulously performed on the march.[31] The ancient Israelites actually carried their god with them while campaigning, in the form of the Ark of the Covenant. A prominent

---

[26] Aristotle, *Politics*, at 470.   [27] Ayala, *De Jure*, at 4.

[28] See Vegetius, *Military Institutions*, at 75–6. On the Roman attitude to war, see Dawson, *Origins*, at 109–65.

[29] *The I Ching or Book of Changes*, translated by Richard Wilhelm and Cary F. Baynes (London: Routledge and Kegan Paul, 1951), at 31–5. (Written 8th–7th centuries BC and after.)

[30] 24 Proverbs 5–6.   [31] M. E. Lewis, *Sanctioned Violence*, at 23.

feature of ancient war-making was concern over the holiness of military encampments. The Old Testament provided a set of instructions to this end.[32] For the Romans too, the rational waging of war certainly included a significant spiritual dimension. One illustration was the 'taking of the auspices', in which specialist priests, known as augurs, ascertained the view of the gods regarding the resort to war. At the outset of the struggle, there was also a ceremony for the purification of the military equipment, with particular attention paid to the horses and the trumpets. Before departing from Rome, the leader of the army brandished the lance of Mars and shook sacred shields. The door to the Temple of Janus was ceremoniously opened (a curious ceremony whose meaning continues to prove elusive).[33] The assistance of the gods continued to be sought throughout the campaign. For the besieging of cities, the Romans had formulas and rituals designed to induce the enemy's gods to desert them (the *evocatio*). They also performed a *lustratio urbis* (a formal purification ceremony) around the town walls. These practices may be scorned as mere superstition, but that would be too hasty a judgement. The deeper point about them is the way in which they indicated that war-making was a methodical and painstaking affair, a far cry from a mere blind lashing out at enemies.[34]

Yet another way in which rational or rule-governed behaviour was associated with war was in the conduct of the hostilities and the notion that, to some extent at least, a duty of fair play was owed to the enemy and that, accordingly, there were restrictions on the manner in which destruction could be dealt out to the opposing side. This is a decidedly high-minded notion, associated rather more with theory than with practice; but it has a long historical pedigree. Ancient China offers perhaps the best illustration of it, where the Confucian tradition was strongly in favour of openness and fair play in war – sometimes, it must be said, at the expense of practicality. It was common for the day and place of battle to be fixed by mutual arrangement between the antagonists. Some writers held it to be a point of honour to attack the enemy at its strongest, rather than its weakest, point, on the ground that it was ignoble to exploit the weakness of another. There was even a tradition by

---

[32] See Deuteronomy 23: 9–14.

[33] Garlan, *War*, at 41–3. On the Temple of Janus, see Livy, *Early History*, at 54; and Virgil, *Aeneid*, trans. Cecil Day Lewis (Oxford: Oxford University Press, 1966), 7.607–15. (1st edn 19 BC.)

[34] Ferguson, *War and Peace*, at 9. On ritual aspects of war-making generally, see Mansfield, *Rites of War*, at 26–40.

which an army would discontinue a war when the ruler of the opposing side died. (On at least one occasion, this practice was exploited by an enemy state which successfully repelled an invasion by staging a mock funeral of its ruler!)[35]

It is hardly surprising that the idea of waging war according to rules has operated (if at all), chiefly within cultural areas in which there was a substantial set of shared values, usually of a religious nature, between the opposing sides. Ancient India provides a striking illustration. Within the world of the Vedic religion, there was a substantial recognition of moral kinship even between enemies in war. In fact, of all the ancient societies, India went the furthest, at least in the legal writings, in prescribing rules for the waging of war.[36] The Code of Manu (which evolved over a long period, largely in the first millennium AD), for example, forbade a warrior in a chariot from striking an enemy who was on foot. Enemies should not be slain when fleeing. The killing of prisoners of war was strongly condemned in favour of ransom. Certain tactics were forbidden, such as the use of concealed or barbed weapons or the killing of enemies in their sleep.[37] There was even some evidence of these rules being observed in practice. For example, the wholesale sacking of cities was uncommon in Indian warfare. There were rules too against molesting non-combatants.[38] An indication of their effectiveness was provided by a Greek observer in the third century BC, who reported seeing peasants calmly working their fields while a battle raged nearby.[39]

In Greece, the position was broadly similar to that of India. That is to say that, within the Greek cultural world, there was a belief that war should be waged with at least a certain degree of moderation. It was even possible for belligerent states to agree on the rules of war before the hostilities were under way, in the manner of a duel. The geographer Strabo reported, for example – though only long after the asserted fact – that, in the Lelantine War of the late eighth century BC, the warring states of Khalkís and Eretria agreed on the conditions under which they would conduct the war. Specifically, they agreed that long-range missiles would not be used.[40] In a testimony both to the warlike character of the Greeks and to their feeling of cultural unity, the cities of the Amphictyonic League of Delphi agreed that, in the event of war, the combatant states

---

[35] M. E. Lewis, *Sanctioned Violence*, at 38–9, 65–7.   [36] See Armour, 'Customs of War'.
[37] Anonymous, *Laws of Manu*, at 137–8.   [38] Basham, *Wonder*, at 127.   [39] *Ibid.* at 128.
[40] 5 Strabo, *Geography*, trans. Horace Leonard Jones (London: William Heinemann, 1928), at 19.

would refrain from either destroying cities or cutting off water supplies.[41] Plato held that wars amongst Greeks should be fought in a limited manner. Both sides should be allowed to recover and bury their dead after a battle. Battle should be waged only against the armed forces of the other side, not against the population in general. In such intra-Greek conflicts, the belligerents ought to 'press their quarrel only until the guilty minority are brought to justice by the innocent victims'. There should be no ravaging and burning of private homes, nor should fellow Greeks be sold into slavery.[42]

This idea of fair play towards the enemy was also a prominent feature of Roman practice (and legend). Roman tradition held up Camillus, the hero of Rome's early wars against neighbouring Veii, as the exemplar of restraint and mercy in war-making. As late as the sixteenth century, he received the plaudits of Alberico Gentili as 'that general most observant of the laws of war and of justice in war'.[43] The idea of moral equivalence between warring states was also apparent in Cicero's confident assertion that enemies in war had 'some respect for religion and for established custom' and would accordingly refrain from desecrating temples – in contrast to mere 'piratical savages' who observed no such niceties.[44] Most notably, the Romans insisted that promises made even to enemies in war must be scrupulously kept. Cicero pointed with hearty approval to the example of Regulus, a Roman general who was captured in 255 BC by the Carthaginians during the First Punic War. He was allowed by his captors to return to Rome to take part in a debate over whether Rome would exchange a group of Carthaginian prisoners for himself. He gave his solemn word that, if the Roman Senate did not agree to the exchange, then he would return to his captivity in Carthage. Once in Rome, Regulus spoke out, successfully, against the proffered prisoner exchange. Then, true to his word, he returned to his own captivity in Carthage, spurning his family's tearful pleas for him to remain in Rome.[45]

We should not, however, be deceived into believing that chivalrous practices were anything like a universal feature of war. Against truly foreign foes, such as barbarians, scruples about war methods were often conspicuously absent. In Roman history, the outstanding example of

[41] Robert A. Bauslaugh, *The Concept of Neutrality in Classical Greece* (Berkeley: University of California Press, 1991), at 54.

[42] Plato, *Republic*, at 227–30.   [43] Gentili, *Law of War*, at 310.

[44] 2 Cicero, *The Verrine Orations*, trans. L. H. G. Greenwood (London: William Heinemann, 1935), at 431.

[45] Cicero, *On Duties*, at 138–43.

unrestrained, if not downright genocidal, warfare was Julius Caesar's wholesale slaughter of Gauls in his campaign of conquest in the first century BC. Moreover, the rational craftsman's approach to war could easily work against ideas of restraint in war, a point dramatically illustrated in India by the *Arthaśāstra* of Kautilya. This was a manual of statesmanship – including the waging of war – written in the third century BC by a Brahmin minister in the service of a monarch of the Maurya Dynasty. In sharpest contrast to the religiously based ideas of the Code of Manu, this work took a coldly utilitarian approach to warmaking, showing no regard for the tournament style of combat. Kautilya unapologetically favoured measures of stealth and deception to bring victory – including the copious employment of spies, a liberal resort to ruses and deceptions (such as the booby-trapping of temples), the use of poison, the destroying of wells and the sowing of dissension in the enemy's ranks.[46] The struggle for moderation in war has been a long one – and one whose successes even to the present day are decidedly modest. Perhaps the most that can confidently be said is that the struggle has ancient roots.

Marking off peace from war

Before there could be any systematic thought devoted to war as a distinct sphere of human endeavour, it was necessary that war be contrasted with something that was *not* war. That war and peace are opposite to one another may seem the most obvious proposition imaginable. But it is important to appreciate that this contrast has not been a universal feature of human social life. In particular, in situations of endemic or constant conflict between two peoples, such a contrast is not possible, any more than a science of meteorology would be possible in a society in which the weather never varied. In such a case, war would be, in a certain conceptual sense, invisible by virtue of its very ubiquity. There could be no distinct 'institution' or 'state' of war, no set of rules peculiar to war, no such thing as a declaration of war, no such thing as war aims. The clearest example of endemic conflict from the classical world was the relation between civilised and barbarian states, which was commonly seen as one of natural and permanent hostility. Plato took this view,

---

[46] Kautilya, *Arthaśāstra*, at 367–8. Our present text, which was only rediscovered in 1905 after many centuries of oblivion, bears evidence of emendation later than the third century BC.

holding that, between the Greeks and the barbarians, there was more or less natural and permanent war.[47] The Arabs had a specific label for endemic conflict consisting of interminable raiding and counter-raiding: *razzia*, which they clearly distinguished from formal war.

The practice of making some kind of explicit division between times of war and times of peace was fairly widespread amongst societies all over the world, even amongst prehistoric peoples, although the particular procedures adopted naturally varied greatly.[48] In precolonial Africa, the Fante sent a herald to the enemy to declare war, sometimes even to arrange the time and place for a battle. Various southeastern Nigerian peoples indicated the existence of war by laying plantain leaves and piles of powder and shot on paths that would be travelled by their enemies-to-be.[49] From pre-Columbian America come reports of the initiation of war by a chief of the Michoacán area. A feast was held; and at midnight, a priest burned a number of balls of tobacco, invoking certain deities. Two men were then dispatched to place two balls of tobacco, together with two blood-stained arrows and some eagle feathers, in the territory of the enemy (or in the house of the enemy chief, or in the enemy's chief city or temple).[50] Other methods of indicating the outbreak of war have included the seizure of cattle and the lighting of beacon fires.[51]

In more developed societies, the rituals were sometimes decidedly more elaborate. The war-initiation ritual of the Aztecs of pre-Hispanic Mexico offers one of the most striking illustrations. It was a three-stage process. First, ambassadors were dispatched, with a gift of shields and swords, to give the other side an opportunity to submit peaceably to Aztec rule. Twenty days were allotted for consideration of this offer. If there was no response, or if the response was negative, then the process was repeated, and a second mission sent. This time, the Aztec ambassadors anointed the right arm and head of the other ruler, set a tuft of feathers on his head and gave a further gift of weapons. Another twenty-day interval followed. If there was still no resolution, then a third mission was sent, which addressed a warning primarily to the warriors of

---

[47] Plato, *Republic*, at 229.
[48] For an informative survey of methods of declaration of war amongst primitive peoples, see Davie, *Evolution of War*, at 292–6.
[49] R. S. Smith, *Warfare*, at 53–4.
[50] J. Eric S. Thompson, *Maya History and Religion* (Norman, Okla.: University of Oklahoma Press, 1970), at 121.
[51] Viswanatha, *Ancient India*, at 129.

the other side rather than to its rulers. Once again, weapons were given as a gift. Only if this third request-*cum*-warning produced no result did the Aztecs commence military operations – having deliberately foregone any possibility of surprise and having even supplied their foes with weapons.[52]

In ancient India, officials called *dutas* were charged with delivering ultimatums to the other side. Their Hellenic counterparts were heralds, whose messages apparently were expected to be delivered in dulcet tones, since the Greek word for herald, *keryx*, comes from the verb meaning 'to sing'.[53] Over time, the mere presence of heralds was taken to signify the existence of a war.[54] Another interesting Greek custom was to send a lamb across the frontier into the territory of the enemy-to-be, signifying an intention to reduce that state's territory to mere pasture-land.[55]

We are best informed about the Roman practice. In the early history of Rome, when conflicts were with the neighbouring peoples of central Italy, there seems to have been no clear demarcation between war and peace. Conflicts with the nearby Volscians and Aequians, in particular, appear, on the evidence of Livy, to have been more or less constant. Later, however, during the Republican period, Rome devised (or borrowed) an elaborately ritualistic two-stage process for declaring war (*bellum indicere*) against foreign states. The central role was played by a twenty-member body called the College of Fetials.[56] The first step was a formal request for satisfaction (*rerum repetitio*) delivered by four fetials to the other state, which then had thirty days in which to respond. This formal demand (which was not expected to be acceded to) amounted, in effect, to an official statement of the *casus belli* of the conflict. The actual act of declaration took place three days later (i.e., on the thirty-third day after the delivery of the *rerum repetitio*). This was made by the Senate, ratified by the Centurial Assembly and then communicated to the opposing state by having the fetials hurl a magical spear, dipped in blood or pointed with iron, into the enemy's territory. Cicero praised this fetial process as constituting 'a fair

---

[52] Soustelle, *Daily Life*, at 206–8.

[53] Contemporary epithets described them as 'quick', 'clear-voiced', 'sonorous'. Garlan, *War*, at 44.

[54] See Bederman, *International Law*, at 213–14.   [55] Garlan, *War*, at 48.

[56] For the best known early account of the fetial procedure, the origin of which was attributed to Ancus Marcius, the third king of Rome, see Livy, *Early History*, at 69–71. For recent accounts and analyses, see Wiedemann, 'Fetiales'; and Watson, *International Law*.

code of warfare'.[57] One point that may be noted about the Roman practice was that the expression 'declaration of war' (*indictio belli*) was actually not so precise as one might wish. It could refer to the announcement of war *either* to the Roman people themselves – officially warning them that challenging times were now at hand – *or* to the enemy side. It will be seen that this ambiguity was to be a continuing feature of international law and practice.

In later times, the formalities of the fetial procedure were gradually dispensed with. One problem was that the ritual was difficult to perform when the enemy was located far from Rome, since it was then inconvenient for the fetials to travel to the enemy's frontier for the hurling of the spear. This was remedied, at first, by means of a legal fiction. A spot in the Roman forum was designated as 'enemy territory' for the purpose of the fetial procedure, and the spear was then thrown at that designated patch of ground. A second change made, probably in the second half of the third century BC, was for the *rerum repetitio* and the declaration to be combined into a single process and performed by legates appointed by the Senate instead of by the fetials. These legates were empowered to present the formal demands to the other side and then to inform the other side straight away that Rome was making war against it in the event of their rejection.[58] The obsolescence of the fetial procedure did not, however, mean the abandonment of the idea that wars must be properly declared. A formal declaration process of some kind continued to be insisted on. Cicero, for example, pronounced that '[n]o war is just unless it is waged after a formal demand for restoration, or unless it has been formally announced and declared beforehand'.[59]

The significance of these various rules for the commencing of wars should not be exaggerated. It should be noted, for one thing, that the mechanics of declaring war were set out in the *domestic* laws of the countries concerned, and so cannot be said to constitute rules of international law in the true sense. In addition, it should not be supposed that formal declarations of war were anything like universal, even in societies which had well-developed procedures. We are informed of an attack by Aegina against Athens in about 500 BC, which was not preceded by

---

[57] Cicero, *On Duties*, at 15.

[58] Rich, *Declaring War*, at 57. There were a few occasions in which the fetial procedures were revived. The latest would appear to have been in AD 178 by Emperor Marcus Aurelius. Watson, *International Law*, at 60.

[59] Cicero, *On Duties*, at 15–16; and Cicero, *Republic*, at 69.

any formal declaration.[60] Nor, apparently, was it thought necessary to have a formal declaration of war in the case of certain small-scale, one-off operations of a punitive character.[61] Declarations were also thought not to be required against barbarian groups. No declaration of war, for example, preceded Caesar's conquest of Gaul in the first century BC. Despite these reservations, the implications for international law of such a sharp demarcation of the boundary between war and peace were immense. Most outstandingly, it made the idea of a *state* of war easy to envisage. In such a conception, war would cease to reside in the actual physical clash of the opposing sides, but instead would become a period of time whose commencement and termination points were precisely identified. This notion would not be clearly articulated until the seventeenth century AD, but the conceptual seeds of it clearly existed much earlier.

These various features of war just identified should not be thought of as anything like a systematic empirical account of warfare in ancient history. Instead, they should be seen as key components of the *idea* of war, in the *most* general terms, as it began to reach a fairly advanced stage in various ancient societies. The number of real wars which actually embodied all of these features to a high degree was probably very small indeed in practice. The principal point to grasp, however, is that this conception of war – even though highly idealised – would play a powerful role in moulding legal ideas about war over the coming centuries. Lawyers did not create from a vacuum, or set out rules on war in the abstract. They worked with conceptions that were given to them from the real world. But it must always be appreciated that the 'real' world contains ideas as well as practices. With regard to war, the ideas that the real world contained were very powerful ones, which exerted a hold over the human imagination to the present day (and doubtless far beyond). And none of these was more powerful, more tenacious or more far-reaching than what will be termed the concept of the just war in the generic sense.

War as an instrument of justice

One of the most momentous ideas in human history was the notion that war could and should be employed in a socially productive fashion, for the subduing of evil and the promotion of good – that it should be an instrument of law, rather than of greed or ambition. This is the just-war

---

[60] Herodotus, *Histories*, at 369–70.   [61] Harris, *War and Imperialism*, at 174.

doctrine, stated in its broadest terms. It rests upon a key underlying idea: that the normal condition of international affairs is one of peace.[62] This is the notion that international life is fundamentally orderly, notwithstanding the swirling dance of power politics on the surface. This deeper-level order might be either intellectually rich or threadbare as the case may be. That is to say, it might consist of little or nothing beyond a bare prohibition against resorting to war in general terms. Or it might consist of a dense thicket of detailed rules of conduct applicable to a wide range of situations, with a prohibition against war being only one component part of the broader package. In all events, just-war doctrine then sets out the conditions under which, as an exception to the general rule, it *is* permissible to resort to armed force. Broadly speaking, just-war theories permit armed force to be used either for the vindication of legal rights or, more generally, in an altruistic fashion for the promotion of general community values.

Universal peace

The idea of peace as the normal condition of human affairs was far from a natural one. For a very long time, the prevailing view in the ancient world was that war was simply a constant feature of the political landscape, as routine as the coming and going of the seasons of the year. Plato, in *The Laws*, had one of his speakers voice what was probably a common opinion: that peace was 'only a fiction' and that 'all states by nature are fighting an undeclared war against every other state'.[63] Aristotle believed, famously, that the human species was intrinsically social in nature; but this intrinsic sociality was taken no further than the level of the city-state.[64] Relations between independent city-states were therefore regarded as inherently competitive. With barbarians especially, peace was seen to be impossible in principle. In Aristotle's view, conflicts against barbarians were 'by nature just'. He compared war against barbarians to the use of force against wild beasts or against rebellious or disobedient persons – 'such men as are by nature intended to be ruled over but refuse', as he put it.[65] Even within the Greek city-state world, however, conflict was so common as to be entirely unremarkable. Even Plato's ideal republic was a society strongly geared

---

[62] See generally Zampaglione, *Idea of Peace*.   [63] Plato, *Laws*, at 47.
[64] Aristotle, *Politics*, at 59.   [65] *Ibid.* at 79.

towards war-waging, with defence from enemies being one of the fore-most, if mundane, tasks of the philosopher-kings. This matter-of-fact acceptance of the constancy of warfare goes far to explain why even thinkers as profound as Plato and Aristotle gave so little serious thought to war.[66]

The position of Rome, at least during its early history, was similar to that of Greece. In its early period of expansion, Rome considered itself, at least in principle, to be permanently at war with any state with which it did not have a treaty of friendship or alliance (*foedus*). The chief Roman conceptual division was therefore not between a 'state of peace' and a 'state of war' in the modern sense, but rather between a state of passive or notional hostility as opposed to a state of *active* conflict. Moreover, the word *pax*, normally translated as 'peace', actually referred to the condition prevailing after a successful war. Cognate with the word 'pact', *pax* was an agreement to abstain from active hostilities.[67] Traces of this brooding and suspicious conception of peace were in evidence well into the imperial period. The Roman lawyer Pomponius, in the second century AD, while conceding that states which did not have treaties with Rome were 'not precisely ene-mies', pointed out that certain marks of war were nonetheless present. Specifically, if any Roman property passed into the hands of such states, then the Roman owner would lose title to it, as in a war. Similarly, a Roman free person who was captured by such a state became a slave.[68]

The conception that peace was the natural condition of the world would seem to have been first articulated in China, in the Confucian tradition. On this view, the world was, at least in principle, a single ordered society, with the terrestrial world functioning as a sort of mirror of its heavenly counterpart, with all of its parts in (ideally) perfect harmony. Some parts of this great cosmos, of course, were more harmonious and advanced than others. In particular, China itself (naturally) was seen as the centre of civilisation, the 'Middle Kingdom' with barbarian states surrounding it on all sides. With China as the embodiment of civilised life, its emperor possessed a sort of natural-law entitlement, again in principle, to rule the entire world (*Tianxia*, or 'all under Heaven'). From this perspective, there was no room for

---

[66] See Ostwald, 'Peace and War'.
[67] Harris, *War and Imperialism*, at 35; Bainton, 'Early Church', at 207; and Ziegler, 'Friedensverträge'.
[68] Justinian, *Digest*, 49.15.5.

a Hellenic-style conception of natural and perpetual war against the outlying barbarian kingdoms. Armed action was necessary on specific occasions for specific purposes, such as the subduing of rebellions or for the protection of the Middle Kingdom from invasion. But these were seen to be in the nature of emergency corrective measures, designed to restore the turbulent or dysfunctional elements to their natural place in the grand cosmic scheme of things. There was no idea of the world as being *intrinsically* turbulent or lawless.[69] According to the Confucian view, therefore, even barbarians were not utterly alien. They were merely imperfectly integrated into the great global order. The best way of dealing with them was gradually to reform them by setting a good example of what a fully civilised society was like. This normal peaceful relation with the neighbouring barbarian states was symbolised by the ritualistic exchange of 'gifts' or 'tribute' between the Chinese government and envoys from the barbarian states.

Not until later did similar ideas begin to take hold in the West. It was the stoic philosophers who were chiefly responsible for this development, beginning in about the third century BC. Most outstandingly, the stoics elaborated the concept of a law of nature or natural law (*jus naturalae*), which was a set of universal norms, applicable to all nations and peoples at all times. The idea – one of the most powerful and far-reaching ever devised by humankind – goes back at least as far as Aristotle, who posited the existence of a body of general laws 'which everywhere has the same force and does not exist by people's thinking this or that'.[70] He also described this general law of nature as comprising 'all those unwritten principles which are supposed to be acknowledged everywhere'.[71]

This core idea of a universal law of nature was taken much further and developed more systematically by the stoics after Aristotle's death. They propounded a thoroughgoing cosmopolitan theory, which held the whole of humankind to comprise a single moral, if not political, society.[72] In the words of Cicero, who was strongly influenced by stoicism on this point, 'the whole human race is seen to be knit together'

---

[69] Hsu, *China's Entrance*, at 8–9. See also Charles O. Hucker, *China's Imperial Past: An Introduction to Chinese History and Culture* (Stanford: Stanford University Press, 1975), at 55–7, 78–86.

[70] Aristotle, *Ethics*, at 124.

[71] Aristotle, *Rhetoric*, in *The Basic Works of Aristotle*, ed. Richard McKeon (New York: Random House, 1941), at 1359.

[72] See, for example, Marcus Aurelius, *Meditations*, trans. Gregory Hays (London: Weidenfeld and Nicolson, 2003), at 38–9. (Written *c.* 175.)

by this universal natural law.[73] He insisted that '[t]here is one, single justice. It binds together human society and has been established by one, single, law'.[74] It is important to note that this idea of natural law did not entail any conception, even in theory, of any universal *political* sovereignty, as in the Chinese case. Even at the height of the Roman Empire's power, Europeans never adopted the Chinese view that the Roman state embraced literally the entire world. The supreme ruling force in the world, in the stoic view, was not an emperor but rather the law of nature as such, which was supreme by virtue of its own innate power. It ruled the world by the force of reason, not by the strength of swords.

This cosmopolitan outlook of the stoics naturally entailed a rejection of the earlier idea of the universe as a theatre of perpetual strife. In a global society that was orderly and rational, living at all times under the sway of a universal law, conflict and disorder must inevitably be seen as a pathological state of affairs, a sign that something was, somehow, 'wrong' – but at the same time repairable, once the rule of natural law was brought fully to bear. There was no room in such a philosophy for permanent or endemic war. On the contrary, it was now important to realise that peace must never be lost sight of, even in cases where war occurred. As Cicero put it, war 'should always be undertaken in such a way that one is seen to be aiming only at peace'.[75]

It is well to take note of a very important difference between the Chinese and the Western notions of cosmopolitanism and world peace, which would have a powerful, if subtle, impact on the historical experience of the human species. The Western conception of cosmopolitanism would ultimately become the basis of our modern international law. The Chinese one would not, because, in contrast to its Western counterpart, it was neither international nor legal. It was not international because the Chinese version of cosmopolitanism was, in a manner of speaking, too radical. In positing that the whole world was a single *political* community, China effectively rejected any notion of a world of *independent* political communities bound together by the rule of law rather than by the sovereignty of a single emperor. The Chinese can therefore be said to have been the pioneers of the concept of world government, but not of international law as it later came to be known. Chinese cosmopolitanism was, ironically, provincialism writ large, without the element of pluralism that would become so essential a feature of the

---

[73] Cicero, *Laws*, at 108.   [74] *Ibid.* at 112.   [75] Cicero, *On Duties*, at 32.

aptly named law of nations that Europeans would later devise. In addition, the Chinese approach to the marriage of justice and war was not
legal in character, but moral. The Confucian tradition had a low view
of law as an instrument of social control, electing to rely instead on
authoritarian rule by a sovereign of unimpeachable benevolence. For
these reasons, the Chinese possessed the notion of a global moral community long before the West, but they did not use it to produce a body of
international law combining justice and war.

The natural-law outlook of the stoic philosophers, for all of its
sophisticated idealism, was too cerebral a system to attract anything
like widespread adherence. The honour of propounding universal moral
principles would fall, instead, to the great universal religions, most
notably to Christianity, which had a pacifist strain powerful enough
to match, or even exceed, that of Confucianism in China. And it would
be under the general auspices of Christianity that pacifist thought (if not
practice) would reach its highest pitch prior to the twentieth century.
Before turning to the medieval Christian version of peace, with its many
implications, we must take note of the kinds of justifications for war that
were offered by pre-Christian societies, since the continuity with medieval thought in that area would prove to be very strong.

War in the name of justice

The immediate implication of the idea of peace as a general condition of
the world at large, with war as an exception, was that any resort to war
required at least some kind of affirmative justification: specifically, a
belief that the only acceptable reason for undertaking war was to uphold
some larger community ideal, such as the rule of law. This was the
essence of what will be referred to as a just-war outlook in the generic
sense of that term. Mythology, once again, provides some instructive
early examples, though sometimes very crude ones. Some ancient gods
achieved renown for doing battle in the name of order against the chaos –
with chaos embodied in the form of a frightful monster. We can point to
Zeus's victory over Typheus in Greek mythology, or Marduk's triumph
over Tiamat in Mesopotamia as ready examples. Other gods did battle
against various forms of human wickedness. The Egyptian hero-god
Horus, for example, had a number of war attributes, including the
punishment of evil-doing. In Mesopotamian religion, the chief active
god, Enlil, was in part a god of war. His war functions, however, were
part of a larger persona. He was actually a sort of guardian and enforcer

of the divine laws of the universe, whose wrath was reserved for violators of these laws. In Norse religion, the original war god, Tiw, was also a god of justice. In Greece, Zeus had many war functions, but he was also the god who watched over the making and keeping of oaths. Much the same was true of Roman Jupiter. He was, amongst many other things, a sort of patron deity of the Roman armies (which bore his symbol of the eagle on their shields), and at the same time, like Zeus, a guardian of oaths. In the Zoroastrian faith as well, Mithra, one of the foremost gods, was similarly a deity both of war and of justice. He also presided over the tribunal which weighed the good and evil deeds of deceased persons prior to their dispatch to Paradise or Hell (as the case may be).[76]

Similar ideas were abroad in the sublunar world, where it was often seen as important to have at least a colourable claim to a just cause before taking up the sword. An early illustration is found in Thucydides' account of the opening stages of the Peloponnesian War in the late fifth century BC. He clearly considered the war to have been, at its root, a power struggle made inevitable by the steady growth of Athenian power. But in the diplomatic discussions leading up to the war, accusations of wrong-doing in such forms as treaty violations and wanton aggression figured prominently.[77] In other ancient civilisations too, it was common for states that contemplated waging offensive war to produce a plausible allegation of misconduct by their foes that would be generally acknowledged.

One common justification for war was the mistreatment of nationals. The Aztecs, for example, resorted to war over the mistreatment of travelling merchants, and also (rather more expansively) over a refusal by foreign peoples to enter into trading relations with them.[78] The molesting of diplomatic envoys was a common *casus belli* in the ancient world. In Mesopotamia, for instance, the deliberate insulting of a diplomat was treated as actually constituting a declaration of war.[79] The Bible relates that, in ancient Israel, David made war against the Ammonites because of their brutality towards Israeli envoys.[80] In Rome too, the mistreatment of ambassadors was a common justification for war, as

---

[76] Mary Boyce, *Zoroastrians: Their Religious Beliefs and Practices* (London: Routledge, 1979), at 7–10, 27.
[77] Thucydides, *Peloponnesian War*, at 48–62, 72–82.
[78] Soustelle, *Daily Life*, at 203–4.
[79] Linda S. Frey and Marsha L. Frey, *The History of Diplomatic Immunity* (Columbus, Ohio: Ohio State University Press, 1999), at 20.
[80] 2 Samuel 10: 1–7. See also Good, 'Just War'.

were self-defence claims.[81] Even in one of the most egregious examples of aggressive war, the conquest of Gaul in the first century BC, Julius Caesar was careful to impute various acts of wrongdoing to the Gauls as the justification for his invasion.[82]

There can be no doubt that many, if not all, of these formal causes were merely 'cover stories' given for public consumption or for formal purposes, with the true cause of the conflict lying elsewhere, in such considerations as political rivalry, greed for power and the like. The Greek historian Polybius, in commenting on the matter, carefully distinguished 'pretexts' for wars from true 'causes'.[83] Self-defence claims were particularly subject to manipulation, as Rome demonstrated by sometimes deliberately allying itself with small states which were enemies of Rome's intended foe – and then declaring war to assist its new-minted ally. This device was used in a range of instances, from the Third Samnite War of 298–290 BC (in aid of the Lucanians) to the war against Mithradates VI of Pontus in 88 BC (to restore claimants to the thrones of Bithynia and Cappadocia).[84]

In this connection, it is interesting to note the assessments made, after the fact, of Alexander the Great's conquests of the fourth century BC. According to Arrian, Alexander carefully itemised his grievances against the Persians, referring to the invasion of Greece a century and a half earlier, and also accusing the present Persian king, Darius, of complicity in the assassination of his father and of aiding rebels against Alexander within Greece.[85] Later writers, however, expressed grave doubts as to the legitimacy of the mighty warrior's conquests. Polybius, for example, maintained that, in reality, Alexander was motivated by nothing more than a thirst for glory, combined with a shrewd awareness of the weakness of his foes.[86] Seneca, the dramatist and stoic essayist, echoed this conclusion in the first century AD, contrasting Alexander unfavourably, as a 'robber and looter of nations', with Hercules, who (despite his somewhat infirm basis in historical fact) had struggled selflessly for the

---

[81] On the justifications for Rome's various wars, see Harris, *War and Imperialism*, at 163–254; and Rich, *Declaring War*, at 109–18.

[82] Julius Caesar, *The Conquest of Gaul*, trans. S. A. Handford (Harmondsworth: Penguin, 1951), at 28–38. Not everyone was convinced. See Harris, *War and Imperialism*, at 174–5.

[83] Polybius, *Rise*, at 183–5.

[84] For a host of Roman examples of this technique, see Harris, *War and Imperialism*, at 175–254.

[85] Arrian, *The Campaigns of Alexander*, trans. Aubrey de Sélincourt (Harmondsworth: Penguin, 1971), at 127–8.

[86] Polybius, *Rise*, at 183–5.

benefit of the general public against evils of various kinds.[87] Seneca's views were endorsed by his nephew, the epic poet-*cum*-historian Lucan, who denounced Alexander as a mere robber.[88] Unfavourable assessments of Alexander in this vein continued to be a staple of European natural-law writing.[89]

There were, however, some more encouraging reports from the classical world. Herodotus related that, in the midst of a war between Sparta and Athens around 500 BC, Corinth withdrew its forces from the Spartan side because of a fear that it might be acting wrongfully, thereby bringing a halt to a Spartan invasion of Attica.[90] More striking (and also better documented) is the example of a legal claim by one state against another for aggression. In 240 BC, the Achean League took advantage of a succession crisis in Argos to invade the city-state with a view to overthrowing its government. The attempt failed; and Argos made a legal claim against the League for this act of aggression, with the city-state of Mantinea acting as the arbitrator. It is not clear whether the League consented to these proceedings, but the result was that Mantinea upheld Argos's claim and assessed a token fine of half a talent against the League.[91] In Roman history, there were even instances in which Rome actually declined to wage war because the necessary provocation was absent. In 192 BC, it decided against declaring war on the Seleucid Empire for lack of a sufficient reason. (Later that year, its ruler, Antiochus III, thoughtfully filled in this awkward lacuna by invading Rome's Greek sphere of influence.)[92]

Despite all of this evidence of concern over the justice of resorting to war, it cannot be said that the Romans produced any very elaborate thought on the subject. Some very brief remarks by Cicero in the first century BC are the most that we have on the relation of war and justice.

---

[87] Seneca, 'On Favours', in *Moral and Political Essays*, trans. John M. Cooper and J. F. Procopé (Cambridge: Cambridge University Press, 1995), at 208–9. See also Cicero, *On Duties*, at 109.

[88] Lucan, *Pharsalia*, trans. J. D. Duff (Cambridge, Mass.: Harvard University Press, 1927), at 591–3. On Alexander's *casus belli* against Persia, see Michael Austin, 'Alexander and the Macedonian Invasion of Asia: Aspects of the Historiography of War and Empire in Antiquity', in Rich and Shipley (eds.), *War and Society*, at 197–223.

[89] See, for example, Grotius, *War and Peace*, at 170, 546, 505.

[90] Herodotus, *Histories*, at 367.

[91] Sheila L. Ager, *Interstate Arbitrations in the Greek World, 337–90 BC* (Berkeley: University of California Press, 1996), at 118–19. A talent was a very large currency unit (or rather unit of weight), consisting of twenty-five kilograms of silver.

[92] Rich, *Declaring War*, at 87–8.

He identified two just causes of war: punishment of the enemy for wrongdoing, and the repelling of an attack.[93] In the coming centuries, however, European thought would become very considerably more elaborate on this subject. This development was made possible by the fact that Christian doctrine brought the key idea of peace as the normal condition of humanity to a larger audience, and with greater emotional force, than the stoic philosophers ever achieved in their wildest dreams.

[93] Cicero, *Republic*, at 69.

2

Loving enemies and hating sin

Let us do evil, that good may come.

St Paul[1]

The real evils in war are love of violence, revengeful cruelty, fierce and implacable enmity, wild resistance, and the lust of power, and such like; and it is generally to punish these things ... that, in obedience to God or some lawful authority, good men undertake wars.

St Augustine[2]

The idea of a world living in peace under the rule of a universal law of nature was one of the most far-reaching in human history. But it was far from being widely held. In fact, in the ancient world, it appeared only in the two ancient civilisations previously noted: China, under the auspices of Confucian thought; and Rome, under stoic influence, reinforced by Christian ideas. In many parts of the world, such as sub-Saharan Africa, the dominant view remained one of endemic hostility between neighbouring states.[3] Islamic society represented a kind of mid-way position between these extremes. It held relations within the Islamic fold to be peaceful, without regard to race, language or cultural heritage, while positing ceaseless hostility against the infidel world outside. This point is often unappreciated because of Islam's famous, and largely deserved, principle of toleration of *individual* members of other faiths who dwelled within the Islamic fold. When it came to relations between Muslim and infidel *states*, however, the picture was importantly different. There, an unrelenting hostility was the norm. Where Islam made an important contribution to legal ideas about war was on the subject of internal, rather than international, conflict. In this area, Muslim legal

[1] Romans 3: 8. [2] Augustine, *Contra Faustum*, in *Political Writings*, at 164.
[3] Bozeman, *Conflict in Africa*, at 124–5, 203.

thought devised solutions to important problems that would elude
Western European writers until the nineteenth century.

Christianity, in contrast to Islam, was the heir to the classical tradition
of natural law.[4] Moreover, Christian thought was even more insistent
than its stoic and Roman progenitors on the existence of a residual or
background condition of peace in world affairs. This was the result of a
powerful strain of radical pacifism inherent in Christian doctrine – and
largely absent from Islam. Indeed, this Christian bias towards pacifism
was so strong that early Christian writers were hard-pressed to find *any*
justification for a resort to war. With some effort, this intellectual
challenge was successfully met, resulting in the development of a rich
corpus of just-war doctrine that has never been surpassed in its detail,
subtlety and consistency. It should not be thought, however, that intellectual coherence was the sole force at work in medieval legal considerations of war. Lawyers are practical people, even if theologians and
monks and professors are not (or not always). They were attuned to
developments on the ground, in the practice of states; and they brought
much of this practical knowledge to bear on their considerations of war.
In the course of time, these practical concerns would greatly overshadow
the doctrinal considerations of the just-war expositors.

Islamic perspectives

In their views on war, the Muslim and Christian traditions presented a
sharp contrast.[5] Christianity had a strong pacifist strain, deriving from
the gospels of the New Testament. The Quran, in contrast to the gospels,
breathes the vigorous air of a martial people, urging the believers to exert
themselves for the faith, to '[m]arch forth on the Way of God'.[6] There
are many references to war in the Quran (some forty-one in eighteen
suras), but it is a herculean task to forge a coherent doctrine from them.
On the one hand are found exhortations to the faithful to '[f]ight against
them [infidels] till strife be at an end and the religion be all of it God's'.[7]
On the other hand, there are a number of express condemnations of
aggressive warfare.[8] In the course of its development, Muslim

---

[4] Natural law did play some role in Islamic thought, though nothing like so significant a one
as in Christianity. See generally A. Ezzati, *Islam and Natural Law* (London: Islamic College
for Advanced Studies Press, 2002).
[5] See generally Haleem (ed.), *Crescent and Cross*.   [6] Quran, Sura 9: 38.
[7] *Ibid.*, Sura 8: 40.   [8] See, for example, *ibid.*, Suras 2: 186–7; 2: 190; and 4: 92–3.

jurisprudence came to distinguish between three different levels of officially administered violence. First was fully fledged foreign war, which was known as *Akham al-Hiraba*. Second was war against internal insurgents – i.e., within the Muslim community – known as *Akham al-Bughat*. At the lowest level was state violence or coercion in the form of routine law enforcement, known as *Akham al-Tariq*. Our concern will be with the first and second of these.[9]

Battling the infidel

The single most striking feature of Muslim thought about war was the absence of a belief that the natural condition of international affairs was one of peace. In fact, it held precisely the opposite view: that, between the community of the faithful and the infidel world, there was inevitable and perpetual enmity, comparable to the never-ending 'natural' condition of war between the Greek and barbarian worlds of classical times. The infidel world was even known as the *Dar al-Harb*, meaning 'house of war' in Arabic, in contrast to the Muslim world or *Dar al-Islam* ('house of Islam'), which was the abode of peace and harmony. The everlasting enmity between these two 'houses' was what Muslim writers had in mind when they wrote of war – using the expression *Akham al-Hiraba* (*Hiraba* being a form of the word *Harb*). No specific wrong-doing was required on the part of the infidels to justify war against them. No declaration of war was necessary, nor was any permanent peace treaty possible. Instead, there was constant, if often desultory, conflict, consisting largely of seasonal raiding or campaigning by land in southern France, or by sea off the coasts of Sicily and Italy, or against the Byzantine Empire in the eastern Mediterranean. This was not, or not necessarily, defensive war on the part of the Muslims. On the contrary, there was a certain expansionist ethos to Islam, in that it was seen as inherently praiseworthy for the true faith to expand as much as possible, to bring as large a portion of the earth as possible under the enlightened rule of the Muslim law (the *Shar'ia*). Non-believers living within the *Dar al-Islam*, however, were not compelled to adopt the Muslim faith. They were allowed to retain their own religions provided that they refrained from disturbing the peace of the community and that they submitted to certain civil disabilities such as liability for extra taxation.

---

[9] On Islamic conceptions of war, see generally Khadduri, *War and Peace*; and Løkkegaard, 'Concepts'.

The idea of endemic warfare between the Muslim and infidel worlds naturally made it virtually impossible to devise any body of rules for determining when a transition from peace to war was justified.[10] In addition, the absence of any sense of moral community between Muslim and infidel states was inauspicious for the development of rules on the conduct of armed conflict. As a result, Islamic writers did not develop any very deep or extensive body of ideas about foreign war.[11] In practice, however, Muslim jurisprudence displayed considerable inventiveness and flexibility in devising ways to circumvent some of the practical inconveniences entailed by the doctrine of perpetual strife. One useful device was truces. Even though, strictly speaking, fully fledged peace could not exist between the *Dar al-Islam* and the *Dar al-Harb*, temporary pauses in hostilities were allowed. The Quran itself provided some support for this practice, admonishing the faithful that agreements with polytheists should be kept by the Muslim side so long as they were observed by the infidels.[12] Truces were held to be terminable at the will of the Muslim party – subject, however, to the proviso that due notice must be given to the other side prior to the recommencing of hostilities. There was some diversity of opinion as to the maximum permitted length for truces, with ten years as the outside figure.[13]

A related means of mitigating strife between Christians and Muslims was the devising of an intermediate category between the hitherto starkly opposed *Dar al-Harb* and *Dar al-Islam*, known as a 'house of truce' (*Dar al-Sulh*) or 'house of covenant' (*Dar al-'Ahd*). This category consisted of infidel states which were in a position of contractual subordination to the *Dar al-Islam*, recognising Muslim overlordship and paying tribute. Such states could be left in peace under their nonbelieving rulers. This device could be put to wide use by the simple means of deeming routine gifts to constitute the necessary 'tribute', somewhat in the manner of the Chinese tributary system.[14] Yet another useful source of flexibility was the granting of safe-conducts (*aman*) to individual infidels. In time, these safe-conducts also came to be granted to collectivities, such as cities (mainly the Italian trading cities) or even whole countries, although these collective *aman* could only be granted

---

[10] See, however, Kelsay, 'Religion, Morality', for the view that Islam did, to some extent, develop a body of just-war doctrine comparable in spirit to that of the Christian world.

[11] Donner, 'Sources', in Kelsay, *Just War*, at 52; and Joseph Schacht, *An Introduction to Islamic Law* (Oxford: Clarendon Press, 1964), at 76.

[12] Quran, Sura 9: 4; and Sura 9: 7.   [13] B. Lewis, *Politics and War*, at 175.

[14] *Ibid.* at 176–7.

by an imam, in the form of an order known as a *berat*. Secular rulers played a role by concluding agreements with Christian states, known as 'capitulations'. The original purpose of these agreements was to settle the kinds of *berat* that imams would be allowed to grant.[15]

The *Akham al-Hiraba* was not the only form taken by hostility between the Muslim and the infidel worlds. Two other types of conflict should also be noted. One was known as *razzia*, meaning perpetual raiding across the frontier of the enemy, undertaken on the personal initiative of the raiders themselves.[16] The practitioners of this form of combat, known as *ghazis*, lived 'ordinary' lives with their families in villages, engaging on a part-time basis in raiding missions against infidels. *Ghazis* held an honourable place in Muslim society, operating defensively as frontier guardians and offensively (when possible) as pioneers of future conquests. The most famous *ghazi* warriors were a clan in northwestern Asia Minor known as the Osmanlis, who, beginning in the thirteenth century, graduated from border warfare to full-scale imperialism as the founders of the Ottoman Empire, which endured into the twentieth century.

The other form of interstate – or rather interfaith – strife that calls for particular notice was the *jihad*. This term had Quranic roots, with the first treatise on the subject dating from the eighth century AD, by the Syrian jurist 'Abd al-Rahmān al-Awzā'ī.[17] The word *jihad* is linguistically quite distinct from *harb*, which is the standard Arabic word for 'war'. It comes from an Arabic root meaning to strive, to exert oneself, to take extraordinary pains. The essence of *jihad*, therefore, was total dedication to a cause, even to the point of self-sacrifice. The concept did not, at least originally, have an exclusively military connotation. Striving and dedication can take many other forms. There could be, for example, a '*jihad* of the tongue' and a '*jihad* of the pen', referring to speaking and writing of virtue and to denouncing evil. In mystical and ascetic traditions, there was a doctrine of a 'greater *jihad*' or '*jihad* of the heart', meaning an interior struggle against one's *own* sinful inclinations, with military activity relegated to the status of a 'lesser *jihad*'.[18] A saying was attributed to Muhammad that 'the best *jihad* is [speaking]

---

[15] 1 Shaw, *Ottoman Empire*, at 163.
[16] For the linguistic origin of this term, see Donner, 'Sources', in Kelsay, *Just War*, at 34–5.
[17] Løkkegaard, 'Concepts', at 272–3.
[18] B. Lewis, *Political Language*, at 71–2; and B. Lewis, *Politics and War*, at 175–6. See also D. C. Watt, 'Islamic Conceptions of the Holy War', in Murphy, *Holy War*, at 141–56; and Firestone, *Jihad*, at 16–18.

a word of justice to a tyrannical ruler'.[19] In the course of the Middle
Ages, *jihad* came to be downplayed in the Islamic world. In the thirteenth and fourteenth centuries, the jurist Ibn Taymiyyah held that, in
its military form, it referred only to defensive war.[20] The concept would
be revived, however, in the nineteenth century and later, in the context
of anticolonial and anti-Western campaigns.[21]

Strife within the Muslim world

To the subject of conflict within the Muslim world, Islamic jurisprudence
brought a considerably greater degree of sophistication than it did to
questions of foreign war. The crucial conceptual distinction made by the
medieval Muslim jurists was between two categories of state-wielded
coercion within Muslim society: first, against ordinary criminal bands;
and second, against organised and ideologically inspired insurgents. The
criminal groups such as highway robbers – the counterparts of the ancient
Roman *latrociniae* – were known as *muharib*. This term was cognate with
harb ('war'), indicating that these brigands were, in a manner of speaking,
equated with fully fledged enemies of Muslim society. Quite different,
however, was the other type of internal enemy, known as *bughat*, which
we should translate as 'rebels' or 'insurgents', a category unknown to
Roman law.[22] Two characteristics in particular distinguished the two
types of miscreant. First, *bughat* were animated by a doctrine or belief
of some kind and not merely by greed for plunder. The doctrine held
might be misguided or heretical, but the important point was that
the *bughat* fought as a patriot for a cause. The second distinctive feature
of a *bughat* group was the possession of some kind of internal organisa-
tional structure of a governmental or quasi-governmental nature. This
might take the form of a disciplined fighting arm comparable to a regular
military force. Or it could consist of the effective possession of a territory
in which the insurgents exercised de facto sovereign powers such as
taxation or the handing down of judicial decisions.

---

[19] Firestone, *Jihad*, at 17.
[20] Løkkegaard, 'Concepts', at 274; and Hillenbrand, *Islamic Perspectives*, at 241–3. On *jihad*,
see generally Peters, *Jihad*; Peters, 'Jihad'; and Morabia, Arnaldez and Morabia, *Gihâd*. For
comparisons between *jihad* and Western just-war ideas, see Kelsay and Johnson (eds.),
Just War and Jihad.
[21] See Chapter 10 below for this development.
[22] See generally Khaled Abou El Fadl, '*Bughat*', in Johnson and Kelsay (eds.), *Cross, Crescent,
and Sword*, at 149–76; and Fadl, *Rebellion and Violence*, at 237–49.

Bughat were entitled to certain legal protections that were denied to *muharib*. For example, it was not lawful for a ruler to wage a war of extermination against *bughat*, nor to pursue them in flight. *Bughat* also could not be held accountable for blood shed or for property seized. They could not be imprisoned, enslaved or ransomed when captured, nor could property be confiscated from individual warriors (although property belonging to the rebel 'government' itself could be taken). The *bughat* leaders were conceded to have the 'right' to raise taxes lawfully in areas which they controlled, with the result that persons who paid taxes to them were not liable to make a second payment to the legitimate government. Similarly, judgments handed down by courts in insurgent-controlled areas were entitled to recognition by the legitimate authorities.[23] Not until the nineteenth century would European lawyers devise a similar legal conception, which would be known as 'recognition of insurgency'. In the Middle Ages, however, European legal thought about war became very highly developed in other directions – towards the devising of a body of just-war doctrine for dealing with war against foreign states.

Christian soldiers

On the Christian side of the great religious divide of the medieval world, the legal outlook on war had a dual ancestry: the natural-law tradition inherited from stoic philosophy and Roman law, and Christian doctrines derived from scripture. The Christian side of the inheritance, in particular, offered something unprecedented in the Western world – a doctrine of radical pacifism, which urged believers to love their enemies and to turn the other cheek when struck. These two traditions were very different in many ways, but they agreed on one crucial point: the thesis that the 'natural' state of the world is one of peace, with war as an exceptional and perverse state of affairs requiring some kind of explicit justification. Stated in Islamic terms, it could be said that, according to the European natural-law view, the entire world was a 'house of peace', with no such thing as a 'house of war'. The great achievement of the lawyers, philosophers and theologians of Christian Europe was to devise a coherent set of beliefs – known as just-war doctrine – that married these two streams of thought together while

---

[23] Fadl, *Rebellion and Violence*, at 237–49.

managing, in the process, to circumvent some of the more awkward consequences of the extreme pacifism of the Christian heritage.

On turning the other cheek

In the early Middle Ages, the principal challenge facing writers on war was to reconcile the divergent (or apparently divergent) views of classical natural law and Christianity. Natural law accepted that war was permissible for (broadly speaking) the enforcement of law. The Christian gospels held (or appeared to hold) that war was impermissible under any circumstances.[24] The most immediate practical question was one of personal ethics rather than of high state policy: whether individual Christians could, or should, perform military service.[25] The predominant view of the early Church fathers, most notably of Tertullian, was that they should not, on the authority of the gospel teachings. It should be noted that there was a parallel view that Christians should not resort to the law courts either, since they, like armies, were organs of state coercion.[26]

Gradually, this position was modified, as a result of several factors.[27] One was an increasing tendency of Christian writers to see the Roman Empire as a divinely approved political vehicle for the furthering of the Christian faith and for the safeguarding of civilisation in general. Even the most devout Christians could appreciate the value of a vigilant and disciplined military force against enemies of the faith, whether internal or external. The increasing threat that barbarians presented to the Roman Empire made this task particularly urgent. Consequently, Christian writers began to stress the virtues of defending the broader community, and the faith itself, against external foes. It became common for them to lavish praise onto the Roman state and military as a model (or at least a potential model) of disciplined and devoted community service. Saint Ambrose of Milan, writing in the late fourth century, lauded '[t]he virtue which leads people to protect their country from barbarians in time of war, or which in peacetime makes them defend the weak or protect their friends from robbers'.[28] Even

---

[24] See Haines, 'Attitudes'.

[25] See generally, on this subject, Cadoux, *Early Christian Attitude*, at 96–160. See also Helgeland, Daly and Burns, *Christians and the Military*; and Childress, 'Moral Discourse'.

[26] Cadoux, *Early Christian Attitude*, at 67.   [27] See Brière, 'Étapes'.

[28] Ambrose, *De Officiis*, at 193. On Ambrose's views on war, see F. H. Russell, *Just War*, at 12–15.

Tertullian, the most pacifistically inclined of the Church fathers, stressed that Christians prayed dutifully for the Roman emperors and their armies.[29] In much the same vein, Christian writers also began to stress the positive value of the law-enforcement activities of magistrates against internal wrongdoers. No less an authority than Saint Paul praised magistrates as 'God's agents' labouring on behalf of the community at large – agents whose tasks naturally included the distasteful, but necessary, chore of punishing wrongdoers.[30]

These tendencies were summed up in the late fourth and early fifth centuries by Augustine of Hippo.[31] Following from earlier writings, he explained that the gospel exhortation to pacifism should be understood as a limitation only on the purposes for which force could be used. In particular, the gospels forbade only the use of force for egoistical ends. The position was very different, however, when force was employed altruistically, to protect *others* – i.e., to safeguard the community of faithful from its oppressors and enemies. That was a praiseworthy public service. In such a case, the real blame for any violence lay with the wrongdoer, not the law enforcer.[32] '[I]t is the injustice of the opposing side', averred Augustine, 'that lays on the wise man the duty of waging wars'.[33] Good men, he contended, could wage war for the purpose of 'bringing under the yoke the unbridled lusts of men' and for the rooting out of vice.[34]

In the mid twelfth century, his views were incorporated into the *Decretum* of Gratian, whose labours brought forth a de facto official canon-law code for the medieval Catholic Church.[35] They were also endorsed by Thomas Aquinas, the foremost of the medieval Catholic theologians, in the thirteenth century. He too made a close connection between permissible war and domestic law enforcement. '[J]ust as it is lawful for [rulers] to have recourse to the sword in defending [the] common weal against internal disturbances', he pronounced, 'so too it is their business to have recourse to the sword of war in defending the

[29] Tertullian, *Apology*, trans. T. R. Glover (London: William Heinemann, 1931), at 151–7. (1st edn *c*. AD 211.)

[30] Romans 13: 2–4.

[31] For a convenient collection of Augustine's principal writings on war, see Augustine, *Political Writings*, at 162–83. On Augustine's contribution to just-war doctrine, see Brière, 'Conception'; Markus, 'Saint Augustine's Views'; and Langan, 'Elements'.

[32] Augustine, *Contra Faustum*, in *Political Writings*, at 170.

[33] Augustine, *City of God*, at 862.

[34] Augustine, Letter No. 138, in *Political Writings*, at 179–80.

[35] See Causa 23 of the *Decretum*, in Gratian, *Gratianus in Jurisprudence*, at 18–30.

common weal against external enemies'. There was no sin, he insisted, following Augustine, in resorting to force when 'commissioned by another' for the common good.[36]

By this mode of reasoning, the medieval Catholic Church succeeded in extricating itself from the snare of radical pacifism which the gospels appeared to command. Indeed, it may have succeeded all too well, as evidenced by the deep involvement which the Church began to take in military affairs. In the ninth century, a number of popes actively engaged in martial labours. Leo IV, in addition to fortifying the city of Rome (thereby creating the 'Leonine City'), built a battle fleet which inflicted a defeat on Muslim forces in 849. Later that century, Pope John VIII also organised a naval force against the Muslims, but less successfully. He was reduced to buying his foes off with tribute instead, thereby becoming a rather disgruntled denizen of the Islamic 'house of covenant'. Churchmen were also enlisted by rulers to give their imprimatur to armed action, if only safely after the fact. After the Battle of Fontenay, for instance, in 841, in which the forces of Charles the Bald and Louis the German bested those of their brother Lothair, a council of bishops duly pronounced the victors' war to have been just. In 1155, after the slaughter of over 1,000 rebellious citizens of Rome by the troops of Holy Roman Emperor Frederick I, Pope Hadrian IV personally celebrated mass for the soldiers and absolved them of any sins committed during the operation.[37]

As the Middle Ages progressed, the image of the Church Militant became more pronounced.[38] It was increasingly pointed out that the virtues of the religious devotee and of the soldier had a great deal in common. The qualities of steadfastness, courage and dedication to larger causes were common to both endeavours.[39] The conjunction of the monastic and military lives reached its peak in the various crusading orders in the Holy Land (the Templars and Hospitalers) and Spain (the orders of Santiago and Calatrava and the like). The soldiers in these bodies were not actually in holy orders, but they lived under a discipline that was clearly monastic in flavour and inspiration. Back on the European home front, this association took the form of knight errantry

---

[36] Aquinas, *On Law, Morality and Politics*, at 221–2.
[37] Verkamp, 'Moral Treatment', at 230–2.
[38] See generally Harnack, *Militia Christi*; and Thouzellier, 'Ecclesia Militans'.
[39] On military imagery in early Christian writing, see Cadoux, *Early Christian Attitude*, at 161–70.

and chivalry, in which piety and warfare were, at least theoretically, combined in the most intimate possible way. As early as the tenth century, the ceremony of the dubbing of knights (sometimes, revealingly, called 'ordination') included the knight's laying of his sword on an altar, with the taking of an oath that the weapon would be used solely for the protection of the weak and downtrodden against sinners and oppressors.[40] Further evidence of the happy alliance between war and religion is found in the popularity of warrior saints, such as George and Maurice. Above all was the cult of Saint Michael (actually an archangel rather than a saint). A kind of Christian counterpart of the Zoroastrian Mithra, Michael was the foremost embodiment of the just warrior, since he would lead the heavenly host against the forces of Satan in the titanic battle preceding the Last Judgment. His iconography was significant. In medieval art, he wielded, naturally, a sword. But he also carried the scales of justice.[41]

The mature just-war doctrine

Once the hurdle of Christian pacifism had been overcome, the intellectual path was open towards an elaboration of a theory of just wars along the lines adumbrated by Cicero and other writers in the classical, natural-law tradition. Its essence may be stated with the utmost brevity: a just war was a war waged for the enforcement of right and the eradication of evil. In approximately the period between 1050 and 1300, a number of European writers, mostly theologians, proceeded to construct a detailed doctrine on this basic conceptual foundation, which stands as one of the most impressive intellectual achievements of medieval thought.[42] There were naturally disagreements about many of the specific aspects of just-war doctrine; but essential elements of it were broadly agreed. In particular, it was usually agreed that five main principles or criteria were necessary in order for a war to be just in the strict sense.

---

[40] Verkamp, 'Moral Treatment', at 238–9. On chivalry, see generally Keen, *Chivalry*; and Kaeuper, *Chivalry and Violence*.
[41] See, for example, Luca Signorelli, *Madonna and Child with Saints and Angels*, at the National Gallery of Art in Washington (Acc. No. 1961.9.87).
[42] For a masterful treatment of just-war thought, see F. H. Russell, *Just War*. For an excellent brief account, see Barnes, 'Just War'. See also Vanderpol, *Droit de la guerre juste*; Vanderpol, *Doctrine scolastique*; Regout, *Doctrine*; Brière, 'Étapes'; Brière, *Droit de juste guerre*; and Bacot, *Doctrine*.

The first was *auctoritas*: the proposition that a just war could be waged only by the command of a sovereign. This principle reflected the pacifist view underlying just-war theory as a whole, according to which a just war was one waged in defence of others rather than of oneself – with the direct implication that the just warrior had to hold a commission from his community (i.e., from his ruler) to justify the shedding of blood. A notable feature of *auctoritas* was that it was commonly held to be necessary on *both* sides of the conflict, and not on the just side only. This requirement had the effect of excluding domestic law-enforcement operations against bandits, pirates and the like from the category of just wars.

The second criterion of a just war was *personae*. This meant that only certain categories of persons were allowed to engage in armed conflict. Some, such as women, children and the aged or infirm, were excluded by the dictates of nature. Another important excluded category was ecclesiastics, whose professional calling was held to be incompatible with the shedding of blood. (Clerics, incidentally, were forbidden to practise surgery on the same ground.)[43] Some writers, with a practical bent, extended this principle to conclude that clergy were also entitled to exemption from taxes levied for war purposes.[44]

The third principle was known as *res*. Meaning literally 'thing', it really meant a thing in contention, the object of the quarrel, the *casus belli*. This concept meant, in effect, that a just war must have a well-defined objective. The *res* might take a corporeal form, such as a territory whose title was disputed. But it could also take an incorporeal form such as a demand for compensation for an injury inflicted. An important implication of this principle was the exclusion of endemic conflict from the category of just war – that is, it meant the rejection by Europeans of any doctrine like the Muslim one of the *Dar al-Islam* versus the *Dar al-Harb*.

The fourth principle was of the highest importance: the requirement of a just cause, or *justa causa*. This meant that, in order for a war to be permissible, it had to be waged in the pursuit of a valid legal claim. *Res* and *justa causa* had an intimate relation, with *res* referring to the claim that was being made and *justa causa* to the legal validity of that claim in the eyes of the law and, more broadly, to the permissibility of resorting to force to obtain the *res*. This principle of *justa causa* is what most

---

[43] Fourth Lateran Council (1215), Canon 18, in 1 Tanner, *Decrees*, at 244.
[44] Bonet, *Tree of Battles*, at 165.

persons would intuitively regard as the very heart of just-war theory. It may therefore come as something of a surprise that relatively little attention was given to it by medieval writers, who typically confined themselves to the most general comments on this topic. Augustine, for example, stated that a just war was 'one that avenges wrongs, when a nation or state has to be punished for refusing to make amends for the wrongs inflicted by its subjects or to restore what it has seized unjustly'.[45] This broad formulation was endorsed verbatim by Thomas Aquinas in the thirteenth century.[46]

A very important point about *justa causa* was that it was strictly an *objective* question. That is to say, the legal claim on which a war was waged must actually be valid in order for the war to be just. A sincere, but erroneous, belief in the rightness of one's legal cause would not suffice. Consequently, a war could not be just on *both* sides, any more than both parties to a lawsuit could have the law supporting their respective claims. That meant that a ruler should take the greatest care before resorting to war to be sure that the law was actually in his favour. To this end, it was advisable that the ruler should consult with legal experts, who in turn should give their advice conscientiously, without fear or favour.[47] It should be appreciated, however, that *justa causa* was not a narrowly legalistic principle, referring only to the validity of the legal claim without regard to the broader context of the dispute. Prudential elements played a part as well. One of these was a requirement of necessity – that a war would not be just if an alternative and non-forcible way of resolving the crisis was available. There was also, if only implicitly, a requirement of proportionality – that a war should not be waged if the good which was expected to flow from it was outweighed by the evils that it would entail.[48]

The final criterion was *animus*: 'rightful intention'. This was a requirement that a just war be waged not out of hatred but out of love, for the purpose of correcting evil and bringing the enemy to the path of righteousness. *Animus* may be thought of as a sort of subjective or mental counterpart of *justa causa*. *Justa causa* determined whether an action as such was permissible in principle; while *animus* concerned the

---

[45] Augustine, *Quaestionum in Heptateuchum*, quoted in Aquinas, *On Law, Morality and Politics*, at 221.

[46] Aquinas, *On Law; Morality and Politics*, at 221. On Aquinas's views on war, see Gmür, *Thomas von Aquino*; Tooke, *Just War*, at 170–80; and F. H. Russell, *Just War*, at 267–71.

[47] Vitoria, *Law of War*, at 306–7; and Suárez, *Three Virtues*, at 828–31.

[48] See Vitoria, *Law of War*, at 304; and Suárez, *Three Virtues*, at 816–17.

extent to which the actor's soul was endangered by performing that act. *Justa causa* was therefore the natural realm of the lawyer, and *animus* of the theologian. Of all of the elements of the just-war schema, this was the most distinctively Christian one, since it functioned as the key means of reconciling the Christian duty of universal love with the resort to force. It is perhaps not surprising, then, that *animus* received rather more attention from the theologians than *justa causa* did. To Augustine, nothing was more reprehensible than the love of violence for its own sake, or the quest for personal glory or booty. 'The real evils in war', he warned, 'are love of violence, revengeful cruelty, fierce and implacable enmity, wild resistance, and the lust of power, and such like'.[49] Aquinas was very careful to stress that the lack of the correct *animus* would make a war unjust, even if the requisite objective *justa causa* was present.[50]

A clear implication of this principle of *animus* was to exclude personal hatred from the sphere of just war-making. There must be hatred only of the wrong-doing that had made the war necessary, but not of the wrong-doer. Augustine stressed that war must be waged, if at all, with reluctance, out of regrettable necessity and 'with a certain benevolent severity'.[51] Aquinas agreed, insisting that a just war must be motivated solely by a desire for 'the advancement of good or the avoidance of evil' with no element of 'private animosity'. Indeed, to wage a just war was actually to confer a positive benefit onto the misguided enemy, by preventing his sinful enterprise from succeeding and thereby imperilling his soul. Augustine made an analogy with a father applying corporal punishment to a son for corrective purposes, with a motive of love.[52] The fourteenth-century clerical writer, Honoré de Bonet, echoed this view by likening a just war to the administration of medicine to the sick – painful and unpleasant in the short term, but done for the good of the patient himself.[53] It may be noted, in this connection, that Aquinas's discussion of warfare appeared in the section of his great *Summa Theologica* that dealt with charity. The waging of war with the correct *animus* was therefore a means by which a Christian could be true to the gospel command to return kindness for hatred, to love one's enemy as one's friend. As Francisco Suárez, a Spanish Jesuit writer of the sixteenth and seventeenth centuries, would later put it (with a trace of idealism),

[49] Augustine, *Contra Faustum*, in *Political Writings*, at 164.
[50] Aquinas, *On Law, Morality and Politics*, at 221, 226–7.
[51] Augustine, Letter No. 138, in *Political Writings*, at 178.   [52] *Ibid.* at 178–9.
[53] Bonet, *Tree of Battles*, at 125.

'war is not opposed to the love of one's enemies; for whoever wages war honourably hates, not individuals, but the actions which he justly condemns'.[54] Here too, the analogy with domestic law enforcement is clear. The criminal law is applied with a view to reintegrating the wrongdoer into society. The miscreant may justly be punished for his specific wrongful acts; but he retains his humanity, his membership of the society and his fundamental rights. And he is to be welcomed back into the community when and if he abjures his wrongdoing.

As a final caution, it should be noted that the very expression 'just war' is apt to mislead or cause confusion in certain important respects because it could be employed in either a narrow or a broad sense. In its narrow sense, it might be thought to refer to the presence or absence of the single factor of *justa causa*. But the expression in the Middle Ages had a broader meaning than that, referring to the entire five-fold scheme of characteristics. That meant, for example, that a war might be unjust in this broad sense even if the particular criterion of *justa causa* was met. It is perhaps best to think of a just war in the medieval European usage as, so to speak, an ideal war, i.e., a resort to force that was wholly altruistic, entirely unsullied by such evils as greed or love of violence. Any resort to arms in which one or more of the criteria was lacking would, to that extent, fall short of being a 'true' war, i.e., it would be contaminated (as it were) by certain impure elements.

The very prototype of a just war in this medieval sense was a war for the defence of the Christian world as a whole against a common outside enemy who threatened the faith or the faithful, carried out under the *auctoritas* of the pope. This highest category of war was referred to by the thirteenth-century theologian Hostiensis as a 'Roman war' (with 'Roman' referring, of course, to the Roman Catholic Church rather than to the historical Roman Empire).[55] In the sixteenth century, the Spanish Dominican scholar Francisco de Vitoria spoke in terms of what he called a 'perfect' war, by which was meant a war that was 'complete in itself', lacking in nothing.[56] There was a distinctly Platonic element to this way of thinking, with imperfect practices here on earth being measured against an ideal model. No mundane conflict would ever be *perfectly* just, simply because perfection was not given to mere mortals. But in war-making, as in all other

---

[54] Suárez, *Three Virtues*, at 802.
[55] John of Legnano, *Tractatus*, at 275–6. See also F. H. Russell, *Just War*, at 129–30.
[56] Vitoria, *Law of War*, at 301.

endeavours, it was the duty of good Christians to strive to their utmost in pursuit of the high ideals of their faith.

The contours of the just-war outlook

Our purpose is not to study the specific doctrines of medieval Christian just-war doctrine as such, but rather to investigate the conception of war that underlay and pervaded it and which flowed from it. It is therefore more important to survey the broader features of the just-war outlook than to burrow into its many nooks and crannies. Our principal attention will be on various aspects of just-war thought which are especially apt to be overlooked or misunderstood, as well as on those elements which would play an important role in the future development of legal conceptions of war.

Just-war doctrine and natural law

It has been observed that just-war thought had a dual heritage – secular natural-law theory from the classical world, and Christian doctrine from the gospels. There was assumed to be no conflict between the two – as indeed, there hardly would be in an era when many of the expounders of natural law were theologians. We should be wary, however, of characterising just-war doctrine too lightly as being 'Christian' or 'theological' in nature. Looked at as a whole, the just-war framework owed rather more to secular natural-law thought than to specifically Christian doctrines. Most particularly, it would be wrong to see a just war as a war for the propagation of the Christian religion. A holy war, as this would be known, was altogether foreign to natural-law principles of just war, which are our present concern. Nor had supernatural elements, such as divine commands, any place in it. The ethos of just-war doctrine, in brief, was that of the lawyer rather than the priest, of the rationalist rather than the zealot.

This intimate association between just-war doctrine and natural law (which, incidentally, would endure into the nineteenth century) had a number of important implications. The most obvious one was to confer onto medieval just-war theory the universal character that was so striking a feature of natural-law thought. The law of nature was applicable not simply to Christians but also to the entire human community (and indeed, to the animal world as well). Moreover, the content of this body of law was discernible through the application of human reason, an attribute possessed by Christians and non-Christians alike. The divine law of Christianity, in contrast, was based not on reason but on revelation from a deity on high – a revelation to which only Christians, by definition, were attuned. Where natural law was immanent in the natural world, and present within the mind of each person, divine law consisted of commands from, as it were, 'outside' of nature (i.e., 'supernatural' in the most literal sense). No human could presume to fathom the mind of God, but every human could discover and apply the law of nature.[57] This secular and universal character of natural law, more than anything else, distinguished Christian – or rather European – thought on war, and international law generally, from that of the Islamic world. There was no room in the natural-law tradition for such a religiously based classification of states as existed in the Muslim position on war.

This universalist ethos inevitably placed severe limits on the extent to which a state could be lawfully attacked simply because it professed a pagan faith – a point that the Catholic Church readily conceded. As early as the pontificate of Pope Gregory I (590–604), there was an express prohibition against the forcible conversion of non-believers.[58] This was reinforced in the thirteenth century, when Pope Innocent IV (who, in his earlier role as Sinibaldo Fieschi, had been a distinguished canon lawyer) held that non-adherence to the Christian faith was not wrongful in and of itself. Infidels and pagans, he insisted, were subject to natural law as Christians were – and thereby were entitled to all the benefits of that law, including the right to be secure in their lawfully acquired possessions. So long as the infidels committed no wrongful *acts* against Christians – such as forbidding them to preach the gospels – there was no cause to molest them or to dispossess them of their kingdoms.[59] Conquests of pagan territories therefore had to be justified in terms of orthodox just-war doctrine, i.e., some kind of identifiable *justa causa* had to be found, some specific act of wrongdoing on the part of the infidels.

This point had important legal implications for the various crusades against Muslim and pagan parts of the world. For the crusades to the Holy Land, the *justa causa* was the unlawful occupation of the Holy

---

[57] See Aquinas, *Treatise on Law*, at 166–72, 256–7; and Vitoria, *On the Power of the Church I*, in *Political Writings*, ed. Anthony Pagden and Jeremy Lawrance (Cambridge: Cambridge University Press, 1991) at 71.

[58] Housley (ed.), *Documents*, at 112 n. 10.

[59] F. H. Russell, *Just War*, at 199–200. See also Bonet, *Tree of Battles*, at 127.

Land by Muslim aggressors, who proceeded to compound their sins by interfering with the access of Christian pilgrims to the holy places.[60] Much the same justification was given for the crusading in Spain, since Spain too was seen as having been unlawfully taken by way of aggression. The very name for the Spanish crusading effort – the *reconquista* (i.e. 'reconquest') – revealed the legal nature of the enterprise.[61]

One other aspect of the natural-law heritage of medieval thought on war should be stressed. That is, that natural law possessed no very strong theory of the state. It was a set of rules directed to individual human beings (and animals), but not to states as corporate entities. The rulers of states were, of course, subject to natural law, but not in any fundamentally different way from ordinary persons. Societies in the Middle Ages were seen more as agglomerations of individuals, all of whom were responsible for their actions according to the law of nature. In the context of warfare, that meant that the soldiers fighting in the opposing armies – or at least those of higher status such as knights – were not seen as mere cogs in a state machine, or as dutiful patriots answering their country's call in its hour of need. They were regarded, much like their rulers, as individual persons who had made a conscious choice to risk their mortal souls (not to mention their bodily frames) by taking up arms in a cause that might – or might not – be just. This position illustrates an important point about medieval conceptions of natural law: that that law did not, at least in principle, make any distinction between the moral standards of rulers and subjects. The mightiest emperor and the meanest peasant were equally subject to its exacting standards.

This universalist view of natural law had the effect of placing just-war theorists in a dilemma which they never satisfactorily resolved. On the one hand, notions of individual responsibility implied that soldiers or feudal underlings should carefully judge the lawfulness of any war in which their ruler or lord might order them to serve. At the same time, though, conservative churchmen were very reluctant to foment revolt against established authority. In practice, 'lesser subjects' (as Vitoria referred to them) were expected dutifully to discharge their required

---

[60] See, for example, Bonet, *Tree of Battles*, at 126–7; and Suárez, *Three Virtues*, at 823–5. On the legal character of the crusades, see Pissard, *Guerre sainte*; Alphandéry, *Chrétienté et l'idée*; Villey, *Croisade*; Brundage, *Medieval Canon Law*; Walters, Jr, 'Just War and Crusade'; and Tyerman, *Invention*.

[61] On Spanish crusading, see Villey, *Croisade*, at 193–208. On the crusade concept in northeastern Europe, see Lotter, 'Crusading Idea'.

service unless the cause in which they were enlisted was patently unjust.[62] The chief point for present purposes is that a medieval war was not such a unitary thing as we would be inclined to suppose, in which contending states, as monolithic corporate entities, were pitted against one another. Rather, it was an aggregation of small 'wars' waged by the individual combatants against one another. This meant that the individual members of the opposing armies were, at least in principle, actual enemies of one another on a person-to-person basis, since each individual on the enemy side was seen as an actual evildoer, personally responsible for his wrongs in the eyes of both God and man.

The just war as law enforcement

Stated in the very briefest and most general terms, the idea of war as a law-enforcement operation was (and remains) the very essence of just-war thought in its most general sense. This conception was very strongly present in the European Middle Ages, and its consequences were both numerous and momentous. For one thing, it meant that a just war could not be seen as a conflict between legal or moral equals, in the manner of a duel or a sporting contest. Instead, every armed conflict must be seen as a case of right and wrong, of crime and punishment or (as lawyers might say) of delict and sanction. This is admittedly to oversimplify the situation somewhat, since there were some marginal cases in which wars might be unjust on *both* sides. An example would be a case of two greedy would-be conquerors trying to overcome one another, in the manner of thieves coming to blows over the division of their loot. Another example would be duelling, to which the Catholic Church was sternly opposed.[63] Nevertheless, it was generally held in the Middle Ages that, even if a war could be *un*just on both sides, it could not be just on both, any more than it was possible for there to be two magistrates at swordpoint against one another with no sign of criminality.

   Another important implication of the law-enforcement frame of mind was that a resort to war could involve no rupture of the basic moral, social and legal bonds binding the warring states together. War involved no suspension of ordinary legal rights and duties. It merely constituted a more drastic method than usual of implementing them.

---

[62] Vitoria, *Law of War*, at 307–9, 321; Augustine, *Contra Faustum*, in *Political Writings*, at 165; and Suárez, *Three Virtues*, at 832–3.
[63] See Council of Trent (1563), 25th session, chapter 19, in 1 Tanner, *Decrees*, at 795.

There would be, of course, no *civil*-law relation between the contending states, since they were not under the rule of a common sovereign. But the *natural*-law ties between the warring parties continued in full force and effect even during the conflict. Again we may resort to the analogy of the magistrate and the criminal. It would not be suggested that, as between them, no law existed. On the contrary, the criminal remained fully part of the society, subject to its civil laws. It was merely that, as a wrongdoer, he was required to make appropriate amends for his misdeeds or to undergo appropriate punishment. The same was true of warring states. Despite the conflict between them, the states always remained as fellow members of the global community and, as such, continuously subject to the natural law which ruled it. This principle was manifested most concretely in the rule that faith was to be kept with the enemy in war, e.g., that armistice agreements, safe-conduct guarantees and the like should be scrupulously observed.[64] This consideration also meant that there was no room for any concept of a *state* of war, in the sense of a distinctly marked out period of time in which a special legal regime was substituted for the ordinary one that generally prevailed. There could not be, since the basic dictates of natural law were never suspended. Medieval just-war theory, in other words, knew no state of war but only *acts* of war – either wrongful acts by the unjust side or lawful ones by the just party – that occasionally punctured the general state of peace, but without ever displacing it.

This notion of war as an act (or series of acts) meant that war was seen in what might be called unilateral terms – i.e., as a use of force (lawful or unlawful as the case may be) by one party against another. Hence the expression 'just war' should be understood to mean the justifiable commission of a forcible act by a state. This is somewhat counterintuitive from the modern standpoint, which tends to see war as a single conflict involving a *mutual* clash of arms. In medieval terms, though, a situation of mutual conflict would comprise *two* wars, since two parties were committing acts of war. One of the two wars would be just and the other unjust. More precisely, it would be said that one side was fighting a true war – i.e., a just war in the sense of a war that approached the ideal of a use of force in the name of right – while the other side was engaging in mere banditry.

---

[64] See Ambrose, *De Officiis*, at 197–9, 395–7; and Augustine, Letter No. 189, in *Political Writings*, at 182.

Finally, it will be readily apparent that the law-enforcement model of war left no room for neutrality for third states. For one thing, since there was really no such thing as a state of war in just-war thought, so there could hardly be a distinct status of neutrality either. The rights and duties of third states simply remained as they always were, since war involved no suspension of natural law. This logical point was reinforced by a moral one: that third states could no more be 'neutral' during a war than ordinary citizens could be 'neutral' with regard to the capturing of an accused criminal by a magistrate. In fact, neutrality in such a situation would fall dangerously near to being a wrongful act in itself, since it was arguable that ordinary citizens should assist their rulers in the discharging of their noble tasks. The medieval attitude towards neutrality found an apt literary reflection in Dante's *Divine Comedy*, in which the vestibule of Hell was populated (and thickly at that) by persons who had done neither good nor evil in their lives. Declining to answer the call of justice was no way to save one's soul.

Offence and defence

It would be a great error to equate a just war, in its medieval incarnation, with a defensive war. It is true that wars of aggression were roundly and consistently denounced. Augustine, for example, condemned wars of conquest as mere brigandage on a large scale.[65] It is also true that, in a certain manner of speaking, all just wars were defensive in the very broad sense that they were designed to defend the world against wickedness, to prevent evil from overcoming good. (In fact, the English word 'war' (as well as the French *guerre* and Spanish *guerra*) is cognate with the German *Wehr*, which means defence or resistance.)[66] Even punitive action, after the crime, could be said to be defensive in a broad sense, insofar as it might be designed to prevent a recurrence of the wrongdoing in the future. Just wars were, however, offensive in the sense that the enforcement action of a magistrate is offensive. (Again, the law-enforcement image provides the key to understanding.) Law enforcement by a magistrate could be said to be defensive in the broad sense of being designed to protect or safeguard society from evildoing. But his action is offensive in the sense that he actively searches out criminals and

---

[65] Augustine, *City of God*, at 142.
[66] The general German word for 'war' is *Krieg*. On medieval terminology relating to war, see Haggenmacher, *Grotius*, at 98–105.

brings them to justice. It should also be appreciated that this detective action might take place at some point of time substantially *later* than the original criminal act. The magistrate's action could then be said to be a response to crime, but it could not be said to be a defence against the actual *commission* of a crime. A just war might therefore be thought of as a kind of licensed aggression – licensed, that is, by the satisfaction of the various just-war criteria laid down by the law of nature.

Self-defence may therefore be seen to be very different from a just war, in a variety of ways. For one thing, self-defence was discussed almost entirely as a prerogative of *individuals*, undertaken on their own initiative, whereas the waging of just wars was the prerogative of states, as stressed by the principle of *auctoritas*. In the fourteenth century, John of Legnano, who was a professor of civil law at the University of Bologna, characterised self-defence as a species of what he called a 'particular war' – i.e., a 'war' waged by one person on his own behalf – as opposed to a 'universal war', involving the whole community.[67] In addition, while the Catholic Church clearly approved of just wars, it continued to be wary of self-defence, on the ground that it was egoistic action, undertaken by a person strictly for his *own* benefit rather than for that of the community, as in the case of a just war. As such, it was directly contrary to the divine command of the gospels to turn the other cheek – so that a Christian who engaged in it imperilled his immortal self and risked eternal damnation.

At the same time, though, individual self-defence was held to be permitted instead by *natural* law, which recognised a fundamental right of self-preservation as a 'natural' or instinctive feature of the human species (and of all other species as well).[68] Strictly speaking, states had a natural-law right of self-defence too, against aggressors; but this was little developed in medieval writing. A situation of an aggressive attack by one state against another would be analysed in terms of the presence and absence of a *justa causa* rather than of the exercise of self-defence. Not for many centuries to come would self-defence be applied in any systematic way to states.[69]

Self-defence differed from just wars not only as a matter of broad principle but also in a host of specific ways. For one thing, its status as an inherent natural-law right meant that no permission was required from

---

[67] John of Legnano, *Tractatus*, at 276–7. On John of Legnano, see Ballis, *Legal Position*, at 51–8.

[68] See John of Legnano, *Tractatus*, at 278–80.   [69] See Chapter 3 below.

any higher authority for its exercise. In other words, the just-war principle of *auctoritas* was inapplicable to it. Also inapplicable was the just-war principle of *personae*, so that self-defence was available to ecclesiastics, whereas participation in just wars was not. John of Legnano, followed by Bonet, held self-defence to be exercisable by sons against fathers, by vassals against lords, by monks against abbots and even by slaves against masters.[70] (Interestingly, it was held by John of Legnano that heavenly bodies possessed no right of self-defence, apparently because they were not 'receptive of foreign impressions'.)[71] Another notable difference between self-defence and just warfare concerned the taking of property. A self-defender was entitled to use force to recover any of his *own* property that his attacker might have purloined, provided that he acted in the immediate aftermath of the theft.[72] A fighter in a just war, however, could go further in two respects. First, he could capture *any* property to which his enemy had lawful title. Second, the *quantity* of property captured was allowed to exceed in value the loss caused by the unjust party's original wrongdoing.[73] A final difference between self-defence and just war – and perhaps the most striking one – was that self-defence action did not have to be directed against an *unlawful* attack. In other words, a *justa causa* was not required. The reason was that self-defence was seen as an exercise of a primeval right of survival under any and all conditions – a right possessed by wrongdoers as well as by champions of justice.[74]

Perhaps the most important restriction on self-defence was that it was only allowed against an *ongoing* wrong, such as an assault. It must not be either preventive (prior to the attack) or punitive (subsequent to the attack). Self-defence, in other words, was the act of preventing the wrongdoing from being consummated, i.e., of warding off the assault as it was actually occurring. In the words of Vitoria, 'Self-defence must be a response to an immediate danger, made in the heat of the moment or *incontinenti* as the lawyers say.'[75]

---

[70] John of Legnano, *Tractatus*, at 289–91; and Bonet, *Tree of Battles*, at 170–1. Bonet, however, held that clerics could use force to defend property only in a case of strict necessity. *Tree of Battles*, at 140–1, 145.

[71] John of Legnano, *Tractatus*, at 281.   [72] *Ibid.* at 297–302.

[73] Vitoria, *Law of War*, at 304–5, 317–18, 322–3.

[74] Bonet, *Tree of Battles*, at 171. Self-defence against lawful force might, however, be punishable under the local civil law of the place in which it occurred.

[75] Vitoria, *Law of War*, at 300.

In practice, some extremely slight leeway was allowed for individual self-defence, in both temporal directions. Preemptive action was permitted, according to John of Legnano, when a foe was 'bold and ready to strike'.[76] There was some slight tolerance for action after the fact as well. Vitoria held that natural law allowed an individual who had been assaulted to strike back at his attacker even if there was no threat of a further blow. This was in the interest of allowing the victim to avoid 'disgrace and humiliation' or 'dishonour and loss of face'.[77] Also, action in hot pursuit to recover property was allowed, immediately after a robbery. But these were marginal considerations. In principle, the rule was that self-defence served only the very limited purpose of fending off a blow in the course of delivery or preventing the consummation of an ongoing attack. It differed critically from a just war in having no law-enforcement component, and in being preventive rather than remedial in character.

The 'rights' of war

Medieval just-war doctrine was notably lacking in any idea of moral equivalence, or equality of rights, between a just and an unjust belligerent. The unjust side, by definition, had no right whatever to use force against the just side, any more than a criminal has a 'right' to use violence against a magistrate. Indeed, the pacifist heritage of medieval Christianity gave rise to doubts over whether even fighters on the just side possessed a positive right to commit violence. Some bishops held that killing was sinful, even in a just cause, and that penance was therefore required. In the fourth century, Basil the Great pronounced that soldiers should abstain from communion for three years following their belligerent actions.[78] The laws of Henry I of England in the early twelfth century prescribed forty days' penance on bread and water (as well as additional deprivations in Lent) for any soldier who had killed in 'a national war or defence of his lord'.[79]

There were at least a few instances in which these strictures were actually followed in practice. The best-known case occurred after the Battle of Hastings of 1066, when the Norman bishops laid down an elaborate schedule of penances, carefully geared to the particular actions and attitudes of the participating troops. Simply for fighting in a just war, a penance of three years was prescribed. One year of penance was required of a fighter for each enemy soldier that he knew that he had

---

[76] John of Legnano, *Tractatus*, at 304.   [77] Vitoria, *Law of War*, at 299–300.
[78] Verkamp, 'Moral Treatment', at 224.   [79] Haines, 'Attitudes', at 380.

killed. If a soldier struck an enemy but was unsure whether death had ensued or not, the penance was forty days. If the number of opponents that a soldier killed was not known, then there was to be penance of one day per week for the rest of the soldier's life (or the building or endowing of a church as a substitute). There was a special rule for archers, who shot from afar and naturally would not know the effects of their acts: penance for three Lents. The most extreme sanction was reserved for those with the improper *animus*. These killings were straightforward homicide (even if the cause was just), requiring seven years' penance. Even the commander himself, Duke William of Normandy (now to become King William I of England), made amends for the conflict (which incidentally had been expressly authorised by Pope Alexander II) in the form of the endowing of Battle Abbey, which still stands as a tangible monument to the force of the medieval law of just wars.[80]

Persons fighting for an unjust cause were naturally in an even less envious position. There naturally could be no question of their being accorded a legal immunity for their acts. Any killing done by them was mere homicide, with each soldier being individually responsible for his own guilty acts.[81] There were various specific legal indications of this difference of position between individual just and unjust fighters. One of these concerned the availability of what was called, borrowing from Roman law, an *actio mandati*. This referred to a legal right of the warriors to be indemnified for their expenses by the authority on whose behalf they were fighting.[82] Persons fighting for a just cause had an *actio mandati* against their superior. Those on the unjust side had no such right *vis-à-vis* their sovereign.[83] There was asymmetry too with regard to the acquisition of legal title to property captured in war. Fighters for an unjust cause could not receive good legal title to any enemy property which they captured. As unjust warriors, they were on a par with mere thieves, who of course received no title to goods that they stole. They could not legally enslave captured persons from the just side. Nor were fighters on the unjust side entitled to be ransomed.[84]

---

[80] Verkamp, 'Moral Treatment', at 224–5.
[81] See, for example, Suárez, *Three Virtues*, at 813.
[82] On the *actio mandati*, see John of Legnano, *Tractatus*, at 259. See also Vitoria, *Law of War*, at 304–5, 322; and Suárez, *Three Virtues*, at 820. The *actio mandati* was only allowed for expenses incurred over and above what the soldiers had a prior duty to contribute by virtue of, say, feudal obligations. It was also not available to persons who served for a wage.
[83] F. H. Russell, *Just War*, at 150–5. See also Ayala, *De Jure*, at 24–5; and Belli, *Military Matters*, at 64.
[84] See, for example, Belli, *Military Matters*, at 59–60.

More generally, it may be said that the nature of just wars ruled out, *a priori*, the idea that the laws of war could apply even-handedly to the two sides. That was clearly impossible, given that only one side had even a pretence of a right to use force at all. The entire tenor of the laws of war consisted in placing restraints on how vigorously the *just* side could prosecute its cause. It was no part of the law of war, in the medieval mind, to mark out a level playing field for the two sides to contend on an equal footing.

There was one important caveat to this general principle of no rights of war for unjust warriors. That was that fighters in an unjust cause did not thereby forfeit their fundamental natural-law right of self-defence, which (as noted above) did not require a *justa causa*. This was, of course, another indication of the point that self-defence action, rooted in the primitive species instinct of self-preservation, was conceptually quite distinct from general just-war doctrine. It only remains, in this context, to observe that this caveat had an importantly limited reach. By its nature, it could justify the unjust warriors in fending off attacks on them by the just side; but it did not entitle them to take offensive action against their foes on the just side. This point, incidentally, nicely illustrates the essentially offensive character of just-war action.

For the overwhelming part, just-war doctrine, in its treatment of the conduct of hostilities by the just side, remained resolutely lodged at the level of broad general principle, and indeed of only one general principle at that: necessity. That meant that the just side was permitted to use whatever degree of force was strictly necessary in the particular circumstances of the case to bring about victory. Beyond that point, *all* force became unlawful. As Vitoria explained, any measures that had the effect of weakening the enemy's resources were lawful, even if they entailed the killing and plundering of innocent persons. By the same token, however, such drastic acts would *not* be permissible if the struggle could be 'satisfactorily waged' without resorting to them. The purpose of war, it must always be remembered, was not the destruction of the enemy for its own sake but rather the obtaining of justice.[85] This principle of necessity imported a balancing test – a weighing of the suffering caused by the war, against the military advantage at stake.

> [C]are must be taken [cautioned Vitoria] to ensure that the evil effects of the war do not outweigh the possible benefits sought by waging it. If the

---

[85] Vitoria, *Law of War*, at 317, 326–7.

storming of a fortress or town garrisoned by the enemy but full of innocent inhabitants is not of great importance for eventual victory in the war, it does not seem to me permissible to kill a large number of innocent people by indiscriminate bombardment in order to defeat a small number of enemy combatants.[86]

This principle of necessity was Janus-faced, however. If it sometimes pointed in the direction of moderation, it could as easily point in the direction of licence. On the side of licence, necessity could permit the just side to take extreme measures to ensure victory. As Suárez tersely pronounced, 'if an end is permissible, the necessary means to that end are also permissible'.[87]

Apart from this general principle of necessity, just-war doctrine laid down hardly any specific rules of war, to be observed in all circumstances by the just side.[88] The principal one was a logical outgrowth from the principle of *personae*. Just as that principle precluded persons in the specified categories from being participants in war, so it also implied that those same persons should be exempted from being targets of war measures. This inference was expressly articulated by the Second Lateran Council of 1139, which ruled that there should be no molesting of certain categories of noncombatants, such as clerics, pilgrims, merchants and peasants.[89] Even this specific rule was actually rooted in the principle of necessity, in that it was taken for granted that such harmless persons as the ones identified would, in the nature of things, pose no actual military threat. Virtually the only specific rule laid down in the Middle Ages that did *not* arise from necessity was another stricture by that same Lateran Council: a flat prohibition against the use of 'that murderous art of crossbowmen and archers' in wars within the Christian world.[90] (These black arts continued to be permitted against infidel enemies.) Such a specific ban on a type of weapon was, however, unique (and, on the evidence, not very effective). On the whole, the jealous lordship of the principle of necessity was very nearly unchallenged in the Middle Ages.

---

[86] *Ibid.* at 315–16.   [87] Suárez, *Three Virtues*, at 840. See also Hartigan, 'Saint Augustine'.
[88] See Cole, 'Aquinas', at 67–71.
[89] Second Lateran Council (1139), Canon 11, in 1 Tanner, *Decrees*, at 199. This rule on noncombatants was renewed by the Fourth Lateran Council (1215), Constitution 22, *ibid.* at 222. See also Bonet, *Tree of Battles*, at 153–4, 188. On immunities of various noncombatants, see Keen, *Laws of War*, at 189–217.
[90] Second Lateran Council (1139), Canon 29, in 1 Tanner, *Decrees*, at 203.

Making peace – the jus victoriae

One of the most distinctive and instructive aspects of medieval just-war theory was its treatment of peace arrangements. One should speak of 'arrangements' rather than of 'treaties' in this connection because just-war doctrine did not envisage that wars would be concluded by a process of negotiation. Instead, it concerned itself with situations in which one side triumphed militarily over the other; and it proceeded to consider what kinds of terms or penalties the winning side was permitted to impose onto the losing one. The set of rules governing the rights of winners was sometimes known as the *jus victoriae* ('law of victory'). By the nature of the situation envisaged, this *jus victoriae* was a law of *diktats* rather than a law of treaties.[91]

One possible misunderstanding should be dispelled at the outset: the supposition that the just side would necessarily be the one doing the dictating. For all of the idealism and other-worldliness of the theologians who elaborated the medieval just-war schema, there was no general illusion that the virtuous side would inevitably triumph.[92] On the contrary, medieval writers were fully aware that history and scripture were both replete with instances in which the wicked had vanquished the innocent on the field of battle. This was explained in a variety of ways, such as by holding that God, acting in ways not fathomable by fallible humans, chose to allow evil-doers to prevail (presumably only temporarily), possibly as a means of punishing evil acts committed on some prior occasion by the just side. What medieval just-war theory did hold, though, was that, *if* the wicked side happened to prevail in a war, then its victory could represent nothing more than a purely material triumph, a successful exercise of power but not of right. The determination of legal right was exclusively a function of the principle of the law in its objective (if silent) majesty, and in particular of the principle of *justa causa*. It would therefore also be entirely wrong to suppose that medieval just-war theory viewed war as a means of determining which side was legally in the right. Power and right, to put it simply, had no necessary connection whatever with one another.

This meant that a just war was very different from a duel – i.e., from a situation in which two rivals agreed with one another in advance that the outcome of their combat would decide the issue between them and also

---

[91] For a systematic exposition of the *jus victoriae*, see Suárez, *Three Virtues*, at 840–51.
[92] See, for example, Gentili, *Law of War*, at 32, 298–9.

preclude any future quarrelling on the subject. The evil of duelling therefore lay in the way that it converted – or purported to convert – a dispute over legal right into a mere contest of brute strength, with the winner acquiring recognised legal rights by virtue of his armed triumph. A just war was importantly different. It was purely remedial in nature and, as such, was not a source of legal rights on its own. Rather, a just war was merely a means of *enforcing* a right which had an entirely independent prior existence. That enforcement effort might be successful or not as the case may be. But if the unjust side happened to have the better of the conflict, it thereby acquired no legal rights which it did not possess beforehand. That meant, in turn, that there was no bar to the just side's reasserting its claims on some future occasion when the strategic outlook appeared more auspicious. Such a situation was therefore more in the nature of truce than of a true peace. Much later in history, as will be seen, the ethos of the duellist would enter the realm of war.[93] In the Middle Ages, however, the two processes were seen as entirely foreign to one another.

The *jus victoriae*, in short, was strictly a law as to what terms a just side could impose onto an unjust one (assuming, necessarily, that the fortunes of war happened to favour it). Its guiding principle was the key concept of *animus*, which clearly dictated that peace settlements must be infused by a spirit of moderation and fairness on the victor's part. A just victor, as Augustine emphasised, must be animated by 'the benevolent design' of restoring 'the mutual bond of piety and justice' between the contending parties, which is their normal and natural relation.[94] Gratian was of like mind, holding that the very purpose of war was 'to procure more easily for the vanquished a participation in piety and justice'.[95] Oppression and mere vindictiveness must therefore be strictly eschewed. 'Just as violence is the portion of him who rebels and resists', Augustine admonished, 'so mercy is the due of him who has been conquered or captured'.[96] Vitoria, in the sixteenth century, was rather more specific on the point, emphasising that the effect of victory (for the just side, that is) was that the victor thereby became the judge of his foe's wrongdoing. In discharging this judicial role, the victor was obligated to 'use his

---

[93] See Chapters 4 and 5 below on this later development.
[94] Augustine, Letter No. 138, in *Political Writings*, at 178–9.
[95] Gratian, *Gratianus in Jurisprudence*, at 23.
[96] Augustine, Letter No. 189, in *Select Letters* (Cambridge, Mass.: Harvard University Press, 1953), at 331.

victory with moderation and with Christian humility'.[97] He must be scrupulously fair to his vanquished foe – and in particular he must spurn any temptation to extract unreasonable rewards for himself. 'He must give satisfaction to the injured [i.e., to himself]', cautioned Vitoria, 'but as far as possible without causing the utter ruination of the guilty commonwealth'.[98] There was no justification, he added, 'for plundering and robbing the unfortunate victims of defeat of all they possess'.[99]

Two notably important prerogatives were allowed to victors in just wars. First was the right to be indemnified by the losing side for the expenses incurred in prosecuting the struggle. This was on the thesis that the ultimate responsibility for the conflict lay with the unjust side because of its obstinate refusal to respect the legal rights of the just party. It was therefore only right that it should fully compensate the just party for all the expenses that it incurred, including the cost of prosecuting the war. The second key prerogative was the right to impose punishment onto the defeated side or to demand some kind of guarantees or assurances that the wrongful conduct would not be repeated. Here too, the principles of justice and proportionality were the watchwords. Any punishment inflicted must, however, be carefully tailored to the original wrongdoing; and there must be no indulgence in mere vengeance or malice. 'Punishment should fit the crime', asserted Vitoria; 'it would be intolerable if we were allowed to occupy the whole kingdom of France because they had plundered a few cattle or burnt a single village'. Similarly, it would be 'barbarous and inhumane' to depose an enemy sovereign who fought for an erroneous cause in good faith.[100] In sum, the idea that a victor could dictate whatever terms it wished to a vanquished foe was completely foreign to the medieval just-war mentality.[101]

Outside the cloister

The mature framework of medieval Christian just-war thought was very impressive for its intellectual coherence and consistency. At the same time, however – and perhaps for that very reason – it must be said that it

---

[97] Vitoria, *Law of War*, at 327.   [98] *Ibid.*
[99] Vitoria, Letter to Miguel de Arcos, 8 Nov. 1534, in *Political Writings*, ed. Anthony Pagder and Jeremy Lawrance (Cambridge: Cambridge University Press, 1991) at 332.
[100] Vitoria, *Law of War*, at 324–6.
[101] On the medieval *jus victoriae*, see generally Brière, 'Juste victoire'.

exuded the musty odour of the scholar's chamber rather than the bracing air of the field of battle. Just-war doctrine might be described as a distinctly 'top-down' approach to war. That is to say, that it was deductive in character, based on a very small number of very general principles, derived from general natural law and Christian scripture rather than from any careful empirical analysis of war itself. Just-war writing therefore always had a certain aura of artificiality, an intricacy and detail that appealed more naturally to the subtle debater or logician than to the battle-hardened general. Never, in short, has writing about war been so largely the province of people so far removed from the actual practice of the subject.

It is therefore surprising to find that the doctrinal writings on war had any effect at all on rulers and warriors in the real world. But there is at least some evidence that they did. Notice has already been taken of the penances prescribed after the Battle of Hastings. In 1158, we find no less a figure than Holy Roman Emperor Frederick I, when preparing to attack Milan, carefully laying the legal groundwork for the operation. He set out the reasons for the conflict and obtained express confirmation of them from the bishop of Brixen. He even took scrupulous care to claim the correct *animus*, sternly (if perhaps a trifle optimistically) cautioning his knights that 'it is not lust for domination that drives us to battle, but a fierce rebellion' on the part of the wicked and refractory Milanese.[102]

On the whole, however, evidence of the impact of just-war thought on state practice in the Middle Ages was decidedly modest. Realists will naturally find it especially difficult to believe that the principle of *animus* in particular was ever very much in evidence in medieval warfare. Even the principle of *personae*, in which the Church might be thought to have taken a particular interest, was evidently interpreted with an impressive degree of flexibility. *The Song of Roland* portrays Bishop Turpin laying into the enemy forces with a gusto worthy of Roland himself. In the more factual realm, there was the example of Pope John X personally leading his forces to victory against Muslim armies in 915. In 958, Pope John XII embarked on a decidedly un-holy military campaign against Capua and Benevento with a view to enlarging the papal domains.

The just-war theory of the churchmen was not, however, the only framework in which legal issues about war were discussed. That doctrine was supplemented by a body of law known as the 'Law of Arms' (or *jus*

---

[102] Verkamp, 'Moral Treatment', at 230.

armorum), which departed in several respects from the just-war thought of the Church writers. It was more down-to-earth, more suited to the everyday needs of the practising soldier, dealing with such matters as ransom arrangements for prisoners, the taking and dividing of spoils, truces and safe-conducts and so forth. It also took greater account of the realities of feudal life. This law of arms derived in large part from Roman miliary law (*jus militare*), preserved in outline form by the seventh-century encyclopedist Isidore of Seville. The treatise of Vegetius, dating from the fifth century AD, continued throughout the Middle Ages to act as a useful and prestigious source of information about Roman ways of war-making. Other contributions to the law of arms included judicial opinions handed down in cases dealing with war matters, dealing with such questions as ransom or entitlement to captured property. Finally, there were precedents in the practices of states, as handed down through the transnational guild of heralds. Heralds considered themselves (fancifully) to be descended from the Roman *fetiales*. Be that as it may, these ornaments of medieval life performed a variety of tasks such as advising on ceremonial points (often of great interest in the Middle Ages), undertaking diplomatic missions, adjudicating entitlements to coats of arms and so forth. They also constituted a kind of collective memory of practices associated with war. In that hierarchical and protocol-conscious era, every major armed force travelled with a herald in its company, for the conducting of such on-the-spot tasks as the negotiation of truces or the delivery of surrender demands to towns about to undergo a siege.[103]

The first systematic exposition of the law of arms was by John of Legnano. His work, written around 1360, was recast into somewhat more popular form by a Benedictine monk and legal scholar from Provence named Honoré de Bonet (or Bouvet), in his famous *Tree of Battles* of 1386–7.[104] A further restatement came from Christine de Pisan, in *The Book of Deeds of Arms and of Chivalry* of 1410. In the sixteenth century, this stream of writing on practical aspects of war merged with the more theoretical writings of the theologians, most outstandingly in the writing of Vitoria. His work was undertaken in the wake of the Spanish conquests in the New World, to which he turned his attention in detail. He also, in contrast to his medieval forebears, wrote in detail on aspects of the conducting of hostilities.[105] The result

[103] On medieval heralds, see Keen, *Chivalry*, at 134–42.
[104] On Bonet's work, see Wright, '*Tree of Battles*'.
[105] See generally Vitoria, *Law of War*, at 314–26.

was a body of writing about war which, for the first time, dealt squarely with harsh practical questions rather than with abstract generalities. The effect was to make legal writing on the subject of war more rich and varied, if also rather less intellectually coherent, than the more high-minded doctrinal writers of the Middle Ages had envisaged. We shall look briefly at a few of the principal concerns of this amorphous body of law and practice.

Declaring war

The commencing of wars provides a good example of an area in which inherited practice filled a vacuum left by doctrine. Just-war theory did not explicitly require the issuing of a formal demand for redress prior to resorting to war. This is somewhat curious, since it might have been reasonable to require a formal demand for justice by the just party before it resorted to the extreme measure of war to vindicate its rights. It may be that the analogy between war-making and law enforcement was responsible, since it was not common for magistrates to give prior warnings to criminals of their forthcoming arrest. In all events, the gap was filled, at least in part, by borrowing from Roman precedents. By the twelfth century, it was reasonably common – but by no means universal – for some kind of formal notice to be given to the enemy side prior to the launching of a war.[106] Various specific procedures were employed for this purpose. One was the dispatching of heralds to the court of the opposing ruler to present a formal demand for the redress of an alleged grievance, in the nature of what later ages would call an ultimatum. Sometimes, ultimatums were very detailed, replete with flowery language and elaborate politeness, as in 1528, when Francis I of France commenced war against Charles V of the Holy Roman Empire.[107] Declarations could also, however, be extremely terse, as in the case of the declaration of war by Savoy against Milan in 1427.[108] The use of heralds to declare war remained common in Europe into the sixteenth century and did not fall into complete disuse until the seventeenth century.[109]

---

[106] On medieval declarations of war, see Nys, *Droit de la guerre*, at 105–12.
[107] Declaration of War by France, 22 Jan. 1528, 4(2) Dumont 502–10.
[108] Declaration of War by Savoy, 21 Aug. 1427, 2(2) *ibid* at 193.
[109] On the use of heralds, see 3 Nys, *Droit international*, at 31–3; and Garrett Mattingly, *Renaissance Diplomacy* (Harmondsworth: Penguin, 1955), at 29–31.

There were other means of instituting war, such as by the dispatching of letters of defiance (as they were aptly termed). These were, strictly speaking, formal renunciations of feudal obligations.[110] The historian Jean Froissart has left a description of this process in his account of the inauguration of the Hundred Years War between England and France in 1337. The English parliament entrusted to the bishop of Lincoln the task of taking documents to the king of France, formally rescinding the homage that Edward III had previously given as a vassal to King Philip VI of France (with respect to French territories held by England). The message also formally asserted Edward III's claim to the French crown, which Philip VI was accused of unlawfully usurping. 'We give you notice', the French king was informed, 'that we shall claim and conquer our heritage of France by the armed force of us and ours, and from this day forward we challenge you and yours'. The message concluded by announcing that 'we consider you as our enemy and adversary'. Froissart clearly stated that King Philip VI did not consider any response to be necessary. Instead, he simply granted the bishop safe passage back to England.[111] Various symbolic acts could also function as declarations of war, such as the unfurling of flags. Italian city-states sometimes adopted the practice of throwing down a gauntlet, i.e., of sending a bloody glove to the opposing side.[112] The imprisonment of all nationals of the enemy-state-to-be was another device. According to Vitoria, a refusal by a state to admit nationals of another state into its territory, or a mass expulsion of nationals of another state, likewise amounted to 'an act of war'.[113]

The formal announcing of war was sometimes a dual process – of announcement to the enemy, coupled with a parallel proclamation to the declaring ruler's own population. This was the case in the English

---

[110] Haggenmacher, *Grotius*, at 233–7. See, for example, a letter of 1315 from Robert, the son of the Count of Flanders, to his feudal superior, King Louis X of France, informing the French king that he (Robert) was adhering to his father's cause in a conflict between Flanders and France (while carefully stating that he would continue to render fealty and homage to Louis), at 1(2) Dumont 23.

[111] Froissart, *Chronicles*, at 59–60. See the text of a letter of defiance from the children of the deceased Duke of Orléans to his slayer John, Duke of Burgundy, of 18 July 1411, together with the response, at 2(1) Dumont 343. For other examples of letters of defiance, see letter from John, Duke of Burgundy to Charles VI, 24 Sept. 1415, 2(2) *ibid.* at 54; and letter from the Duke of Prussia to the king of Poland, 1454, 3(1) *ibid.* at 199.

[112] Redslob, *Histoire*, at 152.

[113] Vitoria, *On the American Indians*, in *Political Writings*, ed. Anthony Pagden and Jeremy Lawrance (Cambridge:Cambridge University Press), at 278.

declaration of war against France in 1557. Two groups of heralds were put to work that day. One of them was dispatched to announce war to the French government, while the other one proclaimed the news in London.[114] As we shall see, declarations of war to the warring state's own population would become an ever larger feature of declarations of war with the passage of time.

Conducting the hostilities

It has been observed that the just-war theorists, applying the rules of natural law, based their views on the conduct of hostilities on a single principle: necessity. In practice, this did not bode well for the moderation of the horror and destruction of war, since each side would naturally incline to regard itself as the just one and would just as naturally err on the side of generosity in deciding what actions were needed to bring its enemy to book. The Law of Arms, however, offered some semblance of hope for moderation. In particular, the codes of knighthood that were so important a part of medieval chivalry exalted the practices of fair play and generous treatment of vanquished foes. The ethos of the tournament was clearly apparent in these ideals. And war itself, to some extent, took on ritualistic trappings, perhaps in part as a survival of ancient practices. The besieging of cities in particular became a highly ritualised activity in the Middle Ages, governed by an elaborate code of rules and practices.[115]

Probably the most important practical impact of chivalric ideals was in the realm of treatment of prisoners. Monarchs who were at war with one another sometimes entered into agreements on the treatment of prisoners, as in the case of France, England and the Holy Roman Empire in 1528.[116] The most striking innovation, though, was the discontinuance of the ancient practice of enslaving prisoners of war (at least in wars between Christians). Ransom was substituted, concerning which an elaborate body of rules and practices grew up.[117] It was seen as a legal entitlement for prisoners, with the amount of the ransom 'agreed' on a contractual basis between each individual prisoner and his captor. But this (comparatively) humane practice was not universally followed. A well-known departure from it occurred at the Battle of Agincourt in

---

[114] Nys, *Droit de la guerre*, at 111.   [115] See Keen, *Laws of War*, at 119–33.
[116] England-France-Holy Roman Empire, Treaty of 15 June 1528, 4(1) Dumont 515.
[117] On ransom in medieval warfare, see Keen, *Laws of War*, at 156–85.

1415, when King Henry V of England ordered all but the most important
of the French prisoners to be killed.[118]

The rules and practices of knighthood and chivalry did little in
practice to mitigate the horrors of war. They played a greater role in
literature of the romance writers, such as Chrétien de Troyes, than of
lawyers such as John of Legnano. For the most part, medieval warfare
presented a shocking picture of horror and brutality.[119] From the annals
of the Hundred Years War of the fourteenth and fifteenth centuries came
a picture of war that was at the furthest remove from romance. There
were relatively few pitched battles. A more typical method of warfare was
the *chevauchée*, which was a raiding expedition by mounted soldiers,
dedicated to the destruction of crops, pillaging of property and general
weakening of the enemy's war-making capacity. Further scope for suffering by civilians was offered by the euphemistically named 'free companies' of soldiers, who hired themselves out to the highest bidder
during war – commonly turning their hands, with remarkable nimble-
ness, to free-lance plundering during times of peace or truce. These
bodies were also known, with ominous accuracy, as *les écorcheurs*
('scorchers'). Nor did the activities of free-ranging knights always measure up to the high standards of the medieval romances. Saint Peter
Damian (a bishop of Ostia in the eleventh century), for example,
grumbled that the swords wielded by knights errant had created more
widows and orphans than they had protected.[120] By the end of the
sixteenth century, knighthood had sunk to the level of satire at the
hands of Miguel de Cervantes.

To their credit, the lawyers were consistent spokesmen for moderation in war. John of Legnano and Bonet both condemned gratuitous
violence, pillaging, molesting of civilians, the mistreatment of prisoners
of war and the like.[121] Of more practical import were certain advances
from secular rulers, who began to take at least some steps to bring their
often unruly armed forces under some kind of control. A crucial step
was the promulgation of codes of conduct for armed forces by the rulers
who led them. An early example was produced by Florence in 1369. King
Charles V of France followed suit in 1374. In England, King Richard II
issued a set of ordinances on war at Durham in 1385, superseded in 1419

---

[118] Keen, *Chivalry*, at 221.
[119] For general surveys of medieval war, see Contamine, *Middle Ages*; and Maurice Keen
(ed.), *Medieval Warfare: A History* (Oxford: Oxford University Press, 1999).
[120] Haines, 'Attitudes', at 380.   [121] See Bonet, *Tree of Battles*, at 153–4, 188.

by a set of *Statutes and Ordinances to Be Kept in Time of War*, proclaimed by Henry V. In 1432, Holy Roman Emperor Sigismund issued a code for the conduct of his forces in the forthcoming military campaign against the Hussite forces in Bohemia.[122] From Charles the Bold of Burgundy came a set of rules on war in 1473. These various codes were designed to instill a sense of discipline in the armed forces, for the furtherance of effective war-waging, as well as for the protection of innocent parties from the rapacity for which medieval armed forces were all too justly famous.[123] The practical impact of these initiatives was limited. But they were an important beginning – if no more than that – in the daunting struggle to curb the excesses of war.

Neutrality

The position regarding neutrality provides perhaps the best example of a body of law growing up entirely through state practice, with no assistance whatever from formal just-war doctrine. The logic of the just-war outlook clearly had no room for neutrality. In a war between good and evil, between law enforcement and crime, the duty of third parties clearly was to support the just side – or, at the barest minimum, to refrain from providing any assistance to the unjust party. The problem with this approach is, however, all too obvious. It was typically difficult, or even impossible, for third states to know on which side right lay in any given contest. There was also the problem that the political interest of particular third states might militate against taking sides in a struggle. In all events, it certainly was not common in practice for third states to plunge into wars without very sound reasons.

Moreover, there were a number of very practical issues, beneath the notice of the theologians and philosophers, which cried out for solution. The most obvious of these concerned the carriage of goods by sea. What was the position of neutral-owned goods found on board enemy ships, and (more commonly) of enemy-owned goods found on board neutral vessels? To these questions, answers were hammered out by the mercantile trading communities themselves. The most prominent statement of the rules in this area was the so-called *Consolato del Mar* ('Consulate of the Sea'), which was apparently compiled by and for the merchant

---

[122] For the text of which, see 2(2) Dumont 236–40.
[123] Contamine, *Middle Ages*, at 119–21.

community of Barcelona in the thirteenth century on the basis of pre-existing practice.[124] The approach adopted by the *Consolato* on neutral property at sea has been called the character-of-the-cargo principle. That is, that a belligerent state could capture property belonging to enemy nationals even if that property was being carried on a neutral ship on the high seas – though any neutral goods on board must be left alone. By the same token, if neutral-owned property was located on an enemy ship, then the ship itself, together with any enemy property on board, could be captured – but here too, the neutral-owned property was immune from capture. In addition, belligerents were authorised by the *Consolato* to visit and search neutral ships on the high seas, to ascertain whether they were carrying any enemy-owned property or not, or anything in the nature of war materials (such as arms or ammunition) to the enemy state. This was a small beginning to what would eventually become an immensely detailed body of law about the rights and duties of neutrals. For present purposes, it is only necessary to note that this body of law had its genesis in the practical concerns of seamen and traders, not in the exalted ruminations of just-war theorists.[125]

Reprisals

Another very practical problem facing medieval rulers was what to do about small-scale injuries which did not justify the drastic step of war. The most obvious example was an injury committed against an individual national by a foreign party or foreign government, such as the plundering of a travelling merchant by a highwayman in a foreign state. The solution that was devised to this problem was the process that became known as reprisal. Unknown to Roman law, it constituted one of the more striking legal innovations of the Middle Ages. It is of particular interest for present purposes because, more than any other aspect of medieval conflict, it represented just-war principles operating in their purest form. And yet, paradoxically, it was not at all certain that reprisals constituted war at all. They certainly bore very little resemblance to what would be called war in later centuries. Because of the large – and often puzzling and contentious – role that reprisals would play in the

---

[124] See generally Stanley S. Jados, *Consulate of the Sea and Related Documents* (University, Ala.: University of Alabama Press, 1975).

[125] On neutrality in medieval practice, see Neff, *Rights and Duties*, at 7–26.

later history of war, it is well to take a careful look at their medieval origin.[126]

Reprisals arose out of Germanic law and practice, operating at first in the unedifying context of family feuding, in which revenge for an injury by an evil-doer could be taken against members of the perpetrator's family. By the High Middle Ages, it was being applied by analogy to states. The essence of it may be stated very simply. When a person was injured by a foreigner and was unable, for some good reason, to obtain compensation from the very person who committed the wrong, satisfaction could be had, as a last resort, by seizing property belonging to any fellow-national of the wrongdoer. Terminology was rather loose in this area. In its *very* narrowest sense, the word 'reprisal' referred to the retaking of stolen goods by the true owner from the very person who had stolen them. This original meaning is directly reflected in the word itself – from the French *reprendre*, meaning simply to take back or recover. A reprisal in this narrow and literal sense was permitted by general natural law. By a very slight extension, it was also regarded as permissible to seize property from the thief that was equivalent in amount to that taken, if the stolen property had been, say, consumed or lost.

This right of reprisal in the strict sense had to be exercised on the spot, at the time of the theft or very soon thereafter. It therefore bore a strong resemblance to self-defence – to the point that it may justly be thought of as self-defence of property rather than of person. It is therefore not surprising to find John of Legnano classifying this form of reprisal, along with self-defence, under the broad heading of 'particular war', meaning a 'war' waged by an individual on his own behalf and on his own authority.[127] In this very narrowest use of the term 'reprisal', there was of course no component of collective responsibility.

If satisfaction could not be obtained from the thief himself at the time of the offence, the victim could attempt to pursue the wrongdoer in the courts of the state in which the act occurred. If – but only if – justice was denied to the victim or was, for some reason, not available, then self-help would be allowed. This self-help could be exercised back in the victim's

---

[126] On reprisal in the Middle Ages, see generally Mas Latrie, *Droit de marque*, on which this discussion draws heavily. See also Nys, *Droit de la guerre*, at 37–54; and Brière, 'Évolution', at 251–6.

[127] John of Legnano, *Tractatus*, at 277. Strictly speaking, John of Legnano was positing the *absence* of a right of self-defence on the thief's part against the victim's recovery effort. The effect, however, was to place the recovery of stolen property on a par with self-defence.

home state; and it would be directed not against the thief himself, but against fellow-nationals of the thief who happened to reside there at the time. Specifically, the remedy would be the seizure of property from the thief's fellow-nationals, as compensation for the wrongdoing. This was a reprisal in the extended, and more common, sense of the word. To take this rather drastic step, the victim of the theft needed the express consent of his *own* sovereign. In other words, *auctoritas* was necessary, as it was for a just war. The *auctoritas* came in the form of what was called a 'letter of reprisal', which was an official authorisation to the victim, by his ruler, allowing him to seize property belonging to fellow-nationals of the thief who were resident in the sovereign's jurisdiction.

This process of taking reprisals (as it was commonly termed) was very closely analogous to a just war. To obtain the requisite letter of reprisal, the applicant had to establish that a wrong had actually been committed – i.e., that there had been a denial of justice by the authorities in the wrongdoer's country. This was, of course, the establishing of a *justa causa*. The letter would specify the aggregate amount of property that could be taken – an amount equal to the loss from the original theft. The issuance of letters of reprisal was often publicly proclaimed by heralds, also in the manner of wars. The particular persons who would be despoiled in this manner were of course, by hypothesis, entirely innocent of the original wrongdoing. They were nonetheless regarded as fair targets on the thesis that the wrong being remedied was not, strictly speaking, the original theft, but rather the subsequent denial of justice – a failure for which the foreign *state* was responsible, and, by extension, all of its members. The solace of these innocent sufferers, for what it was worth, was that they were entitled to be indemnified by the original wrongdoer, whom they could pursue in the courts of their own country.

The execution of letters of reprisal by the holders was subject to a number of interesting restrictions. For example, it was common for the letters to stipulate the allowance of a period of grace before the seizures could begin.[128] Another common limitation on reprisals was the exemption of certain categories of persons or property from them. Ecclesiastical property, for example, was typically exempted. This was reinforced by a pronouncement of the Catholic Church's Second Council of Lyons in 1274 (with the penalty of excommunication brandished).[129] Also immune from reprisals in most cases were travellers,

---

[128] Mas Latrie, *Droit de marque*, at 20.
[129] Second Council of Lyons (1274), Constitution 28, in 1 Tanner, *Decrees*, at 330.

pilgrims, ambassadors and the like, as well as merchants attending fairs.[130] It was also common for foreign nationals who were permanent residents of the issuing state to be exempted. Scholars were frequently exempted too (an early precedent being an exemption granted by Holy Roman Emperor Frederick I to scholars of the University of Bologna in 1155).[131]

Once the reprisal process was under way, it was subject to continuing judicial oversight. Property that was seized had to be brought before officials, who would certify that it fell within the terms of the reprisal grant (or order its release if it did not). The value of the property taken would also be officially assessed. At least in the early stages of the proceedings, the property was held by way of pledge. That is, it was simply sequestered and not confiscated or sold. (For this reason, reprisals were sometimes given the label *pignorationes* or *pignora*, from *pignus*, which was the old Roman law of pledge.) Once the quantity of property seized reached the stipulated value (i.e., the value of the original loss), seizures had to stop. If the original thief failed to come forward, at this late stage, to make amends, then the seized property could be sold and the proceeds paid over to the holder of the letter of reprisal. It should be added that the reprisal process operated exclusively against *property*. No violence was permitted against the persons of the foreign nationals, nor could they be imprisoned or held hostage or the like. The objects of the reprisal action were, however, legally obligated to acquiesce in the process, since it was carried out under colour of the prevailing local law.

The account just given describes the reprisal process in its mature form. The practice evolved gradually, beginning as early as the ninth century amongst the cities of northern Italy. By the thirteenth century, the practice had expanded northward. A request to the king of England for a letter of reprisal is known, for example, from 1295.[132] There was express provision for such letters in an English ordinance of 1353, as well as in a French maritime ordinance of 1400.[133] The law and practice in this area first received detailed scholarly attention from Bartolo of

---

[130] John of Legnano, *Tractatus*, at 314, 319–20.
[131] See H. Koeppler, 'Frederik Barbarosa and the Schools of Bologna: Some Remarks on the 'Authentica Habita'', 54 *English Historical Review* 577–607 (1939), at 593–606.
[132] Mas Latrie, *Droit de marque*, at 10.
[133] For the English enactment, see 27 Edw. 3 c. 17, in 1 A. Luders and T. E. Tomlins (eds.), *Statutes of the Realm* (London: 1810), at 339. On the French ordinance, see Ludwig Gessner, *Le droit des neutres sur mer* (2nd edn, Berlin: Carl Heymann, 1876), at 37.

Sassoferrato, the famous medieval lawyer, who wrote a short treatise on the subject early in the fourteenth century.[134] His treatment was liberally drawn upon later that century by John of Legnano and Bonet.[135]

The analogies between the reprisal process and just wars were many and obvious – the need for *auctoritas*, the requirement of a *justa causa*, the exemption of certain categories of persons, the precise definition of the *res* (i.e., the value of the original loss), the exact equivalence between the remedy and the original damage. Indeed, here was the application of just-war principles with what could (at least in principle) be called clinical precision. Moreover, the process could fairly be considered actually to be a war in the true sense, since it involved the exercise of coercive power – albeit in a delegated form, by the victim of the theft, rather than by the armed forces of the victim's state. For these reasons, Bonet could conclude of reprisals, though rather guardedly, that they constituted 'a kind of war'.[136]

In one important sense, however, reprisals failed to qualify as wars. That is, that they amounted to a delegation to the letter holder of a portion of his ruler's *sovereign* powers – i.e., the ruler's right to determine the distribution of property amongst persons located in the territory over which his sovereign powers extended. Reprisals were therefore, in the final analysis, really an exercise of domestic law enforcement – albeit *delegated* law enforcement – rather than a resort to war properly speaking. The close analogy of reprisals to war was really, then, a vivid demonstration of the powerful conceptual affinity between law enforcement and just wars.

Certain types of reprisals, however, approached rather nearer to true wars than those just described. It was observed that letters of reprisal typically permitted property seizures only within the territorial jurisdiction of the issuing sovereign. Sometimes, though, letters authorised the holder to seize property outside the territory of the issuing ruler, on the high seas – an area over which the letter holder's ruler exercised no sovereign power. Ordinarily, the seizing of property on the high seas was piracy plain and simple. If the capturing was done under authority of a letter of reprisal, however, then it was commonly regarded not as an act of piracy, nor as an exercise of sovereign right, but rather as a true act of war. It was a limited kind of war, to be sure, since it was prosecuted only by the holder of the letter. But it was seen as war nonetheless. A letter of reprisal authorising

---

[134] On Bartolo, see Keen, *Laws of War*, at 219–21; and Nys, *Droit de guerre*, at 44–9.
[135] See John of Legnano, *Tractatus*, at 307–31; and Bonet, *Tree of Battles*, at 173–5.
[136] Bonet, *Tree of Battles*, at 173.

action on the high seas in this manner was sometimes (though not universally) known by the special term of 'letter of marque'. This expression apparently derives from the German word *Mark*, meaning frontier, referring to the right to take action beyond the frontier of the issuing state. It must be borne in mind, however, that medieval terminology was not consistent and that the expressions 'marque' and 'reprisal' were sometimes used interchangeably or synonymously.[137]

Taking to the seas to capture property was, naturally, a risky business. It is therefore not surprising that holders of letters of marque sometimes sub-delegated their rights to persons with some useful prior experience in the hazardous art of seizing private property on the high seas. As a result, simple piracy and lawful war-making were sometimes distinguished from one another by nothing more than the ink patterns on a letter of marque. Vitoria recognised this. While cautiously approving of letters of marque as remedies for wrongs done, he also warned of the risk of their misuse as a cover for piracy.[138] Land-based reprisals too offered ample scope for abuse, if the authorisations for them were too prodigally granted. In addition, there were some who objected in principle to the whole idea that innocent persons should be made to suffer for the acts of others. The Catholic Church, most notably, took this view. Its pronouncement on reprisals at the Second Council of Lyons of 1274 condemned them as 'oppressive and contrary to the laws and natural equity'.[139]

Some steps began to be taken to limit the possible abuses that could arise. Two treaties concluded by Genoa and Aragon, in 1378 and 1386, for example, spelled out certain procedural protections necessary before letters of reprisal could be issued.[140] At the same time, it should be appreciated that, while there was no denying that reprisals were capable of abuse, those were rude times; and the scope for alternative and gentler remedies was not great. For present purposes, the important point is that the historical roots of the law and practice of reprisals lay very squarely at the heart of medieval just-war theory, even if only by analogy – an association that would continue, with important consequences, for a very long time to come.[141]

---

[137] The usage adopted here, of associating 'reprisal' with seizure within the territory of the state, and 'marque' with action on the high seas, was used in Nys, *Droit de guerre*. Mas Latrie, *Droit de marque*, however, adopted the opposite association.

[138] Vitoria, *Law of War*, at 318.

[139] Second Council of Lyons (1274), Constitution 28, in 1 Tanner, *Decrees*, at 330.

[140] Mas Latrie, *Droit du marque*, at 44.

[141] See Chapters 3 and 6 below for further developments.

All of these innovations in state practice served to indicate that warfare was a decidedly more complex phenomenon than the expositors of natural-law and just-war theory were able to take account of. But the world of state practice was also changing by the sixteenth and seventeenth centuries, in some very fundamental ways. The Thirty Years War of 1618–48 represented, in many ways, the last – and most horrific – spasm of medieval-style warfare, with devastation and savagery on a scale far greater even than that of the earlier Hundred Years War. In the wake of that experience, new approaches to statecraft in general and to war in particular began to emerge and, with them, new legal conceptions.

PART II

New forces stirring (1600–1815)

[I]t seemed to be to the advantage of human interests to ... make a kind of business of war and to reduce it into the form of an art.

Samuel Pufendorf

In the seventeenth and eighteenth centuries, the nation-state (along with much else) emerged in recognisably its modern form. Along with it came modern international law – appropriately labeled as 'the law of nations'. The decisive contribution in this direction was made early in the seventeenth century by the Dutch lawyer (and theologian) Hugo Grotius, in his famous treatise *On the Law of War and Peace*, first published in France in 1625.[1] Grotius spoke of this law of nations in careful contrast to the older law of *nature*, which had dominated international legal thought throughout the Middle Ages. For our purposes, the new law of nations had two outstanding features that distinguished it from the older natural law. The first was that it focussed on the rights and duties of states as such – i.e., that it was a law applicable *only* to states.[2] It was therefore in sharp contrast to the older natural-law way of thinking, in which principles of universal application had been applied, with as little distortion as possible, to the conduct of rulers and private individuals alike. The second innovation of the law of nations was to concentrate on the external actions of states and thereby to forgo considerations of good faith and mental attitude and the like.

When this new approach was applied to the ever-relevant subject of war, the result was a discarding of the core just-war principles of *justa causa* and *animus*, in favour of a formalistic approach to war. A just war would now be seen as a war in which the full range of external formalities was in place. The result was a stress on the external features of war, with ever greater account taken, for better or for worse, of state practice as the guide to international law, rather than the eternal verities of nature. International legal thought about war, in short, was drifting steadily from Heaven down to Earth.

This change was a momentous one – perhaps the single greatest conceptual leap that has ever occurred in the history of international law. It entailed the emancipation of statecraft in general, including international law, from the principles of interpersonal morality, which had been so pronounced a feature of natural-law thought. The pioneering figure was the Italian political writer Niccolo Machiavelli, whose very name became a by-word for wickedness and depravity amongst moralists. He was the first to stress, in the most straightforward terms,

---

[1] On Grotius, see generally W. S. M. Knight, *Life and Works of Hugo Grotius* (London: Sweet and Maxwell, 1925); Edward Dumbauld, *The Life and Legal Writings of Hugo Grotius* (Norman, Okla.: University of Oklahoma Press, 1969); and Tuck, *Rights*, at 78–108.
[2] Grotius, *War and Peace*, at 639.

the view that the qualities that made for successful stewardship of a state were not (to put it mildly) the same as those for gaining entrance to the Kingdom of Heaven. Statecraft was increasingly becoming a science in this period, with the central concern being the dispassionate identification of the corporate interest of the state as such – followed by the rational and single-minded devotion to the promotion of that interest. This new science of statecraft was humanistic in flavour, as it dealt with the conduct of human beings whose activities and interests were resolutely planted in the hurly-burly affairs of the real world. Moreover, it operated according to a body of principles peculiar to itself. It even came to be taught as an academic subject, at least in German universities, under the name of 'cameralism'.

This new law of nations, like the new statecraft, was seen as a purely human creation, a product of the free will of man, again contrasting with the older law of nature, with its à priori and universal character.[3] It was, so to speak, a 'bottom up' system of law, crafted by the states of the world themselves in an empirical fashion, for dealing with practical issues which faced them. The principal 'legislative' devices for this new law of nations were treaties and customary practices (or 'usage' in the standard terminology of the time). Its doctrines and methods were therefore derived not from broad principles of morality but rather from a coldly unsentimental analysis of human political life as it was actually lived. In all these respects, this new law contrasted decisively with the 'top down' character of natural law, with its rationalistic style of deductive reasoning from lofty principles of great generality.

It would be an error, however, to suppose that this new law of nations entirely superseded the older natural law. Far from it. Natural law continued, throughout this period, to provide the basic framework for thinking about war. But it no longer held unchallenged sway to the extent that it previously had. Instead, the two bodies of law entered into a kind of partnership – somewhat warily, to be sure. The distinguishing feature of mainstream international law thought in this period was, therefore, its dualistic character, as these two types of law – of nature and of nations – co-existed and interwove to create what we now call international law. In principle, the foundation of international legal thought continued to be the law of nature, as in the Middle Ages. Indeed, this period was the great age of systematic natural-law jurisprudence, culminating in the middle of the eighteenth century in the

---

[3] *Ibid.* at 23–4.

encyclopedic writing of the German legal philosopher Christian Wolff.[4] The law of nations was originally seen as playing only a secondary and supplementary role, to be used on a somewhat ad hoc basis when rules of natural law were, for some reason, difficult to apply in practice.

In the course of time, however, the law of nations loomed ever larger and the law of nature ever smaller. This trend became particularly apparent in the work of Wolff's follower and populariser, Emmerich de Vattel. Vattel, significantly, was a practising diplomat as well as a treatise writer. His famous book on *The Law of Nations* in 1758 was the most accessible and thorough treatment of international law in its dualistic form. In his book, Vattel placed a great deal more stress on the law of nations – or 'voluntary' law as he termed it, following Wolff – than previous writers had. Nowhere was this more true than in his treatment of war. By the nineteenth century, the voluntary law would acquire an overwhelming dominance. But the two preceding centuries (our present period) constituted the age of transition, when the old law and the new functioned in tandem, in a workable – if sometimes untidy and uneasy – partnership. The line of international legal writing extending from Grotius to Vattel, with its dualistic character, will be referred to (for lack of a generally accepted label) as the mainstream tradition of international law.

The new prominence of nation-states on the European scene was abundantly apparent in the area of war. Its most obvious manifestation was the establishment of standing armies as instruments of the over-all national interest, in place of the feudal levies and ad hoc calls to arms of the general population that had characterised medieval warfare. The innovator in this regard was the Ottoman Empire, with its famous (and feared) Janissary Corps, founded in the fourteenth century. Amongst the Christian powers, France was the first to follow suit, in the fifteenth century. The members of these new forces undertook long-term service, in return for cash payment, thereby making soldiering into a career-long occupation for ordinary persons for the first time. (In fact, the word 'soldier' derives ultimately from the Latin 'solidus', a Roman gold coin, thereby indicating the tie between military service and the payment of a money wage.) The new ethos of professionalisation also extended well above the ranks of the common soldiers, as warfare began evolving above the realm of craftsmanship into something like a fully fledged

---

[4] For an English translation of a small portion of Wolff's great corpus of natural-law writing, see Wolff, *Law of Nations*.

science. Ever higher levels of technical expertise were now required in warfare, in such areas as ballistics, fortress design and naval architecture. With the establishment of military academies for systematic instruction, warfare entered fully into the spirit of what has been called, with some justice, the Age of Reason.[5]

An important corollary of this increasing professionalisation of warfare was an increasing tendency to separate military and civilian populations in a variety of ways. One way was visually. The custom of providing soldiers with uniform clothing ('uniforms' for short) began during the seventeenth century. So did the practice of housing soldiers in barracks instead of quartering them on civilian populations. Soldiers were even separated from civilians, in many cases by nationality, as it became common for European armies to be manned to a large extent by foreign mercenaries on long-term service rather than by patriotic nationals. Armed forces also began to be provisioned through regular commissary arrangements, to minimise the reliance on 'contributions' from civilian populations (as they were euphemistically termed).[6] In short, the armed service was on its way to becoming a distinctive way of life.

This increasing professionalisation of military life had many positive features, which international lawyers were not slow to recognise and applaud. The foremost effect was to advance the idea that warfare was a contest between the professional standing armies, with the ambient civilian populations to be as little affected as possible. The result was to reduce, if only modestly, the degree of suffering of civilian populations, which had been such a ghastly feature of the Thirty Years War (of 1618–48) in particular. The new military style also tended to promote moderation in warfare as between the contending fighters themselves. One reason for this was that the new standing armies were so expensive that rulers were often loath to take undue risks with them. Generals often avoided pitched battles where possible because of the risk of the destruction of their forces at a fell swoop. As an alternative, war of manoeuvre became the standard strategy, with the goal being to place

---

[5] On styles of warfare in this period, see generally George Clark, *War and Society in the Seventeenth Century* (Cambridge: Cambridge University Press, 1958); Anderson, *War and Society*; and Geoffrey Parker, *The Military Revolution: Military Innovation and the Rise of the West, 1500–1800* (Cambridge: Cambridge University Press, 1988).

[6] On this important aspect of war, see generally Martin van Creveld, *Supplying War: Logistics from Wallenstein to Patton* (Cambridge: Cambridge University Press, 1977); and John A. Lynn (ed.), *Feeding Mars: Logistics in Western Warfare from the Middle Ages to the Present* (Boulder, Colo.: Westview, 1993).

one's troops in enemy territory, so as to compel the enemy to bear the brunt of supporting them.

Another force in the direction of moderation of war was the comparative uniformity of military strength amongst the major European powers. France was the leading military power during this period. But even it possessed no decisive technological or numerical superiority over the various coalitions that were constantly assembled against it. The result was that there was only modest scope for territorial gains or losses. The style of warfare that emerged from these trends was succinctly summed up by an acute observer from across the Atlantic. Alexander Hamilton described the situation thus:

> The disciplined armies always kept on foot on the continent of Europe ... have ... been productive of the signal advantage of rendering sudden conquests impracticable, and of preventing that rapid desolation which used to mark the progress of war prior to their introduction. The art of fortification has contributed to the same ends. The nations of Europe are encircled with chains of fortified places, which mutually obstruct invasion. Campaigns are wasted in reducing two or three frontier garrisons, to gain admittance into an enemy's country. Similar impediments occur at every step, to exhaust the strength and delay the process of an invader. Formerly, an invading army would penetrate into the heart of a neighbouring country almost as soon as intelligence of its approach could be received; but now a comparatively small force of disciplined troops, acting on the defensive, with the aid of posts, is able to impede, and finally to frustrate, the enterprises of one much more considerable. The history of war, in that quarter of the globe, is no longer a history of nations subdued and empires overturned; but of towns taken and retaken; of battles that decide nothing, of retreats more beneficial than victories; of much effort and little acquisition.[7]

It is small wonder that the historian Edward Gibbon could complacently characterise the age as one in which warfare consisted of 'temperate and undecisive contests'.[8]

It was also an age of politeness and formality. The eighteenth-century Dutch international lawyer Cornelius van Bynkershoek observed (with disapproval) that rulers of his time were 'so addicted to flattery' that 'princes even in the midst of hostilities resort to adulation; so that now

---

[7] Hamilton, *Federalist Papers*, No. 8.
[8] 2 Edward Gibbon, *The History of the Decline and Fall of the Roman Empire*, ed. David Womersley (London: Penguin, 1994), at 513. (1st edn 1781.)

enemies invoke prosperity upon each other, call each other friends, and pretend to be sorry for their mutual losses'.[9] Others saw the situation in a more positive light. The Scottish philosopher and historian Adam Ferguson was pleased to note that, in the late eighteenth century, 'war is made with little animosity, and battles are fought without any personal exasperation of those who are engaged; so that parties are, almost in the very heat of a contest, ready to listen to the dictates of humanity or reason'.[10] It was reported that, in 1666, France dispatched an envoy to England – whilst the two countries were at war – to express commiseration for the Great Fire of London that year.[11]

There was, however, a darker side to this picture of moderate warfare. If this first era of modern statecraft was strikingly rational in its ethos, it was just as strikingly amoral. Indeed, from the standpoint of the new statecraft, the period might be known more aptly as the Age of Calculation than as the Age of Reason. This calculation was in the spirit of the new sciences of mathematics and mechanics, with the goal being the maximisation of the national interest. The ethos of the period was therefore relentlessly utilitarian, with little place for sentiment, moralism or ideology. Alliances were formed and dissolved in a kind of perpetual stately waltz, danced to the lilting strains of the European balance of power. Exemplifying the new style of rulership, near to the point of caricature, was that veritable crown prince of eighteenth-century political rationalists, the Austrian Count Kaunitz-Rittberg. He boasted of his mastery of the arcane art of 'political algebra' which enabled him, with the unerring certainty of the mathematician, to thread his way through the intricate diplomatic mazes of the time.[12] It is hardly surprising, then, that war took on the aura of a chess game, particularly in the northwestern part of Europe, with its flat terrain, network of canals, dense clustering of rich cities and chains of fortresses with their state-of-the-art geometrical designs.

This age of calculation was nothing resembling an era of peace. On the contrary, the major European powers oscillated into and out of war with one another, in various ever-shifting combinations, with monotonous regularity.[13] From modern perspectives (and some contemporary ones

---

[9] Bynkershoek, *Questions*, at 26.   [10] Anderson, *War and Society*, at 188.
[11] Bynkershoek, *Questions*, at 26.
[12] Walter L. Dorn, *Competition for Empire 1740–1763* (New York: Harper and Row, 1963), at 296–7.
[13] For an insightful analysis of the militaristic character of this period, see Speier, 'Militarism'. For a notably lucid account of the political and diplomatic contexts of wars of the period, see McKay and Scott, *Rise of the Great Powers*.

too), it was a depressingly materialistic time, with no ideological divides, no great causes, no spirit of heroic self-sacrifice. In the practice of states, if not the ruminations of scholars, the just-war ethos was very little in evidence. Lawyers in the mainstream tradition of international law, still in thrall to classical just-war thought, spoke out against this trend, but to little practical avail. Cynical statesmen – and they abounded during this period – had little trouble conjuring up a cause for war whenever one was needed. Voltaire at his most sarcastic has left us with a bitterly satirical picture of an eighteenth-century-style *casus belli*:

> A genealogist proves to a prince that he is the direct descendant of a count whose relatives had made a family pact three or four hundred years ago with a house whose very name has left no memory. This house had remote pretensions to a province whose last owner had just died of apoplexy. The prince and his council conclude without difficulty that the province belongs to him by divine right. This province, which is some hundreds of leagues distant, protests in vain that it does not know him, that it has no wish to be governed by him, that one must at least have a people's consent before legislating for it. These discourses do not even reach the ears of the prince whose rights are incontestable. He immediately finds a great number of men who have nothing to do nor to lose. He dresses them in heavy blue cloth at 110 *sous* the ell, puts a heavy white cord round their hats, makes them turn left and right, and marches to glory.[14]

According to Vattel, actual state practice was scarcely less absurd than this. He maintained that the war between France and the Netherlands in 1672 resulted from the irritation of the French King, Louis XIV, over the issuing of certain medals and the spreading of offensive jokes.[15] He also pointed out that, when the Northern War between Russia and Sweden broke out in 1701, one of the Russian 'grievances' was that Czar Peter I had not been shown proper honours when passing through Riga.[16]

These trends placed mainstream international-law writers, who were conservative by instinct, in a dilemma. They bemoaned the amorality of their age even while approving of certain of its more positive features, such as the moderation of warfare. Some commentators, however, went decidedly further towards embracing the new trends than the mainstream writers did. We shall look particularly at two dissident schools of thought about the legal nature of war that emerged during this period.

---

[14] Voltaire, *Philosophical Dictionary*, ed. and trans. Theodore Besterman (Harmondsworth: Penguin, 1971), at 232. (1st edn 1764.)
[15] Vattel, *Law of Nations*, at 120.   [16] *Ibid.* at 245.

One of these descended from the writing of the English political theorist Thomas Hobbes. The Hobbesian school of thought entailed a frank acceptance of the ways of power politics. Most pertinently for legal purposes, it rejected the fundamental natural-law principle that peace is the normal condition of interstate relations. The Hobbesians did not go so far as to renounce natural law entirely, but they accepted it only in a radically stripped-down form, with an obsessive concentration on the single principle of the quest for security in a brutally hostile world.

The other dissident line of thought will be called (for lack of any widely accepted term) the 'contractual' viewpoint. It adopted a model of war as a duel between states, entered into by mutual consent, thereby justifying the alternate label of the 'duelling' view of war. It rejected another of the basic tenets of just-war thought: the idea that victory in war could not, in itself, be a source of legal rights. Both of these new philosophies were more strongly in tune with the trends of contemporary power politics than the mainstream tradition was.

At the same time that these intellectual challenges to mainstream legal thought were being posed, conditions in European geopolitics were changing too. Particularly in the second half of the eighteenth century, new factors began to undermine the forces that had favoured moderation in the waging of war. For one thing, the focus of military activity shifted from the Low Countries to Central and Eastern Europe, where religious and ethnic hatreds assumed a prominence foreign to the older ethos of the 'sport of kings'. In the Balkans, the long retreat of the Ottoman Empire brought Muslim, Catholic and Orthodox interests into conflict. The near-annihilation of Prussia in the Seven Years War of 1756–63 – averted only by the spectacular generalship of Frederick II – provided vivid evidence that 'temperate and undecisive contests' were ceasing to be the norm. In addition, forces of ideology and nationalism began to stir, first with revolts in Corsica against Genoese and (later) French rule, and then with the American Independence War of 1775–83 – but most of all with French Revolutionary Wars that began in 1792 and extended, with brief interludes of peace, until 1815.

From the military standpoint, the French Revolutionary period witnessed some striking changes. First came the *levée en masse* of 1792, which swelled the revolutionary armies to a size far beyond that of the typical eighteenth-century force. This innovation made possible – and necessary – a new formula for victory in war: the devastating defeat of enemy armies with a single blow, which became the hallmark of Napoleonic warfare. After the hammerblow victory would come a humiliating peace treaty, possibly installing a new, French-supported government (as in the Netherlands, Naples, the Rhineland and Spain) or imposing large financial payments to France (as in the case of Austria). In addition, this period witnessed the world's first systematic attempt at 'total war' between whole economies, as the French 'Continental System' and the British practice of large-scale blockading and manipulation of neutral commerce were brought into opposition.

When the situation is perceived through legal lenses, however, a much more conservative picture of the French Revolution era emerges. The striking thing was how little, rather than how much, impact the upheavals had on the law of nations. It was one of history's more dramatic demonstrations of how it is that the doctrines and structures of international law are more deeply rooted – and correspondingly slower to evolve – than the surface events that claim the attentions of journalists and of some historians. The period produced no revolutionary international legal theorist comparable to William Godwin or Thomas Paine, no monumental treatise on 'Revolutionary International Law'. Resorts to arms were justified in largely traditional terms, with legal grievances identified.[17] The various French innovations in land warfare also had relatively little impact on the laws of war. As it happened, the principal international legal developments of the period had to do with the law of neutrality rather than of war as such.[18] From the standpoint of the legal conception of war, the key developments were the two dissident schools of thought, which predated the French Revolution by a century and more. These would slowly but steadily push the old natural-law doctrines of just wars into a marginal position. That process would culminate in the nineteenth century. But its early, and decisive, stages occurred during this period.

[17] For detailed information on the technical legal causes of war during the Revolutionary period, see Blanning, *Origins*.
[18] See Neff, *Rights and Duties*, at 69–85.

3

War in due form

A definite formality in the conduct of war was introduced by the law of nations, and . . . particular effects follow wars waged in accordance with such formality. . . . Hence arises the distinction . . . between a war which, according to the law of nations, is formally declared and is called legal, that is a complete war; and a war not formally declared, which nevertheless does not on that account cease to be a legal war.

Hugo Grotius[1]

The just-war tradition, inherited directly from the Middle Ages, continued to be the dominant framework for legal analyses of war throughout the seventeenth and eighteenth centuries. For example, the Dutch judge Cornelius van Bynkershoek, writing in 1738, defined war as 'a contest of independent persons carried on by force or fraud for the sake of asserting their rights'.[2] Vattel, in a similar spirit, referred to the right of states 'to use force to obtain justice, if it can not otherwise be had, or to follow up one's rights by force of arms'.[3] In the 1760s, William Blackstone, the influential English legal commentator, defined war as 'an appeal to the God of hosts to punish such infractions of public faith as are committed by one independent people against another; neither state having any superior jurisdiction to resort to upon earth for justice'.[4] These expressions of just-war sentiments, however, were anachronisms by the time they were pronounced. In reality, a number of important departures from past ways occurred, which, when fully developed in the nineteenth century, would take the legal conception of war far away from its medieval roots. The rise of the new law of nations, or

[1] Grotius, *War and Peace*, at 57.   [2] Bynkershoek, *Questions*, at 15.
[3] Vattel, *Law of Nations*, at 135.
[4] 2 Blackstone, *Commentaries*, ed. J. W. Ehrlich (New York: Capricorn, 1959), at 332. (1st edn 1769.)

'voluntary' law, alongside the old law of nature, gave to this period its distinctive dualistic stamp. There were now two kinds of just war: the natural-law kind, assessed according to the classical five-fold schema of the Middle Ages; and the voluntary-law kind, which looked to external formalities instead, thereby effectively dispensing with the key principles of *animus* and *justa causa*.

Wars that were unjust in this new voluntary-law sense – 'imperfect wars' as they came to be commonly called – began to be separated out from just (or 'perfect') wars in a quite different way from before. They began, during this period, to be excluded from the category of war altogether. This trend would reach its full maturation only in the nineteenth century, in the form of 'measures short of war'. But the early stages were apparent during the present era. Reprisals were the most prominent example of imperfect wars, but there were other kinds too to which our attention will be turned. They attracted comparatively little attention from lawyers at the time. In the light of the important future that lay in store for them, however, some careful attention to them will be in order.

Breaking new ground

The tenacity of the medieval just-war outlook was much in evidence throughout the seventeenth and eighteenth centuries even if it increasingly took on the air of a rear-guard action. Hugo Grotius strongly reaffirmed it in many respects.[5] He took great pains, as had Augustine, over a thousand years earlier, to refute the idea that the Christian religion enjoined absolute pacifism.[6] Echoing Augustine's suspicion of using force in self-help, he averred that 'it is more honourable to avenge the wrongs of others rather than one's own'.[7] He strongly endorsed the orthodox natural-law position that peace was the natural, or residual, condition of humankind. Thoroughly in the ethos of classical just-war thought, he defined war as an '[a]rmed execution against an armed adversary'. A decision to resort to war was just, he pithily remarked, 'if it consists in the execution of a right' and unjust 'if it consists in the execution of an injury'.[8] Also in the medieval vein, Grotius condemned unjust wars as mere brigandage.[9]

---

[5] See Tooke, *Just War*, at 195–230.   [6] See, for example, Grotius, *War and Peace*, at 57–90.
[7] *Ibid.* at 505.   [8] Grotius, *Commentary*, at 30. See also Grotius, *War and Peace*, at 555–6.
[9] Grotius, *War and Peace*, at 778.

On the particular, and vital, subject of *justa causa*, Grotius was rather more precise than his medieval forebears had been. He specified three types of just cause: defence against an impending or ongoing wrong; action to obtain what is owed; and the infliction of punishment for past wrongdoing.[10] Defensive war, the first category, differed from self-defence in the narrow and strict sense, in being directed against impending or threatening dangers rather than against an ongoing attack. This point will be explained more fully in due course in the context of self-defence. The second just cause, obtaining what is owed, could encompass several things. It might refer to the forcible repossession of some physical thing, such as territory, that was being wrongfully withheld. It could also refer to the extracting of compensation for some past misdeed, in which case it was regarded as tantamount to the recovery of a debt. The third kind of just war, for punishment, was, as the label indicated, punitive rather than compensatory in character. The measure of injury that could be inflicted under this heading was determined by the degree of moral turpitude of the wrongdoer, rather than by the amount of loss suffered by the victim (as under the second heading).[11] It may be noted that these three just causes corresponded temporally to the future, the present and the past. Defensive wars were future-oriented in being directed against impending wrongs. Wars to obtain things owed were concerned with ongoing wrongs. Punitive wars dealt with past misdeeds. This list of just causes acquired virtually canonical status, to be routinely endorsed by international lawyers for centuries to come.[12]

For all of Grotius's ties with the natural-law tradition of the past, however, it must be appreciated that his innovations were far more significant. For present purposes, three of these will be singled out. The first was the devising of a conception of a new body of law, which he called the law of *nations*, distinguished from the law of *nature* which had previously been the sole corpus of law dealing with war. Second was the distinction that he made between what he called 'primary' and 'secondary' action. Third was the articulation, for the first time, of a conception of a *state* of war. Each of these calls for a brief explanation.[13]

---

[10] *Ibid.* at 171. See also Haggenmacher, *Grotius*, at 176–85.

[11] Grotius, *War and Peace*, at 502–3. [12] See, for example, Vattel, *Law of Nations*, at 243–4.

[13] For expositions of Grotius's views on war, see generally Tooke, *Just War*, at 195–230; Haggenmacher, *Grotius*; Onuma (ed.), *Normative Approach*; and Johnson, *Ideology*, at 209–32.

Consider first the articulation of the concept of the law of nations. It is this achievement, more than any other, that entitles Grotius to his status as the 'father of international law'. Central to this conception of a law of nations was the idea that the legal relations that prevailed between nation-states were of a unique character, qualitatively different from those governing interpersonal contacts. No such distinction had been made in the Middle Ages. At that time, the law applicable to human relations, the *jus gentium* (or 'law of peoples') had been seen as merely a sub-category of the general, all-encompassing law of nature. No special body of law existed that was uniquely applicable to rulers. Instead, sovereigns were bound, at least in principle, by the same ethical and legal standards as their subjects were.

The source of this new body of law lay in the conscious will of the states themselves. Instead of being (so to speak) handed down from above, it welled up from below, blossoming out of the practices of the countries of the world. Its binding power came not from the command of God or the nature of things but rather from the 'mutual consent' of the states – either all or 'a great many' of them – and its function was the down-to-earth one of promoting the advantage of 'the great society of states'.[14] Where the law of nature was determined for all time to come by the over-all character of the universe, the law of nations was more flexible, more adaptable to local conditions. For this reason, Grotius sometimes referred to the law of nations as the 'volitional law', to reflect its origin in the collective will of the states of the world.[15] Later writers, most notably Christian Wolff and his follower Vattel, employed the expression 'voluntary law', which may have been coined by the German philosopher and polymath Gottfried von Leibnitz. (To avoid confusion, the term 'voluntary' law will be used in this discussion from here on.)[16]

The result of Grotius's innovation was to confer onto the mainstream tradition of international law a distinctively dualistic character, with these two bodies of law – natural and voluntary – constantly intertwining with one another in ways not always readily apparent to the

---

[14] Grotius, *War and Peace*, at 15.   [15] See, for example, *ibid.* at 38, 624.
[16] Actually, the voluntary law of Wolff and Vattel differed in some important respects from Grotius's law of nations, chiefly in being a law that was mandatory for all states (notwithstanding its label). Grotius's law of nations, in contrast, was contractual in nature. For the purposes of this history, the distinction is not germane, since the voluntary law of Wolff and Vattel shared with the Grotian law of nations the key feature of being concerned with the external actions of states in their practical dealings with one another.

unpractised eye. The partnership was not, however, seen as an equal one. The deeper and more fundamental of the two kinds of law was the law of nature. Grotius had no intention of discarding that foremost ornament of Western civilisation. The voluntary law of nations was seen to operate as a sort of help-mate to the law of nature, filling it out and supplementing it when necessary for practical reasons. It was therefore a kind of interstitial or secondary law. In the course of this period, however, the law of nations steadily gained the upper hand over the older law of nature in questions concerning war.

Perhaps the single most important difference between the contents of these two bodies of law was that the voluntary law was held to control only the external features of life, while the natural-law rules dealt with questions of intrinsic justice. Questions of conscience or of inner disposition were left as the preserve of the natural law. That clearly meant that the principle of *animus* was disqualified from any role in the voluntary law of war. More importantly, the principle of *justa causa* was left out of the voluntary-law fold as well. It had begun to be undermined, cautiously and tentatively, at the hands of ecclesiastical natural-law writers in the sixteenth century, most notably Vitoria. Like his medieval predecessors, Vitoria denied that it was possible for a war to be just on both sides because the principle of *justa causa* operated in a sternly objective manner. In a legal dispute, one side must be right and the other wrong. Vitoria tempered this doctrine, though, with a key concession: that, if the party lacking the *justa causa* nevertheless held its position in good faith, its lack of an objective *justa causa* would be excused. This would occur in a situation of what Vitoria called 'invincible error' (or doubt or ignorance): a state of affairs in which it was not possible, even with the best efforts, to discover where justice actually lay in the case at hand. Strictly speaking, it was still the case that one party would have a *justa causa* while the other would not. But the war would nonetheless be just on both sides in the limited sense that both sides were free of blame.[17]

Grotius and his followers reached much this same conclusion, holding that situations of invincible doubt brought the voluntary law into play in place of the natural law. The voluntary law would look not to the substantive justice of the legal claims but instead to 'a definite formality

---

[17] Vitoria, *On the American Indians*, in *Political Writings*, ed. Anthony Pagden and Jeremy Lawrance (Cambridge: Cambridge University Press, 1991), at 282–3; and *Law of War*, at 312–13.

in the conduct of war'.[18] Provided that all of the external formalities
connected with war were duly observed – in particular that the rules on
the *conduct* of hostilities were obeyed – the voluntary law would treat
both sides as fighting justly. Vattel would later refer to this new conception
of just war as 'lawful war in due form'.[19] He expounded its essence very
succinctly: 'If the enemy observes all the rules of formal warfare [he
explained], we are not to be heard in complaint of him as a violator of
the Law of Nations; he has the same right as we to assert a just cause; and
our entire hope lies in victory or a friendly settlement.'[20]

The existence of two different sets of criteria for just wars naturally
gave rise to the possibility that a given war might be, at the very same
time, just in one sense and unjust in the other. For example, a war in
which all of the elements of the medieval just-war framework were
present would be just according to natural law; but it would be unjust
according to the voluntary law if some or all of the required formalities
(such as a declaration of war) were missing. Conversely, a country might
begin a conflict without a *justa causa*; but its war would be treated as just
in the eyes of the voluntary law if all of the formalities were duly
observed. This may have been a superficial conception of 'justice', but
it had the signal virtue of being far more easily applied in practice than the
old natural-law standards, which were now increasingly relegated to the
realm of conscience or of moral obligation. In all events, the voluntary-law
approach of exalting form over substance would hold sway over the law of
war well into the twentieth century.

The second major innovation of Grotius was the making of a distinction between what he called 'primary' and 'secondary' rights. Primary
rights were rights exercisable against an actual wrongdoer. The right to
recover one's property from a thief is an example (i.e., a reprisal in the
original sense of that term). The source of these primary rights was the
general law of *nature*. Secondary action referred to measures taken
against persons other than an actual wrongdoer.[21] The natural law, in
Grotius's view, simply did not permit secondary action under any
circumstances. No one, he insisted, was liable under natural law for
the deeds of another person.[22] Such vicarious liability was a feature
exclusively of the voluntary law. The most outstanding illustration of

[18] Grotius, *War and Peace*, at 57.   [19] Vattel, *Law of Nations*, at 257–8.
[20] *Ibid.* at 305.   [21] Grotius, *War and Peace*, at 634–5.
[22] *Ibid.* at 539–45, 624. There was one exception to this principle, which is not germane to the
present discussion: the liability of heirs for debts of a decedent.

secondary action was war, because war entailed the killing of persons not on the basis of any personal wrongdoing but merely because of their membership of the enemy armed force. In fact, it would seem that, for Grotius, the core defining feature of war was that it consisted of secondary, rather than primary, action.

This view had some momentous implications. One was that it transferred the *entire* law of war, at a stroke, from the realm of natural law into that of the voluntary law. The effect was to open the way for treating war in a more flexible manner than before, as a man-made institution whose rules could be crafted – and recrafted as necessary – by human beings themselves to serve their own purposes. The law of war, in short, was being transplanted from Heaven to Earth.

Another noteworthy implication of Grotius's theory of war as secondary action was that it marked a departure from the medieval view of war as a conflict between rival individuals who were all personally responsible for their deeds. It will be recalled that, in the medieval scheme of things, all enemies in war had been considered to be wrongdoers in their own right, in the sense that all of them were held (if not very realistically) to have made a conscious choice to associate themselves with their leader's cause. Medieval war, in other words, had been seen as primary, rather than secondary, action.

Grotius's conception in effect recognised the reality of modern political life by discarding this notion of universal personal responsibility. It was now possible to treat persons fighting in an opposing army, even for an unjust cause, not as evil-doers but instead as dutiful patriots in a rival cause. A mere 'obstinate devotion to one's party', in Grotius's view, was not in itself cause for punishment.[23] The soldiers on the opposing side were therefore subject to being killed not because of any personal wickedness or acts of wrongdoing on their part, but rather by virtue of their *status* as members of the opposing armed force. War, in other words, was now being seen, more than ever before, in *national* rather than in interpersonal terms. This 'nationalisation' (as it may be termed) of the conception of war was given its most famous expression in the eighteenth century by the novelist, political theorist and musician Jean-Jacques Rousseau. In *The Social Contract*, written in 1762, he maintained that 'War . . .is not a relation between men, but between states', with the result that 'in war individuals are enemies wholly by chance, not as men, nor even as citizens, but only as soldiers'.[24]

---

[23] *Ibid.* at 651.   [24] Rousseau, *Social Contract*, at 56.

The third major innovation of Grotius was the propounding of the concept of a *state* of war. The essence of the idea may be stated quite simply: that war ought not to be seen in terms of specific *acts*, but instead as a legal condition in which specific acts take place. On this point, Grotius was expressly critical of the definition of war received from Cicero, as 'a contending by force'. The new view, he posited, was to see war as 'a condition' – more precisely as 'the condition of those contending by force, viewed simply as such'.[25] He explicitly distinguished between 'the state of war', on the one hand, and 'its acts', on the other. A *state* of war can exist even in the absence of any *acts* of war on the part of either side. 'War', concluded Grotius, 'is the name of a condition which can exist even when it does not carry forward its operations'.[26] This was contrary to the medieval doctrine, which had seen war in terms of individual coercive acts or operations occurring within a state of peace that was permanently in force.

This idea of war as a condition or state won wide support amongst international lawyers in the succeeding generations. Bynkershoek, for example, writing in 1737, held war to be '[not] merely the act of fighting, but also the state of things obtaining during war'.[27] In the middle of the eighteenth century, Wolff added his support. War in the strict sense refers, he maintained, 'rather to the status than to the action'.[28] Vattel followed him, giving what became a standard capsule definition of war: 'War', he pronounced, 'is that state in which we prosecute our rights by force'.[29] At the same time, however, it must be said that mainstream international lawyers actually made little practical use of the idea during this period. As will be seen in due course, it was actually the dissident schools of thought which had clearer notions of a state of war, which would reach their full elaboration only in the nineteenth century.[30] But the first steps were taken by Grotius and his followers in the present period.

Perfect war

The older and newer conceptions of just war, deriving respectively from the natural and the voluntary law, had a certain similarity of character,

---

[25] Grotius, *War and Peace*, at 33.
[26] *Ibid.* at 832. For a sharp criticism of Grotius in this regard, see Grob, *Relativity*, at 179–81.
[27] Bynkershoek, *Questions*, at 16.   [28] Wolff, *Law of Nations*, at 311.
[29] Vattel, *Law of Nations*, at 235.   [30] See Chapters 4 and 5 below.

in that both entailed judging particular wars against a sort of notional 'ideal' war. As the Italian scholar Alberico Gentili put it, a just war was a war that was 'perfect in all its parts'.[31] According to the natural law, such a perfect or ideal war was one that accorded exactly with the five-fold schema expounded in the Middle Ages. From the standpoint of the voluntary law, a perfect war was one in which all of the requisite external formalities were present.[32] Therefore, the stress, in the voluntary law, was on such factors as the presence of a declaration of war, the full (as opposed to merely partial) commitment of armed forces and so forth. An effect was to confer onto war a decidedly ritualistic flavour that had been entirely lacking in the medieval just-war analysis but which accords more strongly with modern stereotypes. The principal legal features of this new, formal style of conflict may be briefly identified.

Declaring war

The most obvious mark of a perfect war from the voluntary-law standpoint was the issuing of an express declaration of war.[33] It will be recalled that medieval just-war theory had no requirement of a formal declaration, just as it had no conception of war as a state or condition. War, in the medieval view, had been regarded as an ad hoc operation of a law-enforcement character. It has been observed, however, that, even in the Middle Ages, states sometimes issued formal declarations of some kind to their foes. The new voluntary law, with its roots in state practice, was naturally suited to take this body of pre-existing practice and mould it into a rule of law. The pioneer figure was Gentili, who, with his reverence for Roman precedents, was the first writer who strongly insisted on the need for a declaration of war, denouncing a resort to arms without a prior declaration as 'unjust, detestable, savage'.[34] Invoking (as he often did) the analogy of civil litigation, he insisted that war 'is no more a secret strife than are the contests of the Forum . . . . Before we enter upon legal proceedings we ask in civil fashion for what is due us or what is our own.'[35]

Grotius approached the question with rather more exactitude, making a distinction on the basis of his dichotomy between primary and secondary action. Against a primary enemy (i.e., against someone who

---

[31] Gentili, *Law of War*, at 12–14.   [32] Grotius, *War and Peace*, at 97.
[33] *Ibid.*   [34] Gentili, *Law of War*, at 140.
[35] *Ibid.* at 132.

had personally committed a wrongful act), a declaration was not required by the victim prior to his taking remedial or punitive action. The reason was that the hostile relationship between wrongdoer and victim was already fully in force, by the nature of the situation. A 'demand for settlement' was required only when secondary action was to be taken, i.e., against fellow nationals of the wrongdoer who would not necessarily have any reason to think that they were about to be attacked.[36] In other words, a declaration of war, according to Grotius, was required by the law of *nations* (i.e., by the voluntary law) but not by the law of *nature*, since the law of nations ruled the realm of secondary action while the law of nature reigned over primary acts.

It was one thing to require the formality of a declaration.[37] It was quite another to agree on just what degree of formality was required or on what, precisely, would qualify as a declaration, or on what the consequences would be if this required formality was lacking. In all of these areas, uncertainty would continue for a long time to come. On the question of what a declaration of war should consist of, we find Gentili in favour of adherence to the old Roman fetial practice. He held the declaration process to be a two-stage affair: consisting of, first, a request for satisfaction (on the analogy of civil litigation) and, second, the actual declaration of war. Moreover, there must then be an interval of thirty-three days, as in the old Roman practice, before material hostilities could be commenced. The purpose was to allow the accused state to decide rationally whether to yield to the demand or to contest it.[38]

The dominant view of international lawyers, however, was that the law prescribed no particular formality for declarations of war. Nor did lawyers ever succeed in agreeing on a definition of a declaration of war. As a result, a welter of different methods was employed, directed to various different audiences – sometimes to the enemy state, sometimes to the world at large, sometimes to domestic populations and sometimes to all of these at once. The most common view of lawyers was that declarations of war should be directed to the enemy state, and this could be done in various ways.[39] There were, for example, vestiges of the venerable medieval practice of using heralds to declare war. In 1635, King Louis XIII of France announced his country's entry into the Thirty Years War in grand style, by sending a herald to Brussels, with trumpets and medieval fanfare, to declare war against Spain. The last recorded use

[36] Grotius, *War and Peace*, at 634–5.   [37] See, to this effect, Vattel, *Law of Nations*, at 255–8.
[38] Gentili, *Law of War*, at 133–5.   [39] See, for example, Wolff, *Law of Nations*, at 364–6.

of heralds to declare war to an enemy state appears to have occurred in 1657, when Sweden went to war against Denmark.[40]

The more modern method was to declare war by way of public proclamation directed to the opposing side.[41] As befitted a polite and formal age, it was urged that this be couched in suitably dignified terms, with a careful avoidance of invective, defamation or similarly undignified language. Christian Wolff offered some helpful advice on this subject to rulers of his day.

> In declarations of war [Wolff solemnly abjured] the facts are to be reviewed and to them are to be applied the principles of the law of nature and nations; a thing which can be done without any harshness of words and without argument prompted by ill will. . . . [F]ar be it from you to call your enemy a breaker of treaties and a traitor, for whom there is nothing so sacred that he does not desecrate it . . . . [I]t is sufficient that the acts and the principles of the law of nature and nations applicable to them are to be understood by others, and it is not required that you should set forth your opinion of the vices of your enemy. If then you do this, it is not done with the intention of instructing others, but of harming your enemy, or detracting from his reputation, and can proceed from nothing else than from hatred towards the enemy and from desire for vengeance and other perverse impulses akin thereto.[42]

An alternative means of declaring war was to issue a conditional statement to the opposing side, to the effect that, if certain specified demands were not met, then war would result. This process was sometimes known as *denuntiatio* or as *indictio*. Later, the term 'ultimatum' would be commonly used.[43] Ultimatums would have their heaviest use in the nineteenth century; but they also featured in this period, chiefly in wars in Central and Eastern Europe. In 1710, for example, Russia issued an ultimatum to the Ottoman Empire and followed it up on the very same day with a declaration of war.[44] Sometimes, ultimatums sparked declarations of war in return. In 1736, for example, when Russia demanded satisfaction from Turkey for alleged violations of a treaty, Turkey responded by declaring war.[45] In 1787, the same thing happened

---

[40] Nys, *Droit de la guerre*, at 111–12.
[41] See, for example, Wolff, *Law of Nations*, at 364–6; and Vattel, *Law of Nations*, at 255.
[42] Wolff, *Law of Nations*, at 382.
[43] See Grotius, *War and Peace*, at 635–7; Wolff, *Law of Nations*, at 364–73; and Vattel, *Law of Nations*, at 254–5.
[44] Shaw, *Ottoman Empire*, at 230–1.   [45] *Ibid.* at 244–5.

in reverse. When the Ottoman Empire issued a conditional declaration of war against Russia (to be rescinded if Russia evacuated both the Caucasus and the Crimea), Russia countered with an unconditional declaration of war against Turkey.[46]

In practice, declarations were often pitched at least as much to the world at large as to the enemy state. As Vattel explained, the wondrous advances in communication that had occurred by the 1750s naturally ensured that news of a declaration of war by public proclamation would reach the enemy state with great promptness, thereby obviating the need for separate direct notice to it.[47] These broadly directed declarations served various purposes. Enlisting public opinion on the side of the declaring state was one obvious consideration, or the allaying of suspicions that might arise. For example, when King Gustavus Adolphus of Sweden entered the Thirty Years War by invading Germany in 1630, he issued a proclamation to the world setting out his reasons.[48] In much the same vein, an English declaration of war against the Netherlands in 1652 contained a general appeal to 'all Lovers of Truth and Justice' to acknowledge that country's 'most righteous Cause' for resorting to armed force.[49] The Dutch declaration against England, in turn, expressed the equal and opposite hope 'that all Kings, Republicks, and States' would see the Dutch cause to be 'true and founded on Justice'.[50] There was also a more pragmatic reason for taking care to trumpet the existence of a war to the world at large: to warn third states that there were now certain risks involved in trading with the belligerent powers. In particular, neutral merchant ships carrying contraband of war (such as armaments) to the opposing side would be subject to capture, and the contraband cargo to confiscation.

The issuing of formal public declarations of war in this manner became fairly common from about the middle of the seventeenth century to the middle of the eighteenth.[51] Declarations naturally varied in style between different countries and different times. But there came to be a clear family resemblance amongst declarations in the practice of the European states of the period. For example, it was common, though by

---

[46] *Ibid.* at 258.   [47] Vattel, *Law of Nations*, at 255.
[48] Manifesto on the Reasons for Taking Up Arms and Entering Germany, July or Aug. 1630, 5(2) Dumont 608.
[49] Declaration of War by England against the Netherlands, 31 July 1652, in 3 Anonymous, *General Collection*, at 36–44.
[50] Declaration of War by the Netherlands against England, 2 Aug. 1652, in *ibid.* at 45–59.
[51] See Grotius, *War and Peace*, at 603–4.

no means universal, for declarations of war to contain detailed accusations of wrongdoing on the part of the opposing state, coupled with an
earnest assertion that the declaring state was being driven to the drastic
step of war only by 'extreme necessity'.[52] Sometimes, the catalogues of
grievances were very extensive. In its 1652 declaration against England,
for example, the Netherlands boasted of a veritable 'Cloud of Reasons',
exhaustively recited, for taking up arms.[53] Sometimes, declarations
contained detailed narrations of particular incidents leading to the
conflict.[54] So strong (it might appear) is the urge of humans to have at
least a claim of right on their sides. Sometimes, however, declarations
were very terse affairs, comprising little more than a bare announcement
of the fact of war. An example was the one issued by France against the
Netherlands in 1672:

> The ill opinion which his Majesty hath for some time past entertain'd of
> the Conduct of the States General [i.e., the Netherlands], having pro-
> ceeded so far that his Majesty without the diminution of his Glory cannot
> any longer dissemble the Indignation wrought in him for their acting so
> little conformably to the great Obligations, which his Majesty and the
> Kings his Predecessors have so bountifully heap'd upon them; his Majesty
> hath declar'd, as he does now declare, that he hath determin'd and
> resolv'd to make War against the said States-General of the United
> Provinces, both by Sea and Land; and so consequently commands all
> his Subjects, Vassals and Servants, to fall upon the Hollanders; and
> forbids them for the future to have any Commerce, Communication or
> Correspondence with them, upon pain of Death.[55]

In addition to the enemy-state-to-be and the world at large, there was
a third audience to which declarations of war were directed: the domestic population of the warring state.[56] The purpose here was to inform the
population of special duties to which they might become subject by
virtue of the war. Nationals of the declaring state might, for example, be
requested or required to leave the territory of the enemy state or to
discontinue trading with the enemy. A declaration might also announce
the seizure of enemy property within the territory of the declaring state

---

[52] See, for example, Declaration of War by England against the Netherlands, March 1672, in
4 Anonymous, *General Collection*, at 254–8.
[53] Declaration of War by the Netherlands against England, 2 Aug. 1652, in 3 *ibid.* at 45–59.
[54] See, for example, Declaration of War by the Netherlands against France, 8 May 1702, in 1
ibid. at 422–30.
[55] 1 *ibid.* at 167–8.   [56] See, for example, Vattel, *Law of Nations*, at 255.

or the expulsion of enemy nationals.[57] A common provision of declarations, such as the French one of 1672 just cited, was an exhortation to all the subjects of the declaring state to 'fall upon' the enemy. Dutch declarations of war commonly included this feature.[58]

Declarations of war sometimes took the form of the issuing of an order for taking 'general reprisals' against the enemy state. These were in contrast to 'special reprisals', inherited from medieval practice. The difference between the two can be stated quite simply. Special reprisals were an authorisation to someone who had been the actual victim of a denial of justice, to seize property belonging to nationals of the country that had been responsible for the wrong. General reprisals were an authorisation to *all* nationals of the reprisal-taking state to capture property belonging to persons from the target country, with no pretence that the captors had personally suffered any kind of wrongdoing. Special reprisals, in other words, set only the wronged party loose on nationals of the target state. General reprisals mobilised the entire country against the enemy. Consequently, an authorisation of general reprisals was regarded as fully tantamount to a declaration of war.

One further difference between the two types of reprisal should be noted. In the case of special reprisals, property could only be seized up to the value of the original loss actually suffered by the victim. In the case of general reprisals, there was no limit to the amount of property that could be taken from enemy nationals. Indeed, the more the better, since general reprisals were truly war. The Second Anglo-Dutch War was inaugurated in 1664 by England's issuance of a general Order of Reprisals. The same was true of the commencement of the war against France in 1689 by England and the Netherlands.[59]

International lawyers did not succeed, however, during this period – or any other, as will be seen – in crafting a rigorous definition of a declaration of war. As a result, a number of state actions were of more or less ambiguous character in this regard. In practice, it came to be accepted that *any* unambiguous sign or signal of an intention to resort

---

[57] For a good example, see Declaration of War by Spain against France of 3 May 1689, in 1 Anonymous, *General Collection*, at 272–4.

[58] See, for example, the declarations by the Netherlands against England of 2 Aug. 1652, in 3 *ibid.* at 45–59; by the Netherlands against France of 9 Mar. 1689, in 3 *ibid.* at 256–67; by the Netherlands against France of 8 May 1702, in 1 *ibid.* at 422–30; by the Holy Roman Empire against France of 15 May 1702, in 1 *ibid.* at 430–3; and by France against Spain of 9 Jan. 1719, in 4 *ibid.* at 382–4. On these three distinct types of declaration of war, see Vattel, *Law of Nations*, at 255–8.   [59] Grewe, *Epochs*, at 368.

to war could function as a declaration of war. An especially clear (if nonetheless only implicit) signal of intention to go to war was the provision of aid to a state's enemy when there was no pre-existing obligation to do so. For example, when England began openly to provide assistance to the Dutch insurgents against Spain in 1585, this was taken by Spain to be a de facto declaration of war.[60] Similarly, in 1778, France concluded a military alliance with the American colonies, in their independence struggle against Britain.[61] Britain, not surprisingly, regarded this act as an 'unprovoked and . . . unjust . . . aggression'.[62] But it did not trouble to issue a formal declaration of war against France, clearly regarding it as obvious to both parties that they were now at war.

Other state actions were also commonly, if not very clearly, regarded as functional equivalents of a declaration of war. A good example was the issuing of letters of marque. During this period, the common practice of states was to issue letters of marque not, in the medieval fashion, during peacetime to a single individual as a measure of reprisal, but instead during war as a means of augmenting the issuing state's naval capacity on short notice.[63] Letters of marque would therefore be issued on a large scale, in the spirit of general reprisals. A ship holding such a letter would function as a sort of auxiliary to its state's naval forces, capturing enemy vessels as the opportunity presented itself in the course of normal trading (in return for a share of the proceeds of any captures made). Such vessels were known, by the eighteenth century, as 'letter-of-marque ships' or sometimes even, for short, simply as 'letters of marque'.[64] (Ships that were specially fitted out by private entrepreneurs to engage in the full-time, rather than part-time, pursuit and capture of enemy property at sea were known as 'privateers'.)[65] In the light of this practice, it is not surprising that states regarded the act of issuing letters of marque as tantamount to a declaration of war. Much

---

[60] Geoffrey Parker, The Dutch Revolt (London: Penguin, 1985), at 216–19.

[61] France-USA, Treaty of Alliance, 6 Feb. 1778, 46 CTS 447.

[62] Quoted in 3 Phillimore, Commentaries, at 90. For accounts of the legal aspects of this affair, see ibid. at 90–3; Twiss, Law of Nations, at 67; and Kent, Commentaries, at 189. For documentation, see 2 C. de Martens, Causes célèbres, at 140–253.

[63] For the text of a letter of reprisal, issued by France in 1778, see Théodor Ortolan, Règles internationales et diplomaties de la mer (Paris: J. Dumaine et Cosse et N. Delamotte, 1845), at 456–8. For the text of a letter of marque, issued by Britain in 1812, see Thomas Gibson Bowles, Maritime Warfare (2nd edn, London: W. Ridgway, 1878), at 109–11.

[64] See, for example, the British case of Le Coux v. Eden, 2 Dougl 595 (1781).

[65] N. A. M. Rodger, The Wooden World: An Anatomy of the Georgian Navy (Glasgow: William Collins, 1986), at 130.

the same was true of 'hostile embargoes', which were requisitions of ships belonging to the nationals of the target country. Such an act was regarded as so egregiously and inherently hostile in nature as to amount to a declaration of war. (Hostile embargoes were to be distinguished from 'civil embargoes', which were non-discriminatory requisitions in an emergency, not directed against the nationals of any particular state.)[66]

In the light of the absence of a clear definition of a declaration of war, no clear answer can be given to the question of how frequent declarations were in practice during the seventeenth and eighteenth centuries. The broader the definition of 'declaration', obviously the more numerous will be the cases in which they appeared. And, conversely, the narrower the definition, the fewer will be the number of instances. Moreover, even when declarations were issued, it sometimes happened that hostilities were already in progress. This was the case in the War of the Spanish Succession in 1701, as well as in the Seven Years War of 1756–63, when British and French forces had already clashed on both land and sea by the time that the declarations were promulgated in 1756.

Perhaps the only statement that can confidently be made is that it was common – though far from universal – for states to give at least some kind of more or less clear signal to the enemy, to the home population and to the world at large that war was about to ensue. *Formal* declarations, in the form of either public proclamations or ultimatums, went into and out of fashion amongst European states for no very obvious reasons. From about the middle of the seventeenth to the middle of the eighteenth centuries, formal declarations were common. After the Seven Years War, however, they were frequently dispensed with. Declarations were sometimes issued during the French Revolutionary wars, and sometimes not. But the practice became widespread again in about the middle of the nineteenth century.[67] Unresolved and controversial questions, however, would continue to bedevil the subject of declarations well into the twentieth century – and possibly beyond.

As if all this uncertainty as to the definition of a declaration of war were not sufficient occupation for even the subtlest of lawyers, there was

---

[66] On these types of embargo, see 1 Carlos Calvo, *Dictionnaire de droit international public et privé*, 2 vols.(Paris: Gillaumin 1885), at 289–90. An embargo of either type was distinct in turn from what was called an *arrêt de prince*, which was a general prohibition against departure of any ships from the state's ports, with no element of sequestration. The typical reason for such an act would be to prevent the spread of sensitive news.

[67] For a survey of incidents of armed hostilities without declarations of war during this period, see Maurice, *Hostilities*, at 12–45.

doubt too over what the consequences were – if indeed there were any at all – of going to war without issuing a declaration first. Grotius's view of the question is especially instructive – or rather non-instructive. The lack of a declaration of war meant, essentially by definition, that the war was an imperfect one (i.e., that it was an unjust war in the voluntary-law sense of the term). But imperfect war was still war. So it was not apparent that the lack of perfection really made any practical difference to the belligerents. This point, as it happens, was not explored with any thoroughness until the nineteenth century; and even then it would continue to be the source of much puzzlement.[68]

Conducting the hostilities

In perhaps no area did the new voluntary law of nations effect such fundamental and lasting changes as in the area of rules on the conduct of hostilities. In particular, the voluntary law introduced two major innovations, as important as any that have occurred in the entire history of the law of war. First was an insistence on strictly even-handed treatment of the two belligerents, without regard to where justice lay in the underlying dispute. Second was that the voluntary law looked towards the establishment of a set of fixed rules, of a code of conduct, instead of relying exclusively on the general principle of necessity to determine the lawfulness of individual acts of war. A few words on each of these points are necessary.

First, on the even-handed treatment of the opposing sides. The natural-law position, as inherited from medieval just-war doctrine, was radically asymmetrical. The unjust side had no right whatever to commit acts of war, which were wholly the prerogative of the just party.[69] In practice, there was some cautious hedging by natural lawyers in this regard. In the sixteenth century, Vitoria had conceded that individual soldiers on the unjust side should not be regarded as being personally blameworthy if they were merely discharging duties owed to their lawful superiors. '[E]ven though the war may be unjust on one side or the other', he concluded, 'the soldiers on each side . . . are all equally innocent'.[70] The later writers in the mainstream tradition reached the same conclusion, but they did so by relying on the voluntary law as a supplement to the natural law. Grotius illustrated the position with

---

[68] See Chapter 5 below for further developments in this area.
[69] See Grotius, *War and Peace*, at 718–19.   [70] Vitoria, *Law of War*, at 321.

reference to the capture of enemy property. According to the voluntary law, soldiers on both sides, on an equal basis, obtained what he called 'external' legal title (*externum dominium*) to captured property. At the same time, however, the soldiers on the unjust side were under a *natural-law* – i.e., purely moral – duty to restore the property to the original owner.[71] Gradually, the rigid natural-law position was quietly discarded, so that, by the middle of the eighteenth century, Vattel could present the voluntary-law principle of even-handed treatment as one of the most fundamental principles of the law of war.[72]

The other major innovation wrought by the introduction of the voluntary law was the introduction of the idea of a fixed set of rules for the conducting of hostilities. In theory, the natural-law principle of necessity – allowing all action that conduced to the defeat of an unjust enemy and forbidding everything beyond that – remained in force.[73] Reliance solely on the general principle of necessity had some clear drawbacks, however. The principal one was that it risked turning warfare into an open-ended licence to commit atrocities. The solution, in the standard manner of the period, was to supplement the old law of nature by the newer voluntary law, which would lay down a set of fixed rules about war that would apply equally to the two sides and which would be independent of considerations of necessity. As Vattel put the matter:

> How could it be determined accurately [he demanded] just how far it was necessary on a given occasion to carry hostilities, in order to bring about the successful termination of the war? .... [A]s between Nation and Nation, we must lay down general rules, independent of circumstances and of certain and easy application. Now, we can only arrive at such rules by considering acts of hostility in the abstract and in their essential character. Hence, ... the voluntary Law of Nations limits itself to forbidding acts that are essentially unlawful and obnoxious .... On the other hand, it permits or tolerates every act which in its essential nature is adapted to attaining the end of the war; and it does not stop to consider whether the act was unnecessary, useless, or superfluous in a given case.[74]

The basis on which the code of conduct was to be built up, in other words, was to look to the 'essential nature' of various acts of hostility in deciding whether to permit or forbid them, while studiously ignoring

---

[71] Grotius, *War and Peace*, at 716–21.   [72] Vattel, *Law of Nations*, at 305–6.
[73] See Grotius, *War and Peace*, at 567–77; and Vattel, *Law of Nations*, at 279–80, 305.
[74] Vattel, *Law of Nations*, at 295.

the specific circumstances or context in which those acts occurred. An illustration of this approach in action concerned the question of the use of poison in war. It was generally agreed that poisoning was permitted by the natural law where necessary under the circumstances, but flatly prohibited by the voluntary law.[75]

It should not be thought that the voluntary law contained no component of necessity. It did, but in an importantly different way from the older natural law. Under the natural law, necessity had operated as *both* a constraining and a permissive force, i.e., it determined both what was allowed and what was forbidden. Under the voluntary law, the code of conduct replaced necessity on the permissive side, so that the code determined what conduct was allowed. Necessity in its constraining capacity, however, was retained, with the effect that acts that were allowed, in principle, by the 'normal' laws of war (i.e., by the code of conduct) would nonetheless be prohibited if they had no connection whatever to the winning of the war. If there was 'the clearest evidence' (in Vattel's words) that a given act of war had no effect whatever on the outcome of the struggle, then that act would be unlawful even under the voluntary law.[76] This dualistic character of the law on the conduct of war – combining a code of rules about the conduct of war with a principle of necessity in this newer and more limited sense – continues in force to the present day.

Although the idea of a code-of-conduct approach to the moderation of war represented a major landmark in the legal history of war, it cannot be said that, in practice, very much concrete progress was actually made in that direction in the seventeenth and eighteenth centuries. Nothing resembling a full written code of laws of war was agreed, even amongst the European states. There was broad agreement amongst the publicists, however, on a few points. Pillage was held to be prohibited, as was the killing of persons who had surrendered. Assassination of rival rulers by traitorous or deceitful means (such as the suborning of their guards) was likewise barred, although the killing of rival rulers by dint of one's *own* stealth or boldness was allowed.[77] Serious progress in the codification of the laws of war, however, would only come later, in the nineteenth century and beyond.

---

[75] See Grotius, *War and Peace*, at 651–3; and Wolff, *Law of Nations*, at 450–1. For dissent on this count, see Vattel, *Law of Nations*, at 288–9, holding poisoning to be against natural law.

[76] Vattel, *Law of Nations*, at 295.

[77] Grotius, *War and Peace*, at 653–6; Pufendorf, *Nature and Nations*, at 1308; and Vattel, *Law of Nations*, at 287–8.

The considerable advance made in the moderation of warfare after about 1650 really owed more to state practice – i.e., to the prevailing conditions and styles of war – than to the urgings of international lawyers. But progress there was. Much of it resulted from the increasing professionalisation of war which was so striking a feature of this period. Major steps were taken, for example, in the disciplining of armed forces. Various states promulgated codes of law for their armies, with punishment meted out for infractions. The increasing isolation of military from civilian populations was a feature of both peacetime and wartime. In war especially, the belief was gaining ever firmer hold that hostilities should be confined to the armed forces of the two sides, with as little molestation of civilian populations as possible. The visible fruits of this trend were proudly observed by Vattel:

> At the present day [he noted] war is carried on by regular armies; the people, the peasantry, the towns-folk, take no part in it, and as a rule have nothing to fear from the sword of the enemy. Provided the inhabitants submit to him who is master of the country, and pay the contributions demanded, and refrain from acts of hostility, they live in safety as if they were on friendly terms with the enemy; their property rights are even held sacred; the peasants go freely into the enemy camp to sell their provisions, and they are protected as far as possible from the calamities of war. Such treatment is highly commendable and well worthy of Nations which boast of their civilization.[78]

Even changes of sovereignty were of little moment to ordinary people, since it was generally accepted that transferred areas would retain their prior rights, laws and way of life.[79] The Treaty of Westphalia, for example, expressly provided that any cities that underwent transfers of sovereignty were nevertheless to retain all of their rights.[80] A change of sovereign therefore meant little more than a change in the identity of the party holding (as it were) the title deeds to the territory.

Moderation was apparent in a number of other respects as well. For example, the treatment accorded to prisoners of war improved – from, it must be confessed, a very low base. The old medieval practice, in which individual prisoners negotiated ransom arrangements with the particular individuals who had captured them, gave way to a new practice. The holding of prisoners was now, in a manner of speaking, nationalised, in

---

[78] Vattel, *Law of Nations*, at 283.   [79] *Ibid.* at 309.
[80] France-Holy Roman Empire, Treaty of Münster, 24 Oct. 1648, 1 CTS 271, Art. 117.

that prisoners were held by the enemy force as a whole rather than by individual captors. It became common for European states, in wars with one another, to arrange for exchanges of prisoners during the conflict – not so much out of tenderness of feeling as to relieve the governments of the expense and trouble of guarding their charges. Prisoner-exchange cartels (as they were customarily called) typically stipulated that prisoners would be exchanged on a person-for-person basis, with higher-rank prisoners being treated as multiples of lower-rank ones. There were very elaborate arrangements to this effect between, for example, France and the Netherlands in 1672 and between France and Savoy in 1690.[81]

Bilateral friendship treaties between European maritime states were a useful source of protections for merchants in wartime. These agreements commonly included provisions for periods of grace, giving merchants of either state that were located in the other at the outbreak of a war a liberal amount of time (three months or six months were common figures) to gather their possessions and depart without molestation. An early example was a treaty between the Netherlands and France in 1662, stipulating a six-month grace period.[82] By the eighteenth century, such agreements were commonplace amongst the European maritime states.[83] Vattel even held the granting of grace periods to be mandatory.[84]

Peace-making

In principle – i.e., according to the *natural* law – the medieval *jus victoriae* was still in force, inclusive of a duty on the unjust side in a war to indemnify its opponent for the costs incurred in bringing it to book.[85] In reality, wars were terminated in quite different ways. Gentili was the first international-law writer to discuss peace-making in a post-medieval fashion, and his treatment remained remarkably unaltered through the next three centuries and more.[86] He identified three

---

[81] France-Netherlands, Cartel, 21 May 1675, 13 CTS 379; and France-Savoy, Treaty of Exchange and Ransom, 19 Oct. 1690, 19 CTS 79.

[82] France-Netherlands, Treaty of 27 Apr. 1662, 7 CTS 139, Art. 13. See also the later arrangement France-Netherlands, Treaty of Commerce and Navigation, 20 Sept. 1697, 21 CTS 371, Art. 42, which provided for a nine-month grace period. See also Netherlands-Portugal, Treaty of Peace and Alliance, 6 Aug. 1661, 6 CTS 375, Art. 16, which did not specify a particular time interval.

[83] Bynkershoek, *Questions*, at 28–9; and G. F. von Martens, *Compendium*, at 282–3.

[84] Vattel, *Law of Nations*, at 256.   [85] Grotius, *Commentary*, at 267–8.

[86] See Gentili, *Law of War*, at 360–403.

methods of terminating wars – although only two of them merited the name of peace-making in a true sense. Sometimes, wars merely, so to speak, 'petered out'. One side, or both, simply elected to stop prosecuting the struggle. In Gentili's opinion, this did not truly amount to peace but merely to the discontinuance of material hostilities.[87] The two means by which a true peace could be made were, first, by what Grotius called 'pure surrender' (and which later lawyers would call 'subjugation') and, second, by negotiated settlement. Regarding subjugation, the natural law continued to hold to the old *jus victoriae*.[88] In practice, however, the *jus victoriae* was effectively obsolete in this era since subjugation was little in evidence, apart from the striking case of the effacement of Poland from the political map of Europe by a trio of voracious neighbours in the second half of the eighteenth century.

This period, on the whole, was an era of negotiated peace agreements, with crowns, territories, fortresses, colonies, economic privileges and the like assiduously traded about by statesmen like so many hogsheads of tobacco or boatloads of slaves. In Vattel's opinion, the primary function of peace treaties was not to *resolve* the issues over which a war had been fought, but rather simply to preclude any further armed conflict on the matter by setting out a workable – and permanent – compromise.[89]

> [T]he only recourse [Vattel insisted] is to compromise the claims and grievances on both sides, and to put an end to all differences by as fair an agreement as can be reached. In so doing the original grounds of the war are left unsettled, as well as any controversies which the various acts of hostility may have given rise to; neither of the parties is condemned as unjust, a proceeding which scarcely any sovereign would submit to; but an agreement is reached as to what each belligerent shall receive in settlement for all his claims.[90]

An important question regarding peace treaties was the effect, if any, that duress had on their legal validity. It was widely held that the general natural-law rule that contracts were vitiated by duress did not apply to peace treaties. The reason, Gentili explained, is that fear is a natural feature of war. Hence it could not be said that any *unlawful* pressure was being applied when a treaty was 'forced' upon another state by, say, the prospect of military annihilation. Gentili went on to condemn a duress

---

[87] *Ibid.* at 360.   [88] See *ibid.* at 291–359; and Grotius, *War and Peace*, at 825–8.
[89] See, for example, Wolff, *Law of Nations*, at 517; and Vattel, *Law of Nations*, at 350–1, 357–8.
[90] Vattel, *Law of Nations*, at 350.

plea as unworthy of a sovereign – comparing it, interestingly, with
a claim of ignorance of the law on the part of a law professor, or a
confession of fear on the part of a soldier.[91] Vattel's explanation was that
even the harshest peace-treaty arrangements were the result of a true
choice on the part of the defeated party – although one that was, to be
sure, made in unpropitious circumstances. The defeated state, he reasoned, 'freely chooses a loss that is present and certain, but limited in
extent, in preference to a disaster, not yet arrived, but very probable, and
terrible in character'.[92] For this reason, the losing side could not be
allowed to resile from a treaty on the ground of duress.

It was generally agreed that the law did not contain detailed requirements as to the specific contents of peace treaties. In practice, though,
peace treaties came to be fairly standardised amongst the European
states in the course of the seventeenth century. They typically provided
for the cessation of all military hostilities between the parties. Express
provision was commonly made for each side to retain full legal title to
any property that it had succeeded in capturing.[93] The mutual freeing of
prisoners of war (if that had not already been achieved by means of
cartels during the conflict) was another typical arrangement. If one side
held more prisoners than the other, it was sometimes agreed, as a sort of
clearing arrangement, that there should be a payment to that side for the
higher expenses that it had incurred in maintaining them.[94]

Another very common feature of treaties was an amnesty provision,
to the effect that all injuries inflicted during the war were to be comprehensively forgiven, to ensure that they did not later become the
source of 'Processes and litigious Strifes', as the Peace of Westphalia of
1648 put it.[95] In that treaty (between France and the Holy Roman
Empire), the amnesty was provided for, in the following terms:

---

[91] Gentili, Law of War, at 363.   [92] Vattel, Law of Nations, at 356.
[93] Grotius, War and Peace, at 809–10. For examples of clauses of this sort, see England-
Netherlands, Treaty of Breda (Peace and Alliance), 31 July 1667, 10 CTS 231, Art. 4; and
Denmark-England, Treaty of Peace, 31 July 1667, ibid. at 287, Art. 5.
[94] See, for example, France-Spain, Treaty of the Pyrenees, 7 Nov. 1659, 5 CTS 325, Art. 41.
The rationale, of course, was that the side holding the larger number of prisoners had
undergone greater expenses for their maintenance than the other had. For examples of
prisoner-release provisions, see Netherlands-Portugal, Treaty of Peace and Alliance,
6 Aug. 1661, 6 CTS 375, Art. 6; England-France, Treaty of Peace, 31 July 1667, 10 CTS
215, Art. 3; Russia-Turkey, Treaty of Peace, 13 June 1700, 23 CTS 25, Art. 9; and Holy
Roman Empire-Turkey, Treaty of Belgrade, 18 Sept. 1739, 35 CTS 381, Art. 10.
[95] France-Holy Roman Empire, Treaty of Münster, 24 Oct. 1648, 1 CTS 271, Art. 91. See also,
to this same effect, England-France, Treaty of Ryswick, 20 Sept. 1697, 21 CTS 409, Art. 10.

[T]here shall be on the one side and the other a perpetual Oblivion,
Amnesty, or Pardon of all that has been committed since the beginning
of these Troubles . . . . [A]ll that has passed on the one side, and the other,
as well before as during the War, in Words, Writings, and Outrageous
Actions, in Violences, Hostilities, Damages and Expenses, without any
respect to Persons or Things, shall be entirely abolished in such a manner
that all that might be demanded of, or pretended to, by each other on that
behalf, shall be buried in eternal Oblivion.[96]

Such provisions were therefore a means by which peace was made in the
most thorough way possible – not simply as between ruler and ruler, but
comprehensively, between all of the fighters right down to the lowest
rank. Amnesty clauses became so standard a feature of European peace
treaties in this period that Wolff regarded them as an inherent part of the
peace process, so that any treaty that lacked an express amnesty provision should be deemed to include one implicitly nonetheless.[97]

One of the most notable general features of European peace treaties
was their non-judgmental character. They commonly refrained from
stating any conclusion as to the legal merits of the two sides' positions in
the original quarrel. Grotius noted, in one of his rare comments on
contemporary events, that the current practice of states was to avoid
imputing blame to the losing side in peace treaties. '[I]t is not customary', he pointed out, 'for the parties to arrive at peace by a confession of
wrongs'.[98] A concrete illustration of this point was the practice of
leaving each state to bear its own costs of the conflict, with no attempt
to place the entire cost of the war onto the unjust party.[99] The contrast
with the medieval just-war frame of mind could hardly be greater.
Questions of good and evil, right and wrong, played no part in this
new style of peace-making, which was a thoroughly unsentimental

---

[96] France-Holy Roman Empire, Treaty of Münster, 24 Oct. 1648, 1 CTS 271, Art. 2. For
further examples, see Denmark-England, Treaty of Peace, 31 July 1667, 10 CTS 287, Art. 3;
England-France, Treaty of Ryswick, 20 Sept. 1697, 21 CTS 409, Art. 3. See also the
component treaties of the Peace of Utrecht of 1713: France-Great Britain, Treaty of
Peace and Amity, 11 Apr. 1713, 27 CTS 475, Art. 3; France-Netherlands, Treaty of Peace
and Amity, 11 Apr. 1713, 28 CTS 37, Art.2; France-Savoy, Treaty of Peace and Amity,
11 Apr. 1713, ibid. at 123, Art. 2; France-Prussia, Treaty of Peace and Amity, 11 Apr. 1713
ibid. at 141, Art.3; and France-Portugal, Treaty of Peace and Amity, 11 Apr. 1713, ibid. at
169, Art. 2. See also Hungary-Prussia, Treaty of Berlin, 28 July 1742, 36 CTS 409, Art. 2;
and Poland-Prussia, Treaty of Peace, 15 Feb. 1763, 42 CTS 361, Art. 1.
[97] Wolff, Law of Nations, at 502.   [98] Grotius, War and Peace, at 809.
[99] Ibid. at 810; and Wolff, Law of Nations, at 504. For details of state practice on this point in
the period, see Camuzet, Indemnité, at 36–8.

business of costs and benefits – a task for political algebraists rather than for moralists.

Imperfect war

The category of armed conflicts known as 'imperfect wars' was never very precisely defined or agreed upon. From the start, lawyers expressed different views on the subject, with some putting the difference between perfect and imperfect wars in material, and others in formal, terms. One of the earliest writers to discuss the subject was Gentili. He identified an imperfect war as an armed conflict comprising isolated acts of hostility 'without an interruption of friendly relations'.[100] On this account, an imperfect war was not, strictly speaking, a war at all, but rather the occurrence of war-like acts during a time of peace. Broadly similar was the view of Jacques Burlamaqui, a professor at the University of Geneva, writing in the mid eighteenth century. In his opinion, an imperfect war was a situation 'which does not break the peace in all respects, but only in certain particulars, the tranquillity of the state subsisting in other affairs uninterrupted'. A perfect war, in contrast, was a total rupture of all relations, laying the foundation for the commission of 'all possible acts of hostility' between the parties.[101]

Grotius took a different approach, using formal rather than material criteria to distinguish perfect from imperfect wars. An imperfect war, in his view, was simply a war in which one or more of the formalities of war was lacking. In a nutshell, it meant an undeclared, as opposed to a declared, war. Ever ready to make analogies to civil-law institutions, Grotius likened this distinction between perfect and imperfect wars to that between marriage and cohabitation – the one being a union entered into with due solemnity and prescribed formalities, and the other lacking the formalities either in whole or in part.[102] He insisted, however, that an imperfect war was still a war, so long as it possessed the key definitional attribute of war – the resort to secondary, as opposed to primary, action (i.e., the taking of action against persons who had not been parties to any act of wrongdoing).[103] It may be noted that, in Grotius's view, an imperfect or undeclared war could be fully the equal of a perfect one in material terms (i.e., in terms of the number of troops committed, the intensity of the conflict and so forth).

---

[100] Gentili, *Law of War*, at 268.   [101] Burlamaqui, *Principles*, at 258.
[102] Grotius, *War and Peace*, at 97.   [103] *Ibid.* at 634–5.

Over the longer term, it was Gentili's view, rather than Grotius's, that prevailed amongst international lawyers. The dominant view came to be that an imperfect war was, as Gentili had intimated, a situation in which *acts* of war occurred without the creation of a *state* of war. This could not be expressed very clearly at the time, since the concept of a state of war was very little developed. In the nineteenth century, there would be a full exploration of the subject, under the label 'measures short of war'.[104] For present purposes, it is only necessary to point out some of the ways in which countries could engage in acts of war without taking the drastic step of entering into a state of war. Three types of situation in particular will occupy us. First will be cases in which the rupture of peaceful relations between the two countries was, for some reason, less than total. Second, and closely related, will be reprisals. Third will be self-defence.

Ruptures less than total

There were various ways in which the armed forces of countries could collide without a state of war being in existence. The best example of such a conflict in history was the naval clash between France and the United States in 1798–1800, often referred to in historical treatments as a 'quasi-war'.[105] No formal declaration of war was issued by either side, although diplomatic and consular relations between the countries were broken off. Economic relations were also severed. The United States Congress approved, by graduated steps, a series of measures that stopped short of a full commitment of armed forces but which also seemed incompatible with a fully fledged state of peace. First came a suspension of economic relations with France, followed by an authorisation to American merchant vessels to arm themselves for the purpose of resisting visit and search by French warships.[106] The commercial and military-alliance treaties of 1778 with France were then declared terminated (on the ground of their breach by France).[107] Finally, and most drastically, the president was given authorisation to instruct American naval vessels to capture French warships anywhere in the world,

---

[104] See Chapter 6 below.
[105] See, for example, Alexander DeConde, *The Quasi-war: The Politics and Diplomacy of the Undeclared War with France 1797–1801* (New York: Charles Scribner's Sons, 1966).
[106] Act to Suspend Commercial Intercourse with France, 13 June 1798, 1 Stat 565; and Act to Authorize the Defence of Merchant Vessels, 25 June 1798, 1 Stat 572.
[107] Act to Declare Treaties with France No Longer Obligatory, 7 July 1798, 1 Stat 578.

irrespective of whether those ships had actually engaged in hostile action. Crews of any captured vessels could be confined.[108] No capturing of French merchant vessels, however, was ever authorised. Nor was there ever any clash between land forces. In due course, the matter was wound up by means of the Convention of Mortefontaine of 1800 – which, incidentally, was not formally designated as a peace treaty.[109]

There was some puzzlement as to whether this crisis amounted to a war or not. The French apparently did not regard it as one. Joseph Bonaparte tactfully referred to the affair as a 'transient misunderstanding'.[110] An opinion by the American attorney-general in 1798 described the contest in somewhat stronger terms as 'a state of maritime war between France and the United States'.[111] When the matter came before the Supreme Court for consideration in 1800,[112] one of the justices expressly held the conflict to be an imperfect war, on the ground that only a special and limited commission had been given to Americans to commit hostile acts, rather than a general one.[113] Another justice similarly described the situation as an imperfect war, which he characterised as 'a war as to certain object, and to a certain extent', and alternatively as 'a qualified state of hostility'.[114] In another case, the Supreme Court referred to the crisis as involving what it called 'partial hostilities', as distinct from 'general hostilities' that were characteristic of war.[115] From a more detached perspective, the British Admiralty Court Judge William Scott referred to the conflict somewhat delphically as a 'state of hostility (if so it may be called)'.[116]

We are on firmer ground in considering one type of limited-liability conflict that was a distinctive feature of statecraft in this particular era: participation in wars as an auxiliary, which entailed supplying troops to another state for employment in a war, but with the sending state not itself becoming a party to the war. Provided that the agreement between the sending and the employing states predated the outbreak of the war,

---

[108] Act Further to Protect Commerce, 9 July 1798, 1 Stat 578.
[109] France-USA, Convention of Mortefontaine, 30 Sept. 1800, 55 CTS 343.
[110] 1 FRUS 583.
[111] Charles Lee, 'Treason', 1 Op A-G 85 (1798), at 99. See also a second opinion by Charles Lee, 'Prize Ship and Crew – How to Be Disposed Of', ibid. at 85 (1798).
[112] Bas v. Tingy, 4 US (4 Dall) 37 (1800).
[113] Ibid. at 40–2 (opinion of Justice Washington).
[114] Ibid. at 45 (opinion of Justice Paterson).
[115] Talbot v. Seeman, 5 US (1 Cranch) 1 (1801), at 50.
[116] The Santa Cruz, 1 C Rob 49 (1798), at 64. On the legal nature of this conflict, see Grob, Relativity, at 37–64.

and that the aid supplied was limited to a predetermined amount, then it was generally agreed that there was no ground for the state against which the troops were used to treat the supplying country as a fully fledged enemy.[117] Vattel explained the position by characterising the transaction as the mere discharging of a debt, affording no legal ground for complaint by any third state.[118] The auxiliary forces *themselves* were, of course, subject to attack by the state that they were deployed against. But the country which sent them remained at peace. This situation was to be carefully distinguished, legally, from an alliance, in which there was an open-ended association or sharing of goals between the allied states so that each one was fully, and without limit, the enemy of the opposing side. It was not always apparent to the naked eye, however, what legal capacity a state was fighting in at a given time. For example, in the Battle of Dettingen in 1743, during the War of the Austrian Succession, British and French troops clashed – but the two *countries*, strictly speaking, did not. Both sets of forces were fighting as auxiliaries, the French for Bavaria, and the British (under the interesting rubric of the 'Pragmatic Army') for Austria. Only later did the two states enter the fray in their full capacities.

The law on auxiliaries allowed great play to the Machiavellian mentality (which was much in evidence in this era), for example by enabling a supplying state to circumvent an inconvenient peace agreement. Frederick II of Prussia demonstrated this technique with characteristic panache. After his famous 'grab' of Silesia in 1740, he formally made peace with Austria in 1742, thereby obtaining full legal title to the province.[119] But he was shortly back in the field – not in his own right, but as an auxiliary to Bavaria. Seldom was a more energetic auxiliary seen. He immediately invaded Saxony and Bohemia in full force, taking Prague, capturing some 15,000 Imperial troops and posing a serious threat to Vienna itself (although the campaign ultimately turned into a major disaster for him).

Reprisals

The classic illustration of the use of force in a limited manner for a limited goal was reprisals – or, more exactly, *special* reprisals. (General reprisals, it will be recalled, were fully tantamount to war.) Special

[117] 2 Rayneval, *Institutions*, at 48–9.   [118] Vattel, *Law of Nations*, at 266.
[119] Hungary-Prussia, Treaty of Berlin, 28 July 1742, 36 CTS 409.

reprisals differed in no fundamental way in this period from their medieval ancestors, although a certain amount of elaboration along existing lines did occur.[120] The essence of reprisals continued to be, as in the Middle Ages, the seizing of property belonging to the fellow nationals of an original wrongdoer. The property was held as a 'gage' or pledge – i.e., it was sequestered rather than confiscated – to induce the wrongdoer to make amends.[121] If the wrongdoer proved contumacious, then matters would proceed to confiscation. One interesting change from medieval practice was that it was generally held during this period that persons as well as property could be seized, effectively as hostages, a process dignified by lofty-sounding labels of 'androlepsy' or 'viricaption'.[122]

During this period, reprisals came to be somewhat more precisely differentiated than before from various other actions to which they bore a certain superficial resemblance. Brief note may be taken of these. Reprisals differed from the recovery of property *actually* taken, in that such a recovery of one's own property was seen as a *natural*-law right. Reprisals, in contrast, were allowed only by the voluntary law.[123] When the natural-law right of recovery was exercised by a state rather than an individual, it was, of course a just war in the older sense – one of Grotius's three categories of just war, as noted above. Reprisals also differed from self-defence action, which was designed (as will presently be seen) to prevent an injury from occurring in the first place. Reprisals, in contrast, were remedial – i.e., designed to obtain compensation for an injury *after* it had occurred. Reprisals were also distinct from *retaliation*, which was a mechanical returning of tit for tat, i.e., the simple inflicting onto one's foe of the *very* wrong that he had originally committed

---

[120] The paucity of scholarly study of reprisals in this period is even more striking than for the Middle Ages.

[121] The word 'gage' in this sense survives in the word 'engagement', used with reference to nuptials, in which the husband- and wife-to-be pledge themselves to one another. On the French law and practice of reprisals in this period, see 2 René-Josué Valin, *Nouveau Commentaire sur l'Ordonnance de la Marine du moi d'août 1681* (3rd edn, La Rochelle: Jerôme Legier, 1776), at 414–26.

[122] See, for example, Grotius, *War and Peace*, at 625–6; Wolff, *Law of Nations*, at 303–5; and Vattel, *Law of Nations*, at 231. This process is of course reminiscent of imprisonment for debt – except that it involved imprisonment for a debt owed by another person, rather than by the captive himself.

[123] In technical terms, reprisals were said to be an institution of the *jus gentium*, or man-made universal law, rather than of the *jus naturale*, which was a universal law that was transcendental in origin. Somewhat confusingly, the right of recovery had been the original, literal meaning of 'reprisal' in the Middle Ages. See Chapter 2 above.

('an eye for an eye' and 'a tooth for a tooth'). This was regarded as mere vengeance and, as such, an outright breach of natural law.[124]

Reprisal also differed from the practice known as *retorsion*, which was a sort of juridical version of retaliation. In the typical situation, one state would enact a law discriminating against nationals of another, and that other would counter by enacting a similarly discriminatory measure. Retorsion was regarded as lawful, on the ground that it was an exercise of ordinary sovereign rights, albeit in an unfriendly manner.[125] It differed from reprisal, however, in having no remedial or compensatory character.

Finally, reprisal must be distinguished from punishment. The difference here was that the extent of lawful punishment was determined by the degree of moral turpitude of the wrongdoer, or (alternatively) by the degree of inducement that was necessary to persuade the evil-doer to alter his wicked ways. The permissible limit of reprisals, in contrast, was determined by the amount of material harm that had been sustained by the wrongdoer's victim. In due course (as will be seen), reprisals would acquire a punitive character. But that did not occur until the nineteenth century. During the present period, as in the Middle Ages, reprisal, being reparation for injury suffered, was quite distinct from punishment.

There was some disagreement amongst international lawyers as to whether special reprisals were wars. In Grotius's eyes, they were, because they consisted of secondary, rather than primary, action. As such, they were entirely in the sphere of the voluntary law (since the natural law, in Grotius's view, allowed no secondary action). He characterised a reprisal as 'an enforcement of a right by violent means' – terminology clearly in the spirit of traditional just-war thought.[126] Reprisals, however, were imperfect wars, rather than perfect ones, because of the absence of the key formality of a declaration of war. Most lawyers, however, declined to follow Grotius on the point and considered reprisals to be distinct from war, by virtue of the fact that, in reprisal situations, relations between the two sides were hostile only to a limited extent.

There was a noticeable ambivalence amongst legal writers on the question of whether reprisals were a good thing or not. Some regarded

---

[124] See Wolff, *Law of Nations*, at 295–6; and Vattel, *Law of Nations*, at 227–8. Retaliation was, and to some extent continues to be, permissible in wartime in response to violations of the laws of war, under the unfortunately confusing label of 'belligerent reprisals'. On this subject, see F. Kalshoven, *Belligerent Reprisals* (Leyden: Sijthoff, 1971).

[125] See Wolff, *Law of Nations*, at 298–300; and Vattel, *Law of Nations*, at 228.

[126] Grotius, *War and Peace*, at 625.

them with favour, as a means by which states could avoid the more drastic step of going to war, by obtaining satisfaction through the more moderate means of property attachments. Wolff and Vattel were both of this persuasion, going so far as to hold that states were positively obligated to resort to reprisals instead of war whenever a viable choice was available.[127] Other observers were rather more sensitive to the potential for abuse and oppression that reprisals offered. Bynkershoek, for example, who was no doctrinaire pacifist, condemned special reprisals, in terms reminiscent of the medieval Catholic Church, as a 'wicked practice', sternly pointing out that the Romans had refrained from stooping to such depths. At a minimum, he contended, scrupulous care should be taken to ensure that letters of reprisal were only issued when 'justice has been clearly refused' to a national by a foreign sovereign.[128]

State practice inclined towards the position of Bynkershoek, and a general consensus emerged that reprisals were relics of a ruder past, unworthy of the civilised condition which European states had created and in which they took such great pride. The result was a considerable acceleration of the trend, which had begun in the Middle Ages, towards restricting special reprisals. This was typically done by way of bilateral friendship treaties between the major European states, which commonly contained provisions that letters of reprisal would only be issued when one state party had culpably failed to grant justice to a national of the other, following a formal demand to that effect by the sovereign of the aggrieved party. Such provisions appeared in the truce agreement of 1609 between Spain and the Netherlands, as well as in the final peace agreement of 1648 between the two countries, and also in the treaty of 1654 which concluded the first Anglo-Dutch War.[129] By the second half of the seventeenth century, these arrangements were a common feature of friendship treaties amongst the major European trading states.[130]

---

[127] Wolff, *Law of Nations*, at 310; and Vattel, *Law of Nations*, at 231–2.

[128] Bynkershoek, *Questions*, at 133–5.

[129] Netherlands-Spain, Truce of Twelve Years, 9 Apr. 1609, 5(2) Dumont 99, Art. 11; Treaty of Peace, 30 Jan. 1648, 1 CTS 1, Art. 22; and England-Netherlands, Treaty of Peace and Union, 5 Apr. 1654, 3 CTS 225, Art. 24.

[130] See, for example, England-France, Treaty to Re-establish Commerce, 29 Mar. 1632, 6(1) Dumont 33, Art. 2; France-Netherlands, Treaty of 27 Apr. 1662, 7 CTS 139, Art. 17; England-Spain, Treaty of Peace and Friendship, 23 May 1667, 10 CTS 63, Art. 3; England-France, Treaty of Peace, 31 July 1667, 10 CTS 215, Art. 3; Denmark-England, Treaty of Peace and Commerce, 11 July 1670, 11 CTS 347, Art. 39; and England-France, Treaty of Ryswick, 20 Sept. 1697, 21 CTS 409, Art. 9.

By the eighteenth century, then, it appeared that special reprisals were largely an extinct practice – though events in the nineteenth century would tell a very different story.

Self-defence and defensive war

On the question of self-defence, as of special reprisals, there was a strong element of continuity from medieval doctrine. Self-defence continued to be seen as an inherent, natural-law right, distinct from war in the true sense and exercisable by unjust parties as well as by just ones (i.e., exercisable against just uses of force as well as against unjust ones).[131] There were also, however, some noteworthy developments in this period. The most important one was the discussion of the subject, for the first time, in terms of the position of states, and not simply of individuals as had been the case in the Middle Ages. This led in turn to the important, if somewhat blurry, distinction between, on the one hand, what will be called self-defence in the narrow sense and, on the other hand, what will be called defensive war. Private persons were confined to self-defence in the narrow sense. This was self-defence as expounded in medieval just-war doctrine, referring to the inherent natural-law right of individual persons to fend off an attack that was in the actual course of delivery.

As in the Middle Ages, there continued to be some very limited scope, at the margins, for acting in self-defence in the very face of an impending attack, as well as in the immediate aftermath of one. Concerning action prior to the attack, Gentili conceded that self-defence was permitted to individuals against a peril which was 'already meditated and prepared'.[132] As he drily remarked, 'One who is prepared to do a deed differs but little from one who does it.'[133] Also as in medieval law, self-defence was permissible for the protection of property as well as of persons, so that a self-help operation to recover stolen property was allowed, provided that it took place in the immediate aftermath of the theft.[134] The principal points to note about self-defence in this period were the ways in which it differed from wars, on the one hand, and from reprisals, on the other.

First, regarding the relation between self-defence and war. It will be recalled that defence had been stated by Grotius as one of the three

---

[131] See Grotius, *War and Peace*, at 172–3. See Wolff, *Law of Nations*, at 305–6, for a dissenting view on this point.
[132] Gentili, *Law of War*, at 66.   [133] *Ibid.* at 409.
[134] *Ibid.* at 138; and Grotius, *Commentary*, at 87.

natural-law justifications for war. It is important to realise, though, that this defensive war (as it will be termed) was *not* the same thing as self-defence in the proper sense. Self-defence in the proper sense continued to be spoken of, as in the Middle Ages, as a prerogative of individual persons, rooted (as before) in the inherent natural-law right of self-preservation.

Defensive war, in contrast, was a right of states. The principal difference between them lay in the scope allowed for preventive action. States were generally regarded as possessing greater latitude than individuals for taking armed action to ward off impending or threatened, as opposed to ongoing, attacks. The reason for this difference in treatment, explained Grotius, was that individuals lived in settled societies, with governments and magistrates who were able to protect them, or at least to provide them with remedies against their assailants after attacks had occurred (such as legal actions for damages). States, however, live in no such settled society *vis-à-vis* one another, with the result that litigation could never be counted on to provide protection or redress. As a consequence, states must, regrettably, be allowed greater scope than individuals to act pre-emptively.[135] As a result, sovereigns – but not individuals – were allowed to take arms in the face of 'an injury not yet inflicted, which menaces either person or property'.[136] As Gentili explained, self-defence in the narrow sense arose in situations of 'true and absolute necessity', whereas defensive war was allowed on the broader basis of 'expediency'.[137]

In brief, self-defence in the narrow sense was designed to prevent an attack from being successfully *concluded*. Defensive war – or preventive war, as it might alternatively be called – was designed to prevent an attack from being launched in the first place. As a result, this preventive feature meant that defensive wars, notwithstanding the label, were essentially *offensive* in nature, thoroughly in keeping with just wars generally.[138]

More specifically, it may be said that self-defence in the narrow sense and defensive war differed from one another in four important respects. First, self-defence in the narrow sense continued to be commonly treated as a right of *individuals*; while defensive war was a prerogative of states. Strictly speaking, lawyers would have conceded readily enough that states had a true self-defence right as individuals did, in addition to their further prerogative of defensive war. In practice, though, self-defence in the narrow sense continued to be instinctively thought of and discussed with

---

[135] Grotius, *War and Peace*, at 184.   [136] *Ibid.* at 172.
[137] Gentili, *Law of War*, at 58, 61.   [138] See Chapter 2 above.

individuals in mind. Second, self-defence in the narrow sense did not encompass preventive action (save in the highly marginal case of allowing a pre-emptive attack when a blow was on the *very* brink of being delivered).[139] Defensive war did allow preventive action. Indeed, that was its very essence. Third, self-defence in the narrow sense, at least in principle, allowed the defender to go no further than the fending off of the actual blow. That is to say, it had to be strictly proportionate to the gravity of the attack. A putative self-defender who went beyond the bounds of proportionality thereby became an aggressor himself.[140] Defensive war, in contrast, allowed the state to inflict whatever degree of force was necessary to remove the threat altogether, including taking steps to ensure against its recurrence.[141] Finally, there was the question of a declaration of war. Defensive war called for a declaration in the same manner as other wars. Self-defence in the narrow sense, it was agreed, did not.[142]

The most worrisome aspect of defensive war, obviously, was the danger of its abuse at the hands of paranoid or unscrupulous statesmen. The lawyers therefore invariably hastened to stress that the right of states to wage defensive war was far from unlimited and that merely speculative dangers could not justify it. Nor, they insisted, was defensive war justified simply for the maintenance of the general balance of power. The impending danger must be reasonably clear and imminent. Gentili, for example, cautioned that the mere 'possibility of being attacked' could not justify a resort to preventive war.[143] Grotius agreed, holding that, if a state was concerned about a build-up of arms or fortification of territory by a neighbouring power, then its only lawful remedy was to build up its own forces on a precautionary basis. He went on to posit, not very helpfully, that 'the degree of certainty required' to justify a preventive war was 'that which is accepted in morals'.[144]

---

[139] Terminology is unfortunately very unclear in this area. It is suggested that 'pre-emptive' should be used to refer to action against an attack that is on the brink of being launched, with 'preventive' used to refer to an attack made as a precaution against a more speculative future danger (i.e., with 'preventive' therefore referring to defensive-war cases of the kind here explained).

[140] Wolff, *Law of Nations*, at 493.

[141] This principle of proportionality had been stressed even in medieval writing. See, for example, Aquinas, *On Law, Morality, and Politics*, at 226. But proportionality had not been so distinctively a feature of self-defence, since it applied to the waging of just wars as well.

[142] See, for example, Gentili, *Law of War*, at 136–8.   [143] *Ibid.* at 184.

[144] Grotius, *War and Peace*, at 549. On balance-of-power considerations in international law during this period, see Vagts and Vagts, 'Balance of Power'.

In all events, the articulation of the distinction between, on the one hand, self-defence in the strict and narrow sense of warding off a blow in the course of delivery and, on the other hand, the broader sense of defence as a *justa causa* for a just war was one of the major contributions of legal thought in this period. From here onwards, it will be necessary to maintain this distinction with the most scrupulous care. The difference between these two conceptions – so subtle and so ill defined and fuzzy at the margins but yet so important – would be very long-lasting in international law, up to our present time (and doubtless well beyond). And the failure to appreciate the distinction between them has led to much confusion.

It only remains to distinguish defensive action, in both its broad and narrow forms, from reprisals. The fundamental difference was that a special reprisal was entirely compensatory or remedial in character, whereas self-defence, in both of its forms, was preventive. In other words, a special reprisal was taken *after* an injury was completed. Self-defence in the narrow sense occurred during the very course of the injury, with a view to preventing its consummation. With defensive war, the contrast was even sharper, since that was designed to prevent the attack from being launched to begin with. Reprisals were therefore, in a manner of speaking, backward-looking, in the sense that they were designed to restore the reprisal taker to the position that he would have been in, had the wrongful act not occurred. Defensive actions, in contrast, were oriented towards either the present (in the case of narrow self-defence) or the future (in the case of defensive war).

There was a contrast too in the amount of injury that could be inflicted in the two types of operation. Since special reprisals were compensatory, property seizures had to halt at precisely the point at which the property seized became equal in value to the damage inflicted by the original injury. Self-defence actions were measured on a different scale. For narrow self-defence, the level of violence allowed was whatever was necessary to ward off the attack. With defensive war, the level of force allowed was whatever was sufficient, in the circumstances, to remove or neutralise the threat. The kind of action taken was also different. In a special reprisal, property was seized or persons held as hostages; but killing was not permitted. In self-defence, killing could be justified if it was necessary to repel the attack; and in defensive war, of course, killing was an inherent feature. Finally, there was the matter of the target group. Self-defence was exercisable *only* against the actual attacker, and defensive war only against the party actually posing the threat. With special reprisals, however, action was taken against fellow nationals of the original wrongdoer who were guilty of no wrong or threatened wrong.

The clarity of these conceptual lines between war, reprisal and self-defence (in the narrow sense) is a vivid indicator of how successful international lawyers were, by the eighteenth century, in devising a coherent body of legal doctrine that dealt more or less adequately with the various forms of international conflict. There was, however, some serious instability in this apparently impressive conceptual structure. Most obviously, within the mainstream tradition itself, there was the dualistic character of legal thought, as the natural-law and voluntary-law components continually jostled against one another – with the long-term drift decidedly in favour of the voluntary law. But there were threats from outside as well, in the form of alternative conceptions of war – conceptions that began by challenging the mainstream position and proceeded, in due course, largely to supplant it.

4

Dissension in the ranks

[T]he state of men without civil society (which state we may properly call the state of nature) is nothing else but a mere war of all against all; and in that war all men have equal right unto all things.

Thomas Hobbes[1]

[T]he belligerents at the outset made an agreement to rest their case with the fortune of battle. [T]his is understood to be the case ... when the revenge for their injuries and the securing of their claims ... are left to the arbitrament of Mars, and both sides enter the conflict with the thought: 'Either I will revenge my right or injury in war, or else I will lose still more.'

Samuel Pufendorf[2]

Until about the middle of the seventeenth century, Western European legal writing on the subject of war essentially grew out of a unitary tradition, stemming from the medieval just-war framework, with its roots in natural-law thought. Even when, during the seventeenth century, the voluntary law was brought in, the natural law remained as the base, with the voluntary law as a sort of superstructure. The seventeenth century, however, also witnessed the emergence of two dissident strains of legal thought as challenges to the mainstream tradition. One of them will be labelled the 'Hobbesian' school after its principal architect, the English political theorist Thomas Hobbes. At its heart was a view of natural law that was radically at odds with its medieval forebear. In particular, it rejected the central tenet of mainstream just-war thought: that natural-law relations were inherently peaceful, with war being an occasional, and pathological, interruption of the general state of peace. In place of this (relatively) idyllic image, the Hobbesians painted

---

[1] Hobbes, *De Cive*, at 13. [2] Pufendorf, *Nature and Nations*, at 1325.

a frightening picture of the state of nature as a condition of perpetual strife, with peace rather than war as the exceptional state of affairs.

The other dissident school of thought is less apparent to the historical eye because, in contrast to the Hobbesian one, it was never strongly associated with a particular writer, nor were its tenets ever set down in a systematic manner. To appreciate its influence, a certain degree of intellectual archeology is called for, and a certain liberty must be taken, in the interest of clarity, in its reconstruction. For the lack of any generally accepted name, this other dissenting tradition will be called the 'contractual' or 'duelling' school of thought. As these labels suggest, it portrayed war as a consensual arrangement between the contending sides – a kind of deadly sporting engagement. We will point out the salient features of each of these new approaches and then proceed to explore the alternative positions that they entailed with regard to a range of specific legal issues concerning war.

Challenges to orthodoxy

In the seventeenth century, two of the most fundamental tenets of the mainstream natural-law tradition came under attack. One was its vision of the state of nature (i.e., the condition in which persons lived prior to the establishment of governments or states) as a comparatively peaceful and orderly world – ordered, of course, by the law of nature itself. The other key tenet was the belief, fundamental to medieval just-war thought, that the law of nature held universal sway, in time of war as well as of peace. Thomas Hobbes and his followers challenged the first of these foundations. The contractual (or duelling) school of thought rejected the second one. In its view, war involved the substitution of a new juridical order for an old one.

Neither approach, it might be noted at the outset, went so far as to reject the very idea of natural law altogether. The Hobbesians believed in natural law – but their view of it was very different from that of the mainstream writers. They pictured natural law as inherently a law of conflict rather than of harmony, a law of war rather than of peace. The contractual writers also believed in natural law. They pictured it in the same terms as the mainstream writers and made important contributions to its development. They were heretical, though, in their belief that the natural law was abruptly suspended in time of war. They therefore saw war not as the enforcement or application of natural law (as in the just-war view) but rather as its negation or suspension. With these very general remarks in mind, we may look in greater detail at these new schools of thought.

The Hobbesian challenge

The world of political and legal theory has not been the same since the career of Thomas Hobbes.[3] On the subject of the legal conception of war, he ranks as the dissenter-in-chief of our period. His *magnum opus*, *Leviathan*, was published in 1651, a generation after Grotius's *On the Law of War and Peace*. At the root of Hobbes's thought was the rejection of the medieval idea that the natural state of the human race was one of peace, occasionally punctuated, in cases of emergency, by episodes of war. Hobbes's opinion was very different. The state of nature, far from being orderly and peaceful, was a brutally competitive world, a seething cauldron of atomistic individuals obsessively seeking to ensure their own *individual* self-preservation, with the hindmost left unsentimentally to the devil.[4] It is true that the principle of self-preservation had been a fundamental tenet of natural-law thought throughout the Middle Ages, carefully recognised as such by Aquinas.[5] That in itself was nothing new. Hobbes's innovation was to put forward a radically stripped-down version of natural law, in which the right of self-preservation stood in forbidding majesty as, effectively, the *sole* fundamental natural right.[6] Accompanying this sole fundamental right was an equally solitary and equally fundamental natural-law duty: to adhere to contracts voluntarily entered into.[7] On these two principles, a vast political and legal edifice was constructed.

The direct implication of this drastically reduced conception of natural law was that the state of nature was a realm of natural liberty and equality – with all persons equally entitled to pursue their own safety as best they could. With no judge or legislator in control, every person was, perforce, his own judge of what was necessary for self-preservation. If one person's quest for his own security necessitated interference with others, then that interference was justified according to the basic natural-law right to security. That is not to say, however, that the person whose freedom was being interfered with had a duty to acquiesce. Far from it. That person had every bit as much right to safeguard his own security as the intervener did – and hence a corresponding natural-law right to resist any attempt by others to infringe it. The

---

[3] For a wide-ranging survey of Hobbes's thought, see generally Sorrell (ed.), *Cambridge Companion*; and Tuck, *Rights*, at 109–39.
[4] See Hobbes, *De Cive*, at 21–42; Hobbes, *Leviathan*, at 80–4; and Hobbes, *Elements*, at 77–81.
[5] Aquinas, *Treatise on Law*, at 250.
[6] Hobbes, *De Cive*, at 26–7; Hobbes, *Leviathan*, at 85; and Hobbes, *Elements*, at 78–9.
[7] Hobbes, *Leviathan*, at 93–8; and Hobbes, *De Cive*, at 43–7.

inevitable result, as Hobbes put it, was that 'men live thereby in perpetual diffidence, and study how to preoccupate with each other; the estate of men in this natural liberty is the estate of war'.[8] This was the famous – or notorious – Hobbesian theory of the state of nature as a 'war of all against all'. In the popular stereotype, this concept of a war of all against all naturally conjures up a horrifying picture of perpetual strife and turmoil. (It must be confessed that Hobbes's lurid prose lent considerable force to this popular image.) It should be appreciated, though, that, from the legal standpoint, the 'war of all against all' must be seen in somewhat more sober terms. Specifically, the Hobbesian state of nature was what might be termed a conflict-of-rights situation: a state of affairs in which, seemingly paradoxically, two people could be in conflict, with each one having right on his side. This was in the sharpest contrast to traditional natural-law thought, in which rights and duties were parcelled out (so to speak) with the greatest care, with one party's right ceasing where another's began and with duties and rights being the inverse of one another. The clearest manifestation of this feature of mainstream natural-law was, of course, the just-war principle of an objective *justa causa*, with its insistence that right could lie on one side only.

It is important to appreciate that this Hobbesian doctrine of over-lapping rights owed nothing to the theological principle of invincible ignorance, which allowed a war to be just on both sides, but only in a limited and contingent manner. As soon as the ignorance was van-quished, so soon would the classical just-war doctrine be applied in all its fullness. In the Hobbesian state of nature, there was no question of ignorance, no doubt as to where right truly lay. It lay on both sides equally, as a matter of fundamental principle – in effect, as a result of the very *definition* of the state of nature itself, which granted the right of self-preservation to all persons equally.[9] It is therefore immediately apparent that no judge, however impartial or learned, could resolve quarrels in which security or self-preservation was at issue, because each contending party would *actually* have right on its side, in the strictest sense of the term.

Hobbes did, however, have a solution to this seemingly intractable problem. The peoples of the world, he surmised, had managed to surmount their piteous plight by banding together into political societies and volun-tarily and collectively transferring their natural rights to a sovereign. From a series of such transfers arose the political units of the world, the various nation-states. Within those states, the natural-law condition of overlapping rights no longer prevailed. It was now superseded by a state of *civil* law, as

---

[8] Hobbes, *Elements*, at 79–80.   [9] Hobbes, *De Cive*, at 27–9, 63.

distinct from natural law. This was a body of rules or commands promulgated by the newly created sovereign. It was known as 'positive' law, a term
familiar from medieval jurisprudence. By substituting this positive, or
man-made, law for the old natural law, the condition of overlapping rights
could be swept aside in its entirety. Rights and duties could now be
allocated by the sovereign with as much exactitude as necessary, so that
one party's rights and other parties' duties would be coterminous – where
the one began, the other would end, and vice versa.[10]

   This strategy of overcoming the drawbacks of natural law did not,
however, actually eliminate the problem of overlapping rights completely. It merely elevated it to the collective, as opposed to the individual,
plane. The anarchic state of nature still existed, but with nation-states,
instead of individuals, as its unhappy participants. '[A]s amongst mas-
terless men', Hobbes averred, 'there is perpetual war, of every man
against his neighbour; . . . so in states, and commonwealths not dependent on one another, every commonwealth . . . has an absolute liberty,
to do what it shall judge . . . most conducing to [its] benefit'. The result,
inevitably, is that states 'live in the condition of a perpetual war, and
upon the confines of battle, with their frontiers armed, and cannons
planted against their neighbours round about'.[11]

   This harsh, if unavoidable, conclusion was to bring about a radical
inversion of the positions of war and peace in international affairs, as
compared to mainstream natural-law thought. War must now be seen
not, as in the medieval natural-law tradition, as an exceptional phenomenon, nor as an emergency law-enforcement operation. Instead, war must
now be regarded as a normal and intrinsic feature of interstate life, and
peace as the exception. This must necessarily be so, in Hobbes's view, so
long as the legal rights of different states overlapped. Any interlude in
fighting, Hobbes maintained, could be no more than 'a breathing time',
as opposed to a settled and stable condition of peace.[12]

   Hobbes did not deny that nation-states *could* be at peace with one
another. But peaceful relations could never be simply taken for granted.
They had to be consciously crafted and carefully nurtured. There was no
great mystery as to how this could be achieved: by means of treaties
between states. To make this possible, it was necessary for Hobbes to
have recourse to the second pillar of his drastically pared-down system
of natural law: the duty to adhere to agreements freely made. The result
was that, for Hobbes, the *entire* content of the law of peace was the product

---

[10] Hobbes, *Leviathan*, at 117, 160–3.   [11] *Ibid.* at 140.   [12] Hobbes, *De Cive*, at 144.

of the voluntary, rather than the natural, law. War, therefore, was the preserve of nature, and peace the product of human artifice. No longer, on the Hobbesian view, could war be seen as an effort to enforce the general values of a community of nations against a misbehaving state (as in the natural-law conception). It was now seen as a condition in which community-wide values were nonexistent, in which the warring states lived in legal isolation from one another, with each one thrown back onto the sole fundamental natural right of survival in a brutal world.

The ideas of Hobbes were better attuned to the international political atmosphere of his period than were those of the mainstream natural lawyers. From the mainstream writers, cries of despair could readily be heard at the amorality and cynicism that were so pervasive a feature of interstate relations. Grotius, for example, despondently observed in his turbulent time 'a lack of restraint in relation to war, such as even barbarous races should be ashamed of', with the result 'that men rush to arms for slight causes, or for no cause at all'.[13] Writers schooled in the medieval natural-law tradition would naturally find much to disapprove of in this period.

Hobbes's approach, though, was more that of the dispassionate scientist than of the outraged moralist. His concern was to describe and explain the world as it actually was – and not to flinch at what he found. On this count alone, he stands out as a wholesale repudiator of the entire medieval tradition. For proof of his thesis of the natural state of war amongst humans, he simply pointed to evidence lying all around. Even in settled societies, he averred, 'men travel not without their swords by their sides, ... neither sleep they without shutting not only their doors against their fellow subjects, but also their trunks and coffers for fear of domestics'. What clearer testimony could there be, he demanded, of 'the distrust they have of each other, and all, of all'?[14] In his coldly utilitarian outlook, his utter disregard of religious idealism, his ready acceptance of competition and rivalry as the natural hallmarks of human existence in a state of nature – in all these respects, Hobbes was singularly well equipped to act as the chief analyst of his competitive era.

The corrosive influence of Hobbes's thought had a massive impact on later writers, although more on political theorists than on lawyers. The philosopher Benedict de Spinoza, for example, followed Hobbes in considering the nations of the world to be in a state of nature *vis-à-vis* one another, with hostility as their normal relation and self-preservation – as determined by each state for itself – as the overriding natural right, enforceable

---

[13] Grotius, *War and Peace*, at 20.   [14] Hobbes, *De Cive*, at 11.

exclusively by 'the right of war'.[15] Also in a Hobbesian vein, Spinoza maintained that, '[i]f ... one commonwealth wishes to attack another ... , it has the right to attempt this, since all it needs to wage war by right is the will to wage war'.[16] The German philosopher Immanual Kant also endorsed the Hobbesian view of war as the natural condition of independent sovereign states. He maintained, like Hobbes, that the division of mankind into separate and independent nation-states constituted, in itself, a sort of permanent state of war.[17] It is true that Kant harboured greater hope than Hobbes that this dreadful condition could be overcome through the steady and assiduous efforts of rulers and peoples. But he believed that this process would have to take as its starting point a Hobbesian base.

Amongst international lawyers, the influence of Hobbes was diffuse but highly significant. Few lawyers addressed his ideas directly. Many, however, would be influenced – more deeply than they themselves knew – by the fundamental Hobbesian idea of a world in which international relations were inherently competitive rather than cooperative. In the nineteenth century particularly, Hobbes would reign as a kind of uncrowned king or hidden imam, of the positivist school of international law.[18]

The contractual or duelling school

The essence of the contractual theory of war may be stated very simply. It rejected the mainstream tradition's law-enforcement model of war, in favour of an image of war as a contract between two parties to settle a quarrel by force of arms – i.e., as a duel. For this reason, it will be referred to, in the alternative, as the duelling theory. This school of thought, in contrast to both the mainstream tradition and the Hobbesian critique, never received a systematic treatment by any single author either in this period or later. It has therefore always been the least conspicuous of the rival positions, appearing in the legal literature in something of a piecemeal fashion. The writer who most frequently betrayed the influence of this mode of thought was the German natural-law author Samuel Pufendorf. But he was not a consistent or thoroughgoing exponent of the contractual view, since much of his thought was along orthodox just-war lines. In fact, he was one of the foremost natural-law scholars of his generation, with his treatise *On the Law of Nature and Nations* (of 1672) standing out as one of

---

[15] Spinoza, *Treatise*, at 305.   [16] *Ibid.* at 295.
[17] Kant, *Perpetual Peace*, in *Political Writings*, at 113. (1st edn 1795.)
[18] See Chapter 5 below for this development.

the most monumental works in that long tradition.[19] In keeping with orthodox natural-law thought, he defined war as 'the state of men who are naturally inflicting or repelling injuries or are striving to extort by force what is due to them'.[20] He also straightforwardly endorsed Grotius's three categories of just causes of wars: to obtain something which is unlawfully withheld; to defend the state against injury (meaning principally *threatened* injury); and to procure reparation for an injury inflicted, as well as guarantees against future misconduct.[21]

The contractual school of thought was a less radical departure from the mainstream tradition than the Hobbesian one, in that it accepted the medieval just-war idea that peace was the normal condition of humankind even in the state of nature. Its departure from orthodoxy consisted of denying that natural law governed relations between the adversarial parties *during* wartime. Relations during war were determined by the agreement made by the parties to lay aside their peaceful relations and resort to arms instead. This contractual arrangement – or 'war contract' as it will be termed – was not of course reduced to writing in the manner of an ordinary contract, but it was real nonetheless. As Pufendorf explained the matter: 'the belligerents at the outset [make] an agreement to rest their case with the fortune of battle . . . , and both sides enter the conflict with the thought: "Either I will revenge my right or injury in war, or else I will lose still more."'[22] His conclusion was that 'practically all formal wars appear to suppose an agreement that he upon whose side the fortune of war has rested can impose his entire will upon the conquered'.[23]

This outlook had a venerable, if not necessarily distinguished, ancestry in the Germanic practice of trial by battle. The Catholic Church, however, strongly condemned duelling, along with trial by battle. Duelling was denounced by the Council of Trent in 1563 as an 'abominable practice . . . introduced by the contrivance of the devil'. Killings in duels were to be punished as homicides. Participants (and their seconds as well) were to be denied Christian burial and have their property confiscated. Rulers who permitted the practice in their jurisdictions were to suffer excommunication, along with advisers and even spectators.[24] It was a hazardous sport for all concerned.[25]

---

[19] On Pufendorf, see Tuck, *Rights*, at 140–65.   [20] Pufendorf, *Nature and Nations*, at 9.
[21] *Ibid.* at 1294.   [22] *Ibid.* at 1325.   [23] *Ibid.* at 767.
[24] Council of Trent (1563), 25th session, c. 19, in 1 Tanner, *Decrees*, at 795.
[25] On the law relating to duelling in the Middle Ages, see John of Legnano, *Tractatus*, at 331–54. On the condemnation of trial by battle, see Bonet, *Tree of Battles*, at 117–18, 195–6. On the objection to duelling as a tempting of God, see Belli, *Military matters*, at 90.

There were, however, some potentially important caveats to the Church's censorious stance. Francisco Suárez, early in the seventeenth century, maintained that, although duelling was contrary to natural law, parties who engaged in it committed no wrong to *one another*. He likened combat by 'mutual and voluntary agreement' to 'a game which is in other respects wrong, but in which there is no injustice committed among the players'. The duellists, to be sure, were offenders – but they were offenders against the general peace of the land, as a sort of criminal conspiracy, rather than against one another. Consequently, neither participant could maintain a private lawsuit against the other for injury suffered, since both were equally guilty of breaching the law. This reasoning was readily applicable to the situation in which the duelling parties were states. So long as there was no world sovereign to inflict punishment on them from the 'outside' (as it were) for engaging in this heinous misconduct, duelling could become, in practice, an effective method of settling quarrels as between the parties themselves.

Two aspects of the contractual outlook on war call for particular attention. The first is the role that it accorded to the voluntary law. It has been observed that, in the mainstream tradition, the voluntary-law component of war had been steadily gaining ground at the expense of the natural-law element, especially at the hands of Vattel. Nevertheless, the law of war was always seen in that school as a partnership between those two kinds of law. The contractual approach, however, held that the *entire* law of war was voluntary or man-made, since the whole of war was a product of the war contract between the parties. This idea had been clearly present in the writing of Grotius, when he held that war was always governed by the voluntary law (or law of nations) rather than by natural law. But Grotius had not followed this idea up systematically, nor had mainstream writers who followed him accepted the thesis. Where Grotius had only hinted, however, the contractual school of thought boldly followed.

The other crucial aspect of the contractual theory of war – and perhaps its most important departure from mainstream thought – concerned the effects of wars. It will be recalled that, according to just-war theory, there was never any pretence that a war actually *resolved* a legal dispute. A just war was purely a remedial or enforcement measure, which might be successful or not as the material fortunes of the struggle dictated. It did not *create* any legal rights for the winning side that that party had not possessed previously. Only the law itself could create or extinguish rights. The contractual theory of war parted company with just-war theory on this important point. The essence of the war contract was that the winner of the duel would acquire full legal title to the *res* that was being fought over, without regard to how strong or weak its legal claim might have been beforehand. As Suárez had stated, a duellist became the legal owner of any property that he captured, on the ground that the two contestants were parties to 'a pact to the effect that the victorious party shall acquire the property of the vanquished'.[26] In the strictest sense of the word, then, might made right according to the contractual perspective. That meant that brute strength could, as such, be a source of legal rights – something that had never been accepted in traditional just-war doctrine.[27]

Grappling with issues

It may be noted that, in a number of notable respects, the mainstream tradition occupied what could be termed a middle way between two extremes represented by the two dissident schools of thought. This fact is illustrated by the rival positions held by the schools on the broad question of what body of law governed issues of war and peace. The two dissident schools had rather dogmatic, and opposing, views on that question. One the one side, we find the Hobbesians, who held that war was governed entirely by natural law, while peace was governed entirely by man-made (i.e., positive or voluntary) law, in the form of treaties between independent states. In fact, to say that war in the Hobbesian view was 'governed' by natural law risks being misleading, since the connection between the two was more intimate than that expression would imply. War was essentially, by *definition*, the state of affairs in which natural law prevailed between two parties, to the exclusion of positive or voluntary law. At the opposite extreme was the contractual school, which viewed war as being governed entirely by voluntary (i.e., contractual) law, and peace by a combination of natural law and treaty law. The mainstream tradition, in contrast to both, saw *both* war and peace as governed by *both* natural law and man-made (i.e., voluntary) law.

It is instructive to see the new ideas in action in specific situations, in order to illustrate the way in which their solutions compared and

---

[26] Suárez, *Three Virtues*, at 852.

[27] It could be contended that might could make right only as between the parties to the duel *inter se*, but with no obligation on the part of third states to recognise any change in legal position. This point would not be made in an explicit way until the 1930s, with the Stimson Doctrine. For this development, see Chapter 8 below.

contrasted with those of the mainstream just-war tradition. On many issues, the three schools were substantially in agreement as to result, but with importantly different reasoning processes involved. In these areas, the two dissident schools of thought often possessed, as will be seen, considerably more definite or coherent views on the issues at hand than the mainstream school did. To other questions, different answers were given. Some of the more notable of these issues may be identified briefly.

War as a state or condition

It has been noted that the writers in the mainstream tradition supported the view of war as a state or condition, distinct from the material hostilities that might occur. That idea, however, played little role in their over-all thinking on war. It was otherwise with the new schools, where the idea of war as a condition was tightly integrated into their respective definitions of war. The Hobbesian position on the matter is easily seen. War must necessarily be a condition, since war was, in effect, defined as the state of affairs which prevailed when two parties were linked only by the law of nature, unadorned by treaty commitments. As Hobbes put it:

> [W]ar consisteth not in battle only in the act of fighting: but in a tract of time, wherein the will to contend by battle is sufficiently known: and there-fore the notion of *time*, is to be considered in the nature of war: ... so the nature of war, consisteth not in actual fighting: but in the known disposition thereto, during all the time there is no assurance to the contrary.[28]

A Hobbesian state of war, therefore, was a condition in which an omni-present possibility of a resort to arms in the exercise of natural-law rights brooded constantly, untempered by treaty obligations. Moreover, it was a condition in which the opposing sides were both *lawfully* entitled to use force, since both were exercising their (overlapping) natural-law rights of survival.

The contractual school of thought had an equally distinct conception of a state of war. In fact, it was the most emphatic of the three on the subject, since it saw a war as a private arrangement by the states concerned, which had the effect of setting up a special legal regime in substitution for the normal one of peacetime. A state of war, in this conception, was the contractual relationship between the two parties, beginning at the time

---

[28] Hobbes, *Leviathan*, at 82. (Emphases in the original.)

of the conclusion of the war contract and concluding with the outcome of the violent proceedings themselves. In short, it was the period of time during which the war contract was in force. During this period, the normal law of nature was suspended, as between the duellists; and a new body of rules, regulating the process of duelling *per se*, was substituted. As in the case of the Hobbesian conception, a state of war was a condition in which two countries became legally entitled to use armed force against one other – although in this case, the source of that entitlement was the war contract between the parties, rather than the general law of nature.

Concerning the basic concept of a state of war, it only remains to take note of why the two dissident schools inevitably attached a stronger legal significance to the idea than the mainstream tradition did. The reason was that the mainstream writers were heirs to the medieval natural-law tradition, which held that the law of nature ruled the affairs of the entire sublunar universe in all times and all places, in war as well as in peace. States of war and peace were accordingly not seen as differing fundamentally from one another – the same law of nature ruled majestically and impartially over both. The two dissident schools both rejected this idea and perceived conditions of war and peace to be radically distinct from one another from the legal standpoint. To the Hobbesians, the law of nature held sway over war and the law of contract or treaty (i.e., man-made law) over peace. The contractual position was a kind of mirror image of this, with the law of nature ruling over peace and man-made law covering war. Both agreed, though, that to go from the one state to the other was necessarily to enter a fundamentally different legal world.

Declaring war

On the annoyingly obscure subject of declarations of war, the dissident schools offered only marginally clearer and more definite thinking than the mainstream tradition did. According to the Hobbesian approach, there could be no reason for two countries that were in a state of nature to declare war against one another, since, by definition, they were *already* in a state of war. A declaration of war might, however, be necessary for informing the domestic populations of the countries of the situation and perhaps also for activating various duties, such as compulsory military service, that the subjects of the warring state might be expected to perform. In situations in which states were bound by treaty to peaceful relations with one another, war would be commenced by the termination of the relevant treaty or treaties, which would then automatically bring a reversion to the state of nature. There certainly was support for this view in state practice, in that declarations of war were commonly held to terminate all treaty relations between the warring states. The Hobbesians merely reversed the direction of causation, holding that, strictly speaking, the termination of treaties created the state of war rather than vice versa.

For the contractual school, the question of how to create a state of war amounted to the question of how, precisely, to go about concluding a war contract. In principle, it is readily seen how this would be done: by the issuing of a challenge to war by one state, which the other state would then accept. That is to say, there would have to be some kind of 'offer and acceptance' or 'meeting of the minds' (to borrow common expressions from the ordinary law of contract) regarding the submission of a dispute to 'the arbitrament of Mars'. There could be room for dispute, however, as to which step in this process best merited the label of 'declaration' – or indeed, whether 'declaration' ought preferably to be seen as referring to the whole process. Perhaps the best example of declarations in this style were ultimatums, with one party making a peremptory demand on the other, with an explicit statement that, if the demand was not satisfied, then a resort to arms would follow. The other state could then either avoid war by complying with the demand, or accept the challenge by refusing to comply and thereby bringing the state of war into existence.

One topic in particular is of value for the way in which it neatly illustrates the different approaches of the three schools to the problem of declaring war. This was the question of whether a single country could unilaterally foist a state of war onto another one without that other country's consent – or even, at the extreme, in the face of its active opposition. The issue, in other words, was whether a purely *unilateral* declaration could effectually create a state of war, or whether *both* sides had somehow to signal their intention to enter into a state of war. There was at least some state practice in favour of reciprocal declarations of war. In 1595, for example, France and Spain each declared war against the other.[29] In 1652, England's declaration of war against the Netherlands was met two days later by a counter-declaration by the Netherlands against England.[30] This practice appears,

---

[29] Declaration of war by France against Spain, 16 Jan. 1595, 5(1) Dumont 512; and Declaration of war by Spain against France, 7 Mar. 1595, *ibid.* at 515.
[30] Declaration of war by England against the Netherlands, 31 July 1652, 3 Anonymous, *General Collection*, at 36–44; and Declaration of war by the Netherlands against England, 2 Aug. 1652, *ibid.* at 45–59.

however, not to have been common, and writers in the mainstream school held such reciprocity to be unnecessary. Grotius held that a single declaration sufficed, since it would be apparent from that point that a war was in progress.[31] It could also be pointed out that the mainstream school's intellectual ancestry in medieval just-war doctrine naturally inclined it to hold that a single country could inaugurate a state of war on its own. This was because the just-war view always saw war in unilateral terms, as a decision by one party to resort to violence against another.

The Hobbesian school was able to reach this same conclusion, but not without a certain degree of intellectual strain. In principle, the Hobbesians were strongly of the view that contracts, once duly arrived at, were binding on the two parties, with no unilateral right on the part of either party to resile from them. A contract could of course be terminated by the mutual consent of both parties. Unilateral termination, however, was difficult to justify. The Hobbesians were able to resolve the problem by either of two possible approaches, which were slight variants of one another. One was to hold that the fundamental natural-law right of self-preservation continued to be operative at all times, even to the point of taking precedence over (or 'trumping') the normal duty to fulfil treaty obligations. Alternatively, it could be argued that every treaty concluded by every state contained a tacit provision (grandly known in Latin as a *clausula rebus sic stantibus*), to the effect that the treaty arrangements were not intended to prejudice the security interests of either party or to deprive either party of the right to take whatever steps were necessary to safeguard its security.[32] Whichever mode of reasoning was used, though, the end result was the same: to allow states to denounce treaties unilaterally whenever that was necessary for self-preservation. A declaration of war, according to the Hobbesian school, would therefore be the invocation of this right, which, by its nature, was a unilateral matter.

On this question of unilateral declarations of war, the logic of the contractual approach was equally definite on the point, but in the opposite direction – i.e., towards requiring the joint or mutual will of *both* sides to create a state of war. One country could no more create

---

[31] Grotius, *War and Peace*, at 637. See also Wolff, *Law of Nations*, at 368–9.

[32] The *clausula rebus sic stantibus* lives on in present-day international law, in the form of a rule of law allowing treaties to be terminated, in certain restricted conditions, in the face of a fundamental change of circumstances. See the Vienna Convention on the Law of Treaties, 23 May 1969, 1155 UNTS 331, Art. 62.

a war on its own than one challenger could unilaterally arrange a duel. A single party of course could issue a challenge unilaterally, but there would be no duel unless the would-be adversary cooperated by accepting it. The challenger might decide instead to ambush his foe on a dark night; but that of course would be a mere criminal act bearing no resemblance to a duel. In the interstate sphere, a declaration of war issued by one state alone could only be, strictly speaking, an offer or challenge to enter into a state of war. The state of war would then actually occur if – but only if – the offer or challenge was duly accepted. Following this line of reasoning, it would be concluded that, if a state issued a declaration of war unilaterally and then proceeded to attack, its action would simply be an unlawful act of aggression. There would be no true state of war; and the victim country would be entitled to compensation for the illegal attack, just as any state was entitled, under general natural law, to recompense for any unlawful damage done to it. If, on the other hand, there was a true state of war – duly agreed upon by *both* sides – then neither side would incur any legal liability for any attacks, whether offensive or defensive, launched against the other.

On a couple of occasions in European history, this question actually arose. One instance occurred in 1780–1, when Britain sought to dragoon a reluctant Netherlands into war, in the course of struggles connected with the American independence conflict. Its real motive was a desire to stop the Netherlands from taking advantage of its status as a neutral in the war that was then raging between Britain and France. Specifically, Britain sought to prevent the Dutch from carrying on much of France's normal trade for it. In its declaration of war, however, Britain made no mention of these matters of high policy, instead putting forward a range of legal-sounding grievances: the alleged failure of the Dutch to honour an alliance arrangement agreed by treaty, the giving of shelter to an 'American pirate' (John Paul Jones) in Dutch ports; fomenting opposition to Britain in the East Indies; receiving enemy privateers in its West Indian ports; and failing to stop the city of Amsterdam from concluding a 'treaty' with the rebellious American colonists.[33] After promulgating the declaration, the British moved swiftly to begin capturing Dutch merchant ships on the high seas.

---

[33] Manifesto of His Britannic Majesty Regarding Relations with the Netherlands, 21 Dec. 1780, in J. B. Scott (ed.), *Armed Neutralities*, at 330–4. See also the Order in Council Granting Reprisals Against the Ships, Goods and Subjects of the Netherlands, 20 Dec. 1780, in *ibid.* at 334–5.

The Dutch resisted these captures by the British as best they could. But they strained, at the same time, to deny that any state of war was really in existence. The reason was that the Dutch were anxious to qualify for membership in a coalition of neutral states which had banded together as an 'armed neutrality' for the mutual safeguarding of their trade against interference by the belligerents. The Netherlands accordingly insisted that its armed resistance against British naval force was merely an exercise of a right of retaliation against unlawful acts by the British, not a resort to war.[34] It has been observed that there were doubts as to the lawfulness of retaliation in natural law.[35] The point for present purposes, however, is that, in the Dutch view, the situation was a case of unlawful aggression by Britain, which was countered by the exercise of an ordinary *peacetime* remedy – i.e., that the crisis was *not* a state of war in the legal sense. The question was never adjudicated. It may be noted, though, that the British stratagem succeeded de facto, when it became apparent that the other Armed Neutrality powers were unwilling to support the Netherlands (i.e., were unwilling to go to war against Britain on behalf of the Netherlands).

In the early part of the nineteenth century, the question of unilateral imposition of a state of war arose again, this time in British prize courts. One case in 1802 presented the question of whether French attacks against Portugal meant that a state of war existed between them, notwithstanding a clear reluctance on Portugal's part (comparable to that of the Netherlands earlier) to become involved in a war. Even though no formal declaration of war was issued by France, Sir William Scott, the eminent British judge, held a state of war to exist, which Portugal's 'submissive conduct' could not prevent. The fact that France persisted in its attacks sufficed to create a state of war between the two countries regardless of the wishes of Portugal.[36] Scott reached a similar conclusion in another case in 1813, concerning the effect of a declaration of war by Sweden against Britain. He noted that Britain had issued no counter-declaration against Sweden, nor had it issued letters of marque or reprisal. But this non-responsiveness on Britain's part did not preclude the existence of a state of war. In reaching this conclusion, Scott forthrightly rejected the contractual theory of war:

---

[34] Netherlands Ordinance Concerning Commerce and Navigation, 26 Jan. 1781, in *ibid.* at 358–64.
[35] See Wolff, *Law of Nations*, at 298–300.   [36] *The Nayade*, 4 C Rob 251 (1802).

A declaration of war by one country only [Scott insisted] is not, as has been represented a mere challenge, to be accepted or refused at pleasure by the other. It proves the existence of actual hostilities on one side at least, and puts the other party also into a state of war.[37]

The matter cannot be regarded as having been definitively settled by these cases and incidents. In the nineteenth century (as will be seen), there would be renewed controversy about the creation of a state of war. Indeed, the underlying issues remain alive to the present day.[38]

Rights of war

The three contending approaches to war put forward instructively different ways of thinking about the law concerning the conduct of war (the *jus in bello* in the technical terminology). The mainstream tradition, reflecting its medieval heritage, was very hesitant to embrace the idea that the death and destruction involved in war could really be inflicted as a matter of legal right, even in a just cause, never mind in an unjust one. Grotius held that, according to the natural law, a fighter in a just war did not possess a 'true and perfect right' to kill, capture and destroy.[39] Instead, he had something rather more limited: an immunity from *punishment* at the hands of earthly authorities. The result was that just warriors possessed what Grotius called an 'incomplete' permission to kill and capture.[40] In this connection, he made an interesting analogy at this point to the position of marriage in the Christian religion. Chastity was the ideal; consequently, sexual relations, even within marriage, could not be positively lawful. The position was that punishment was withheld from persons who indulged in this vice within the strictures of the marital relationship.[41] Later mainstream writers moved away from this highly principled position. Vattel, for example, readily conceded that fighters on the just side in a war had a true legal right to kill their enemies, on the ground that the enemies were acting wrongly in resorting to violence in an unjust cause.[42] The voluntary law, in contrast,

---

[37] *The Eliza Ann*, 1 Dods 244 (1813), at 247. See also, however, *The Success*, 1 Dods 131 (1812), in which Scott pointedly declined to decide whether a single declaration, unresponded to by the target country, created a state of war.

[38] For a survey of state practice on declarations of war in the eighteenth century, see Michael D. Ramsay, 'Textualism and War Powers', 69 *University of Chicago Law Review* 1543–1638 (2002), at 1569–96.

[39] Grotius, *War and Peace*, at 595.   [40] *Ibid.* at 663.

[41] *Ibid.* at 641–3, 663. Due caution is advisable in making comparisons between war and matrimony.

[42] Vattel, *Law of Nations*, at 280.

granted only an immunity from punishment – but, crucially, it granted it to both sides equally.[43]

Both of the dissident schools took a much more 'positive' view (if that is the right word for it) of the right to kill and capture in the course of war. The Hobbesian position was straightforward. Acts of war were regarded as exercises of legal right in the strict sense, i.e., as exercises, by *both* sides, of the fundamental natural-law right of self-preservation. '[I]n the state of nature', Hobbes candidly maintained, 'it is lawful for every one, by reason of that war which is of all against all, to subdue and also to kill men as oft as it shall seem to conduce unto their good'.[44] The position of the contractual school was equally clear. The war contract conferred an affirmative right onto each duellist to kill the other. The dissident schools, in other words, could speak more forthrightly than mainstream writers, in favour of what became known as 'rights of war' – or, in later parlance, 'belligerents' rights' – as rights in the true legal sense, possessed on a wholly equal basis by both sides.

On the question of the general nature of the laws of war, the three approaches held divergent views. To the Hobbesians, the laws of war were, in their entirety, rules of *natural* law. They could scarcely be anything else, given that war was, by definition, a condition governed only by natural law. Moreover, the rights of war were rooted – as pretty much everything was – in the general natural-law principle of necessity. The laws of war, such as they were, were really just the application of that general principle to the particular facts of individual situations as they arose.[45] This picture boded ill for any hopes that the law might moderate the sufferings of war. Bynkershoek, for one, certainly offered little comfort in this direction. He was frankly of the view that war was 'by its very nature so general that it cannot be waged within set limits'.[46] As a direct consequence, 'every force is lawful in war' – including the use of poison or incendiary bombs, as well as the hanging or enslaving of prisoners of war.[47] Later in the century, Rousseau expressed much the same view, holding that war conferred a right onto the belligerents to commit whatever destruction was necessary in order to bring about victory.[48]

The contractualist school was the best placed of the three, at least in principle, to promote a code of conduct governing warfare. Since war, on

[43] *Ibid.* at 305–6.
[44] Hobbes, *De Cive*, at 104. See also Hobbes, *Leviathan*, at 205.
[45] Hobbes, *Elements*, at 103–4.   [46] Bynkershoek, *Questions*, at 16.   [47] *Ibid.* at 16, 26–8.
[48] Rousseau, *Social Contract*, at 57.

that view, was an affair governed wholly by convention rather than by natural law, the contestants were logically free to fix a set of rules for their encounter. The mainstream writers were in the middle, between the wholly conventional-law outlook of the contractualists and the wholly natural-law approach of the Hobbesians. As observed earlier, they held the laws of war to be a combination of natural law and voluntary law, with the voluntary or conventional element gradually gaining the upper hand over the natural-law component. The mainstream approach, therefore, naturally edged towards the contractual one.

On the key issue of the equality of rights of war as between the belligerents, the three schools of thought were in agreement – though for different reasons. From the mainstream standpoint, the equality of standing of the belligerents was a regrettable, but necessary, consequence of invincible ignorance and of the lack of a mechanism for authoritatively determining which side in a war was fighting with justice on its side. The two dissident schools, however, saw this equality not as a grudging concession to an unpleasant reality, but rather as a matter of high principle. From the Hobbesian perspective, it was not merely that the two sides were treated *as if* they were both right. Rather, the two sides actually *were* fighting with equal right on their respective sides. From the contractual standpoint, the same conclusion was equally obvious. The principle of parity of the parties was inherent in the law of contract.[49] Moreover, the long-standing tradition in duelling was to ensure the most scrupulous even-handedness of treatment of the participants.

As to the contents of the laws of war, it has already been noted how limited the progress was in this period towards the compilation of a detailed code of rules. It might have been thought that the contractual school would have the most to offer in this regard, given its view of the laws of war as being wholly man-made. In reality, this promise was unfulfilled. Pufendorf in particular offered heartbreakingly little hope to those seeking to moderate the sufferings of war. He offered nothing significant in the way of specific rules of war, while also rejecting any notion of limitations based on the general concepts of necessity and proportionality. On the contrary, the war contract gave the belligerents a virtually entirely open-ended licence to use force. '[I]n confessing that he is my enemy', Pufendorf pronounced, the opposing belligerent 'allows me a licence to use force against him to any degree, or so far as I may think desirable'.[50] He expressly rejected any argument of

---

[49] Pufendorf, *Nature and Nations*, at 767.   [50] *Ibid.* at 1298.

proportionality on the analogy of the use of force by a magistrate. War, he insisted, was importantly different from law enforcement in that the war contract amounted to a mutual renunciation by each side of the fundamental right to life. As a result, 'it is the law of war that one may go to any length in order to destroy one's enemy':[51]

> Nor is it in fact always unjust to return a greater evil for a less [he insisted], for the objection made by some that retribution should be rendered in proportion to the injury, is true only of civil tribunals, where punishments are meted out by superiors. But the evils inflicted by right of war have properly no relation to punishments, since they neither proceed from a superior as such, nor have as their direct object the reform of the guilty party or others, but the defence and assertion of my safety, my property, and my rights. To secure such ends it is permissible to use whatever means I think will best prevail against such a person, who, by the injury done me, has made it impossible for me to do him an injury, however I may treat him, until we have come to a new agreement to refrain from injuries for the future.[52]

The conclusion was as clear as it was dispiriting: 'The extent of licence in war is such that, however far one may have gone beyond the bounds of humanity in slaughter or in wasting or plundering property, the opinion of nations does not hold one in infamy nor as deserving of being shunned by honest men.'[53] Pufendorf even worried that the effect of moderation might be to 'increase and nourish war', in which case it would be positively 'repugnant to nature'.[54]

To his credit as a humanitarian, Pufendorf struggled to temper these conclusions. He recognised the force of humanitarian considerations but persisted in placing them on a moral rather than a legal plane. He distinguished the rights of war properly speaking from dictates of conscience or humanity. The rights of war in the true sense concerned 'what an enemy may suffer without wrong'. The quite separate moral question concerned the kind or amount of violence that a belligerent could inflict 'without loss of humanity'. Humanitarian considerations dictated that the constraints of necessity and proportionality be observed, as in the just-war tradition.[55] But these humanitarian considerations operated outside the framework of the war contract and hence exerted only a moral restraint, not a legal one. It may be wondered if Pufendorf's role

---

[51] *Ibid.* at 323.   [52] *Ibid.* at 1298.   [53] Pufendorf, *Duty of Man*, at 171.
[54] Pufendorf, *Nature and Nations*, at 1317. On this point, he referred expressly to Hobbes for support.
[55] Pufendorf, *Duty of Man*, at 169.

as a historian of the Thirty Years War may not have unduly blinkered him to the logic of the contractual theory of war. Or alternately, it may be that he simply was not a thoroughgoing partisan of that school.[56] In any event, the contractual theory of war may readily be seen to offer a solution to the problem: altering the contents of the war contract in the direction of moderation. Pufendorf may have been right in his observation that European states in his time seemed disinclined to take this path. But there was nothing in the intrinsic logic of the contractual viewpoint to prevent it.

Competing attitudes towards neutrality

Nowhere was the distinction between the three schools of legal thought about war so sharply etched as in the area of neutrality, a subject which only began to receive sustained attention from legal writers in the middle of the eighteenth century. Although a substantial body of *practice* regarding neutrality had been growing throughout the Middle Ages, medieval just-war doctrine took no account of it, unless it was to deny its validity in principle.[57] The reason is easily seen. In a system in which war constitutes, by definition, a struggle of good against evil, there could be no justification for declining to take a stand. All persons were naturally bound to support the good cause against the wicked one. On the *most* extreme view, it could even be argued that states might have a positive duty to enter any war on the side of the just party. As a more moderate position, third states were assigned the more modest task of withholding support for the unjust side while taking care not to hamper the cause of the just one. Grotius expressly endorsed this position, as did Vattel.[58]

The two dissident schools, in contrast, both looked with a great deal more favour on neutrality than the mainstream tradition did. The Hobbesians, with their conflict-of-rights analysis, were inevitably of the view that neither side in a conflict could ever have a prior claim over the other for the sympathies of third states. With *both* parties fighting for a just cause (their own security), impartiality naturally becomes the logical policy for outside states. Bynkershoek most clearly

---

[56] It may be recalled in this connection that no writer in this period gave a systematic exposition of the contractual theory. Although Pufendorf came near to it in his general outlook, it would be an error to hold him rigorously to all of its conclusions and implications.

[57] See Neff, *Rights and Duties*, at 7–8.

[58] Grotius, *War and Peace*, at 786–7; and Vattel, *Law of Nations*, at 262.

articulated this position, by scornfully rejecting the traditional just-war preference for partiality, holding instead that the justice of a war was simply no business of third states.[59] The contractual school of thought was even clearer in according full recognition to the right of third states to be neutral in time of war. It could hardly be otherwise, since the very nature of a contractual relationship is that the contract has no effect on the rights or duties of third parties. A war is, by nature, only an affair between the two contestants, with the rest of the world free to carry on as usual.

The issue that etched the three schools' positions most sharply concerned the general nature and extent of the rights or powers that belligerent states, as a class, possessed *vis-à-vis* neutrals and, conversely, the rights and powers of neutrals *vis-à-vis* belligerents. Three specific prerogatives that were claimed and exercised by belligerent states should be identified in particular. First was the capture and confiscation of contraband of war from neutral ships on the high seas. (Contraband of war consisted of materials useful to the carrying on of armed conflict, such as weapons and ammunition.) Second was the enforcement of blockades of enemy areas against entry by neutral ships (with the neutral ships, together with their cargoes, subject to confiscation for attempted entry). Third was the visiting and searching of neutral ships on the high seas, in the quest for enemy-owned property or contraband. The challenge facing lawyers in the eighteenth century was, in one sense, backward-looking: to devise some explanation for these three long-standing practices, or else to denounce them forthrightly (and probably without effect) as unlawful. But the task of the lawyers was also forward-looking, since the theoretical basis given for the existing practices would inevitably shape the direction in which the law evolved in the future.

To this task, the Hobbesians brought their conflict-of-rights analysis, together with its close conceptual ally, the principle of necessity. As a concrete illustration of the Hobbesian approach, consider the carriage of arms by neutral individuals to a belligerent destination. The neutrals had a right to engage in this trade, since they were at peace with both parties. At the very same time, though, the opposing belligerent had a right, founded in the principle of necessity, to safeguard its security by capturing and confiscating this weapons shipment to its enemy. In practice, the conflict tended to be 'resolved' in favour of the belligerent state, which naturally tended to be the more determined party, given that it was already at war and therefore naturally in a higher state of desperation than the neutrals. The

---

[59] Bynkershoek, *Questions*, at 61–2. See also G. F. von Martens, *Compendium*, at 321–2.

effective result was that any so-called 'rights' of neutrals, on the conflict-of-rights view, became merely a name for whatever freedom of action happened to be 'left over' to them once the principle of necessity had been fully played out in favour of the belligerents. The conflict-of-rights approach, in short, was, in effect if not in strict theory, a belligerents' charter.[60]

The contractual school of thought took a drastically different view of the nature of neutral rights and duties. In particular, it gave the priority to the rights of neutrals over the rights of the belligerents. This naturally arose out of the very concept of a contract – that it creates rights and duties *only* for the parties to it and leaves third parties entirely unaffected. Consequently, the belligerents in a war were entitled to hurl themselves at one another as energetically as they wished; but they thereby acquired no right whatsoever to interfere with outside parties in their exercises of their normal rights. That was the position of the Abbé Ferdinando Galiani, the Italian cleric and Enlightenment figure who wrote the first comprehensive treatise on the law of neutrality in 1781.[61]

This thesis had some startling implications. For one thing, it implied that neutral traders would have a completely unfettered right to sell and convey goods of *every* sort – even armaments – to either side (or both), as well as the right to trade with *any* port that was normally open, even if it was being blockaded at the time. It also meant that belligerents could have *no* right to visit and search neutral ships on the high seas, or to capture or confiscate any cargoes (of whatever nature). These implications – as alarming to some as they were welcome to others – were, however, too far out of line with established state practice to gain wide acceptance.

One element, though, of contractual thought did find a permanent place in the law of neutrality: the *duty* on the part of neutral states to refrain from any involvement in the hostilities between the warring states. This was analogous to the private-law principle that, although persons who are not parties to a contract (in this case, to a war contract) have no rights or duties under it, they nonetheless incur liability if they impede the performance of it by the parties. In essence, though, the contractual view of neutrality law was that it was a law about the rights and duties of the *neutrals*, in contrast to the Hobbesians, for whom neutrality law was primarily about the rights and duties of *belligerents*.[62]

---

[60] See Neff, *Rights and Duties*, at 45–8.
[61] Ferdinando Galiani, *De' Doveri de' Principi Neutrali verso i Principi Guerregianti, e di Questi verso i Neutrali* (Naples, 1782).
[62] See Neff, *Rights and Duties*, at 51–2.

The mainstream school was slow to reconcile itself to neutrality and to carve out a distinctive position on the question – and when it did, it took, once again, a middle path between the two dissident approaches. Vattel, who was the first writer in this school to treat issues of neutral rights and duties in any detail, simply adopted the Hobbesian analysis, holding that belligerents were entitled to take whatever steps were necessary under the circumstances to bring victory.[63] He recognised no voluntary law of neutrality. Very shortly after Vattel wrote, however, the position changed sharply when a new thesis was advanced that was more in tune with the general ethos of mainstream doctrine on war. The seminal figure was the Danish lawyer Martin Hübner, who wrote a treatise on captures at sea in 1759, the year after Vattel's book was published.[64] Hübner's proposal marked out a middle way between the Hobbesian and contractual positions. He contended that there should be an equitable sharing-out of rights and duties as between neutrals and belligerents, with a clear demarcation between the two and no overlapping of rights. The rights of the two groups would be, on this approach, strictly correlative and coterminous, affording no scope for either party to 'trespass' into the juridical territory of the other. Hübner argued, in other words, for a code-of-conduct approach to the law of neutrality, in opposition to Vattel's necessity-based position – a state of affairs precisely analogous to the opposition in the law of war, where these same two approaches vied for superiority.[65]

The beginnings of such a code-of-conduct view of neutrality were evident in state practice in the seventeenth and eighteenth centuries, with the code emerging from the network of bilateral friendship treaties that bound the major European maritime states together (if somewhat precariously). The principal achievement of this treaty practice was the widespread adoption of the principle that 'free ships make free goods', in the common parlance of the period. That meant that enemy-owned goods (except for contraband) were free from capture if they were being carried on neutral vessels. This new practice marked the abandonment of the medieval character-of-the-cargo principle, according to which enemy property was subject to capture (i.e., was 'good prize' in the legal expression) wherever found. The effect of this new practice was to make maritime warfare less disruptive to economic life than it would

---

[63] Vattel, *Law of Nations*, at 271.
[64] Martin Hübner, *De la saisie.*
[65] On this innovation, see Neff, *Rights and Duties*, at 48–51.

otherwise have been.[66] More importantly, the code-of-conduct approach to the law of neutrality would gain the upper hand in the nineteenth century, when the law of neutrality underwent very substantial development. The important point for present purposes is to note that the code-of-conduct view of neutrality rested, if only implicitly, on a conception of neutrality *per se* that was more positive than the mainstream school of lawyers had ever conceded.

Imperfect wars

The rival positions of the three schools of thought on the subject of imperfect wars is of interest because they foreshadowed some important trends that would emerge in the nineteenth century. It was observed that the mainstream view of the matter was far from coherent. Some writers, such as Grotius, considered imperfect wars to be wars that lacked certain prescribed formalities (chiefly a declaration of war), while others saw them as distinct from wars. On this subject, the dissident schools had considerably more specific ideas to offer.

To the Hobbesians, the distinction between a perfect and an imperfect war was easily stated. A perfect war consisted of the rupturing of *all* peaceful (i.e., contractual) ties between the contending states, while an imperfect war involved the rupture of some of these ties but not all of them. The clearest sign, then, of whether a war was perfect or imperfect was the status of treaties between the contenders. If some treaties continued to subsist, then the war was an imperfect one. It is readily seen from this analysis that the Hobbesian perspective was particularly well equipped to deal with any number of gradations of hostility, with treaties as a sort of surrogate or measuring device. The greater the number, importance and proportion of treaties terminated between the contending parties, the more closely would the conflict resemble a perfect war. It came naturally to adherents of the Hobbesian view to see war – perfect war, that is – as only the final point on a continuum of interstate violence, and also to accept the existence of an indefinite number of intermediate states between perfect war and complete peace.

The contractual school was also able to give a clear account of the subject of imperfect wars. An imperfect war, in its view, would be any de facto armed conflict which occurred in the absence of a war treaty. An accidental or unplanned clash between local armed forces in a disputed

---

[66] See *ibid.* at 29–32.

border area would be one obvious illustration. Another, less obvious, example of an imperfect war would be one that was declared and waged by one state without the consent of the other, i.e., the case (discussed above) of a unilateral declaration of war by one state, contrary to the wishes of the other. Such a conflict would be a case of unlawful aggression from the one side countered by self-defence from the other – a case of 'aggression-and-self-defence', as it will be termed – but it would not be a war. The principal concrete effect of this analysis was that the defending power would have *only* the right of self-defence in the narrow sense of fending off the attack. In the absence of a state of war, it would not possess the full panoply of rights of war. In particular, it would have no right to go onto the offensive itself. In addition, the defending state would have a legal claim against the aggressor for the act of aggression. It must be confessed that there was no explicit analysis along this line during the period in question – and indeed, there would not be until the twentieth century, when the phenomenon of aggression-and-self-defence would finally come to assume a commanding role in international thought on armed conflict. But the ultimate roots of the idea lay here – even if only latently – in the contractual school of thought on war.

Peace-making

Regarding peace-making, the distinctions between the three schools were not vast. All were in agreement that conclusion of wars by way of a peace treaty was the most sensible approach. The Hobbesians and the contractualists, though, had different, and opposite, views of the underlying nature of a peace treaty. To the Hobbesians, a peace treaty was, so to speak, a process of exiting from the state of nature (i.e., the state of war) and re-entering the world of human artifice, in which relations of amity were constructed as an alternative, if often a fragile one, to the natural-law world of fear and suspicion. To the contractualists, the position was the opposite. A peace treaty was a termination of the artificial or man-made regime of the war contract and a reversion to the state of nature, which was inherently peaceful, orderly and rule-governed. In this regard, the mainstream writers were largely at one with the contractual school.

The two dissident schools both rejected the various constraints on victors of the medieval *jus victoriae*. To the Hobbesians, the triumphant side in a war had a natural-law right to impose upon its vanquished rival whatever conditions were necessary to secure its safety over the longer term. Victory in war, effectively by definition, meant the removal of material impediments to the exercise of that fundamental right. It is true of course that, under the Hobbesian conflict-of-rights analysis, the defeated party had an equally fundamental right to safeguard *its* security. The difference was simply that the winning side was in the fortunate position of being able to exercise its right without interference, whereas the losing side was not. Strictly speaking, the victor should not have any right to inflict hardships onto its foe which had nothing whatever to do with the victor's security interest. But this caveat could operate only as a marginal (and rather theoretical) constraint. The essence of the Hobbesian position was that the victor's right was an entitlement to security, unencumbered by any obligation to mete out impartial justice according to some transcendental, objective standard.

The contractual theory of war rejected the medieval *jus victoriae* with equal decisiveness. According to that view, it was a provision of the war contract, agreed at the outset, that the loser threw itself on the mercy of the winner, meaning that the losing side consented in advance to whatever terms the winning party might put to it. If the terms were thought to be too onerous, then the belligerent had the right to reject them and fight on instead in the hope that a turn of the fortunes of battle would rescue it from its plight.

On the specific question of whether peace treaties could be regarded as void because of duress, the two dissident schools joined the mainstream one in replying negatively. But their reasoning differed. To Hobbes and his followers, it was fully accepted, on firm principle, that treaties entered into out of fear were perfectly valid and legally binding.[67] Extreme Hobbesians might even have wondered whether, ultimately, there was ever any other reason to conclude a treaty. The contractualists reached the same conclusion by a different reasoning. Their view was that the war contract contained, as one of its provisions, an acceptance, in advance, to whatever terms the other side might lay down in the event of victory. '[W]hoever resolved to take up war against another', Pufendorf explained, 'when he could have settled the controversy by peaceful negotiations, is understood to have left the decision of the issue to the dice of Mars, and it is, therefore, idle for him to complain of any terms which the fortunes of war have meted out to him'. Again, the comparison with duelling was put forward.[68]

---

[67] Hobbes, *Leviathan*, at 91.   [68] Pufendorf, *Nature and Nations*, at 767.

Both dissident schools also rejected the traditional just-war idea that the just side had a right to be indemnified by the unjust one for the expense of prosecuting the war. According to the Hobbesian view, such an indemnity could be extracted by the winner of a war from the loser – but only in the interest of securing its own future security, not on the basis of any wrongdoing or injustice on the losing side's part, since, in a conflict-of-rights situation, it could not be said that the losing side was legally in the wrong or had acted unjustly. The contractual position reached a similar conclusion on the matter. The war contract was held to grant to both sides equal authority to use force against the other. Consequently, there could be no question of compensation owing to either side for wrongdoing, since any blows struck must be deemed to have been lawfully inflicted and voluntarily suffered.[69]

From this all-too-rapid survey of the three contending schools of thought in action, there is some risk of gaining an unbalanced broader picture. The three approaches to war are perhaps best seen not as implacable opponents of one another but more as counterweights, with the dissident schools of thought acting as balances against the excessively doctrinaire and theoretical ethos of the mainstream tradition. The strength of just-war thought had been its intellectual coherence and comprehensiveness. Its corresponding weakness had been its remoteness from state practice. The Hobbesian and the contractual schools of thought were, so to speak, closer to the ground, more in tune with the changing styles of statecraft and the realities of international relations. But all of them had their characteristic strong points, and all of them survived into the nineteenth century. In that period, they would combine together in ways that were not always obvious, to create the legal picture of war which, in its essentials, continues to dominate the popular imagination to the present day.

[69] See *ibid.*

PART III

War as state policy (1815–1919)

War is a political act by which the States, being unable to reconcile what they believe to their duties, their rights and their interests, resort to armed struggle, and ask that armed struggle to decide which of the two being the stronger will be able by reason of force to impose its will upon the other.

Théophile Funck-Brentano and Albert Sorel

[W]ar is a fact that alters in a variety of ways the legal relations of all the parties concerned. It therefore tells one how the condition of belligerency is created, and what are the rights and obligations of belligerents towards each other and towards neutrals. But it does not pronounce upon the moral questions that occupy such a large space in the writings of the early publicists.

T. J. Lawrence

In the nineteenth century, war reached its pinnacle of legal prestige, when it attained the exalted status of an 'institution of international law'. To a degree unequalled any time before or since, it was frankly recognised by international lawyers as an accepted and routine means of conducting everyday international business. In international politics, as well as in economics, it was a *laissez-faire* era. It was also, in legal terms, a 'positive' era – so much so, as to cause the whole nineteenth century to be grandly denominated as the age of 'positivism'. Positivism was so protean a phenomenon as to defy any neat characterisation. But some of its more salient features may be noted very briefly. As applied to international law generally, and to the activity of war particularly, it may be thought of as an evolved version of the voluntary-law or Hobbesian outlook. That is to say, it perceived law as fundamentally a human creation, a product of culture rather than of nature. No longer, as in the Middle Ages, was there thought to be a body of universal natural law brooding *over* the states of the world. Instead, international law was now seen instead in humanistic and cooperative terms, as a law *between* states, crafted by the states themselves wholly for their own use.

This down-to-earth, humanistic outlook gave to positivism a certain scientific or technocratic ethos. It also gave a broadly utilitarian flavour. It was not the office of lawyers, on this view, to assume the role of lofty social critics or expounders of first principles in the manner of Vitoria or Grotius. Instead, their task was to look to the technical details of drafting treaties, of discerning trends in customary law, of advising governments and so forth. Success and failure in international law-making were measured by the yardstick of utility, not of morals. This abandonment of a concern with first principles and attachment instead to the quotidian issues of daily life naturally served to confer a certain character of amorality onto the positivist outlook. By the same token, though, it meant that international law was now more closely integrated with state practice than ever before, thereby presenting the greatest possible contrast with the situation in the Middle Ages.

The general picture of international relations, in which legal ideas about war were embedded, was very strongly in the Hobbesian image – i.e., as fundamentally anarchic and pluralistic, consisting of rigorously independent nation-states, each with its own distinctive set of interests, ambitions, fears and so forth. Such order as existed was brought about by the conscious agreement of states, either explicitly in the form of treaties, or tacitly as customary law. But this fabric of order was inherently fragile, liable at any time to be broken by states whenever they perceived their security to be under threat in some way. All of this was straightforward Hobbesian thought, very little modified from the time when the master himself wrote in the mid seventeenth century. Perhaps the principal innovation of the nineteenth century in this regard lay in the taking of a more expansive view of security than Hobbes himself had done. In place of Hobbes's essentially defensive stance, with its focus on survival as the supreme goal of political life, there was now a view that a resort to arms could be justified in the general name of the 'vital interests' of states.

This positivist (or Hobbesian) outlook fed directly into legal attitudes towards war. The idea, or ideal, of war as an instrument of justice or a vindication of community values was a thing of the past. War was now forthrightly seen as an instrument for the advancement of rival national interests. Moreover, given the fundamentally anarchic picture of international relations that underlay nineteenth-century legal thought, war was also, and necessarily, an inherent and ineradicable feature of international life. Because each set of state interests was independent of every other, clashes (i.e., wars) were unavoidable. In addition, clashes, when they occurred, did not – indeed *could* not – involve 'higher' questions of general community interest, for the painfully simple reason that there was no such thing as a general community interest. There was *only* a welter of individual state interests, with none occupying a legal privileged position over any other. It is small wonder, then, that the nineteenth century was the age in which the 'sovereign equality of states' – a hallowed expression to lawyers – achieved its status as dogma. Nor is it surprising that the law of neutrality achieved its highest pitch of development during this period, for in the absence of a general community interest in the outcome of wars, it was the most natural thing in the world for third states to insist on going resolutely about their normal business during times of war.

Perhaps the single most outstanding exponent of this positivist view of war was someone who was not a lawyer at all, but a strategist: the Prussian scholar of war and strategy Carl von Clausewitz. Nothing if not candid, he frankly characterised war as 'a clash between major interests, which is resolved by bloodshed'.[1] No lawyer was more emphatic than he in portraying war as a handmaiden of state policy – a pursuit of policy by other means, in his justly famous turn of phrase.[2] This outlook meant that the calculational mentality of war was not merely alive in the nineteenth century, as in the previous era, but also in the very rudest health.

---

[1] Clausewitz, *On War*, at 149.   [2] *Ibid.* at 69, 87, 605.

According to this positivist position, war was, above all else, an exercise of will on the part of a state – i.e., a determination made by a state, reached entirely on the basis of its own interest, that a certain foreign-policy goal will be more effectually pursued by force of arms than by alternative means such as negotiation or the exercise of the unheroic virtue of patience. The 'ideal' war from this positivist perspective was what was sometimes called a 'cabinet war' – meaning a war decided on, in a strictly rational and dispassionate fashion, by the government, after a steely weighing of the likely costs and benefits. As the expression indicates, decisions of such importance were best taken in a 'cabinet' (which originally meant a chamber), safely insulated from such unwelcome meddlers as popular demagogues or the press or tiresome moralists.

The Hobbesian outlook did not, however, have the field of war entirely to itself, even within the broad field of positivist thought. The contractual perspective also made important contributions to the overall positivist synthesis. One of these concerned the manner in which a state of war was initiated. Where the Hobbesians saw the resort to war in unilateral terms, as an exercise of a single state's will, the contractual approach, true to its heritage, saw war in bilateral terms, as a *mutual* decision on the part of two states to settle a quarrel by rolling the dice of Mars. In one respect, however, there was a change in the contractual position in the nineteenth century. The emphasis now was less on a war contract and more on the occurrence of an actual material clash of arms as the means of inaugurating a state of war. Where the Hobbesians saw the essence of war in, as it were, subjective terms, as the product of the will or intention of a single state, the contractualists saw it in objective terms, as a de facto material collision between two states. These two frames of mind will be denominated, for the reasons just set out, as the 'subjective' and 'objective' views of war. These two rival variants of the positivist outlook would contend for the hearts and minds of international lawyers for a long time to come.

In one important area, the contractual perspective held a clearly dominant position: on the law relating to the conduct of war – the *jus in bello* in legal terminology – which made a number of important advances during this period. The idea of war as a rule-governed, even ritualistic contest between professional armed forces reached a very high level of development, to the point that the expression 'law of war' (or more exactly, 'the laws and customs of war') came to refer exclusively to the regulation of the *conduct* of hostilities. The idea of law governing the *resort* to war – the *jus ad bellum* to lawyers – shrivelled into virtual nothingness in the face of the positivist challenge. The decision to resort to war, as observed above, was the prerogative of policy, not of law. Ideally, the prosecution of wars would owe something to the discipline, order and ritual of the parade ground. It would be fought out, in the manner of a tournament, between professional armed forces according to the laws of war, with the losing side then submitting to the winner's terms with as much grace as it could muster under the circumstances. Needless to say, ideal wars in this sense were actually few in number in the extreme. Perhaps the best example of a cabinet war in this period was the Austro-Prussian War of 1866, commenced by Prussia with a limited and carefully defined goal (the exclusion of Austria from the process of German unification) and brought to a swift conclusion by a single decisive blow, in the Napoleonic style.

History, however, is no subject for purists. There were many pressures in the nineteenth century working against the cabinet war as the archetypal kind of armed conflict. For one thing, journalists, demagogues, moralists and other such officious intruders could not simply be wished away. In fact, they became distinctly more, rather than less, influential with the passage of time. As the century progressed, nationalistic and other emotional factors loomed ever larger. This became dramatically apparent in the Franco-Prussian War of 1870–1, when the French government was forced reluctantly into war by the pressures of public opinion – only to be summarily overthrown after its defeat in the field. That same war also brought a disquieting new trend in war to the attention of generals and statesmen: guerrilla and partisan conflict, with the people of a country taking the initiative against an invading army and fighting in furtive ways that were a far cry from the crisp professionalism of the orthodox soldier.

It should be appreciated that many types of armed conflict fell outside the charmed circle of wars properly speaking. These sundry 'measures short of war', as they were now commonly labelled, were the direct descendants of the imperfect wars of the seventeenth and eighteenth centuries, but with some interesting alterations in character. Now as then, they comprised very disparate types of armed action. But they had one outstanding, and greatly under-appreciated, feature: that they were descendants of medieval just wars, meaning that they were measures undertaken either to preserve peace, or to uphold community values of some kind, or to vindicate the rule of law. This aspect of the legal history of war has been almost entirely pushed into the shadows by the prevailing positivist outlook. But these lesser forms of conflict – interventions, reprisals, emergency measures of various kinds – served to keep the old just-war flame from complete extinction. That flame still burned in the nineteenth century, even if at its lowest level in history; and it would flare again, with much light (if little heat), in the twentieth century.

There was one other major category of armed conflict in this period that did not fit neatly into the dominant positivist framework. These were civil wars, which international lawyers had scarcely bothered with prior to the nineteenth century. Now, for a variety of reasons, events conspired to force them onto the legal agenda. Two tendencies especially were at work here. One may be broadly labelled as the trend towards self-determination. In the context of multinational empires, such as the Ottoman or Habsburg domains, it took the form of pressures for autonomy or even outright independence. In addition, in the wake of the American and French Revolutions, populations were far more inclined than they had been before to take dissatisfaction with rulers to the extreme of ejecting them from power. In Latin America, now full of independent states, fragile governments often lacked broad-based popular support or sufficient resources to subdue energetic armed movements. The other factor – and perhaps the principal one – that brought civil conflicts forcefully to the attention of international lawyers arose from the increasing integration of the states of the world. Foreign countries increasingly came to have some stake in civil wars, even if only in the form of an active desire to remain neutral as between the contending factions. In fact, concerns about neutrality stimulated the development of the practice that became known as 'recognition of belligerency', which was one of the most prominent legal innovations of the nineteenth century, together with a related practice called 'recognition of insurgency'. Their effect was to impress something of the character of international wars onto civil conflicts.

At work throughout this period, in a steady and deadly march, was the accelerating advance of technology as applied to war. The new developments in this area were legion – including steam-powered ships, breech-loading rifles, self-propelled torpedoes, artillery with ever greater range and accuracy, land mines and machine guns. By about the turn of the twentieth century, the wonders of science were promising even more exotic, and deadly, means of mass destruction, such as asphyxiating gases. The inventions of submarines and aeroplanes enabled mass slaughter to be introduced to new and exotic fields of combat, under the seas and in the clouds. Even the more conventional and familiar weapons were being produced and deployed in quantities that dwarfed those of previous periods. As rival sets of alliances came gradually to be locked into place by the end of the nineteenth and beginning of the twentieth centuries, fears began to grow that the next war fought between major powers would bring slaughter on a scale undreamt of in past ages.

These fears proved to be all too well founded when, in 1914, 'the iron gates of war' were flung open more widely, and murderously, than at any previous time in history.[3] The Great War of 1914–18 became a destructive cataclysm of world-historical dimensions. It began, however, in the traditional manner of the stereotypical cabinet war, with a decision by the Austro-Hungarian government (with the support of its ally Germany) to present an ultimatum to the government of Serbia in the wake of the assassination of the heir to the Austro-Hungarian throne.[4] It soon became appallingly evident how much suffering could be wrought by the seemingly anodyne-sounding 'legal institution of war'. After that conflict, international lawyers would begin to think in new ways about war. But even then, their minds would work along the lines that had been set down in the nineteenth century – lines which we shall now explore.

---

[3] Virgil, *Aeneid*, 7.622.
[4] The ultimatum of 23 July 1914 demanded that Serbia renounce irredentist ambitions in the Balkans and that it disband an organisation of anti-Austrian agitators operating in its territory, which was alleged to have been responsible for the assassination of Archduke Francis Ferdinand. For the text, see 108 BFSP 695–8. After receiving, and rejecting, a conciliatory Serbian response, Austria-Hungary declared war. For the text of this response, see *ibid.* at 716–20.

5

Collisions of naked interest

International Law, as such, . . . does not consider the justice or injustice of a war. From the purely legal standpoint, all wars are equally just or unjust; or, properly speaking, they are neither just nor unjust. International Law merely takes cognizance of the existence of war as a fact, and prescribes certain rules and regulations which affect the rights and duties of neutrals and belligerents during that continuance. The justice of war in general or of a certain war in particular are questions of the gravest importance and of the most vital interest, but they belong to the domain of international ethics or morality rather than to that of International Law.

Amos Hershey[1]

In the nineteenth century, the two dissident streams of thought on war, together with the voluntary-law portion of the mainstream tradition, were woven together to form a grand, if sometimes uneasy, synthesis to which the label 'positivism' has been affixed. This achievement marked, in many ways, the logical culmination of trends that had been developing since the seventeenth century. One result was to make the law of war more elaborate and detailed than it had ever been before. In fact, it brought so much order and detail to the subject as to make of war an institution of law, as routine and dispassionately studied as, say, the law of inheritance or trusts or contract. Like them, war was an everyday feature of the social world. This particular legal institution was seen as a wholly human creation, largely cut off from its medieval natural-law roots. War was now, so to speak, liberated from its duties of community service and prepared for use as a tool of nineteenth-century European interstate rivalry, in which the contest for power had substantially replaced the quest for justice.

On the subject of war, positivism owed its greatest debts to the two dissident schools of thought. From the Hobbesian tradition, it took the

[1] Hershey, *Russo-Japanese War*, at 67.

167

acceptance of the world as fundamentally competitive and anarchic, with no assumption of peace as the normative condition of international relations. Peaceful relations of course could readily exist, but they could not be taken for granted. From the contractual approach, positivism inherited a ritualistic or sporting ethos, a stress on war as a rigorously rule-bound contest, conducted in what could almost be called a formal manner, by professional armed forces. This meant that legal thought about war had a distinctly rationalistic and limited-war character – an aura of moderation that proved, in the end, to be deceptive. Insofar as it drew from the mainstream tradition, positivism took the voluntary-law component and left the natural-law part, with its rich heritage of just-war thought, largely behind.

From these raw materials, nineteenth-century lawyers managed to construct an impressively detailed edifice of legal rules dealing with the entire phenomenon of war from the opening of the hostilities to the signing of the peace, plus all stages in between – including conduct on the battlefield, the occupation of enemy territory, relations with neutral powers, treatment of prisoners and spies, medical provision for the wounded and much else. As lawyers continually pored over these topics, the result was that war, along with neutrality, became perhaps the most elaborately detailed parts of the whole of international law.

Remnants of just-war thought, however, continued to persist, even in the age of positivism's highest tide. The influential Swiss lawyer Kaspar Bluntschli, for example, writing in the 1860s, unhesitatingly reproduced the traditional view that a resort to war was only lawful if it was preceded by attempts at peaceful settlement, bolstered by objectively valid legal grievances.[2] Similar support for just-war approaches came from the American lawyer H. W. Halleck and the British writer Travers Twiss.[3] Just-war principles, however, had a somewhat ghostly or ethereal quality to them during this period. They were somewhat disembodied principles, lacking any concrete legal consequences – i.e., giving rise to no rights or liabilities that courts would act upon.[4] They therefore exerted no significant effect on the rush of events in the real world. In the common estimation, they were rules of morality rather than of true law.

---

[2] Bluntschli, *Droit international*, at 273–5.
[3] Halleck, *International Law*, at 311–27; and Twiss, *Law of Nations*, at 55–6.
[4] See, for example, Heffter, *Droit international*, at 218–19; and 2 Calvo, *Droit international*, at 21–7.

Positivist thought was no monolithic doctrine. It had something of a patchwork flavour, with the result that the structure that it built, while impressive in its detail, was also riddled with uncertainties and controversies. A detailed investigation of the substantive law of war in the nineteenth century is beyond our present task. But we will take note of one fault line within positivist thought that was notably important: between what will be called its 'objective' and 'subjective' variants. Tension between these two variations on the positivist theme was at the root of many of the controversies that dogged the subject of war in the nineteenth century. But this rivalry would also extend far into the twentieth century, so it is important to take note of its origins in our present period.

If the outwardly impressive legal institution of war that was so grand an achievement of the nineteenth century was beset with internal weaknesses, it was also afflicted – and perhaps more seriously – by various other shortcomings as well. For one thing, it inherited from its Hobbesian ancestry a tolerance for conflict that many have found disquieting. Nor did the limited-war character of positivism prove strong enough to withstand the challenges of new technologies – from machine guns to chemical weapons to submarines and the like – or of new and unsettling ideas, such as popular nationalism. The matter-of-fact, *laissez-faire* approach to war taken by the positivist writers, their clinical and technocratic mode of analysis, their studied agnosticism as between war and peace – all these lend it an unattractive air to those of us who have the misfortune to know what the future of war would bring in a later century. But we should refrain from judging the lawyers of the nineteenth century too harshly or anachronistically. If there were few peace crusaders in their ranks, there was also a welcome dearth of apologists for militarism or aggression. They built – and tolerably well – a system of law that was a creature of its time; and upon this achievement, the historian (if not the moralist) will look with a spirit of understanding.

The positivist synthesis

For present purposes, it may be said that two aspects of positivism were particularly germane to legal conceptions of war in the nineteenth century. The first was the stress on the will of states as the true source of international law. This element had a double ancestry: in the voluntary-law component of mainstream thought, and also in the Hobbesian tradition, with its stress on agreements between states as the only means of escape from the anarchical condition that was the essence of the state of

nature. Positivism accordingly endorsed the 'bottom-up' view of international law that had been implied by the Hobbesian outlook, as distinct
from the 'top-down' ethos of natural law. Rules of international law, since
they derived from agreements between states, were necessarily products of
political processes, outcomes of the highly unsentimental daily man-
oeuvrings of governments. There could be no pretence, therefore, that
international legal rules had any kind of divine basis or eternal validity.
They were pragmatic and ad hoc responses to local conditions and
immediate needs.

The second key aspect of positivism was a scientific or technocratic
ethos, combined with an empiricist outlook. This led to an insistence on
law as a rigorous and objective science. This element was largely new to
legal thought in the nineteenth century. It is true that, in the seventeenth
and eighteenth centuries, there had been a strong movement of systematic jurisprudence, with mathematics exerting a strong pull on legal
thinkers because of its (ostensibly) unique claim to absolute certainty.[5]
Grotius had looked to mathematics (though not very consistently) as a
model for his exposition of natural law. Hobbes too had been strongly
inspired by mathematics and had even attempted (without success) to
make serious contributions to the subject himself.[6] In the nineteenth
century, however, the legal imagination was gripped more by the experi-
mental sciences such as physics and chemistry than by the abstract and
deductive methods of mathematics. The words that Oliver Wendell
Holmes later applied to the English common law were apt for the
positivist mentality: that 'the life of the law has not been logic; it has
been experience'.[7] This attitude lent to positivism a strongly materialistic cast, consistent with much of nineteenth-century thought. The
things which mattered to a positivist were those that could be objectively
observed and measured. Positivism was therefore a thoroughly unspecu-
lative philosophy, rooted in the brute facts of real life as they actually
stood, rather than in the wispy ideals of theologians or in the 'metaphysical' subtleties of natural lawyers.[8]

---

[5] This claim came under increasing doubt in the course of the nineteenth and early twentieth
centuries. See generally Morris Kline, *Mathematics: The Loss of Certainty* (Oxford: Oxford
University Press, 1980).
[6] See Hardy Grant, 'Hobbes and Mathematics', in Sorrell (ed.), *Cambridge Companion*, at
108–28.
[7] Oliver Wendell Holmes, *The Common Law* (Boston: Little, Brown, 1881), at 1.
[8] Auguste Comte, the French sociologist who did more than anyone else to make positivism
into a grand philosophy, derided natural-law ways of thought as 'metaphysical'.

Also strongly in keeping with nineteenth-century science, positivist thought had a distinctly atomistic flavour. In legal terms, this meant that the world was seen as a congeries of political 'atoms' known as nation-states. Just as atoms were seen as the ultimate building blocks of the physical world, wholly indivisible, so were nation-states seen as the building blocks of the international system. Like atoms, nation-states were indivisible and independent. Hence, international law could take no account of internal developments within countries. States could relate to one another by way of treaties, much in the way that atoms could relate to one another through chemical reactions. In principle, though, states were independent of one another; and no state had the right to intervene in the internal affairs of any other. In fact, this period witnessed articulation of the basic principle of the sovereign equality of states – which remains today as one of the foundational principles of international law.[9]

It will readily be seen that this atomistic outlook virtually precluded any deep conception of an international 'community' of states, or any idea (as in medieval natural-law thought) of the states of the world being embarked upon a single collective enterprise, such as the bringing of earthly affairs into line with the dictates of heaven. Instead, each state was embarked upon its *own* adventure – i.e., on its own, never-ending campaign to further its own particular set of national interests, as determined exclusively by itself. As a result, there was a powerfully utilitarian aura about positivism. As utilitarians were obsessed by a perpetual quest for the maximisation of happiness, so were positivist observers of international affairs obsessed by the promotion and maximisation of the national interest. The inevitable result was a straightforward Hobbesian view of the world, in which international relations were seen as inherently competitive.

These factors in combination served to confer a distinctive stamp onto the nineteenth-century outlook on war. From the atomistic and pluralistic element of positivism came a rejection of the venerable natural-law idea that peace must be the natural or residual condition of the world. The eternal pushing and pulling of competing state interests meant that conflict was an inevitable, and normal, feature of international life. In an intrinsically competitive world, without a mechanism

---

[9] See, for example, Wheaton, *Elements*, at 44–5; Halleck, *International Law*, at 81–2, 97–8; Heffter, *Droit international*, at 35–53; 1 Calvo, *Droit international*, at 119–21, 193–5, 261–83; Bluntschli, *Droit international*, at 80–3; and Hall, *Treatise*, at 50–1, 56.

for dispute resolution and without a set of agreed global values or goals, peace could not be seen as a natural condition of the world. On the contrary, war was a constant component of international relations, rather in the way that friction was an inevitable feature of any mechanical system. The furthest that positivism could go in the direction of a general model of world peace was to be utterly agnostic as between war and peace, holding neither of them to be inherently more 'natural' than the other. Each was simply the inverse of the other. Peace was a condition in which war was absent, and war a condition in which peace was absent.

From the moral viewpoint, of course, peace could readily be conceded to be preferable to war. But positivists were not, for the most part, in the business of moralism. Their task was to characterise the world as it actually was. They therefore produced a conception of war as a matter-of-fact tool of international relations. War was seen as a resort to violence to further state interests, whenever that was adjudged to be a more advantageous means than peace. '[S]ometimes', the British lawyer William Edward Hall drily mused, 'wars are caused by collisions of naked interest or sentiment, in which there is no question of right, but which are so violent as to render settlement impossible until a struggle has taken place'.[10] In a similar spirit, the French writer Charles Dupuis tersely defined war as 'the recourse by a State to violence to compel another State to yield to its will'.[11] There were many other formulations in this same vein.[12] War was therefore seen as a state's forcible removal of obstacles in the path of its national interest.

It should not be thought, however, that the positivist outlook in the nineteenth century was anything like monolithic. In fact, on the subject of war in particular, there was a distinct division of positivism into variant forms. For lack of any generally accepted label, we shall refer to these as the subjective and objective points of view. Because of the importance that they would have for the future development of legal conceptions of war, it is necessary to say a bit about them.

Objective and subjective conceptions of war

The two variant versions of positivist thought on the subject of war illustrate the pluralistic character of positivism, in that each one

---

[10] Hall, *Treatise*, at 64.   [11] Dupuis, *Droit de la guerre*, at 1.

[12] See, for example, G. F. von Martens, *Compenduim*, at 275; Wheaton, *Elements*, at 313; Halleck, *International Law*, at 328; and 1 Rolin, *Droit moderne*, at 143.

emphasised a different aspect of the broad positivist outlook. Writers at the time did not recognise this distinction with any great clarity. Indeed, it was common for scholars to consider that war could validly be looked at from either perspective. The two approaches may therefore be thought of as being more complementary than antagonistic. Not until after the First World War (as will be seen in due course) would it become necessary for lawyers to take a firm stand for the one approach or the other.[13] But the division of opinion first became apparent during the nineteenth century.

The subjective viewpoint derived chiefly from the humanistic side of positivism, placing its primary stress on the role of will or intention (hence the label given to it) in the creation of a state of war. A physical attack could not, as such, create a state of war, but only an attack conjoined with the will or intention to institute a war (an *animus belligerendi*, in sonorous Latin). Conversely, a state of war could be brought about by an expression of intention – in the form of a declaration of war – *without* any material armed clash accompanying it. The effect, then, was to place a very strong emphasis on the idea of a war as a state or condition rather than as a set of physical acts – more specifically, as a state in which it is lawful for the contending sides to use armed force against one another. The American lawyer John Bassett Moore endorsed this subjective thesis in his insistence that 'by the term war is meant not the mere employment of force, but the existence of a legal condition of things in which rights are or may be prosecuted by force. Thus if two nations declare war one against the other, war exists, although no force whatever may as yet have been employed.'[14] A key distinction was accordingly now made between *acts* of war and a *state* of war. There could be a state of war without acts of war, for instance after war had been declared, but before either side had deployed its armed forces. Conversely, there could be an act of war without a state of war. The clearest example would be a forcible reprisal, which was universally agreed to be a measure short of war.[15] For the present, the important point is that the distinguishing feature between the two situations, from the subjective point of view, was the intention of the parties and not the presence or nature of physical acts.

---

[13] See Chapter 8 below for this development.
[14] 7 J. B. Moore, *Digest*, at 153–4. For further support of the subjective position, see G. F. von Martens, *Compenduim*, at 275.
[15] See Chapter 6 below for a detailed discussion of this phenomenon.

The objective approach, in contrast, emphasised the empirical and materialistic aspect of positivism. In the spirit of the voluntary law, it looked entirely towards external actions, without regard to the intentions of the parties. Bluntschli expressed the basic idea in holding war to be a 'collection of acts' which carried a host of legal consequences.[16] Taking the objective picture in its purest form, the position was that a statement of intention (such as a declaration of war) could not suffice, on its own, to create a state of war. Only when an *actual* clash of arms occurred would there be a war in the true legal sense. To the objective school, therefore, the expression 'state of war' was little more than a sort of shorthand, referring to the fact that an armed conflict was in progress and that the laws on the conduct of war had been activated. Some writers of the objective persuasion, indeed, went so far as virtually to reject the very conception of a *state* of war as such.[17] Writers of the subjective turn of mind sometimes expressed the distinction between the two viewpoints in terms of a contrast between war in the material sense, meaning a de facto clash of arms, and war in the legal sense, meaning essentially a true state of war. The objective school did not recognise this distinction, holding war in the material and legal senses to be identical.[18]

At the risk of putting the matter in excessively abstract terms, it might be said that the subjective and objective views of war took opposite positions as to the direction of causation in war. To the subjective school, the state of war, created by the will of states, was the primary and fundamental event which gave rise to material hostilities. It gave rise to them in the sense that the state of war created the juridical condition in which it *then* became lawful for the adversaries to engage in armed conflict. To the objective school, the arrow of causation ran in the opposite direction. The material armed clash came first, giving rise to the existence of the state of war. In other words, to the objective school, a state of war was created by the fact of mutual armed conflict, not *vice versa*. But the state of war had no *causal* significance. It was simply an effect.[19]

In practical terms, the conceptual gap between the two schools of thought was not very apparent to the naked eye during the nineteenth

---

[16] Bluntschli, *Droit international*, at 270.
[17] See, for example, Lawrence, *Principles*, at 331–2.
[18] For support of the objective viewpoint, see 1 Pistoye and Duverdy, *Traité*, at 376; 2 Twiss, *Law of Nations*, at 69; 2 Rivier, *Principes*, at 200–2; and 1 Rolin, *Droit moderne*, at 139–43. For the most outspoken presentation of the objective position, see Grob, *Relativity*.
[19] See Kelsen, *Principles*, at 23–4; and 2 Schwarzenberger, *International Law*, at 61.

century, chiefly because it was common for lawyers to hold that a state of war could be created *either* by way of a declaration *or* by the outbreak of de facto material hostilities.[20] The two approaches to war were therefore not seen at the time to be altogether exclusive of one another. There was, however, a difference of opinion concerning a de facto resort to hostilities. On the subjective view, a resort to force by a *single* state sufficed to create a state of war, provided that that was the intention of the attacking state (i.e., provided that the attack was coupled with an *animus belligerendi* on the attacking state's part). If that *animus belligerendi* was absent, then the action would be a measure short of war, such as a forcible reprisal. On the objective view, an outbreak of hostilities marked the commencement of a state of war, provided that those hostilities were mutual rather than one-way. If only one side was using force while the other remained quiescent, then the one state's armed operation would be a measure short of war.

The clearest practical point of division between the two approaches to war, then, concerned the question of whether one state could unilaterally bring a state of war into existence in the *absence* of a formal declaration of war. The subjective position, as just noted, was that it could, by mounting an actual attack and coupling that attack with the *intention* of creating a state of war. The objective position denied that this was possible, holding instead that there could only be a war if and when the victim country fought back against the attack – with the commencement of the state of war then back-dated to the time of the initial attack.[21] As the British-based lawyer Lassa Oppenheim, who was perhaps the purest exemplar of the objective mode of thinking, put it: 'Unilateral acts of force performed by one State against another may be a cause of the outbreak of war, but are not war in themselves, as long as they are not answered by similar hostile acts by the other side.'[22]

The logical implications of this objective viewpoint should be carefully noted (although they were largely missed during the nineteenth century). If one country launched an attack on another, then that other country would have a rather unpalatable, but instructive, choice between three alternatives, which corresponded to three distinct legal

---

[20] See, for example, Wheaton, *Elements*, at 315–17; Halleck, *International Law*, at 352–3; Hall, *Treatise*, at 382; and Bluntschli, *Droit international*, at 277–8.

[21] See, for illustrations, *The Herstelder*, 1 C Rob 113 (1799); and *Société Commerciale d'Orient v. Turkish Government*, Italo-Turkish Mixed Arbitral Tribunal, 16 Dec. 1929, 5 ILR 483.

[22] 2 Oppenheim, *International Law*, at 57.

categories of armed conflict. First, it could fight back against the invader
with its full strength, in which case there would then be a state of war, by
virtue of the requisite de facto clash of armed forces (with the time of
commencement of the war back-dated, as just noted, to the time of the
initial attack).the second possibility was that the state attacked could
decline to fight back. In that case, there would be no state of war. The
first country's attack would be, it is true, an *act* of war, in the sense of
being an armed attack with hostile intention. But there would be no *state*
of war. The attack would instead amount to what lawyers called a
measure short of war, the lawfulness of which would be judged according to general international law (i.e., the law of peace) and not according
to the law of war as such. The phenomenon of measures short of war will
be explored in further detail in due course.[23]

The third possible course of action that a target country could take in
the face of an attack was one that received hardly any attention in the
nineteenth century, but which would later move to the very centre of the
international legal stage. This was a kind of middle way between the two
alternatives just set out. The target state could respond militarily, but in
the strictly limited sense of engaging in self-defence in the narrow
meaning of that term – i.e., by taking up arms for the carefully circumscribed end of fending off the attack, without taking offensive measures
against the other state. For obvious reasons, this will be referred to as a
situation of 'aggression-and-self-defence', to distinguish it from a state
of war properly speaking. This case of aggression-and-self-defence
found only the most shadowy recognition by lawyers in the nineteenth
century, as it was universally expected that a state that was attacked by
another country would opt for either the first or the second of the
alternatives just outlined. That expectation was amply borne out by state
practice. The nineteenth century presented no clear case of aggression-
and-self-defence, as opposed to war or reprisal. In the twentieth century,
the position would change; and aggression-and-self-defence would
move to the very forefront of legal thought.[24] But that would be a
development of the future. For the present, our concern is to note how
elaborately developed the idea of a state of war became in the course of
the nineteenth century – to the point that war was seen, without apology
or irony, as an institution of international law.

---

[23] See Chapter 6 below.   [24] See Chapter 9 below for this development.

War as an institution of law

By the nineteenth century, international law had effectively discarded both of the conceptual foundations on which a generic just-war order rests: the idea that the normal condition of states was one of peace; and the principle that war, when exceptionally resorted to, is an instrument of law enforcement. Instead, war was a thoroughly ordinary and expected feature of everyday international relations, now elevated to the status of an institution of international law. By 'institution' is meant simply a framework of rules of an objective character, ready at all times for application to particular fact situations as they arise. A key feature of this framework was its comprehensive character. That is to say, its rules governed *all* of the relations between the warring parties – and with third states as well – with the result that the law of peace was wholly excluded during war. War and peace, in other words, were now seen as entirely distinct legal states, with no overlap.

This nineteenth-century positivist view of war might be described as an 'essentialist' approach to the subject of war – a view of war as a new mode of existence, a new moral and legal universe that was wholly at odds with the state of peace. A state of war, on this view, was the legal framework within which individual *acts* of hostility took place – with the state of war consisting of the framework rather than of the acts. Moreover, this distinct moral and legal universe was elaborately logical and reasonable according to its own basic premises – every bit as logical and reasonable as the corpus of law governing the state of peace. War and peace were therefore, in a manner of speaking, inverse legal worlds – moral and legal looking-glass images of one another. This radical disjunction was in sharpest contrast to the universalist ethos of medieval natural law. The medieval view of war, in contrast, might be described as 'existentialist' in the sense that it viewed war as a (regrettable) incident or set of incidents embedded within a general and perpetual umbrella of peace. Peace was the framework, in the form of the eternal and unvarying sway of natural law. War consisted of sporadic *acts* of coercion which occurred within that general framework of peace. In the medieval conception, in other words, war had not been seen as an altogether distinct mode of existence, sharply walled off from 'normal' peaceful life, as it was in the nineteenth century.

At the heart of this distinct legal universe was the conception of the state of war. The idea of war as a state or condition was not, of course, new. Grotius had advanced it in the seventeenth century, and it had won the support of mainstream writers afterward. Only in the nineteenth century, however – and especially with the subjective variant of positivism – was it given a central position at the very heart of the legal conception of war. The essence of it may be stated with the utmost simplicity: that a state of war was a legal condition in which it was entirely lawful for the two contending states to rain death and destruction upon one another.[25]

This juridical institution of war possessed three large-scale features (as they might be termed). First was a sharp distinction between times of war and of peace – at both the outset and the conclusion of a war. Second was the idea that war gave rise to a set of legal rules that were peculiar to the state of war as such and which wholly displaced the normal rules of peacetime. Acts that, in normal times, would qualify as homicide, vandalism or piracy could become, in time of war, deeds of heroic patriotism, not merely tolerated but positively honoured. Finally, there was the idea that war, when it broke out, went beyond the transformation of relations between the parties *inter se*, to encompass a transformation of the international legal atmosphere for the entire world. We shall look at each of these in turn. In the process, we will see that, beneath the surface agreement on these very broad features, there swarmed a myriad of uncertainties and controversies, many of them stemming from the division between the objective and subjective views of war that have just been outlined.

Separating war from peace

On the need to mark a precise separation of war from peace, nineteenth-century international lawyers were in virtually unanimous agreement.[26] In the words of a British judge in 1902, it was necessary that peace be demarcated from war 'by a line of the sharpest and most definite kind'.[27] There were solid practical reasons for this. The principal one stemmed from the fact that belligerent acts, such as killing, destruction and capture, were criminal offences if committed in time of peace. Here was the juridical 'magic' of the state of war in its fullest flower – that it transmuted the dark deeds of the pirate and the highwayman into lawful (even praiseworthy) acts of patriotism. But in order to ensure that these acts of zealous public spirit would be free of blame or penalty, it was necessary to know the precise time at which the crucial transmutation

---

[25] See, to this effect, Heffter, *Droit international*, at 218; and 7 J. B. Moore, *Digest*, at 153–4.
[26] See, for example, 3 Fiore, *Nouveau droit*, at 52, 57.
[27] *Janson* v. *Driefontein Consolidated Mines Ltd*, [1902] AC 484, at 504.

occurred. An illustration of the point occurred in the context of the Seven Years War of 1756–63, between Britain and France. British and French forces clashed in colonial areas (most notably North America) and at sea in 1754, but formal declarations of war were only promulgated in 1756. A dispute then arose over the validity of captures made during the pre-declaration period. In the peace negotiations, France contended that the war only began when the declarations were promulgated and that, consequently, any previous captures of its merchant vessels by British warships were mere piratical acts that effected no passage of legal title to the captors. (Captures made as belligerent acts, in contrast, lead to transfers of ownership to the captor country.) That particular dispute does not appear to have been judicially resolved (although it may be noted that Britain retained the ships).[28]

The timing of the commencement of a state of war could be important for third parties as well as for the participants, because they became subject to the strictures of the law of neutrality, but *only* when the state of war was actually under way. For these reasons, states were sometimes so scrupulous as to specify the time of commencement of a state of war to the very minute. In 1885, for example, when Serbia declared war against Bulgaria, it announced that the state of war began at 6:00 a.m. on 14 November.[29] The South African War between Britain and the two Boer republics was similarly precisely timed, commencing at 5:00 p.m. on 11 October 1899.

If there was a general consensus on the need for a precise delimitation of war from peace, there was less agreement on how that delimitation should be effected. The most obvious method was by the issuing of a formal declaration of war prior to undertaking hostilities. If anything, the uncertainty and confusion on the subject of declarations of war was even greater in the nineteenth century than it had been before. Mercifully, it is not feasible to explore all of the doctrinal subtleties (or befuddlements) that proliferated on this subject. It will suffice to survey briefly the range of possible opinions on the subject. First of all, in the interest of clarity, we may identify the two extreme positions, and then take note of the principal in-between views.

At the one extreme, which might be described as the stance of the objective theory of war in its most uncompromising form, would be the position that a declaration of war was not only not required, but also had no significance whatever even if it *was* issued. From this perspective, the

---

[28] 6 Pradier-Fodéré, *Traité*, at 620–1.   [29] Dupuis, 'Déclaration', at 729.

only means of creating a state of war is by way of a de facto mutual armed clash. A declaration might play the role of publicising the *existence* of a war; but a declaration could not, of its own force, *create* a state of war.[30] This view represents the objective theory of war taken to its remorselessly logical conclusion. Travers Twiss at least nodded towards this view, when he maintained that a state of war arose not out of a formal declaration but rather out of 'the aggression of one Nation upon the independence of the other'.[31] There was also some case-law from British courts in support of this position. A judgment concerning the Franco-Prussian War, for example, held that a declaration of war by France against Prussia was insufficient, on its own, to create a state of war in the absence of actual hostilities. The state of war only began, it was concluded, when Prussia responded to the French declaration by engaging in hostilities.[32] A declaration of war could function, on this view, as merely a challenge to the country to which it was directed, to enter into a state of war – a challenge which that state was free to take up or refuse. It could be, in effect, no more than an act of chivalry or politeness, a moral duty but not a legal one.[33]

At the opposite extreme was the position that a declaration of war was required by the law, and in the strongest possible sense – i.e., that, without a declaration, no state of war could exist. The effect, presumably, would be that any war that was fought without a declaration having been issued would be governed by traditional just-war principles – meaning that any killing done by the unjust side would be mere homicide.[34] The French lawyers L.-B. Hautefeuille and Henry Bonfils were perhaps the only notable figures who took this extreme position.[35]

The majority of lawyers took stands somewhere between these extremes, by holding that a state of war could be created by *either* a mutual resort to armed force *or* a unilateral declaration by one party. But there was room for diversity here. Specifically, there was a division

---

[30] In technical legal terminology, it would be said that a declaration of war could have only a *declaratory* and not a *constitutive* function.

[31] 2 Twiss, *Law of Nations*, at 69. He presumably meant aggression that was responded to by the state that was attacked.

[32] *The Teutonia*, 8 Moo NS 411 (1872).

[33] See, for example, Lawrence, *Principles*, at 345–6.

[34] Another logical consequence of the just-war analysis is that neutrality law would not be activated, since that was not recognised in just-war doctrine. According to Hautefeuille, if a country that was the victim of an aggressive attack wished the law of neutrality to apply, it would have to issue an express notification to third states. 1 Hautefeuille, *Droits et devoirs*, at 110.

[35] *Ibid.* at 100–12; and Bonfils, *Manuel*, at 575.

of opinion on whether a declaration of war was required in what might be called a weak sense of the term. This would hold that a declaration was required in the sense that it was a wrongful act to initiate a war without one – *but* that, if armed conflict occured de facto without a declaration, there would nonetheless still be a state of war. That state of war would have been irregularly instituted, but it would have all of the legal effects of a war.[36] It would be, in other words, an imperfect war in precisely the sense in which Grotius had used that term in the seventeenth century.[37] This tended to be the position of lawyers from continental European countries.[38] Lawyers from the English-speaking world, on the other hand, tended to hold that there was no requirement at all that a declaration of war be issued – and that states merely had the *option* of commencing wars by that method. That is to say, that, *if* states elected to issue a declaration of war, then that declaration would be legally efficacious in bringing a state of war into existence.[39]

The picture was made more complicated still (as if that were needed) by the wide scope for flexibility – or confusion – as to what actually counted as a declaration. It continued to be held, as in previous centuries, that international law did not prescribe any specific form that a declaration must take. The common view was that, in the words of the British lawyer Robert Phillimore, all that the law required was that 'fair and reasonable notice of [a state's] intentions' to make war be communicated to the other side.[40] The German lawyer Frederic de Martens put it somewhat more loosely, holding that what was required was some kind of 'concourse of circumstances amounting to evidence that the hostilities were foreseen and that there is no surprise'.[41] Resorting to the imagery of the duel, he held that it was only necessary that 'the two adversaries be aware that they find themselves in the lists and that combat must inevitably take place'.[42] This may have been a sensible conclusion, but it was far removed from what the ordinary person thinks

---

[36] See, for example, Bluntschli, *Droit international*, at 275–6.
[37] Grotius, *War and Peace*, at 57.
[38] See, for example, 1 Mérignhac and Lémonon, *Droit des gens*, at 55–8, which has a useful survey of the opinions of different writers on the subject.
[39] See, for example, Halleck, *International Law*, at 352–3; 3 Phillimore, *Commentaries*, at 85–106; Hall, *Treatise*, at 374–5; and 3 Nys, *Droit international*, at 34–5.
[40] 3 Phillimore, *Commentaries*, at 95.   [41] 3 F. de Martens, *Traité*, at 206–7.
[42] F. de Martens, 'Les hostilités', at 149. See also 2 Calvo, *Droit international*, at 33; and 3 Fiore, *Nouveau droit*, at 56–62.

of as a declaration of war. Some lawyers ranged even further from intuitive views of the matter than Martens did. William Edward Hall, for example – who admittedly had scant regard for the very idea of a declaration of war – contended that '[a]n act of hostility', on its own, was 'in itself a full declaration of intention'.[43]

The question of whether declarations of war were required, and what form they should take, was posed in its sharpest form by the question of the lawfulness of commencing wars by that most robust of methods, a surprise attack. In both the subjective and the objective camps, there was widespread revulsion at the idea of inaugurating a war by so unchivalrous a means.[44] Lawrence, for example, who denied that a declaration of war was required, denounced such attacks as instances of 'international brigandage'.[45] Lawyers, however, were slow to hold states guilty of this nefarious practice. The question first presented itself in concrete form in connection with the Russian naval attack against Turkey at Sinop in 1853, at the outset of the Crimean War. The views of Frederic de Martens, who was in the employ of Russia, are especially enlightening. He conceded that it was not lawful to commence a war by way of a surprise attack.[46] In Russia's defence, however, he also insisted that this particular incident did not fall into that category because, in his view, a state of war already existed de facto between the two countries. Consequently, the attack, although certainly a surprise, had occurred *during* the war – and hence was perfectly lawful.[47]

The most controversial case of a sudden attack at the commencement of a war occurred in 1904 at the outset of the Russo-Japanese War, this time with Russia on the receiving end. Martens was once again on the scene, still in the service of the Russian government – and now denouncing the Japanese attack as a flagrant violation of international law.[48] In this case too, however, there were doubts as to whether the surprise attack actually marked the commencement of the state of war. Japan, like Russia before it, insisted that the two countries were already at war at the time of the attack. It pointed out that it had broken diplomatic relations with Russia with the express statement that it was now reserving 'the right to take such independent action as it [Japan] judges best to

---

[43] Hall, *Treatise*, at 374. See also 1 Pistoye and Duverdy, *Traité*, at 376–7; and Halleck, *International Law*, at 354–5.

[44] See, for example, 3 F. de Martens, *Traité*, at 205–7; 2 Oppenheim, *International Law*, at 103–5; Bonfils, *Manuel*, at 578; and Bluntschli, *Droit international*, at 275.

[45] Lawrence, *Principles*, at 346; see also 2 Oppenheim, *International Law*, at 103–5.

[46] 3 F. de Martens, *Traité*, at 205–6.   [47] F. de Martens, 'Les hostilités'.   [48] *Ibid.*

consolidate and defend the threatened situation, as well as to protect its rights and its legitimate interests'.[49] The majority of legal commentators agreed with Japan, holding that, under the circumstances, it was – or at least should have been – apparent to Russia that peaceful relations between the two countries had been broken *before* the Japanese attack took place.[50]

This 1904 incident was the immediate stimulus for a discussion of the issue at the Second Hague Peace Conference three years later. There appears to have been a broad agreement that, as the law then stood, the issuing of a *formal* declaration of war to the enemy side was not required. The question before the Conference was therefore whether it was desirable to *establish* such a rule. On that point, there was a general consensus in the affirmative. Accordingly, the Hague Convention Relative to the Opening of Hostilities required that, prior to the launching of any 'hostilities', a 'previous and explicit warning' must be given 'in the form either of a reasoned declaration of war or of an ultimatum with conditional declaration of war'.[51] It was generally agreed that this provision did *not* imply that, if hostilities were begun without the required declaration, there would be no state of war. The effect, then, was that the obligation to issue a declaration was merely a 'side requirement', the breach of which would be a wrongful act but which would *not* preclude the existence of a state of war.[52]

It should be noted that the Hague Convention did not actually provide very realistic protection against surprise attacks. During the drafting process, a number of delegations pointed out that a requirement of a prior warning would be of little practical use if the attacking state was permitted to issue its declaration and then launch its attack an instant later. There had been some support for a waiting period amongst earlier writers. Gentili, for example, required an interval of thirty-three days, consonant with the Roman fetial practice.[53] That gallant view, however, went out of fashion amongst lawyers. Grotius held that acts of

---

[49] Dupuis, 'Déclaration', at 731.

[50] See Hershey, *Russo-Japanese War*, at 62–70; Lawrence, *Principles*, at 346–8; and Nagaoka, 'Étude', at 603–5.

[51] Hague Convention III Relative to the Opening of Hostilities, 18 Oct. 1907, 205 CTS 263, Art. 1.

[52] See Strupp, *Éléments*, at 512. On the Hague Convention, see generally Stowell, 'Convention'. Presumably, the launching of a war without a declaration would give rise to liability for damages. There is no record, however, of an actual legal claim to this effect.

[53] Gentili, *Law of War*, at 135. See also Belli, *Military Matters*, at 79–80; and Burlamaqui, *Politic*, at 270.

war could commence immediately after a declaration.[54] So did Wolff and Vattel in the eighteenth century, as well as Bluntschli in the nineteenth.[55] State practice accorded with this harsher view. Sometimes, states even began hostilities after the issuing of a declaration but before its communication to the enemy, as in the case of the United States against Britain in 1812.

At the Hague Conference, the Dutch delegation proposed that a twenty-four-hour interval should be mandated between a declaration and any actual attack.[56] The idea attracted a large measure of support from smaller states. Among the major powers only Russia endorsed it (no doubt mindful of its recent experience at the hands of Japan). The other major powers took the view that, in the conditions of modern war, any provision for a period of grace to the enemy side was not feasible. As a result, the Dutch proposal was defeated by sixteen votes to thirteen (with five abstentions).[57] The practical effect of the Hague Convention, therefore, was very limited; so it is hardly surprising that it played little part in the history of war.

In the area of state practice on the commencing of wars, diversity continued to be the watchword. From about the middle of the century, there was a resurgence in the use of public proclamations of war of the kind pioneered in the seventeenth century. The Crimean War marked the start of this trend, with the British declaration taking the form of a terse notification from Queen Victoria to the parliament that the country was now at war.[58] Sometimes, declarations contained extended recitations of grievances against the other side in the old style. The Russian declaration of war against Turkey in 1828, for example, included an exhaustive recital of the circumstances that had led to the conflict, complete with three annexes.[59] In 1867, Argentina protested that a declaration of war against it by Paraguay contained no statement of reasons – an act that Argentina denounced as 'barbarous, and contrary to the modes of all civilized nations in the present age'.[60] On

---

[54] Grotius, *War and Peace*, at 639–40.
[55] Vattel, *Law of Nations*, at 255–6; Wolff, *Law of Nations*, at 370–2; and Bluntschli, *Droit international*, at 277.
[56] For the text of which, see 3 J. B. Scott (ed.), *Hague Conference Proceedings*, at 254.
[57] *Ibid.* at 170. For the Report to the plenary Conference, by Renault, see 1 *ibid.* at 131–6.
[58] Message of 27 Mar. 1854, 44 BFSP 110.
[59] Declaration of War by Russia against Turkey, 26 Apr. 1828, 15 BFSP 656–62; annexes at 662–7.
[60] Memorandum of the Argentine Government, 8 Apr. 1867, 1(2) *Fontes Juris Gentium*, at 97.

occasion, declarations of war were issued reciprocally, as by China and Japan against one another in 1894.[61] More commonly, though, a single declaration was regarded as sufficient to create a state of war (thereby lending at least some support to the subjective, or unilateralist, viewpoint). Only rarely were declarations given directly to the opposing side, one example being France's declaration of war against Prussia in 1870, which was handed to Chancellor Otto von Bismarck in Berlin by the French *chargé-d'affaires*.[62] For an age in which great stress was placed on war as a clash of competing state wills, it was fitting that the ultimatum would become the method of choice for declaring war. The nineteenth century, indeed, was a sort of golden age of ultimatums, culminating in July 1914 with the most famous one of all: the ultimatum issued by Austria-Hungary to Serbia following the assassination of Archduke Francis Ferdinand, which launched the Great War.

In an era in which war was seen frankly as a matter of policy rather than of law or morals, and in which nationalistic sentiments were playing an increasing role, it is not surprising that the drily polite style of declarations of previous centuries went out of fashion. In its place came elements of bombast, emotion and patriotic self-righteousness. The manifesto issued by the Emperor of Austria in 1866, announcing war with Prussia, is a good illustration. He summoned his subjects to war in the following terms:

> I decide upon fighting [he proclaimed], confident in the goodness of my cause, and upheld by the feeling of the inherent power of a great empire, and in which the Prince and the people are united in one and the same idea, in one and the same hope, those of defending the rights of Austria.
>
> At the sight of my valiant armies, so ready for the fight, which form the bulwark, the rampart against which the forces of the enemy will dash themselves to pieces, I feel my courage and my confidence redoubled, and I can but feel a good hope when I meet the gaze of my faithful peoples, united and determined, and their ready devotion to every sacrifice.
>
> The pure flame of patriotic enthusiasm strives [*sic*] with the same intensity throughout my empire . . . .
>
> But one feeling animates the inhabitants of my kingdoms and provinces: they feel the ties which unite them, the strength which comes from union.[63]

---

[61] Decree of the Emperor of China, Declaring War Against Japan, 1 Aug. 1894, 86 BFSP 301–3; and Proclamation of the Emperor of Japan, Declaring War Against China, 1 Aug. 1894, *ibid.* at 303–4.

[62] See Maurice, *Hostilities*, at 76–8.

[63] Austrian Manifesto of War with Prussia and Italy, 17 June 1866, 63 BFSP 580–4.

Unfortunately for the Emperor, his bold confidence was misplaced. Austria suffered a disastrous defeat in the contest.

The rules of the game

Nowhere was the institutional character of war so clearly present in the nineteenth century as in the rules relating to the conduct of war. In this area, there was no appreciable divergence of view between the objective and subjective variants of positivism. There was general acceptance, without traces of apology or hesitation, of the contractual picture of war as a duel between two sides that were on a legal footing of full and complete equality. Consequently, we find the code-of-conduct approach to the laws of war, which had had its hesitant beginnings in earlier centuries, now coming fully into its own. Now, as then, the essential aim was to displace the general principle of necessity in favour of a menu of specific, context-free rules.

This goal was expressly articulated in 1868, when nineteen European states issued the Declaration of St Petersburg, which had the immediate purpose of banning the use of certain explosive projectiles in war. In the preamble of the Declaration, the parties articulated their desire to '[fix] the technical limits at which the necessities of war ought to yield to the requirements of humanity'. The chief role of international lawyers with regard to war lay in the mapping out of these 'technical limits'. This was necessarily the case since questions of whether or not to resort to war had been allocated virtually entirely to politicians. More than ever before (or since), war was now treated, from the legal standpoint, as a technical craft. Never before (or since) was the reign of Athena, the goddess of crafts, so complete over warfare, or international lawyers so dutifully her acolytes.

The detailed contents of this technical code of laws will not detain us unduly. It is only necessary to take note of the principal initiatives and to make some observations on the general character of the laws of war as they evolved in this period. The seminal step in the detailed codification and exposition of the laws of war came from the United States, with the adoption by the federal government in 1863 of the 'Lieber Code' – a set of rules on land warfare named for the lawyer and political theorist who drafted them. The Lieber Code, in turn, served as the primary inspiration for a multilateral initiative when, in 1874, a set of standards was agreed by a conference of government lawyers in Brussels. The Brussels *projet* (as it was called) was not a legally binding treaty between states but rather a summation of the law of war as it stood at the time.[64] There was also a private codification of the laws of land warfare, by the Institute of International Law in 1880, followed by one on naval warfare in 1913.[65] At the First Hague Peace Conference in 1899, the contents of the Brussels *projet* were substantially replicated in the form of a binding treaty.[66] These 'Hague Rules', as they were appropriately known, were then updated and re-codified by the Second Hague Peace Conference in 1907.[67]

The Hague Rules embodied the dualistic character of the laws of war which had evolved in the mainstream tradition since the seventeenth century. That is to say, they incorporated the general necessity-based approach to the laws of war alongside the newer tendency to lay down specific, context-independent rules of conduct. On the general plane – *very* general, to be sure – the right to adopt means of injuring one's opponent in war was stated to be 'not unlimited'. In addition, though not much more specifically, the infliction of 'unnecessary suffering' was prohibited, together with the use of any weapons calculated to cause it.[68] Here was the principle of necessity, operating as a general limitation on state action.[69]

In the realm of specific rules, the Hague Convention dealt with at least some of the more egregiously harsh practices of war. For example, it prohibited certain types of deceptive practices, such as the misuse of flags of truce. Also banned were policies of granting no quarter to enemy forces or attacking undefended locations. The largest part of the Hague Rules concerned the treatment of prisoners of war and the governing of occupied territories. In these areas, the Rules basically codified principles that had long been widely recognised (if not always observed). There were also, in this period, some attempts to break new ground by prohibiting certain specific classes of weapons. For example, the Hague Rules prohibited the use of poison. Separate rules banning certain newer types of weapons were also agreed. The First Hague Peace Conference adopted three declarations on specific weapons or practices – prohibiting expanding

---

[64] Project of an International Declaration Concerning the Laws and Customs of War, 27 Aug. 1874, in 1 (Supp.) AJIL 96 (1907) (hereinafter 'Brussels *projet*').

[65] 'Oxford Manual of Land Warfare', 9 Sept. 1880, in J. B. Scott (ed.), *Resolutions*, at 25–41; and 'Oxford Manual of Naval War', 9 Aug. 1913, in *ibid.* at 174–201.

[66] Hague Convention II on the Rules of Land Warfare, 29 July 1899, 189 CTS 429.

[67] Hague Convention IV Respecting the Laws and Customs of War on Land, 18 Oct. 1907, 205 CTS 277; reprinted in Roberts and Guelff, *Documents*, at 69–82.

[68] *Ibid.*, Arts. 22 and 23(e).

[69] On the continued importance of necessity in the laws of war, see 3 Phillimore, *Commentaries*, at 78–9.

(or 'dum-dum') bullets, the use of projectiles containing asphyxiating gases and the launching of projectiles from balloons.[70]

Similar progress was made regarding maritime war. An early example was the Declaration of Paris of 1856, which incidentally was the world's first major example of international 'legislation' by means of multi-lateral treaty. The Declaration endorsed the principle that 'free ships make free goods', i.e., that belligerents were not allowed to capture enemy property (except for contraband of war) that was being carried on neutral ships.[71] Also prohibited was the use of privateering in war. By 1860, this Declaration had been ratified by some forty-eight states, including nearly all of the major maritime powers.[72] One of the Hague Conventions of 1907 set out restrictions on naval bombardments of civilian areas.[73] Another one contained restrictions on the use of automatic submarine mines as well as on certain types of naval capture.[74]

Other initiatives during the nineteenth century were directed not so much towards regulating the conduct of hostilities as towards relieving the sufferings of victims of war. The principal event was the founding, in the 1860s, of a private organisation dedicated to the relief of the sufferings of war, the International Committee of the Red Cross. In 1864, the first Geneva Convention concluded under its auspices provided for the immunity of medical personnel (suitably distinguished from combatants) from attack.[75] This Convention was extended to cover maritime warfare by the First Hague Peace Conference in 1899 and then supplemented by further and more detailed arrangements in 1906.[76] Rules for

---

[70] Declaration Concerning Asphyxiating Gases, 29 July 1899, 187 CTS 453; Declaration Concerning the Launching of Projectiles from Balloons, 29 July 1899, *ibid.* at 456; Declaration Concerning Expanding Bullets, 29 July 1899, *ibid.* at 459. The declarations on asphyxiating gases and expanding bullets are reprinted in Roberts and Guelff, *Documents*, at 59–66. The ban on projectiles from balloons was temporary in duration.

[71] Declaration of Paris, 16 Apr. 1856, 115 CTS 1, Art. 2; reprinted in Roberts and Guelff, *Documents*, at 47–52.

[72] Eventually, there were fifty-one ratifications.

[73] Hague Convention IX on Naval Bombardment, 18 Oct. 1907, 205 CTS 345; reprinted in Roberts and Guelff, *Documents*, at 112–16.

[74] Hague Convention VIII on the Laying of Automatic Submarine Mines, 18 Oct. 1907, 205 CTS 331; and Hague Convention XI on Certain Restrictions on Naval Capture, 18 Oct. 1907, *ibid.* at 367. Reprinted in Roberts and Guelff, *Documents*, at 105–8 and 121–4 respectively.

[75] Geneva Convention for the Amelioration of the Wounded, 22 Aug. 1864, 129 CTS 361.

[76] Convention Extending the Geneva Convention of 1864 to Maritime War, 29 July 1899, 187 CTS 443; and Convention for the Amelioration of Wounded and Sick in Armies, 6 July 1906, 202 CTS 144.

the protection of prisoners of war were contained in the Hague Rules of 1899 and 1907, with a special Geneva Convention on the subject concluded later, in 1929.[77]

Of more interest for present purposes than the detailed contents of these rules were certain features of their over-all character that have sometimes received less attention than they merit. One point, often stressed by writers at the time, concerned the strictly even-handed character of the laws of war. The rules were absolutely identical as between the contending parties. This principle of even-handedness was, of course, a direct inheritance from the voluntary-law approach to war of the previous centuries. But it was now shorn of its quasi-apologetic character of earlier years and elevated, with some considerable pride, to the position of high principle. This marked, in turn, a definitive break with the old just-war policy of according *all* rights of war to one side and *none* to the other. The underlying justice of the resort to war now had, it was strongly insisted, nothing whatever to do with the actual conduct of the hostilities. The question of the right to resort to war (*jus ad bellum*, in legal parlance) was banished to the realm of morality, with all of the legal attention now focussed instead on the question of adherence to the laws governing the conduct of war (*jus in bello*, to the lawyers).

The ideal, then, was that war would be fought with more than a trace of the sporting ethos – on the basis of strictly even-handed rules agreed by both sides prior to the conflict, with low practices such as deception kept to a minimum. The sporting outlook naturally meant that the nineteenth-century code of conduct was thoroughly imbued with a limited-war flavour. This was the case with regard to laws governing combat itself, in which (as just noted) certain practices were prohibited and a general sense of fair play was much in evidence. The laws of war therefore meant, in effect, that the basic humanity of enemy soldiers would be recognised at all times. They also meant (or at least implied) the complete absence of any component of interpersonal animosity between soldiers on the opposing sides. A war was strictly a political event, determined from on high by statesmen in pursuit of the national interest. Soldiers were the technicians, the executors of that policy. The troops on the enemy side were fellow technicians. Indeed, soldiers on opposing sides in a war might have more in common with one another than they would with their 'own' civilians, in much the same way as

---

[77] Geneva Convention on Prisoners of War, 27 July 1929, 118 LNTS 343.

other transnational professional communities such as scientists or engineers. This rationalistic and technocratic ethos of positivism, in sum, seemed to point towards the reduction of war to a kind of scientific operation, purged of such primitive and brutish practices as mass slaughter, religious fanaticism and the like. It was – or was meant to be – the final triumph of Athena over Ares.

One of the effects of this professional spirit amongst military forces was an ever greater insistence on the exclusion of civilians from the business of war – either as participants (i.e., as unwelcome meddlers) or as victims. Civilians were barred from participating in war by a general policy of confining the rights of war to members of the armed forces – with the result that civilians who took it upon themselves to attack enemy armed forces risked being treated as mere murderers. By the same token, however, civilians were also to be scrupulously safeguarded from attack – an ideal that was given formal expression in the Declaration of St Petersburg in 1868. '[T]he only legitimate object which States should endeavour to accomplish during war', its preamble grandly proclaimed, was 'to weaken the military forces of the enemy'.[78]

This policy of protecting civilians from the horrors of war was manifested in various specific ways. For example, pillage was prohibited by the Hague Rules, as was the capture of private property generally. This policy of sparing civilians from the horrors of war was also much in evidence in the area of occupation of enemy territory ('belligerent occupation', in legal terminology). A number of restrictions were imposed on states occupying enemy territory, the broad thrust of which was that a military occupation should impinge as little as possible on the civilian population of the area, which was to continue living under its existing laws. Inhabitants could not be suborned from their loyalty to their state – and in particular could not be conscripted into the armed forces of the occupying power. Nor could their property be requisitioned for any purpose beyond the support of the territorial occupation itself. In other words, the inhabitants could not be compelled to lend any support to the broader war effort of the occupying power.

There were other indications of the policy of insulating civilians from operations of war. For example, the practice of expelling enemy alien civilians in time of war and of sequestering their property fell into disuse to a large extent during the nineteenth century. The tendency now was

---

[78] Declaration of St Petersburg, 11 Dec. 1868, 138 CTS 297, preamble; reprinted in Roberts and Guelff, *Documents*, at 54–5.

for nationals of the enemy side to be allowed to remain, provided only that they refrained from providing actual assistance to their country's war effort. It also continued to be a common practice for states to allow a period of grace for enemy merchant vessels to depart peaceably at the start of wars. Bilateral treaties of friendship, commerce and navigation continued to contain provisions to this effect. In 1907, one of the Hague Conventions dealt with the subject, stating a period-of-grace policy to be 'desirable'.[79]

In sum, the nineteenth century witnessed impressive progress in the codification and elaboration of the rules of war – and, in the process, towards a gradual limitation on the destruction and suffering of war. There was optimism on the part of many lawyers that practices of total wars – involving conflicts of whole populations against one another – might now be obsolete. Bluntschli, for example, held this view, asserting that wars of extermination and annihilation – what Clausewitz had called 'absolute wars' – were now illegal.[80] It would become apparent (as will presently be seen) that Bluntschli spoke too soon. But there was no doubt that the lawyers of the nineteenth century could take justifiable pride in their handiwork on the laws of war.

Neutrality

There was no better illustration of war as an institution of international law in the nineteenth century than the maturation of the law of neutrality. Here, as in the laws of war, the ethos of the contractual, or duelling, outlook was especially evident. The general view was that, in war, the contending sides were allowed to throw their fullest might at one another (whilst of course adhering to the laws of war) – but were also barred from directing hostilities against bystanders. The bystanders, however, were subject to legal duties too, and in particular to two fundamental obligations: the duty of abstention, i.e., of refraining from intermixing in the hostilities; and the duty of impartiality, i.e., of taking scrupulous care to treat the belligerents on an even-handed basis. As a consequence, a state of war was *not* simply a matter between the contending parties *inter se*. It inevitably and automatically affected the entire world. Travers Twiss expressed the point clearly

---

[79] Hague Convention VI on the Status of Enemy Merchant Ships at the Outbreak of Hostilities, 18 Oct. 1907, 205 CTS 305, Art. 1; reprinted in Roberts and Guelff, *Documents*, at 97–9.
[80] Bluntschli, *Droit international*, at 281.

when he defined war as 'an alternative state of international relations, which supersedes the relations of peace, whenever Nations prosecute their Right by force'.[81]

This idea of war as a distinct legal condition affecting the world at large had a number of momentous implications. One was that it became more important than ever before that third states be promptly notified when a state of war was in effect, so that they could take the steps required of them by the law of neutrality.[82] Lawyers were virtually unanimous on the importance of this action. Even writers who insisted that a formal declaration of war was not required to the *enemy* maintained that there must be express notification to third states before those countries could become subject to the rights and duties of neutrals.[83] For example, if a state that was the victim of an aggressive attack elected to fight back – and thereby to transform the situation from one of aggression-and-self-defence into a true war – it was not required that it issue a declaration to its attacker. But it was still necessary to issue notification to third states.[84] No state of war would exist, as far as third countries were concerned, in the absence of such a notification. This principle was codified in the Hague Convention of 1907 on the Opening of Hostilities, which expressly required that third states be notified 'without delay' of the existence of a state of war. In addition, the Convention made it clear that this was no mere side requirement, by expressly barring any exercises of belligerents' rights *vis-à-vis* third states that had not been duly notified.

Perhaps the most outstanding trend in the law of neutrality in the nineteenth century, as in the law of war itself, was the dominant hold attained by the code-of-conduct school of thought over its chief rival, the conflict-of-rights (or necessity) approach. Just as the right of belligerents to injure their antagonists was 'not unlimited', so also was their right to impinge on the activities of neutrals subject to a number of legal constraints – with appropriate legal liability to the neutral state if those rules were violated.[85] At the same time, belligerents possessed a number

---

[81] 2 Twiss, *Law of Nations*, at 49.

[82] See, to this effect, G. F. von Martens, *Compendium*, at 279–80; Kent, *International Law*, at 190; Halleck, *International Law*, at 352–3; and 2 Twiss, *Law of Nations*, at 77–8.

[83] See, for example, 3 Phillimore, *Commentaries*, at 107; and 2 Twiss, *Law of Nations*, at 69–71.

[84] See 1 Hautefeuille, *Droits et devoirs*, at 110.

[85] The liability could take either of two principal forms: reprisals from the aggrieved side during the course of the conflict; or a claim for damages afterwards.

of rights *vis-à-vis* neutrals, which had deep historical roots but which were recognised with greater clarity and regulated in greater detail than ever before.[86] Three of these traditional belligerents' rights were of particular importance. First was the right to visit and search neutral merchant ships on the high seas. Second was the right to capture and confiscate contraband of war (i.e., war-related goods such as weapons and ammunition), by way of condemnation by a prize court. Third was the right to enforce blockades, by capturing and confiscating any offending neutral ships, together with their cargoes. To these key belligerent prerogatives, a fourth was added during the course of the century: the right to take action against neutrals for the rendering of what came to be called 'unneutral service'. This right, which, like the others, grew out of earlier practices, was in essence a right by belligerents to capture and condemn neutral ships for engaging in such practices as supplying enemy war fleets with fuel at sea or transporting enemy troops.[87] Neutrals had a corresponding legal duty to submit to the exercise of this range of belligerent measures.

In addition to their passive obligation to submit to these rights of belligerents, neutrals had various affirmative duties to discharge as well – duties which became increasingly burdensome over the course of the nineteenth century. The seminal event here occurred in the 1790s, with the adoption by the United States of neutrality legislation in the face of the French Revolutionary Wars. This American legislation was designed simultaneously to minimise American involvement in the European conflicts while also asserting what the Americans held to be the fundamental rights of neutrals. On the side of minimising involvement, the legislation banned the belligerents from recruiting troops in American territory and from issuing commissions to privateers. It also sought to prevent American nationals from participating voluntarily in the struggles. Significantly, however, the law contained no prohibition against the carriage of contraband of war by private parties – though any such carriage would be undertaken subject to the risk that the cargoes would be captured and confiscated by the opposing side.[88]

---

[86] For a thorough summation of the law of neutrality as it stood at the end of the nineteenth century, see Richard Kleen, *Lois et usages de la neutralité d'après le droit international conventionnel et coutûmier des États civilisés* (2 vols., Paris: A. Chevalier-Marescq, 1898–1900).

[87] On the crystallisation of the principle of unneutral service, see Neff, *Rights and Duties*, at 112–14.

[88] On the American policy, see generally Charles Marion Thomas, *American Neutrality in 1793: A Study in Cabinet Government* (New York: Columbia University Press, 1931).

By the end of the nineteenth century, it was generally agreed that neutral states had a duty actively to police their territories to ensure that it was not being used by any of the belligerents as a 'base of operations' for military action against the other. Most outstandingly, that included a duty to ensure that neither side was fitting out warships in the neutral state's ports. The law on this point received its first major statement in a bilateral agreement between Britain and the United States. This was the Treaty of Washington of 1871, which provided for an arbitration in Geneva the following year, in which Britain was held liable, and assessed damages, for the breach of this duty.[89] At the Second Hague Peace Conference of 1907, an attempt was made to codify the law of neutrality as it then stood, although the effort only achieved modest results. Two conventions were concluded, one on Maritime Neutrality and the other on Neutrality in Land War.[90]

Peace-making

A sharp demarcation of war from peace was generally agreed to be as necessary at the conclusion of wars as it was at their onset, and for the same reason. States should know precisely when their various belligerent activities would cease to be lawful (i.e., would cease to be acts of war and instead become acts of aggression committed during peacetime). And third states should be able to know when the burdens of the law of neutrality were lifted from their shoulders. In general, the nineteenth century witnessed little change in the general law regarding termination of wars. The same three modes of termination that were laid down in previous centuries by Gentili and his followers in the mainstream just-war tradition continued to be widely identified: a de facto halting of hostilities, subjugation and agreement (by means of a peace treaty).[91]

The first method, the de facto halting of hostilities, was not common in practice. An armed conflict between Spain and Chile in the 1860s was ended without a peace treaty, as were hostilities in the same period

---

[89] Great Britain-USA, Treaty of Washington, 8 May 1871, 143 CTS 145.

[90] Hague Convention V on Neutrality in Land Warfare, 18 Oct. 1907, 205 CTS 299; and Hague Convention XIII on Neutrality in Naval War, 18 Oct. 1907, *ibid.* at 395; reprinted in Roberts and Guelff, *Documents*, at 85–94, 127–37, respectively.

[91] See, for example, Heffter, *Droit international*, at 343–5; Halleck, *International Law*, at 845; Hall, *Treatise*, at 557; 3 F. de Martens, *Traité*, at 305; Bonfils, *Manuel*, at 885; 2 Rivier, *Principes*, at 435–61; Despagnet, *Cours*, at 709–10; 3 Fiore, *Nouveau droit*, at 653–4; and 2 Oppenheim, *International Law*, at 275.

between France and Mexico (although diplomatic relations between the two states were only restored in 1881).[92] In the inter-German-Confederation War of 1866, it happened, apparently merely through oversight, that no peace treaty was ever made between Prussia and Liechtenstein – so that, by default, the halting of the hostilities has been considered to have terminated that conflict.[93]

Subjugation was the second standard mode of terminating wars. Subjugation must be understood to mean not simply a crushing military defeat of one party by another. Instead, it referred to something altogether more drastic: the outright disappearance of the defeated party as an independent state. On the continent of Europe, subjugation featured most conspicuously in the unification conflicts in Italy and Germany. In Italy, the dominant power of Piedmont-Sardinia put an end to the independent status of various states such as the Kingdom of the Two Sicilies, Tuscany and the Duchy of Parma and Modena in 1859–60. In Germany, Prussia absorbed Hanover, Nassau, Hesse-Cassel and the Free City of Frankfurt in 1866. The chief field of play for subjugation in state practice, however, was the colonial sphere. Britain's military victory over Upper Burma in 1885, for example, was followed by a formal annexation proclamation in January 1886.[94] The African kingdom of Dahomey was similarly brought into the French Empire by force of arms in 1892–4.[95]

By far the most common of the three methods of termination in this period, as in previous centuries, was by means of a peace treaty between the contending states.[96] Many practices in this area from past centuries continued in evidence. Amnesty clauses, for example, continued to be common, but this was largely through historical inertia since they had lost much of their original purpose. Their original purpose, it will be recalled, had been to ensure that anyone who had committed acts of war during the hostilities would not be held legally accountable for them in the future. Such a provision, however, only made sense on the thesis that acts of war were intrinsically wrongful – a legacy of the medieval Christian pacifist view that all killing was sinful. By the nineteenth century, that outlook was a distant memory. Now that acts of belligerency were seen as *rights* in the true sense of the word, amnesty clauses

---

[92] Stockton, *Outlines*, at 372–3.
[93] On the de facto halting of hostilities, see Phillipson, *Termination*, at 3–7.
[94] Proclamation of Annexation, 1 Jan. 1886, 77 BFSP 980.
[95] On subjugation, see Phillipson, *Termination*, at 9–19.   [96] 2 Rivier, *Principes*, at 454–5.

had lost their original rationale.[97] Nevertheless, they could still be relevant in some marginal cases, such as cases in which territory had been occupied and in which civilian inhabitants had cooperated with the occupying power in some way. An amnesty provision might be included to ensure that those persons would not be punished when the original sovereign resumed rule.[98]

Dark shadows remaining

A certain spirit of sunny optimism pervaded positivism. For one thing, there was a feeling of liberation from the shackles of the past, particularly from the airy idealism of natural-law thought. There was also a refreshing openness about the positivist style, with its emphasis on setting down in codified form, for all the world to see, the standards which states were to meet. There was optimism too that the states actually would adhere to these rules, since they themselves had drafted and ratified the various agreements. The practical men certainly accomplished much, as we have observed. In some ways, however, their goals were as utopian as those of the natural lawyers whom they had supplanted. The idea that the pressures, destruction and suffering of war could really be effectively circumscribed by a network of written rules would be proved illusory by the events of the late nineteenth and early twentieth centuries. We will survey, though only very briefly, some of the ways in which the codes of conduct on war and neutrality proved inadequate to the demands of modern war. First, though, it is well to take note of certain features of the positivist outlook itself which placed important inherent limits on the ability of international law to reduce the horrors of war. Even more disturbingly, certain aspects of positivism may have actively encouraged aggressive war.

Positivism and aggression

Positivist writings did not bristle with moral outrage at the idea of war. Nor did positivism betray any significant utopian leanings. Indeed, the truth was the opposite – that nineteenth-century lawyers tended

---

[97] Phillipson, *Termination*, at 249–50.
[98] See, for example, Italy-Turkey, Definitive Treaty of Peace, 18 Oct. 1912, 217 CTS 160, Art. 4. For a wealth of information on peace-treaty practice in the nineteenth century, see Goldstein, *Wars and Peace Treaties*.

affirmatively to take pride in the strength of their grip on reality. This empirical outlook was far from an unmixed blessing, for it was always a potential (or actual) criticism of positivists that they were all *too* ready to accept the world as they found it, and too hesitant to be critical. If the medieval natural lawyers had erred on the side of being too idealistic, thereby forfeiting the opportunity to influence everyday practice, the positivists may have erred in the opposite direction, of being too anxious that their theories mirror the reality around them. Their influence on daily state practice was greater, but it was bought at the price of a blunting of the critical faculty. For this reason, it is hardly surprising that international lawyers played little part in peace movements in the nineteenth century. Positivist lawyers tended instead to regard war with studied dispassion, to see it as an unavoidable feature of international relations, a morally neutral fact of everyday life, much like the weather. As the American lawyer Amos Hershey put it, international law 'merely takes cognizance of the existence of war as a fact, and prescribes certain rules and regulations which affect the rights and duties of neutrals and belligerents during that continuance'.[99] Another later commentator wryly observed that 'Historians, statesmen, moralists and propagandists continued to discuss the responsibility for and justice of wars, but lawyers gave it up.'[100]

War was seen in instrumentalist terms by the positivists, as an everyday tool of international relations, to be wielded in any situation that lent itself to a military solution. The most famous exhortations of Carl von Clausewitz were to this effect. He relentlessly insisted that war must always be seen as a tool at the service of the general policy, or national interest, of the state – as, in short, a 'political instrument'.[101] War, in his view, was 'merely another kind of writing and language' for the carrying on of political thought. War, in Clausewitz's most famous expression, was 'a continuation of policy by other means'.[102] He described 'policy' as 'the guiding intelligence' in the art of statecraft, with war as 'only the instrument'.[103] Consequently, war differed from peacetime politics only in its methods – the use of violence – not in its fundamental nature or goals.

This rationalistic – and cold-blooded – attitude towards war naturally meant that positivism had a very great affinity with the calculational mentality of eighteenth-century diplomacy. It also raised the suspicions

---

[99] Hershey, *Russo-Japanese War*, at 67.   [100] Wright, 'Changes', at 765.
[101] Clausewitz, *On War*, at 87.
[102] *Ibid.* at 69, 87, 605 (with slight variations of wording).   [103] *Ibid.* at 607.

of people who objected that war was being accepted all too supinely as an every-day means of conducting international politics. The American pragmatist philosopher William James, for example, scornfully held that

> [e]very up-to-date dictionary should say that 'peace' and 'war' mean the same thing, now *in posse*, now *in actu*. It may even reasonably be said that the intensely sharp competitive *preparation* for war by the nations *is the real war*, permanent, unceasing, and that the battles are only a sort of public verification of the mastery gained during the 'peace' interval.[104]

Further reinforcing this positivist tolerance for war was the self-judging feature of positivism inherited from the Hobbesian tradition – the belief that each state decided for itself where its interests lay and how best to achieve them. The result was that it had never, since at least the Middle Ages, been so easy for states to find reasons to wage war. As Henry Bonfils candidly conceded, 'Any dispute, any conflict in which States judge ... their interests to be engaged or their right violated can become a cause of war'.[105] The American statesman and lawyer Elihu Root put the matter with sardonic candour early in the twentieth century:

> [T]here are no international controversies so serious that they cannot be settled peaceably if both parties really desire peaceable settlement, while there are few causes of dispute so trifling that they cannot be made the occasion of war if either party really desires war. The matters in dispute between nations are nothing; the spirit which deals with them is everything.[106]

That positivist thought might be excessively tolerant of war was also suggested by the attitude towards offence and defence in nineteenth-century legal thought. The general view was that those concepts were not relevant to the legal treatment of war.[107] There was no consensus, as there later would be in the twentieth century, that offensive war was wrong *per se* or that defensive war occupied some kind of legally privileged position over offensive war. Most outstandingly, the laws of war, in their sternly even-handed application, were dogmatically blind to questions of offence and defence.

One final way in which the positivist outlook may be said to have provided intellectual support for aggression was in its belief that

---

[104] James, 'Moral Equivalent', at 68.   [105] Bonfils, *Manuel*, at 564.
[106] Elihu Root, *Latin America and the United States*, ed. Robert Bacon and James Brown Scott (Cambridge, Mass.: Harvard University Press, 1917), at 230–1.
[107] 3 F. de Martens, *Traité*, at 185–6.

aggressive war could be a source of legal rights. On this key point, positivism showed its debt to the contractual school of thought on war. Traditional just wars had been, on principle, conservative in character, in the sense that they were designed to maintain a legal status quo – i.e., to restore a wronged party to its previous position or to prevent wrongs from occurring. The nineteenth century, however, was imbued with an altogether more dynamic outlook. There was a realisation that, in some circumstances at least, the status quo 'should' be altered in one direction or another – and that war was often the only means for bringing about such an alteration. Even Bluntschli, who was certainly no militarist, appreciated the force of this point. '[W]ar', he contended, 'is not simply an act of defence against a violation of law and the means of obtaining the maintenance of a violated right: it is a special force which provokes the creation of new rights'.[108]

This frank acceptance of war as a source of new rights elided all too easily into a belief in war as an instrument of destiny, as an important tool for refashioning international affairs in a 'progressive' direction by removing obstacles and eliminating or reducing reactionary forces. Here it is possible to see an affinity between the positivist outlook and imperialist and social Darwinist conceptions of 'progressive' and 'retrograding' states, in the terminology of the Scottish lawyer James Lorimer.[109] As Bluntschli ominously conceded, 'The public life of states is often transformed in the midst of the thunder and lightning of battle; history progresses in the din of the storm.'[110] Such a way of thinking came dangerously near (to put it mildly) to an admission that outright aggression was perfectly lawful.

It would be a mistake, however, to condemn the positivist philosophy as being inherently militaristic. Positivist thought was open to criticism in this regard more in a 'negative' sense, for tolerating aggression and failing to erect barriers against it, than in a 'positive' sense of actually approving of it. If international lawyers in the nineteenth century seldom acted as peace crusaders, they also held back from any explicit endorsement of militarism. Positivism also provided no support for sentiments of extreme nationalism, which was very foreign to the cool rationalism of the 'cabinet war' mentality. It tended to see war as an inevitable feature of the world scene, not in the sense of being the primary driving force of the world, but more in the sense (as noted

---

[108] Bluntschli, *Droit international*, at 282.
[109] 2 Lorimer, *Institutes*, at 31, 39–41.   [110] Bluntschli, *Droit international*, at 282.

above) that physicists saw friction as an inevitable part of any physical system. With their essentially technocratic outlook, positivist writers tended to treat war with the utmost sobriety and dispassion, showing the scrupulous pride of the craftsman or the physician rather than the rantings of the militarist or jingoist. The positivist outlook on war may therefore be described as being drily clinical in character rather than overtly bloodthirsty. How this attitude weighed on the moral scale was (and is) open to healthy debate.

Of the two variants of positivist thought, the subjective one had the more difficult time fending off charges of lending support to militarism. This was because of its view that a state of war could be created by the unilateral will of a single state, combined with the acceptance of the fact that war could be a source of new legal rights for the winning side. The best that could be done to rescue the subjective outlook from charges of support for militarism was to make a distinction between the *power* to create a state of war and the *right* to do so. There was simply no denying, on the subjective theory, that individual states had the power unilaterally to create a state of war. Some lawyers, though, attempted to deny that there was a legal right to do so, in the absence of a *justa causa* of the traditional sort.[111] This 'solution' to the problem of aggressive war amounted, of course, to a reversion to the old – and supposedly discarded – just-war view. Whether this was a very convincing way of dealing with the problem may be gravely doubted, however, because the lack of a *justa causa* carried no concrete legal consequences.

The objective school was in a less awkward position on the matter of legal support for aggression, since it required the cooperation of *both* sides for the creation of a state of war. Oppenheim, for example, firmly maintained that there could not be a true *right* of war on the part of one party unless there was a corresponding *duty* of war on the other side – and there was no such duty. A state that was attacked was under no legal obligation to fight back.[112]

The problem with positivist thought on war was not, therefore, that it was particularly militaristic, but rather that it failed to place any effective legal barrier in the path of statesmen who were. There was no affirmative

---

[111] For lawyers taking this approach, see Heffter, *Droit international*, at 249–52; Halleck, *International Law*, at 247–8; Bluntschli, *Droit international*, at 270; and Funck-Brentano and Sorel, *Précis*, at 233.

[112] 2 Oppenheim, *International Law*, at 57–8, 84–5, 104. See also Funck-Brentano and Sorel, *Précis*, at 231–2.

preference for war over peace in positivist doctrine. Instead, there was a very decidedly *laissez-faire* outlook when it came to armed conflict. Putting the matter in slightly more legalistic terms, it would be said that, if two states were locked in a state of war, they did not thereby commit any legally cognisable wrong either against one another, or against the world at large. There were important legal *consequences* of such a state of affairs, to be sure. The contending states themselves were under a legal duty to adhere to the laws of war during the continuance of the struggle. Third countries, in their turn, became bound by the duties, and also entitled to the rights, of neutrals. But issues related to what lawyers called the *jus ad bellum* – i.e., the lawfulness of a *resort* to war – were quietly dropped from legal consideration. They would return, but not until the twentieth century.

Destruction unlimited

One of the major successes of the nineteenth century, as noted above, was the elaboration of a code of conduct for prosecution of hostilities in considerably greater detail than ever before and, more generally, the advance of a spirit of moderation in the waging of war. That spirit, as in the previous centuries, largely resulted from the practice of effecting a coolly rational balance between ends and means.[113] These conditions, however, along with any fine calculations that were based on them, were subject to change, so that the foundations of moderation in warfare – and of the code-of-conduct approach to war which reflected it – continued to be dangerously insecure. Two factors in particular worked against restraint in war, one psychological and the other material. The psychological factor was the rise of popular nationalism, which brought elements of emotion and short-term passion to bear on problems of statesmanship, sometimes with unfortunate results (as, notably, in the case of France in 1870). The material factor was the unrelenting pressure of new technological developments, which began during this period visibly to outrun the efforts of lawyers and statesmen to restrain them.

The challenges on the material plane were manifold, as was well illustrated by the puzzle of submarine warfare. Lawyers proved unable to reach agreement over whether the traditional rules on visit and search or capture applied to this new weapon. Aeroplanes were another invention whose military utility was unknown but potentially vast. No rules

---

[113] See, to this effect, Clausewitz, *On War*, at 91–2.

existed specifically applicable to them. It may be noted, though, that some attempts were made to restrict the uses of new kinds of weapon prior to their deployment. The Declaration of St Petersburg of 1868 banned the use in warfare of explosive or inflammable bullets – which did not actually exist at the time.[114] A similar attempt to restrict the use of chemical weapons, however, proved a dispiriting failure. It will be recalled that a declaration by the Hague Peace Conference in 1899 forbade the use of asphyxiating gases in projectiles. It was a worthy initiative. But in the Great War of 1914–18, the belligerents energetically circumvented its spirit while largely adhering to its letter, by releasing poison gases from ground-based canisters. An attempt to devise rules on the placing of mines at sea also proved ineffective. When the Hague Convention on Mines at Sea was concluded in 1907, the drafting parties failed to reach agreement on the key issue of whether belligerents would be allowed to mine the high seas. Immediately upon the outbreak of the Great War in 1914, both sides proceeded to do just that.

The problem was not just the advent of brand-new means of destruction, significant as those were. Even ordinary weapons long permitted by the laws of war could be 'improved' to expand their killing power beyond recognition. The metamorphosis of firearms is a good example. Developments in rifles in the nineteenth century, such as the invention of breech-loading weapons, together with significant improvements in range and accuracy, vastly increased the killing power of infantry forces. Much the same was true of artillery. At sea, explosive mines were set in deadly motion in the form of self-propelling torpedoes. But the law was entirely unable to place any kind of limits on these various advances in traditional weapons. In material terms, the gulf between the matchlocks of the sixteenth century and the Gatling gun was immense. In the eyes of the law, however, there was no meaningful distinction between them.

Even regarding 'ordinary' rules of warfare, agreement sometimes proved frustratingly elusive. This was the case especially in the area of neutrality, where there was much uncertainty in the late nineteenth century over the precise extent of belligerents' rights regarding contraband capture and blockade enforcement. In the wake of a failure at the Hague Peace Conference of 1907 to reach agreement on these questions, the London Naval Conference was convened in 1908, with only the major maritime powers participating, in the hope that a smaller and

---

[114] Declaration of St Petersburg, 11 Dec. 1868, 138 CTS 297; reprinted in Roberts and Guelff, *Documents*, at 54–5.

(relatively) like-minded group of states might succeed where the larger gathering had failed. In a manner of speaking, it did. Agreement was even reached on most (but still not all) of the outstanding questions and codified in the Declaration of London of 1909.[115] But this agreement, in the event, never entered into force because political opposition within Britain prevented that country from ratifying it. And without British adherence, the Declaration clearly could not be viable.[116]

In the final analysis, the inadequacy of the laws of war, from the standpoint of limiting the suffering of war, was not merely, and perhaps not even primarily, a technical matter. Rather, it lay in the very nature of the laws of war themselves. For one thing, the law in this area was animated by an underlying *laissez-faire* spirit, with the result that any weapon or category of weapons was permitted unless a specific prohibition against it could be expressly agreed. This gave a natural advantage to developers of new weapons over would-be regulators (a position that continues to prevail in international law). Another inherent feature of the laws of war that limited their effectiveness was the fact that they only placed what might be called qualitative, rather than quantitative, limits on destructiveness. That is, they barred certain tactics (such as no-quarter policies) and certain weapons (such as expanding bullets). But the laws of war never placed an actual ceiling on the total amount of destruction that could be visited by the warring states upon one another. The only restraint in this respect was the principle of necessity, which continued, even now, to play a marginal role in the laws of war, by holding that destruction that was *purely* gratuitous, having no connection whatsoever with the winning of the war, was unlawful. This principle, however, never came close to amounting to a serious restriction on the overall destructiveness of war.

The result of all of these factors was to make the efforts of nineteenth-century lawyers in this area look rather like those of the hapless Lilliputians straining fruitlessly to enchain the Gulliver of total war. At least some contemporary observers looked at the European scene in the late nineteenth and early twentieth centuries with foreboding. As armaments grew ominously in sophistication, as well as in quantity, the rival

---

[115] Declaration of London, 26 Feb. 1909, 208 CTS 338.
[116] On the London Naval Conference and the Declaration of London, see Neff, *Rights and Duties*, at 136–42. See also James Brown Scott, *The Declaration of London, February 26, 1909: A Collection of Official Papers Relating to the International Conference Held in London December 1908 – February 1909* (New York: Oxford University Press, 1919).

alliances became locked into intense arms races in the last years of the
nineteenth century. Worries began to be expressed that, if another war
between major powers should break out, it would be destructive far
beyond all previous measure. In the Great War of 1914–18, these fears
proved to be all too well founded.

Civilians in the firing line

An important part of the limited-war outlook of positivism was its
insistence on war as a business for trained professionals. But the international lawyers of the nineteenth century were not successful, in the
event, in effecting a total separation of civilian from military affairs. In
the late nineteenth and early twentieth centuries, it became increasingly
apparent that civilians were becoming more and more a part of the story
of war – both as victims and as participants. It was sometimes difficult to
determine which of these two trends was the more unsettling.

First, consider civilians as targets of armed action. Although this was
clearly contrary to the prevailing ethos of the laws of war in the nineteenth
century – as expressly stated in the Declaration of St Petersburg – the idea of
total war against whole populations was never thoroughly drained from
legal thought during the period. The juridical beast known as necessity may
have been progressively hidden from view by the code-of-conduct
approach to the regulation of war. But it was never de-fanged. Ironically,
the principle of unlimited war was a legacy of the just-war era, in which the
just side (but not, of course, the unjust one) had the right to use whatever
means were necessary under the circumstances to wear its foe down.
Moreover, the concept of collective responsibility of populations of states
meant that, as a general matter, all persons in the enemy state were enemies,
not just persons in uniform. Bynkershoek, for example, candidly pronounced war to be an 'attempt to subjugate the enemy and all that he has
by seizing all the power that the sovereign has over the state, that is to say,
by exercising complete dominion over all persons and all things contained
in that state'. He expressly contrasted war with civil litigation, where a strict
principle of proportionality prevailed, in which 'we do not exact from a
debtor more than he owes us'.[117]

Bynkershoek had a number of intellectual heirs in the nineteenth
century, especially in the English-speaking world, where writers tended
to cling to the older view of total hostility between warring

---

[117] Bynkershoek, *Questions*, at 15–16.

populations.[118] In the words of H. W. Halleck, for example, the outbreak of war meant that 'the whole state is placed in the legal attitude of a belligerent toward another state, so that every member of the one nation is authorized to commit hostilities against every member of the other, in every place and under every circumstance'.[119] Hall, in particular, went to some length to refute the idea that there could be any absolute separation between civilian life and military campaigning.[120] There was judicial authority to this same effect from the United States Supreme Court, which put the matter in the bluntest terms in 1814:

> In the state of war [it pronounced], nation is known to nation only by their armed exterior; each threatening the other with conquest or annihilation. The individuals who compose the belligerent States, exist, as to each other, in a state of utter occlusion. If they meet, it is only in combat.
>
> War strips man of his social nature; it demands of him the suppression of those sympathies which claim man for a brother; and accustoms the ear of humanity to hear with indifference, perhaps exultation, 'that thousands have been slain'.

Nor, the Court emphasised, were these thoughts merely 'the gloomy reveries of the bookman'. On the contrary, they were living law.[121] In such an atmosphere, the promotion of moderation in warfare was likely to be an uphill task.

From the ranks of the armed forces too, there was dissent from the idea that total war had been, or even should be, eliminated. A forceful voice in this direction was that of Helmuth von Moltke, the chief of the Prussian General Staff. He wrote to Bluntschli on the subject in 1880, expressing grave doubts as to the whole legal project of limiting the means of war. 'The greatest benefit in war', he contended, 'is that it be ended promptly'. The only way that this could be ensured was to permit armed forces to employ 'all means except those that are positively condemned'. He took specific exception to the Declaration of St Petersburg position of targeting only the armed forces of the enemy, insisting instead that it was 'necessary to attack all the resources of the enemy *government*, its finances, its railroads, its provisions and even its prestige'.[122]

---

[118] Dupuis, *Droit de la guerre*, at 1–18.
[119] Halleck, *International Law*, at 345. See also Wheaton, *Elements*, at 314.
[120] Hall, *Treatise*, at 636–8. See also 2 Twiss, *Law of Nations*, at 79–82.
[121] *The Rapid*, 12 US (8 Cranch) 155 (1814), at 160–1.
[122] Letter from Moltke to Bluntschli, 11 Dec. 1880, in 13 RDILC 80–2. For Bluntschli's response, see *ibid.* at 82–4.

Civilians could play a part in modern war in various ways. One was as targets of enemy action, as belligerents became more capable of inflicting economic hardship onto whole populations. This could be achieved chiefly by way of blockades. Doubts had been expressed in some quarters, for example by Hall, as to the legality of 'commercial blockades' (meaning blockades of areas that contained no specific military target such as an enemy army or fleet).[123] The consensus, however, was that these were permitted. British strategic planning even went so far as to rely on blockading as the principal method of conducting war. The American Civil War of 1861–5 was a first experiment in the systematic, large-scale and long-term blockading of a civilian population. Although that blockade fell far short of hermetically sealing the Confederate States off from the outside world, it certainly succeeded in inflicting great hardship on the population and was a tangible factor in the winning of the struggle. Moreover, the United States helpfully devised a number of innovations in the law of blockade that enabled this kind of warfare to be mounted with greater effect.[124] During the Great War of 1914–18, Britain made liberal use of these and went on to devise others as well, in its blockade of the Central Powers – with consequent hardship for civilians not only in the enemy states but in neighbouring neutral countries too.[125]

Civilians were participating in wars not only as victims but also, on some occasions, as participants, supplementing (or even altogether replacing) their regular armed forces. This was especially likely to occur when nationalist passions were inflamed – as was increasingly the case in the nineteenth century. The expression 'wars of national liberation' would later be used to describe such struggles. Early examples included the insurrection in Corsica in the eighteenth century, first against Genoese and then French rule, which caught the imagination of Europe. The American War of Independence was another example. Most potent of all were the various wars of liberation that were waged against French domination in the years following the French Revolution. In the wake of the French defeat of Prussia in 1806, the philosopher Gottlieb Fichte rallied the population at large with his inspirational 'Address to the German Nation'. The response was a 'people's war' waged against the French forces by self-appointed warriors armed more with fervour than with military expertise. Even better

---

[123] Hall, *Treatise*, at 636–8.   [124] See Neff, *Rights and Duties*, at 115–24.
[125] See *ibid.* at 146–59.

known was the 'little war' in Spain (*guerrilla* in Spanish) prosecuted by irregular forces, with some vital foreign support. The Spanish experience was particularly frightening to those who hoped that war would become increasingly ritualised and rule-governed. Atrocities and massacres, committed both by and against the *guerrillas*, became the order of the day, as restraints of war, of which Vattel had been so proud, were cast to the winds.

Further examples of guerrilla warfare appeared later in the century. During the war between Mexico and the United States of 1846–8, Mexican guerrillas, after the defeat of the regular forces, began to conduct irregular operations against the American forces. Reactions to this new form of warfare were devised on the spot by military officers. The American General Winfield Scott responded in 1847 by ordering the trial of any such persons before American military commissions (or 'councils of war' as they were termed), with the death penalty in store for anyone who was found guilty. The problem arose again in Mexico in the 1860s, when irregular forces operated against the French-supported government of Emperor Maximilien. In 1865, he too instituted the death penalty for guerrillas.[126]

In European war, partisan groups made a dramatic appearance (or reappearance) in interstate conflict in the Franco-Prussian War of 1870–1. After the defeat of the main French army in the field at the Battle of Sedan (including the capture of Emperor Napoleon III himself), it was the Prussian expectation that, in the manner of warfare hallowed by the first Napoleon, France would acknowledge its defeat and conclude as favourable a treaty as possible under the circumstances. This assumption failed to take account of the patriotic fervour of the French people. The immediate result of the defeat was the overthrow of the French imperial government. The revolutionary provisional government then made clear its determination to continue the struggle by way of partisan warfare. Units were hastily formed in villages around France, with command structures and uniforms often improvised at short notice; and harassment operations were launched against the German forces. The Germans in turn acted harshly against these *francs-tireurs* (or 'free pullers', referring to the pulling of triggers). In the event, this

---

[126] Nurick and Barrett, 'Legality', at 571. See also Michael O. Lacey, 'Military Commissions: A Historical Survey,' *Army Lawyer* (Mar. 2002), at 43. On guerrilla warfare in history generally, see Robert B. Asprey, *War in the Shadows: The Guerrilla in History* (New York: Doubleday, 1975).

partisan warfare was of only marginal value to the French, who were eventually forced to the peace table. Nevertheless, the experience was a sobering illustration, in the very heart of Europe, of the manner in which patriotic fervour and emotion could interfere with the calculations of rational war planners.[127]

Traditionally minded lawyers were inclined to look on this development with the deepest misgivings. As far back as Roman times, the idea of civilians becoming self-appointed warriors had been frowned on. '[I]t is not lawful', Cicero had asserted, 'for one who is not a soldier to fight [against] the enemy'.[128] In the Middle Ages, the principle of *auctoritas* similarly forbade persons from taking up the sword without the commission of their sovereign. The phenomenon of 'people's war' posed challenges to lawyers, however, because these guerrilla warriors were not mere brigands fighting only for self-enrichment, in the manner of, say, the dreaded medieval 'free companies' or of roving pirate bands. They more nearly resembled the Islamic *bughat*, who fought for a political cause (at least ostensibly, and part of the time). There was, accordingly, some reluctance to place a complete prohibition against armed action that was patriotic in intention, even if unorthodox in method. Small European countries such as Belgium and the Netherlands were especially inclined to take this view. Being worryingly situated between major powers, they naturally objected to rules that would prevent them from drawing on the patriotic fervour of their civilian populations in the event of an invasion.

The rival views on the question of entitlement to engage in hostilities received a thorough airing at the Brussels conference of 1874. Lawyers from the major military powers, most notably Germany, wished to confine combatant status very tightly, to persons who were enrolled in the regular armed forces of states. Any other persons taking to arms would be mere criminals. Lawyers from the small states equally vigorously pressed for combatant status for self-formed groups of patriots. The result, as so often both in law and in life, was a somewhat muddled compromise. The Brussels *projet* conferred the legal privileges of belligerency – i.e., protection from criminal prosecution – onto 'the armed forces' of the contending states (though without providing any

---

[127] On the partisan warfare in the Franco-Prussian War, see Michael Howard, *The Franco-Prussian War: The German Invasion of France 1870–1871* (New York: Collier, 1961), at 249–56.
[128] Cicero, *On Duties*, at 16.

definition of 'armed forces'). But the armed forces were not given a total monopoly on war-making. Civilians were permitted to engage in combat in two specified circumstances. First, they were entitled to form themselves into volunteer units, provided that those auxiliary units (as they might be termed) operated substantially as regular armed forces did. In particular, these units had to satisfy four prescribed criteria. First, they must carry their arms openly. Second, they must be organised into a military-like hierarchy under a leadership whose commands they would follow, in the manner of soldiers. Third, they had to wear some kind of sign recognisable at a distance, so as to distinguish themselves from noncombatants. Finally, they had to conduct their operations in conformity with the laws of war. Provided that all four of these criteria were met, members of auxiliary units would be entitled to all the privileges of authorised belligerents.

The second category of self-constituted warriors who were conceded the privileges of combatants comprised persons who might be described as spontaneous self-defenders. These were persons who took up arms in the direct face of a foreign force attacking their home area. (The auxiliary units just discussed were not confined to the immediate home area of their members.) These persons were conceded the privilege of taking up arms to fend off the attack, on the one condition that they abided by the laws of war in their operations.[129] Two issues, however, could not be agreed by the delegates: whether a person taking up arms on his own initiative in a *non*-occupied area would have combatant status; and whether members of a population could ever have combatant status if they took up arms against the enemy *after* it succeeded in occupying their home area.[130]

These issues arose again at the First Hague Peace Conference of 1899, when the Brussels *projet* was being transformed into a legally binding treaty; but only modest progress was made in resolving them. One change that was made was to impose a second criterion upon spontaneous self-defenders for their recognition as belligerents: the wearing of a sign visible at a distance. Some delegations thought that the law should go beyond the Brussels *projet* by granting combatant status to all forms of resistance against invading armies. Britain, for example, proposed that the Hague Rules (as they were now to be called) should confirm the right of 'the population of an invaded country to patriotically oppose the most

---

[129] Brussels *projet*, Arts. 9 and 10.
[130] For details of the debate over these questions, see 65 BFSP 1048–55, 1076–9.

energetic resistance to invaders by any legitimate means', an initiative that received predictably strong support from Belgium, Switzerland and the Netherlands.[131] Germany and Russia, however, were adamantly opposed to such a broad-based licence to civilians to take up arms.

In the event, the chairman of the sub-committee that undertook the drafting of the Hague Rules, Frederic de Martens, proposed that the matter be dealt with by way of a rather more general and non-committal statement in the preamble to the Hague Convention, to the effect that persons who failed to meet the prescribed legal criteria for combatant status would not be left wholly without legal protection. Such persons, it was pronounced, would remain 'under the protection and the rule of the principles of the law of nations, as they result from the usages established among civilized peoples, from the laws of humanity, and the dictates of the public conscience'.[132] This 'Martens Clause' (as it came to be known) was reiterated at the Second Hague Conference of 1907, when the final version of the Hague Rules was adopted; and it remains a part of international law to the present day.[133] The problem of unlawful combatants, too, remains a challenge to international lawyers to the present day, as will be observed in due course.[134]

Harsh peace-making

Another symptom of harsher times was the dropping of any real attempt to place legal restrictions on the rights of victors in war. Bargaining power was everything, the *jus victoriae* nothing. Most notably, it was widely agreed that there was no legal obligation on the part of a successful belligerent to halt the struggle when its original war aims had been

---

[131] The proposal did not expressly grant belligerent status in such a situation, but it would at least have precluded the infliction of criminal punishment.

[132] Hague Convention II on the Rules of Land Warfare, 29 July 1899, 189 CTS 429, preamble. On the origin of the Martens Clause, see Report to the [First Hague Peace] Conference from the Second Commission on the Laws and Customs of War on Land, in J. B. Scott (ed.), *Reports*, at 140–3.

[133] See, for example, Additional Protocol I to the Geneva Conventions of 1949, 8 June 1977, 1125 UNTS 3, Art. 1(2); Additional Protocol II to the Geneva Conventions of 1949, *ibid.* at 609, preamble; and Convention on Prohibitions or Restrictions of Certain Conventional Weapons, 10 Oct. 1980, 1342 UNTS 137, preamble. See also Legality of the Threat or Use of Nuclear Weapons, 1996 ICJ Rep. 226, para. 78. In modern international law, the Martens Clause has commonly been employed to refer to matters other than combatant status, in particular to the protection of civilian populations from hostilities and to possible restrictions on new types of weaponry.

[134] See Chapter 10 below.

achieved. 'No moral or legal duty exists', Oppenheim bluntly pronounced, 'for a belligerent to stop the war when his opponent is ready
to concede the object for which the war was made'.[135] Peace terms were
also permitted to extend beyond the issues over which the war had
originally been fought and thereby to create new rights which had not
previously existed.[136] The British lawyer John Westlake, speaking in the
spirit of the contractual school of thought, insisted that any exactions on
the losing party, however onerous, could not be seen as penal in character, but instead simply as exercises of the rights of the victor, accepted
in advance by both parties at the outset. '[B]oth opinion and practice',
he maintained, 'allow the victor to ... [insist] on terms having no
relation to the cause of occasion of the war'.[137]

Nor was this a matter merely of scholarly theory. The nineteenth
century provided some notable examples of peace settlements in which
the gains to the winner went far beyond the original causes of the war.
A striking illustration was the Treaty of Guadalupe-Hidalgo of 1848,
which concluded the war between the United States and Mexico.
Although the original territorial dispute had been confined to a portion
of what is now the American state of Texas, the Treaty transferred a large
portion of North America (including the present state of California) to
the United States.[138] (There was even serious pressure within the United
States for the outright annexation of the whole of Mexico.) At the
conclusion of the Franco-Prussian War in 1871, Germany insisted on
the cession of most of Alsace and Lorraine, to which it had made no
prior claim.[139] Similarly, after the Spanish-American War, Spain was
compelled to cede Puerto Rico, the Philippines and various other islands
to the United States, in addition to granting independence to Cuba, the
issue which had originally sparked the war.[140]

The special question of indemnities in peace treaties merits some
consideration, as it provides an instructive insight into the spirit of the
times. In the second half of the century, the old Napoleonic practice of
imposing financial assessments onto defeated states began to come back
into vogue. In the common practice, the payments were labelled as

---

[135] 2 Oppenheim, *International Law*, at 73.

[136] See, for example, 2 Rivier, *Principes*, at 219.

[137] 2 Westlake, *International Law*, at 35. See also, to the same effect, Bluntschli, *Droit international*, at 281–2; and 2 Oppenheim, *International Law*, at 64.

[138] Mexico-USA, Treaty of Guadalupe-Hidalgo, 2 Feb. 1848, 102 CTS 29, Arts. 4, 11.

[139] France-Germany, Treaty of Frankfurt, 10 May 1871, 143 CTS 163.

[140] Spain-USA, Treaty of Paris, 10 Dec. 1898, 187 CTS 100, Arts. 2, 3.

'indemnities' for the victors' expenses in waging the struggle, but without any real attempt at detailed evidence or itemisation of actual costs. That was the case, for example, in a peace treaty of 1873 between the Khanate of Khiva and Russia. Khiva was compelled to pay an 'indemnity' of 2.2 million rubles, which was simply stated to be for the costs incurred by Russia in the waging of the struggle.[141] In 1874, at the conclusion of Britain's successful war against the Ashantee kingdom in West Africa, the peace treaty imposed a payment of 50,000 ounces of gold, also expressed to be an indemnity for the expenses of the war.[142] The most notorious of the financial provisions was the one imposed by Germany on France at the conclusion of the Franco-Prussian War in 1871. The figure arrived at was the largest assessment ever, up to that time: the staggering sum of 5 *billion* francs (some sixty times the size of the indemnity that Prussia had imposed on Austria five years previously).[143]

A few international lawyers (though not many) expressed misgivings about this practice, in terms distinctly reminiscent of the old just-war outlook. In particular, there was some suspicion – exceedingly well founded, it may be surmised – that these so-called 'indemnity' arrangements were actually in the nature of penalties, or of measures to prevent defeated powers from recovering their strength too quickly.[144] French lawyers, it is not surprising to find, were especially inclined to condemn the practice. Bonfils, for example, criticised it as a regression to older ways. He conceded, in the spirit of just-war thought, that the victorious state was entitled to extract an indemnity for the costs that it had *actually* incurred in prosecuting the conflict. But he noted with disapproval that, in practice, the monetary payments were, in reality, 'nothing more than a means by which the victor enriches itself to the detriment of the other and satisfies its cupidity, while profiting from its success'.[145] Of a like view was his fellow French lawyer Théophile Funck-Brentano. Like Bonfils, he admitted that an indemnity in the true sense – i.e., reimbursement for expenses actually undertaken – was permissible. But he went on to point out that this true indemnity was not, in practice, calculable, since it included expenses that trailed far into the future, such as pensions for veterans. There was also the difficulty (or impossibility) of quantifying the

[141] Khiva-Russia, Conditions of Peace, 12 Aug. 1873, 146 CTS 345, Art. 18.
[142] Ashantee-Great Britain, Treaty of Peace, 13 Feb. 1874, 147 CTS 271, Art. 2.
[143] France-Germany, Treaty of Frankfurt, 10 May 1871, 143 CTS 163, Art 7. See also Phillipson, *Termination*, at 274–6.
[144] See, for example, Camuzet, *Indemnité*, at 79.
[145] Bonfils, *Manuel*, at 889. See also, to the same effect, Despagnet, *Cours*, at 713–14.

social disruption caused by the war. He therefore favoured using the expression 'reparation' to refer to the *calculable* portion of an indemnity – which, in his view, was the legal limit of the victorious side's entitlement. Anything beyond reparation (in this strict sense) was mere enrichment of the winning side at the loser's expense, and was not lawful.[146]

In all events, the Prussian exactions of the 1860s and 1870s stimulated a reaction against financial provisions in peace treaties, although the practice was not wholly discontinued. On several occasions, the major powers stepped in to reduce the demands of victorious parties – though on political rather than legal grounds. Perhaps the most striking example occurred in 1878 at the conclusion of the Russo-Turkish War, when the major powers intervened to compel Russia to scale down its original plans for a financial exaction.[147] In 1897, the powers again intervened, following a catastrophic defeat of Greece by Turkey, to moderate the victor's exaction.[148] By about the turn of the twentieth century, indemnities appeared to be fading from state practice. Financial exactions did not feature in the peace settlements of the Spanish-American War of 1898 or the Russo-Japanese War of 1904–5. In fact, the United States agreed to pay $20 million *to* Spain, in conjunction with Spain's cession of the Philippines.[149] Nor did financial exactions feature in the settlements in the various pre-1914 wars in the Balkans (at the insistence of the major powers). Indemnities – or reparations – however, were not fated to disappear from state practice altogether, as the peace-makers of 1919 would later demonstrate, in the wake of the Great War.[150]

In sum, just-war ways of thinking and acting were largely a thing of memory by the nineteenth century. Such notions maintained no more than a kind of ghostly presence, somewhat like mice scurrying in the cracks and crannies of the stately positivist edifice known, suitably grandly, as the legal institution of war. We have seen faint traces of just-war thinking, for example, in the distinction posited by some lawyers between a power to create a state of war, as distinct from a

---

[146] Funck-Brentano and Sorel, *Précis*, at 322–7.

[147] On the role of the great powers in this crisis, see Dupuis, *Principe d'équilibre*, at 350–72.

[148] Shaw and Shaw, *Ottoman Empire*, at 207; and Phillipson, *Termination*, at 87.

[149] Spain-USA, Treaty of Paris, 10 Dec. 1898, 187 CTS 100, Art. 3. The treaty did not expressly state the arrangement to be a purchase of the Philippines. A separate provision transferring Puerto Rico and Guam to the United States made no arrangement for payments of any kind

[150] On state practice regarding financial exaction in peace treaties generally, see Camuzet, *Indemnité*, at 41–77.

true right to do so. We have seen it also in the retention of the principle of necessity in the laws of war, alongside the menu of specific rules governing armed conflict. Misgivings about financial penalties in peace treaties were another sign of it. It might lead observers to wonder if there is some kind of ineluctable and indestructible urge in the individual or collective human psyche to insist on some kind of affinity between substantive justice and the use of force. Be that as it may, there was, in fact, abundant evidence of the survival of the just-war ethos – but outside the edifice of the legal institution of war. Just-war ways may have been largely turned out of the positivist 'house of war' (to borrow the classical Islamic expression). But they remained in buoyant health in the neighbouring, if less imposing, house of 'measures short of war', where we shall proceed to go calling.

6

Tame and half-hearted war: intervention, reprisal and necessity

[I]n cases where a strong state or group of states finds itself obliged to undertake what are practically measures of police against weak and recalcitrant powers, [reprisals] may be a useful alternative to war. They are less destructive and more limited in their operation. It is true that they may be used to inflict injury on small states, and extort from them a compliance with unreasonable demands. But war can be equally unjust, and would certainly cause more suffering.

T. J. Lawrence[1]

The distinction between perfect and imperfect wars, inherited from the seventeenth and eighteenth centuries, continued to exist in the nine-teenth, although under different labels. Perfect wars were the ones that fitted the positivist analysis: conflicts in which one state attempted to force its will upon another, or in which two states reciprocally attempted to impose their respective wills onto one another. As observed above, wars in this proper legal sense were seen as clashes of policy or interest rather than of law. But these fully fledged perfect wars of the positivists constituted, so to speak, only the showy surface of interstate violence. Beneath that surface was another type of armed action by states to which the label 'measures short of war' was commonly given. Clausewitz had recognised this distinction in holding that conflicts between states occupied an entire spectrum of degrees of violence. At the one extreme, he placed the 'pure' type of war, 'a death struggle for total existence'. At the other end was limited war for limited ends, when issues of only slight importance were at stake. In such instances, Clausewitz observed, war becomes reduced to 'something tame and half-hearted'. It will often be

[1] Lawrence, *Principles*, at 343–4.

'nothing more than armed neutrality, a threatening attitude meant to support negotiations, a mild attempt to gain some small advantage'. In these situations, 'the hostile spirit of true war' was lacking.[2] It was the task of lawyers to decide where along this spectrum to make the cut, or dividing line, between conflicts that qualified as wars and ones that did not. On one side of the line was the state of war properly speaking, with the application of the legal institution of war in all its fullness. On the other side were measures short of war, which were regarded as *acts* of war taking place during a *state* of peace.[3]

What distinguished measures short of war from a true state of war was – very broadly speaking – their over-all nature as measures of law enforcement, as opposed to measures of national policy, which were the preserve of true war. Measures short of war were therefore, in essence, the nineteenth-century version of just wars. There was a deep irony here. Where just wars had formerly been seen as 'ideal types' of war – i.e., as wars in the very truest sense – they were now excluded altogether from the category of war in the nineteenth-century sense. Just wars had been, so to speak, 'demoted'. But they were still very much part of the international scene, even if they commanded less attention than wars, both at the time and since. In fact, in some ways, the nineteenth century represented something of a golden age of just wars, albeit in their newer and more modest incarnation.

These nineteenth-century just wars have yet to receive the systematic study that they deserve; and the present treatment can only survey their broader features. They came in a dizzying variety of forms; but, for present purposes, they may be said to have fallen into three principal categories. One was intervention, which referred, during this period, to the use of armed force to promote general community interests. These represented just wars in perhaps their purest form – early versions of what would be known in the United Nations era as enforcement or peacekeeping operations.[4] As such, they constituted a striking innovation on the international legal scene. A second category consisted of reprisals – but reprisals which were now very different in character, in many ways, from past practices. In the nineteenth century, for the first time, reprisals came to be state-to-state affairs, involving the use of armed force, in marked contrast to the past when they had been mere property-sequestration measures directed against individuals. The third

---

[2] Clausewitz, *On War*, at 218.   [3] See, for example, 1 Calvo, *Droit international*, at 802–3.
[4] See Chevalier, 'Sainte-Alliance'.

type of measure short of war was rather different, in that it did not descend from the medieval conception of just wars. It comprised emergency actions of various kinds, falling under the broad heading of necessity. These were exercises of the inherent, primeval right of survival, comprising such actions as self-defence, together with related measures such as rescue missions and punitive expeditions.

It will be readily observed that all three of these categories of measures short of war had one feature in common: that they involved armed action by major powers, either alone or in concert, against lesser ones. There can be few ironies greater than the fact that, in this area of practice which descends so directly from the just-war outlook of the Middle Ages, with its stress on justice and the rule of law, the hard face of power politics should be so ubiquitously present. Brute force and the rule of law have always been uneasy, if sometimes necessary, companions of one another, at the best of times. And the motives of major powers exerting their might to build a better world have ever been open to the readiest suspicion. The nineteenth century was the first period in history in which these disturbing considerations played a major role in international affairs. It would not be the last.

The art of intervention

In considering intervention in the nineteenth century, we must put entirely out of our minds the almost wholly pejorative sense which that term has taken on since the Second World War.[5] In the nineteenth century, it had a much more positive image, connoting action undertaken not in the name of narrow national self-interest but rather in the pursuit of community norms such as preserving the peace, promoting self-determination of peoples or preventing and punishing atrocities. William Edward Hall spoke of intervention as 'a measure of prevention or police', often taken in the interest of preventing the outbreak of a war or of providing some measure of assistance to the state in which it occurred.[6] This conferred onto intervention an aura of selfless action, idealism and community service, presenting a stark contrast to the self-centred Hobbesian frame of mind which prevailed in 'normal' interstate relations. It therefore had the strong

---

[5] On the early uses of the term 'intervention', see Winfield, 'History', at 131–9.
[6] Hall, Treatise, at 281.

flavour of natural law and the just-war ethos to it.[7] For this very reason, however, it aroused great opposition from positivist-minded lawyers, as it was directly antithetical to the fundamental positivist principle of the sovereignty and independence of states and of the rigorous equality of states before the law.[8]

This powerful affinity between intervention and the just-war outlook was nowhere more apparent than in the writing of the century's foremost intellectual champion of the practice, the Scottish lawyer James Lorimer. His approach is of interest because he, practically alone of the major international-law writers of the nineteenth century, stood consciously apart from the prevailing positivist consensus. He frankly deprecated positivist thought as representing what he called the 'negative' or 'national' school of jurisprudence. Positivism, he maintained, was negative in its rejection of any overarching body of ethical thought governing international relations and its reliance instead on treaties and customary practices of states as the sole source of international law. And it was national in its fixation on the isolated nation-state as the ultimate unit of the international community, walled off from other states by the doctrines of sovereignty, independence and non-intervention. Lorimer's positive (or 'cosmopolitan') conception of international law was not, emphatically, to be confused with positiv*ism*. On the contrary, it was a forthright embrace of the natural-law idea that the states of the world formed an interconnected, interdependent moral community. In such a community, as in any community worthy of the name, duties to the society at large must prevail over merely selfish concerns.[9]

In nineteenth-century parlance, intervention did not necessarily imply military action. It could take the form of, say, an offer to mediate in a dispute or an actual war. The British lawyer Robert Phillimore identified no fewer than six kinds of intervention, falling into two broad categories: intervention in the internal affairs of a state (such as the replacing of one government by another), and intervention for the purpose of safeguarding international peace and security. This second category, which Phillimore held to rest on much more solid legal ground than the first, consisted of action for either of two specific purposes: the preservation of the over-all balance of power, or the protection of

---

[7] For a general survey of the subject in its nineteenth-century sense, see Stowell, *Intervention*.
[8] For principled opposition to the lawfulness of intervention, on these grounds, see 1 Calvo, *Droit international*, at 195–8; and Bluntschli, *Droit international*, at 252–4.
[9] 1 Lorimer, *Institutes*, at 9–11.

victims of oppression on religious grounds (what would later be termed humanitarian intervention).[10] The American lawyer Henry Wheaton posited that the number of situations that might give rise to interventions was so large and varied as to preclude the formulation of any set of general legal rules on the subject.[11]

The principal point about intervention, though, was that it was generally (though not universally) regarded as being quite distinct from war.[12] For present purposes, it may suffice to consider interventions as falling into two categories, political and humanitarian. By political interventions are meant those which were designed to bolster the Vienna settlement of 1815 or, more broadly, to safeguard the general peace of Europe against actual or potential threats. By humanitarian interventions are meant those which were designed to rescue a group of foreign nationals from oppression at the hands of their rulers.

Political intervention

Political interventions took a variety of specific forms and occurred in a variety of different conditions. They sometimes took place in internal crises in particular states, in cases of revolutions and the like. At other times, they occurred in the context of interstate conflicts. Sometimes they had the consent of the government of the state in which they occurred, and sometimes not. Non-consensual intervention, consisting of coercive action (as opposed to diplomatic means such as mediation), merited the term 'policing'. Sometimes, the intervening states adopted a stance of impartiality, confining themselves to intervention in the literal sense of 'coming between' two clashing parties. Lorimer referred to this as a 'double intervention'. In later times, it would be referred to as peacekeeping. On other occasions, the intervening states took the side of one party against the other – a 'single intervention' in Lorimer's expression.[13] Sometimes a single state did the intervening on its own initiative, and sometimes it was done by two or more powers in concert.

Some of the early opportunities for intervention were for the purpose of shoring up the 1814–15 European peace settlement which was negotiated at the Congress of Vienna at the conclusion of the Napoleonic Wars. There were some striking features of this peace settlement which

---

[10] 1 Phillimore, *Commentaries*, at 559–61.   [11] Wheaton, *Elements*, at 79.

[12] For a dissenting voice, see Halleck, *International Law*, at 334–43, who held intervention to be 'virtually' a war.

[13] 2 Lorimer, *Institutes*, at 53.

call for notice. Most outstanding for present purposes was the fact that the arrangements made were designed to establish not merely a factual situation but also a legal one, to which was accorded the grand sobriquet of 'the public law of Europe'. This public law of Europe rested, in essence, on two pillars. The first, concerning relations between nations, was the principle of mutual respect by the states of Europe for the sovereignty and independence of one another. States were to be content with the territories that they had been allocated by the peace-makers at Vienna, and none should covet the possessions of the others. The second great principle operated internally in the various European states. This was a respect for legitimacy, for acceptance of established rulers – and a foreswearing of resort to revolutionary excesses. Change, to be sure, could and should occur. But it should occur in a measured and orderly manner without resort to the barricade and the scaffold. This internal principle entailed a strong element of reciprocity. Rulers were bound to cooperate with their subjects in the process of orderly and incremental change, through such means as constitutions and impartial judiciaries. In return, the subjects should be duly respectful of the prevailing laws and institutions, and confine their agitations to prescribed channels. The broad goal was to make arbitrariness and tyranny obsolete, along with their nemesis, revolution.

One of the most innovative aspects of the 1814–15 settlement lay in the fact that it contained an enforcement mechanism, in the form of (more or less) vigilant supervision by the major powers. Its origin lay in the Quadruple Alliance of 1814, comprising the principal powers allied against revolutionary France (Britain, Austria, Prussia and Russia).[14] By 1818, this had become a Quintuple Alliance with the accession of France itself, now safely back under Bourbon rule.[15] Within that group, three of the countries (Austria, Prussia and Russia) associated themselves under the lofty title of the Holy Alliance.[16] These initiatives marked the first time in history that the major powers had formed themselves into a kind of directorate of international society – self-appointed, to be sure – with a view to bringing a degree of order to a hitherto chaotic and anarchic world. From across the Atlantic, Henry Wheaton described the arrangement as 'a sort of superintending authority ... over the international affairs of Europe'.[17]

---

[14] Treaty of Chaumont, 1 Mar. 1814, 63 CTS 83.
[15] Protocol of the Conference of Aix-la-Chapelle, 15 Nov. 1818, 69 CTS 365.
[16] Austria-Prussia-Russia, Holy Alliance, 26 Sept. 1815, 65 CTS 199.
[17] Wheaton, *Elements*, at 79.

A great experiment was in the making. Not even in the Middle Ages – when the doctrine of the just war was most dominant – had there been any suggestion of a league of powers actually devoting their resources on an open-ended basis to upholding the basic values of the world community. In its most benevolent form, this would amount to what Lorimer called 'warlike co-operation in behalf of freedom'.[18] Imbued as he was with the natural-law spirit, Lorimer regarded this form of intervention as not merely a right but also a positive duty.[19] There were naturally those who suspected, both then and later, that the powers were, in reality, rather more concerned with their own interests than with those of humanity at large. Be that as it may, there was no denying that at least the *idea* of a cooperative great-power alliance to secure international peace was a radically new one.

The earliest occasion for armed action by these new-minted watchmen presented itself in the early 1820s, when the outbreak of disturbances in Naples and Sardinia led the monarchs of those two states to appeal for assistance in restoring order. Austria duly sent troops to both, in each case subduing the revolutionary forces and restoring order and legitimacy. In the wake of the Naples intervention, the three Holy Alliance countries issued a statement carefully characterising the two Austrian actions not as wars but as 'temporary measures of precaution' motivated by a spirit of 'justice and disinterestedness'. The exclusive goal of the Holy Allies, the world was assured, was to safeguard 'the free exercise of legitimate authority' and to combat the twin scourges of 'Revolution and Crime'.[20] In 1823, France undertook a similar operation to restore the Spanish King Ferdinand VII to full power after insurgents took control of the northern part of the country. Further interventions by the major powers, in various combinations, in the 1830s led to the independence of Belgium (from the Netherlands) and of Greece (from the Ottoman Empire).

Interventions by the Concert of Europe (as the system of major-power cooperation came to be commonly known) continued to occur, albeit very sporadically, throughout the nineteenth century and even

---

[18] 1 Lorimer, *Institutes*, at 224.

[19] 2 *ibid.* at 121–7. Lorimer was conscious that, in the face of the positivist consensus of his time, his position was a minority one. For agreement with Lorimer, see 1 Fiore, *Nouveau droit*, at 517–26.

[20] Declaration of the Allied Sovereigns of Austria, Prussia and Russia on the Breaking up of the Conference of Laibach, 12 May 1821, in Albrecht-Carrié (ed.), *Concert of Europe*, at 55–7.

into the twentieth. One of the most notable later initiatives occurred in 1886, when the powers imposed a naval blockade of Greece, to compel it to halt an offensive which it had launched against Bulgaria.[21] In 1897–8 came armed action once again against Greece, this time in response to its occupation of Crete (which was then part of the Ottoman Empire). In one of their most impressive cooperative efforts, no fewer than six major powers (Britain, Austria-Hungary, France, Germany, Italy and Russia) combined to blockade the island to prevent the landing of Turkish troops, with the inevitable bloodshed that would have resulted.[22] They then compelled Greece to evacuate the island, while also insisting that Turkey grant a special autonomous status to it, as a condition for its remaining part of the Ottoman Empire.[23]

There were similar developments in the Western Hemisphere in the twentieth century, with the United States assuming the leading policing role. The decisive event was the promulgation, in 1904, of what became known as the 'Roosevelt Corollary' to the Monroe Doctrine. President Theodore Roosevelt announced that, in 'flagrant' cases of '[c]hronic wrongdoing' on the part of Western Hemisphere states, or of 'an impotence which results in a general loosening of the ties of civilized society', the United States might be compelled, with due reluctance, to exercise what was frankly termed 'an international police power'.[24] The purpose was to forestall intervention by European powers and thereby to uphold the Monroe Doctrine, by ensuring that the American republics scrupulously complied with their international obligations – chiefly by paying their debts and according proper treatment to foreign traders and investors.

The Roosevelt Corollary was no idle pronouncement. In the ensuing years, the United States intervened on a number of occasions in Caribbean and Central American states with a view to restoring order, protecting foreign nationals and safeguarding foreign investments. The Dominican Republic was occupied by the American forces on this basis

---

[21] On this incident, see Barès, *Blocus pacifique*, at 40–4; and Hogan, *Pacific Blockade*, at 126–30.

[22] See Notification of the Blockade of the Island of Crete, 19 Mar. 1897, 89 BFSP 446. See also Barès, *Blocus pacifique*, at 45–56.

[23] An adequate history of the Concert of Europe from the legal standpoint has yet to be written in English. See, however, Dupuis, *Principe d'équilibre*; and Holbraad, *Concert of Europe*. For a valuable collection of documents, see Albrecht-Carrié (ed.), *Concert of Europe*.

[24] Bartlett (ed.), *Record*, at 539.

for some eight years, from 1916 to 1924. Haïti was under American occupation for even longer, from 1915 to 1934. These actions, however, were not considered to be true wars.[25]

Humanitarian intervention

The other principal form of intervention was humanitarian. As the term implies, its purpose was to prevent the occurrence, or continuation, of some kind of human tragedy, such as extreme oppression by a ruler of his subjects or a massacre of a civilian population in the course of some kind of unrest or rebellion. No form of armed activity had a more distinguished intellectual pedigree than this one. It was the quintessential example of a just war in the medieval sense: a war fought for the vindication of right against wrong, free from the odour of self-interest (since foreigners were the beneficiaries of the action). Hugo Grotius, in thoroughgoing medieval spirit, even held that states had a right to intervene to rescue foreigners from oppression by their sovereign, even though the hapless subjects *themselves* lacked any right to resist or rebel on their own behalf.[26]

Humanitarian intervention in its modern guise was first articulated – though not actually undertaken – in 1791, with the joint issuing of the Declaration of Pillnitz by Austria and Prussia, in response to events in revolutionary France. They declared that they regarded the precarious situation of the king of France to be 'an object of common interest to all the sovereigns of Europe' and not merely to France alone. They also announced a willingness to 'act promptly in a mutual agreement with the necessary forces' to restore the beleaguered king to his rightful status.[27] Although this announcement (which was not acted on) smacked more of political reaction than of humanitarianism, it contained the two key conceptual elements of humanitarian intervention: a statement that seemingly internal or domestic events could be a matter of common concern to the world at large even in the absence of any direct material interest; and a willingness to use force to set the situation aright.

One of many problems with humanitarian intervention lay in identifying clear illustrations of it. There were many crises in the nineteenth

---

[25] See generally Graham-Yooll, *Imperial Skirmishes.*
[26] Grotius, *War and Peace,* at 583–4.
[27] On the Declaration of Pillnitz, see Blanning, *Origins,* at 86–9.

century (and later) in which humanitarian considerations played at least
some part. But it would be difficult, if not impossible, to point to any in
which humanitarian considerations were the *sole* factor at work. Bearing
this important caveat in mind, it may be said that the first major case,
arguably, of humanitarian intervention occurred in the Greek independence crisis of the 1820s. It began when Britain, France and Russia first
attempted to mediate between the Greeks and their Ottoman rulers and
ended by their taking joint military action against the Turks.[28] Britain and
France blockaded the Dardenelles Straits, as well as the Morea, to prevent
further supplies from reaching the Turkish forces. They also blockaded,
and then destroyed, the principal Ottoman-Egyptian fleet in Navarino
harbour, with the loss of some 8,000 lives. As a result, the Ottoman
Empire was forced to accept the full independence of the Kingdom of
Greece. In their joint note to Turkey in 1830 on the subject, the intervening powers asserted that they were acting '[t]o fulfill an imperious humanitarian duty'. Their motives, they proclaimed, were the wholly selfless
ones of safeguarding the general peace of Europe and consolidating the
Ottoman Empire itself.[29] Further great-power intervention with at least
some humanitarian component took place in Lebanon in 1860, when
French troops were dispatched (with the nominal consent of the Ottoman
government) in the aftermath of communal violence.[30] In the Cretan
crisis of 1897–8, referred to above, there was also a strong humanitarian
element, with the major powers intervening to put a stop to Ottoman
oppression of Greeks.[31]

It is hardly surprising to find that lawyers most sympathetic to just-
war and natural-law ideals should pronounce themselves in favour of
humanitarian intervention. One of them was the Italian writer Pasquale
Fiore, who went so far as to maintain that there was a positive duty to
intervene on the part of peoples struggling for liberty and independence.[32] In the spirit of Lorimer, he denounced *non*-intervention in
such cases as 'an egoistic policy' that was 'contrary to the laws of all'.[33]

---

[28] See France-Great Britain-Russia, Protocol of Conference, 19 July 1828, 78 CTS 457.

[29] Note to the Porte, 8 Apr. 1830, in Albrecht-Carrié (ed.), *Concert of Europe*, at 121–2. On
the Greek intervention, see Barès, *Blocus pacifique*, at 18–25.

[30] On the Lebanon crisis, see Shaw and Shaw, *Ottoman Empire*, at 142–4. For the consent of
the Ottoman government, see Convention for the Pacification of Syria, 5 Sept. 1860, 122
CTS 487. For diplomatic correspondence regarding the crisis, see 51 BFSP 278–490.

[31] Shaw and Shaw, *Ottoman Empire*, at 206–7; and Dupuis, *Principe d'équilibre*, at 391–400.

[32] 3 Fiore, *Nouveau droit*, at 2–3.

[33] 1 *ibid.* at 517–26. See also, to the same effect, Wheaton, *Elements*, at 95–7; Sadoul, *Guerre
civile*, at 59–60; and 1 Rolin, *Droit moderne*, at 162–6.

It is equally unsurprising that more orthodox positivist lawyers tended to look on humanitarian intervention with the gravest misgivings, since it appeared to be in flagrant contradiction to the pluralist ethos of positivism, with its stress on the sovereign independence of states and opposition to intervention by states in the internal affairs of one another.[34] Some writers took an in-between position, deprecating intervention in general but cautiously allowing it in very extreme cases of humanitarian abuses.[35]

Humanitarian intervention would continue to be one of the most controversial subjects of international law throughout the twentieth century and (doubtless) well into the twenty-first as well. Our concern, though, is a more limited one: to emphasise that humanitarian intervention was not regarded as a war by the positivist standards of nineteenth-century international law, thereby demonstrating, more dramatically than any other single development, how wide a gulf separated the nineteenth-century positivist view of war from the medieval natural-law one. That the purest possible example of a traditional just war, according to the old natural-law view, was now regarded as no war at all signified, more than any other single development, how dramatically the legal conception of war had been transformed between the Middle Ages and the nineteenth century.

Reprisals

At the beginning of the nineteenth century, it was easy to suppose that reprisals were a thing of the past. Special reprisals, as observed earlier, had been viewed with misgivings since their inception in the Middle Ages; and the restrictions placed on them in bilateral friendship treaties led, as was intended, to their virtual disappearance as a 'normal' practice of states. General reprisals still existed, but were regarded (as noted earlier) as fully tantamount to war and therefore no longer possessed, as it were, a distinct identity. Such a sanguinary assessment would, however, be proved very wrong, for the nineteenth century actually witnessed a dramatic rebirth of reprisals – or perhaps it would be better said to have witnessed the birth of a new kind of reprisal. This new kind

---

[34] See, for example, 1 Phillimore, *Commentaries*, at 623–4; Hall, *Treatise*, at 286–8; 1 Pradier-Fodéré, *Traité*, at 663; and Rougier, 'Théorie'.

[35] See, for example, Bluntschli, *Droit international*, at 252–5. For a thorough survey of legal views on humanitarian intervention prior to 1945, see Fonteyne, 'Customary Doctrine', at 214–36.

of reprisal differed from its medieval ancestor in three important, and related, respects. First, there was a considerable expansion in the kinds of action that a reprisal could consist of. The new kind of reprisal was not confined to the sequestering of property. Instead, it could consist of *any* act that was unlawful in the normal course of affairs but which was justifiable exceptionally, as a self-help measure against prior wrong-doing – including, crucially, a resort to military force.[36]

The second major change might be described as the 'nationalisation' of reprisals. That is to say, that reprisals were no longer directed against individual nationals of the target country located within the territory of the reprisal-taking state. Instead, the new kind of reprisal was directed against the target country as such, typically in such a form as an occupation of part of the target state's territory or the mounting of a blockade against some or all of its ports.

The third major difference between the new kind of reprisal and the old was that reprisals were no longer backward-looking or remedial in the sense of being designed simply to obtain monetary compensation for a past injury, in the manner of a civil lawsuit. Reprisals were now more apt to be coercive, or even punitive, in nature, designed primarily to compel a state government to alter its conduct in the future.[37]

It may be noted that this new style of interstate reprisals was a kind of hybrid of erstwhile special and general reprisals. It resembled general reprisals – i.e., wars – in being conducted collectively, by the nation at large, under government auspices, rather than by the specific private individuals who had been the victims of the original grievance. But the new reprisals also resembled the old special reprisals in being limited in character. Special reprisals, it will be recalled, had been limited in amount to the value of the loss caused by the original act of wrongdoing. Nineteenth-century reprisals were not delimited quite so precisely as that; but that basic principle remained in effect, in the form of a general requirement of proportionality between the amount of force being used and the goal being sought.[38]

One important effect of these changes was considerably to blur the once-sharp distinction between reprisals and war, to the point that it

---

[36] See Heffter, *Droit international*, at 211–16; 3 Phillimore, *Commentaries*, at 18–20; and 2 Oppenheim, *International Law*, at 38–41.
[37] Kelsen, *Principles*, at 20–2.
[38] Naulilaa Incident Arbitration (*Portugal v. Germany*), 31 July 1928, 2 RIAA 1011, at 1028. (Hereinafter 'Naulilaa Arbitration'.)

now began to take a very sharp legal eye to decide between them. But the essence of the distinction can be stated readily enough. Reprisals were resorts to force usually on a limited scale (in the manner of the imperfect wars of previous centuries), for the limited purpose of compelling the target country to perform its legal obligations. The British lawyer Robert Phillimore made the point with great clarity by defining reprisals squarely in just-war terms, as the employment of armed force to vindicate a right.[39] A reprisal, in short, was a law-enforcement operation; whereas a war was an attempt by a state to bend another to its will.

Reprisal à la mode

These various changes in the character of reprisals came about largely as a matter of state practice, with legal doctrine (as so often) lagging behind. Indeed, a number of legal writers largely ignored the changes and treated reprisals entirely in the traditional fashion.[40] Some, however, were alert to the new developments. The American scholar T. J. Lawrence, for example, writing early in the twentieth century, pointed out that the term 'reprisal' was now used 'in a bewildering variety of senses'.[41] The principal point about the new kind of reprisal, for present purposes, is its just-war character. This was apparent in, for example, Henry Wheaton's pithy definition of a reprisal as a 'forcible means of redress between nations', clearly implying the righting of a wrong.[42] His definition of 'war' offered a most instructive contrast: 'a contest by force between independent sovereign States' – with no suggestion of a legal claim at issue.[43]

Wars, in short, were the pursuit of *policy* by armed means; while reprisals, like the just wars of old, were the pursuit of *justice* by armed means. This is apparent from the standard definition of reprisal that was articulated by an arbitral panel in 1928, which pronounced a reprisal to be 'an act of legal self-help by the injured State, responding *after an unsatisfied demand* – to an act contrary to international law by the offending State. It has the effect of momentarily suspending, as between

---

[39] 3 Phillimore, *Commentaries*, at 18–20.
[40] See, for example, Halleck, *International Law*, at 297–310; 2 Twiss, *Law of Nations*, at 20–1, 27–9; and Woolsey, *Introduction*, at 181–4.
[41] Lawrence, *Principles*, at 334. See also Bonfils, *Manuel*, at 603; and Westlake, 'Reprisals and War', at 128–9.
[42] Wheaton, *Elements*, at 310.   [43] *Ibid.* at 313.

the two States, the observance of this or that rule of international law.'[44] The requirement that a reprisal be a response to a prior unlawful act was, of course, simply the classical just-war requirement of a *justa causa*. As in the traditional medieval just-war theory, this requirement was an objective one, with no defence for unjustified action taken in good faith. If the precipitating act was later adjudged *not* to have been unlawful, then the so-called 'reprisal' action would not be a true reprisal but rather a wrongful attack or act of aggression, for which damages would be owing.

Although nineteenth-century reprisals differed from their earlier counterparts in being directed against foreign state assets, rather than private ones, they sometimes still took the traditional form of a sequestration of property, or the seizure of a gage. A good illustration was the French seizure of the Turkish port of Mytilene in 1901. The purpose was to induce Turkey to provide satisfaction to France for a number of alleged infractions of international law to the detriment of French nationals, which France carefully identified in a diplomatic note. There was no violence or destruction. Moreover, the action was successful in inducing Turkey to reach a settlement of the dispute with France, after which France duly evacuated the captured area. It was observed, apparently without irony, that the incident was 'a truly ideal reprisal', involving no loss of life, no infringement of the interests of third parties and a wholly satisfactory outcome (for France, that is).[45] Equally satisfactory, it may be assumed, was a similar action by Britain against Nicaragua in 1895, following the arrest of the British consul, in connection with a dispute over Britain's entitlement to provide protection for the Moskito Indians in the Atlantic coast area of Nicaragua. Britain sent three warships to the port of Corinto, occupied it and delivered an ultimatum to Nicaragua, giving it twenty-four hours to respond. Nicaragua yielded and concluded a claims-settlement treaty with Britain.[46]

Sometimes, reprisal actions took a rather more violent form, such as the blockading of some or all ports of the target state. They sometimes even comprised artillery bombardments of civilian areas. In 1854, for example, American warships bombarded Greytown in Nicaragua (also known as San Juan del Norte) in response to the mistreatment of some

---

[44] Naulilaa Arbitration, at 1026. (Emphasis in the original.)
[45] See generally Moncharville, 'Conflit franco-turk'.
[46] See Great Britain-Nicaragua, Protocol for the Settlement of Claims, 1 Nov. 1895, 182 CTS 106.

American nationals which Britain was unwilling to remedy. (Britain at that time exercised the ruling power in the area.)[47] It was not always easy to distinguish reprisals from merely punitive measures. In Fiji, for example, in 1840, a group of islanders robbed an American launch that had run aground. Since the particular wrongdoers could not be found, a village of some sixty huts was burned to the ground in response. Shortly afterward, after the killing of two Americans and the wounding of another, two more villages were burned, with some fifty-seven islanders killed.[48] Britain followed a similar policy in the Pacific, carrying out reprisal-style operations, usually involving the burning of villages in the absence of any means of identifying specific individuals responsible for attacks.[49]

The basic legal contours of reprisals – and especially their affinity to former just wars – were best spelled out rather later than our present period, in 1934, by the Institute of International Law. But the principles set out at that time represented a good summation of nineteenth-century practice. There must be, it was stated, an express demand for satisfaction made to the target state prior to the action. The force employed cannot be unlimited (as in a war) but instead must be proportionate to the gravity of the offence. There could be no expansion of aims during the course of the operation; and coercive measures must be brought to a halt as soon as the satisfaction was obtained. Against a lawful reprisal (i.e., one in which a *justa causa* was present), there was no right of resistance – subject, however, to the proviso that, if the reprisal-taking state used disproportionate force, then the target country could respond forcibly.[50] All of these elements bore the clear stamp of just-war thinking, while by the same token contrasting with the prevailing position on wars.

---

[47] For diplomatic correspondence regarding this incident, see 46 BFSP 859–88.
[48] Cox, *War*, at 55.
[49] For a vivid account of this policy in action, see Papers Relating to the Punishment of Natives for Outrages Committed by Them in the Solomon Islands and Other Groups of the Western Pacific, 16 June 1881, 1881 Parl Papers, Vol. LX, at 521–38. See also Papers Relating to Armed Reprisals Inflicted upon Natives of Various Islands in the Western Pacific by HMS 'Diamond', 1886 Parl Papers, Vol. LXI, at 425–76; and Report Rear Admiral and Commander-in-Chief to Assistant High Commissioner for the Western Pacific, 3 July 1886, in Papers Relating to the Recent Operations of HMS 'Opal' Against Natives of the Solomon Islands, 1887 Parl Papers, Vol. LII, at 619–44.
[50] Institute of International Law, *Tableau général (1873–1956)*, at 167–70.

Reprisal and war

It was sometimes no easy matter for the untrained eye to distinguish reprisals from wars. An apt illustration was provided by what historians commonly refer to as the Opium 'War' between Britain and China in 1839–42. The affair was actually a reprisal action. It was sparked by allegations of mistreatment of British nationals following their arrest for unlawfully importing opium into China. It may be noted that the British government's objection was directed not against China's opium restrictions as such, but rather against alleged inhumane treatment of the British nationals whilst in Chinese custody. In April 1840, Britain issued an Order in Council citing 'injurious proceedings of certain officers of the Emperor of China towards officers and subjects of Her Majesty' and authorising reprisals against China 'with a view to obtaining . . . satisfaction and reparation'. Chinese ships and cargoes were to be captured – but, at least initially, only to be detained rather than confiscated. Confiscation would follow, it was specified, only in the event that the requisite satisfaction was not forthcoming.[51] Moreover, the Treaty of Nanking of 1842 was by no means a typical peace treaty. For one thing, it was not formally designated as such. Its preamble referred, gingerly, to the desire of the two states to end 'the misunderstandings and consequent hostilities' which had occurred. The first article, however, did state that '[t]here shall henceforward be peace and friendship between the two countries'. In addition, the treaty provided for a financial indemnity to the British for the wrongdoing, elaborately itemised to account for the specific injuries to the British nationals as well as for the cost to Britain itself of waging the conflict, clearly indicating that the affair concerned reparation for injury inflicted rather than the subjection of China to the will of Britain.[52]

In certain types of disputes, the line between reprisals and war was inherently blurry. The most notable illustration was debt claims. If a debtor state owed money to foreign investors or lenders and failed to pay it, the creditors' home countries sometimes assisted in the debt collection with a show of armed force, the most famous instance occurring in 1902–3, when Britain, Germany and Italy resorted to naval action against Venezuela. Such a measure could readily be seen either in terms

---

[51] Order in Council for the Seizure and Detention of Chinese Vessels and Goods, 3 Apr. 1840, 28 BFSP 1087–8.

[52] China-Great Britain, Treaty of Nanking, 29 Aug. 1842, 93 CTS 465, Arts. 1, 4–6, 12.

of reprisal, as the obtaining of compensation for a wrong done in the past (i.e., a failure to pay debts when they fell due), or in terms of war, as coercive action forcing a country to do something that it preferred not to do (i.e., pay money that was presently owing).

Some lawyers, though only a minority, held that there was no real distinction between armed reprisals and wars.[53] Other writers held reprisals to be, somewhat vaguely, a sort of half-way condition – 'neither wholly warlike nor wholly peaceful', in the words of T. J. Lawrence.[54] The prevailing view, however, was that forcible reprisals were not war, but instead consisted of *acts* of hostility occurring during a *state* of peace.[55] As Hall put it, reprisals were 'acts of war in fact, though not in intention'.[56] As to the legal distinction between reprisals and wars, the two schools of positivist thought differed in predictable and characteristic ways. In general, those of the subjective persuasion held that reprisals were not wars because of an absence of an intention on the part of the reprisal-taking state to that effect. Those of the objective viewpoint held that reprisals differed from wars in being one-way resorts to armed force, with the target country refraining from fighting back. In practice, these two ways of looking at the matter came to much the same thing, since, in cases of a one-way use of force, there would commonly also be an absence of an *animus belligerendi* on the part of the state using force.

In reality, nineteenth-century lawyers distinguished war from reprisals according to a broader and somewhat looser range of criteria, which may be briefly noted – with the criteria basically mirroring the ways in which old just wars differed from modern positivist ones. Most strikingly, as noted above, reprisals required a *justa causa*, while wars did not. In addition, the conduct of reprisals was subject to a principle of proportionality, as wars were not. That is to say, there had to be at least a measure of equivalence between the injury done by the reprisal-taker and the injury that it had originally suffered.[57] If the reprisal-taking state strayed beyond the bounds of proportionality, then its acts ceased to be measures of lawful self-help and became, instead, unlawful acts of aggression.[58] In a true war, in contrast, each side was entitled to throw its entire strength against the enemy, without any quantitative

---

[53] See, for example, Despagnet, *Cours*, at 592–6.   [54] Lawrence, *Principles*, at 344.
[55] 7 J. B. Moore, *Digest*, at 153–4.
[56] Hall, *Treatise*, at 365. See also Lawrence, *Principles*, at 334.
[57] Naulilaa Arbitration, at 1028.   [58] See Hall, *Treatise*, at 367–8.

limit (provided, of course, that the laws of war were observed in the process). In addition, in a reprisal, captured property could only be sequestered (or held as a gage), not confiscated. According to British prize courts, private property was wholly exempt from capture in a reprisal; whereas in a war, capture of private property at sea (though not on land) continued to be allowed. After 1907, it was generally agreed that the Hague Convention on the Opening of Hostilities applied only to wars and not to reprisals. On this point, however, the distinction was not really so great as might first be supposed, since reprisals had to be preceded by a formal demand for redress, which clearly would bear at least a strong family resemblance to an ultimatum. The difference probably was that the demand for redress would not necessarily have to be accompanied by an express threat to resort to force, as an ultimatum would. This point, however, never received judicial attention.

War and reprisals also differed with regard to their impact on treaties between the states concerned. While there was disagreement amongst lawyers on whether a state of war automatically terminated treaties between the warring parties, there was universal accord that a reprisal situation did *not*. It was also common for diplomatic relations between the states to continue while reprisal action was being taken, whereas diplomatic relations were invariably ruptured during a war. Yet another key difference between war and reprisal concerned the rights of the victorious party. In a reprisal case, the victorious party was entitled *only* to appropriate satisfaction for the actual wrongdoing that had precipitated the incident. In a war, the victorious party was entitled to dictate to its defeated foe whatever terms its superiority of power allowed. In other words, the principles of the medieval *jus victoriae* governed reprisal situations, but not wars.

Probably the single most important of all the differences concerned third parties: that reprisals did not trigger the application of the law of neutrality, as wars of course did. That meant that a clear external sign that a given resort to arms was a war rather than a reprisal was the exercise of any of the normal rights of belligerents *vis-à-vis* neutral states (such as the visiting and searching of neutral ships at sea or the enforcement of blockades). More specifically, the position was that such an exercise of belligerents' rights must necessarily be *either* a lawful belligerent act within the framework of a state of war, *or* an *un*lawful act of aggression or piracy in a state of peace – with, not surprisingly, a heavy presumption in favour of the existence of a state of war. This point was instructively illustrated in 1884–5, when France took military action against China, as a reaction to China's support of insurgents in northern Vietnam, which at the time was the French protectorate of Tonking. France referred to the crisis as a 'state of reprisals' rather than as a war.[59] The French Prime Minister Jules Ferry was said to have described the action, intriguingly, as 'a policy of intelligent destruction'.[60] Diplomatic relations between the two countries remained intact. The French action, however, included the blockading of a number of ports in Formosa. Britain objected to the French characterisation of the conflict as a reprisal, insisting that, if the blockades were enforced against third states, then the conflict must necessarily be a war rather than a reprisal.[61] In the event, the conflict ended without a definitive resolution of the point.

On a later occasion, this same issue was pressed forcefully by a third state, with revealing results. This occurred in a crisis in 1902–3, involving action by several European powers against Venezuela. A coalition of three European states (Britain, Germany and Italy) mounted a blockade against Venezuela, for its failure to satisfy various claims of injuries to their nationals. There was also a shelling (by German ships) of a Venezuelan fort. The United States, like Britain in the Formosa case, insisted that a blockade could only be enforced against third states if there was a true, legal state of war. Otherwise, the Americans insisted, its ships would be under no duty to respect the 'blockade' – and would refuse on principle to do so.[62]

Britain, on the basis of its own precedent from the Formosa affair, supported the American position and duly acknowledged that the fracas was indeed a war. Prime Minister Arthur Balfour, when asked in Parliament whether the country was at war, scornfully replied: 'Does the honourable and learned gentleman suppose that without a state of war you can take the ships of another power and blockade its ports?'[63] This must rank as history's most off-hand declaration of war. The Foreign Minister, Lord Lansdowne, confirmed the position by stating that the establishment of the blockade *ipso facto* created a state of war.[64] Germany took a similar position.[65] Moreover, the treaty concluded at the end of the crisis between Britain and Venezuela echoed Lansdowne

---

[59] Perels, 'Droit de blocus', at 470.
[60] Lawrence, *Principles*, at 336. See also 2 Westlake, *International Law*, at 14–15.
[61] Granville to Waddington, 11 Nov. 1884, 76 BFSP 426–7.
[62] Note from US to British government, 13 Dec. 1902, in 1903 FRUS 454–5.
[63] Remarks of Balfour, Parl. Deb., vol. 116, ser. 4, col. 1491, 17 Dec. 1902.
[64] Lansdowne to Herbert, 13 Jan. 1903, 96 BFSP 481.
[65] Basdevant, 'Action coercitive', at 262–3.

by expressly stating that the British blockade had 'created, *ipso facto*, a state of war' between the two countries.[66] T. J. Lawrence expressed the somewhat cautious conclusion that the Venezuelan incident was 'undoubtedly a war, though a little one'.[67]

In the course of the nineteenth century, states devised a type of blockade tailored specially for reprisals, as distinct from a true blockade employed in war. This reprisal-style operation was known, in somewhat unfortunate terminology, as a 'pacific blockade'. A pacific blockade was distinguished from a belligerent blockade in two ways. First, it was enforced only against ships of the country whose territory was being invested, i.e., there was no interference with third-state vessels. A belligerent blockade, in contrast, was enforced against the ships of the whole world (including those of the blocking power itself). Second, in a pacific blockade, ships of the target country, when captured, would only be sequestered, pending resolution of the crisis. In a belligerent blockade, the ships and their cargoes would be confiscated by means of a judicial proceeding in a prize court. This conclusion was set out by the Institute of International Law (a private scholarly body) in a resolution in 1887, in the wake of the great-power action against Greece of the previous year.[68]

A classic illustration of a pacific blockade was the Don Pacifico affair of 1850, involving Britain and Greece. In response to the mistreatment of a British national (Don Pacifico) at the hands of a mob in Greece, Britain demanded redress from the Greek government. When this was not forthcoming, Britain invested five ports in the Gulf of Lepanto with blockades, capturing some fifty to sixty ships in the process. All of these vessels, however, were Greek, since Britain scrupulously refrained from capturing third-state shipping. The British even allowed Greek ships to pass through the blockades, if they were transporting cargoes belonging to non-Greek nationals. Britain also confined itself to sequestering the

---

[66] Great Britain-Venezuela, Exchange of Notes Renewing and Confirming Former Treaties, 13 Feb. 1903, 192 CTS 413. See also, however, a companion agreement, of the same date, which stated, more cautiously, that 'it may be contended' that a blockade *ipso facto* means war. Great Britain-Venezuela, Protocol for the Settlement of British Claims, 13 Feb. 1903, *ibid.* at 414.

[67] Lawrence, *Principles*, at 342. See, to the same effect, 2 Westlake, *International Law*, at 15–16. On this incident, see generally Hogan, *Pacific Blockade*, at 149–57; and Kotzsch, 'Blockade'.

[68] 'Blockade in the Absence of a State of War', in J. B. Scott (ed.), *Resolutions*, at 69–70. For the report on which the resolution was based, see Perels, 'Droit de blocus', at 463–74, which contains a good summary of the range of scholarly opinion on the question. See also Barès, *Blocus pacifique*, at 149–50; and 1 Rolin, *Droit moderne*, at 131.

Greek ships rather than condemning them, thereby further signalling the action as a reprisal rather than a war.[69] (The action, incidentally, produced the desired effect, in the form of a claims-settlement agreement between the two states.)[70]

The discussion so far has been concerned with ways in which the reprisal-*taking* country would indicate the legal character of its action. It should be appreciated, though, that it was within the power of the target country to upset those plans by transmuting what began as a reprisal into a war.[71] It could achieve this feat in either of two ways: by issuing a declaration of war, or by electing to fight back.[72] Lawrence candidly opined that any 'powerful and high-spirited nation' would react to a reprisal by declaring war.[73] This transformational power in the hands of the target country was nowhere better illustrated than in a bizarre incident, not lacking in comic-opera elements, between France and Mexico: the so-called 'Pastry War' of 1838. The affair began as a forcible reprisal by France against Mexico, for Mexico's alleged failure to pay compensation to France for losses suffered by a French pastry cook in Mexico whose shop was looted by a mob. France sent a fleet to Veracruz, which demanded the payment of 60,000 pesos compensation, plus assurances against future mistreatment, plus the granting of some trading concessions. With Mexico's failure to respond within the time given, France broke diplomatic relations with Mexico, declared a blockade of Veracruz and strengthened the armed force.[74] It also bombarded and then occupied a fort on the outskirts of the town. France carefully held to the view, though, that its action was a reprisal and not a resort to war. To that end, it notified Britain that the occupation of the fort was merely by way of security – i.e., the taking of gage.[75] Mexico, however, in a brazen (if not altogether prudent) display of high spirits, upset France's plans by declaring war.

The incident is instructive because it gave rise to arbitral proceedings in which the legal nature of the hostilities was considered. On the subjective theory of war, the conflict would be held to be a war purely

---

[69] Hogan, *Pacific Blockade*, at 105–14.
[70] Great Britain-Greece, Convention for the Settlement of Claims, 18 July 1850, 104 CTS 159. On pacific blockade, see generally Barès, *Blocus pacifique*; and Hogan, *Pacific Blockade*.
[71] Hogan, *Pacific Blockade*, at 70; and 2 Oppenheim, *International Law*, at 127.
[72] See Hall, *Treatise*, at 365–6; and 2 Oppenheim, *International Law*, at 83, 104–6.
[73] Lawrence, *Principles*, at 343.
[74] For the blockade notification of 1 June 1838, see 26 BFSP 725–7.
[75] Count Molé to Earl Granville, 19 Sept. 1838, *ibid.* at 897.

on the unilateral intention of Mexico. On the objective theory of war, in contrast, a war would exist only if there was an *actual* and *mutual* clash of arms between two states (with the commencement date of the war then back-dated to the time of the *initial* use of armed force). The concrete question at stake in the arbitration concerned the status of Mexican ships captured by France: whether France held them by way of sequestration (as it would in a case of reprisal or the taking of a gage), or whether it had title to them by way of capture according to the laws of war (if the conflict was a true war). The decision of the arbitrator (the queen of Britain) was that the conflict was a war and that France consequently acquired full title to the ships. Unfortunately, the reasoning in the decision was not set out in great detail. It would appear, though, that the decision in favour of war was based not on the Mexican declaration alone but rather on an overall survey of the facts of the case, indicating, if only rather ambivalently, support for the objective theory of war.[76]

Opposition to reprisals

The nineteenth century has been described as 'the classic epoch of reprisals'.[77] Many lawyers strongly approved of them, on the ground that they were preferable to the more drastic device of war. Both Wolff and Vattel had expressed this view in the eighteenth century, holding that states were obligated to employ reprisals instead of war, on the general principle that less drastic remedies should be used instead of harsher ones wherever possible.[78] In the nineteenth century, T. J. Lawrence echoed their position, judging reprisals to be 'a useful alternative to war'.[79] In a similar vein, Hall praised reprisals as 'a means of constraint much milder than actual war, and therefore . . . preferable'. He approved of pacific blockade as 'a convenient practice, . . . a mild one in its effects even upon [the target] country', pointing out that it could function 'as a measure of international police, when hostile action would be inappropriate and no action less stringent would be

---

[76] Responsibility for Acts of War (*France* v. *Mexico*), 1 Aug. 1844, 1 RAI 545. See also 'Note doctrinale', *ibid.* at 560–79. For a short account of the crisis, see Barès, *Blocus pacifique*, at 32–5.

[77] Charles de Visscher, *Theory and Reality in Public International Law* (Princeton: Princeton University Press, 1968), at 296.

[78] Wolff, *Law of Nations*, at 310; and Vattel, *Law of Nations*, at 231–2.

[79] Lawrence, *Principles*, at 343–4.

effective'.[80] Echoing (no doubt unconsciously) Augustine's view of just wars as exercises in 'benevolent severity', Hall even maintained that reprisals had many benefits for the target countries as well as for the reprisal-taking states.

> It is true [he conceded] that [the] very mildness [of reprisal action] may tempt strong powers to employ it against weak countries on occasions when, if debarred from its use, they would not resort to hostilities; but it is not to be forgotten that weak countries sometimes presume upon their weakness, and that the possibility of taking measures against them less severe than war may be as much to their advantage as to that of the injured power.[81]

A number of lawyers dissented from this approving and permissive attitude towards reprisals, maintaining that reprisal actions offered all *too* many conveniences as compared to war – with the result that states might seek to pursue their national policies under the heading of reprisal instead of war, precisely to exploit some of the legal distinctions between them. Even lawyers who looked with favour on reprisals conceded this. Lawrence, for example, admitted that states which were minded to launch a surprise attack on an enemy could do so by characterising the conflict as a reprisal instead of as a war, so as to avoid the strictures of the Hague Convention of 1907.[82] The British writer John Westlake also acknowledged that pacific blockades had the effect of 'increas[ing] the power of the strong over the weak'. Also, by 'confusing the bounds of the use of force in time of peace [pacific blockade] impairs the certainty which is so important in international relations'.[83] Ernest Nys, a Belgian lawyer and legal historian, objected that a state should not be allowed to resort to force to compel another to bend to its will while at the same time denying that there was a state of war. If that were allowed, he objected, then the state taking the reprisals would be free of all burdens imposed by the law of neutrality. It would be able, for example, to have warships fitted out for it in neutral ports and to use neutral ports as bases of naval operations – neither of which would be allowed in a true war.[84] (In response, it might be pointed out that a state acting under the banner of reprisals would also be unable to reap the *benefits* of the law of neutrality. For example, it would not be able to visit and search

---

[80] Hall, *Treatise*, at 371–2.   [81] *Ibid.* at 372.
[82] Lawrence, *Principles*, at 344.   [83] 2 Westlake, *International Law*, at 18.
[84] 2 Nys, *Droit international*, at 587. See also 1 Rolin, *Droit moderne*, at 110–12.

third-state ships on the high seas or to enforce blockades or to capture arms that were shipped to the target country.) The French lawyer Paul Pradier-Fodéré condemned reprisals as contrary to 'true civilisation'. He maintained that they entailed injuries to innocent persons and that they poisoned relations between states. Far from preventing wider wars, he believed, they were more likely to lead to them. Like Nys, he condemned them as a means by which powerful states imposed their will onto weaker ones without shouldering the inconveniences that a declaration of war would entail. Reprisals, in his view, were merely 'a fact and not an exercise of right' – and, as such, were for all practical purposes simply a type of war.[85]

There certainly was no lack of cases in which the rules governing reprisals were abused by the major powers. It was not uncommon for reprisals to go beyond the limits of merely putting an end to specific acts of wrongdoing, sometimes leading to permanent annexations. This occurred in 1815, following British reprisals against the Kingdom of Kandy in the interior of Ceylon, which were sparked by the mistreatment of some British nationals. Another notable case was the French occupation of Algeria in 1830, which began as a reprisal action, to avenge an insult to a French consul three years earlier. It ended as an annexation that endured until 1962. The (so-called) Opium War between Britain and China was another illustration. Although, as noted above, it was essentially a reprisal operation, some of the benefits that accrued to Britain from it – notably the opening of five Chinese ports to British trade and residence and the cession of Hong Kong Island – went beyond the scope of the precipitating grievances.[86]

During the drama of the Venezuelan blockade crisis of 1902–3, the Foreign Minister of Argentina, Luis Drago, took the initiative of pressing for a complete legal prohibition against forcible reprisals in one particular class of cases: those in which states defaulted on contractual obligations to private creditors, a position that became known in legal circles as the 'Drago Doctrine'. It won the endorsement of the United States (which had pointedly refrained from participating in the Venezuelan blockade) and, in a slightly limited form, of the Second Hague Peace Conference of 1907. The Conference adopted the Porter Convention (named for the American delegate who played the leading role in its drafting), which provided that armed force could be resorted

---

[85] 6 Pradier-Fodéré, *Traité*, at 487–9.
[86] China–Great Britain, Treaty of Nanking, 29 Aug. 1842, 93 CTS 465, Arts. 2, 3.

to in contract-debt cases *only* if the debtor country failed to submit the matter to arbitration (or if it failed to carry out an arbitral judgment).[87] This marked the first occasion in which the international community agreed to a restriction on the use of armed force. Some favoured going further in this direction. The Argentine legal scholar Carlos Calvo, most notably, contended that international law, properly understood, barred the use of armed force for the collection of *any* kind of pecuniary claim.[88] Westlake, in a similar vein, favoured extending the Porter Convention rules to pecuniary claims in general. These broader proposals, however, failed to win acceptance.[89]

Emergency action

The third category of measures short of war, after interventions and reprisals, consisted of what may broadly be characterised as acts of necessity. These were acts taken in the face of a dire emergency, and involving some kind of infringement of the normal legal rights of other states – with the infringement being excused in the particular case by the exigencies of the emergency situation. Such acts differed from reprisals in that reprisals were responses to prior *unlawful* acts by target states, whereas acts of necessity required no prior unlawfulness.[90] The measures taken were justified wholly by the danger faced by the state taking the action. This meant, in turn, that acts of necessity lacked any character of hostility towards the parties whose rights were invaded. There was no intention on the part of the country resorting to the emergency measures to impose its will onto another state. Its only motive was to preserve itself from danger.

Acts of necessity differed from intervention and reprisals in having been regarded, since the Middle Ages, as quite distinct from just wars properly speaking. They were rooted in the primordial human instinct of survival, which Thomas Aquinas had identified as one of the three

---

[87] Hague Convention II, Respecting the Limitation of the Employment of Force for the Recovery of Contract Debts (Porter Convention), 18 Oct. 1907, 205 CTS 250. It may be noted that the Porter Convention only restricted armed *reprisals*, leaving open the possibility of actual war. On this treaty, see G. W. Scott, 'Hague Convention'.

[88] Hershey, 'Calvo and Drago Doctrines', at 26–8, 31.

[89] Westlake, 'Reprisals and War', at 134–7.

[90] For this reason, Oppenheim maintained that necessity was not a true *right* because there was no duty on the affected state's part to submit to the measures. Necessity was merely a defence to a legal claim that might be brought. 2 Oppenheim, *International Law*, at 177–81.

fundamental natural inclinations of humans (the other two being the
propagation of the species and the quest for wisdom).[91] Pufendorf had
recognised the principle of necessity as an omnipresent 'wild card' in the
law, more fundamental even than the duty to adhere to agreements. If
adherence to an agreement would threaten the very life of the state – or,
by slight modification, a fundamental value or interest of the state – then
the obligation need not be performed.[92] Necessity therefore meant, in a
certain immediate or technical sense, breaching the law. More importantly, though, it meant stepping *outside* the law in the interest of self-
preservation – an interest that was seen to be of higher worth than the
rule of law itself.

   Sometimes, acts of necessity, instead of taking the 'negative' form of
declining to carry out obligations under a treaty, took the more robust
and 'positive' guise of armed action. The archetypal illustration was
provided by Britain in 1807, when it landed armed forces in Denmark,
destroyed part of the Danish fleet at Copenhagen and took possession of
the remainder. The two countries were not at war. Nor was there any
contention or pretence of any wrongful act on Denmark's part towards
Britain. The purpose of the attack was to prevent advancing French
armies – who, to put it mildly, *were* enemies of the British – from
invading Denmark, capturing the Danish fleet and then using it to
challenge British supremacy on the high seas. In 1914, at the outset of
the Great War, came another famous, or notorious, case of necessity in
action: the German invasion and occupation of Belgium. Germany
frankly conceded that the act was prima facie unlawful, as a violation
of Belgium's neutrality (of which Germany itself was a guarantor). It
contended, however, that the invasion was justified on the ground of
imperious necessity. The German contention was that France was about
to attack it through Belgium and that it was entitled to assurances from
Belgium that it would prevent the attack, as its neutrality obligated it to
do. Belgium's failure to give a credible assurance to that effect entitled
Germany, on its argument, to take the initiative itself, in the only
effective way possible, to forestall the anticipated emergency.[93]

   Acts of necessity fell into various sub-categories, classifiable in various
ways. Here, for the sake of convenience, they will be discussed in, so to

---

[91] Aquinas, *Treatise on Law*, at 250.   [92] Pufendorf, *Nature and Nations*, at 295–309.
[93] On the German invasion of Belgium see Barbara Tuchman, *The Guns of August* (New
York: Macmillan, 1962), at 313–24. See also Henri Davignon, *Belgium and Germany: Texts
and Documents* (London: T. Nelson and Sons, 1915).

speak, temporal order: first, action taken in the very face of the peril (self-defence and the rescue of nationals); second, action taken in the immediate aftermath of a crisis (hot pursuit); and finally, action taken after a certain time interval (punitive expeditions).

Self-defence

Self-defence continued, throughout the nineteenth century, to play only a shadowy and peripheral role in international law, remaining, as before, at a safe juridical remove from war properly speaking.[94] Treatise writers seldom bothered to deal with it, except insofar as it was subsumed under the broader heading of the general right of self-preservation.[95] The American writer (and military general) H. W. Halleck had some interesting, if fairly conventional, thoughts on the subject. He carefully distinguished self-defence action from belligerency. Self-defence, in keeping with the view that had prevailed since the Middle Ages, was regarded as defensive in the strict sense of fending off an attack. That meant, in Halleck's view, the defence of the physical territory of a state from attack by outside forces, by such means as building and manning fortifications at the borders. Any activity that strayed outside the borders of the state was, *ipso facto*, outside the scope of self-defence and in the quite distinct realm of belligerency.[96]

If the nineteenth century contributed nothing significant in the way of doctrine on the subject of self-defence, it did provide an incident in state practice that remains in the everyday repertoire of international lawyers to the present day. This was the *Caroline* affair of 1837, involving Britain and the United States. It arose out of an insurrectionary situation in Upper Canada, in which insurgent forces took refuge in United States territory and mounted attacks on British authority from there (with support from some sympathetic American nationals). The soon-to-be-famous ship called the *Caroline* was owned by some American sympathisers and supporters of the insurgents and was to be used for transport service in support of the rebel forces. The British authorities, however, forestalled these plans by mounting a preemptive action.

---

[94] See Descamps, 'Influence', at 469–75.
[95] See, for example, Halleck, *International Law*, at 91–2; Twiss, *Law of Nations*, at 3–5; 3 Phillimore, *Commentaries*, at 312–21; Hall, *Treatise*, at 265–80; and 1 Oppenheim, *International Law*, at 177–81. See also Alexandrov, *Self-defense*, at 19–27.
[96] Halleck, *International Law*, at 93–4.

British forces crossed into American territory, without the consent of the American government, took possession of the *Caroline* and terminated its nautical career by sending it over Niagara Falls (with some loss of life in the process).[97] This bold (if somewhat high-handed) British initiative provoked an outcry in the United States. Most notably, President Martin Van Buren denounced it as 'an outrage of the most aggravated character', characterising it as 'a hostile though temporary invasion of our Territory'.[98]

This was hardly a case of self-defence in the classic sense of one state defending itself against an aggressive attack by another. Although the British operation took place on American territory, it was in no sense directed against the United States as such. Nor was there any suggestion of an American invasion of Canadian territory. Instead, the operation was directed against a band of individual miscreants, acting on their own behalf, who happened to be using American territory as a base of operations and (they hoped) as a sanctuary. The affair, in short, was more in the nature of an act of trespass, or an extraterritorial law-enforcement operation, although Britain's justification for its action was couched in the language of self-defence. It described the operation as 'a justifiable employment of force for the purpose of defending the British territory' from unprovoked attacks by insurgents taking refuge in American territory.[99] The American Secretary of State, Daniel Webster, conceded that a response of this kind could be justifiable – but only in a case of 'clear and absolute necessity'.[100] In Webster's formulation, which was to become the canonical formulation of self-defence in the narrow sense, there must be 'a necessity of self-defence, instant, overwhelming, leaving no choice of means, and no moment for deliberation'.[101]

It is well to take some note of the distinction between self-defence and forcible reprisals. To some extent, the gap between the two was narrower than it had been in past centuries, now that reprisals no longer consisted only of property sequestration as in earlier times. For the most part, though, the traditional distinctions between the two types of operation continued to hold good. One was that a reprisal, now as ever, required the occurrence of a prior act of legal wrongdoing. Self-defence, however,

---

[97] For a general account of the *Caroline* affair, see Kenneth R. Stevens, *Border Diplomacy: The Caroline and McLeod Affairs in Anglo-American-Canadian Relations, 1837–1842* (Tuscaloosa: University of Alabama Press, 1989).

[98] Message from the President to Congress, 8 Jan. 1838, 26 BFSP 1372–3.

[99] Fox to Webster, 12 Mar. 1841, 29 *ibid.* at 1127.

[100] Webster to Fox, 24 Apr. 1841, *ibid.* at 1133.   [101] *Ibid* at 1137–8.

rooted as it was in necessity, was not dependent on any prior wrong-doing, a point appreciated since the Middle Ages.[102] The most obvious difference between self-defence and reprisals lay in the timing. Self-defence was the warding off of a blow *as* it was being struck (in the present tense, as it were), to prevent the wrong from being consummated; whereas reprisal was punitive or remedial action taken *after* the completion of the offence. In the twentieth century, these distinctions would become seriously blurred; but for the present, the two types of operation were still tolerably distinct.[103]

Rescuing nationals in peril

The rescuing of nationals who faced perils in foreign territory was yet another form of action under the broad heading of necessity. It closely resembled self-defence in that it was action taken against an actual ongoing danger. There were some differences, though. One was that it was perhaps more accurate to characterise rescue missions as defences of *others* rather than as *self*-defence, since the persons rescued would not be the ones carrying out the operation. As such, this action – along with humanitarian intervention – was the nineteenth century's purest illustration of a just war in the classical medieval sense.

Sometimes, the danger to the nationals was posed directly and deliberately by foreign governments. A striking example occurred in 1868, when various British nationals, including a consular official and British government envoy, were held captive by Emperor Theodore of Ethiopia. As a first step, Britain stopped the planned shipment of equipment and skilled personnel to Ethiopia. When that failed to induce cooperative behaviour, an ultimatum (as it might fairly be termed) was presented to Theodore, informing him that a military expedition was being mounted that would 'force a concession which you have hitherto withheld from friendly representation'. Delivering up the prisoners, it stated, was 'the only means of preserving your country from war and your own power from overthrow'.[104] The military force was duly dispatched. It defeated the Ethiopian forces in a pitched battle in April 1868, and the Emperor immediately released the prisoners. This crisis is instructive in another respect: as an illustration of how rescue missions, like other interventions,

---

[102] Grotius, *War and Peace*, at 172–3.   [103] See, on this point, Chapter 9 below.
[104] Lord Stanley to Theodore, 9 Sept. 1867, 60 BFSP 1088.

could readily evolve into something rather larger. In this case, the British force, after releasing the prisoners, went on to lay siege to the town of Magdala, which it duly captured. During this phase of the proceedings, Theodore himself was killed. The British forces then retired from the country with no attempt made at annexation (though with a considerable haul of booty).

The dangers to foreign nationals were sometimes posed by insurgent forces rather than by government ones. An especially revealing instance occurred in 1873, involving dangers to British and German nationals. The danger in question arose out of civil strife in Spain, in which insurgent forces (ominously named the *Intransigentes*) had taken to the seas and begun extorting money from seaside towns with threats of bombardment. The British government acted to protect its nationals. In so doing, however, it carefully instructed its armed forces that Spanish ships were to be seized only in situations of 'absolute necessity'.[105] The British fleet was instructed to 'require' the Spanish insurgent force to refrain from bombarding Malaga and 'to enforce this demand if it refused'.[106] The German policy was similar: naval vessels were to 'prevent the bombardment of towns until such time as the life and property of Germans are in safety'.[107] In the event, the British and Germans captured two Spanish rebel ships, detained the rebel leader as a hostage and transferred the vessels to the government in Madrid.[108]

Another striking example of the rescue of nationals from insurgent action was a joint military operation mounted by a group of major powers in China in 1900, for the relief of persons besieged for some eight weeks in the diplomatic compound in Peking by the so-called Boxers. This action was difficult to classify legally. Prime Minister Salisbury of Britain insisted that the operation did not amount to a war, on the ground that the acts of the Boxers were not attributable to the Chinese government. The conflict, that is to say, was not a clash between *public* forces of the two countries. The German Foreign Office agreed.[109] The Chinese government, however, seems to have taken a different view. In effect, it ratified the action of the Boxers, when the Dowager Empress praised them as a loyal militia. This statement has

---

[105] Granville to Adams, 11 Aug. 1873, 65 BFSP 756–7. See also Granville to Lyons, 20 Aug. 1873, *ibid.* at 769–72.

[106] Hammond to the Secretary to the Admiralty, 30 July 1873, *ibid.* at 747.

[107] Munster to Granville, 9 Aug. 1873, *ibid.* at 759–60.

[108] For correspondence relating to this incident, see generally *ibid.* at 744–92.

[109] Grob, *Relativity*, at 201–3.

been described by some historians (if not lawyers) as a declaration of war. It may also be noted that an American court held the conflict to constitute a true war, on the ground that the American government was 'prosecuting its right ... by force of arms'.[110]

Rescue missions, like reprisal actions, sometimes resulted in long-term political dominance of the state in which the rescue took place, or even, in the most extreme case, to outright annexation. The most notable example occurred in Egypt in 1881–2, when a group of discontented Egyptian military officers, resentful of the increasing Western influence in their country, seized effective control of the government. This takeover, which was accompanied by mob attacks against Westerners, led to armed intervention by the British and to the forcible removal of the nationalist government from power. From that point, Egypt became a de facto dependency of Britain.[111] A number of American interventions in the Caribbean also involved rather expansive ideas about what was necessary to give effective protection to American interests. A striking illustration was the American occupation of the Dominican Republic in 1916. The immediate concern was a threat to American interests posed by a revolution. The operation, however, soon turned into an eight-year occupation of the country.[112]

There was comparatively little scholarly debate in this area. Elihu Root conceded that rescue operations like the subduing of the Boxer Rebellion in China necessarily involve 'an impeachment of the effective sovereignty' of the territorial state. Moreover, they often lead to abuses such as the showing of 'arrogant and offensive disrespect' to the host country. But he concluded that 'international custom' gives to states the right to intervene with armed force to protect their nationals, provided that certain criteria are met. Basically, there must be 'unquestionable facts which leave no practical doubt of the incapacity of the government of the country to perform its international duty of protection'.[113] This was not an easy standard to apply in practice. As a general statement of legal principle, however, it was difficult to fault.

---

[110] *Hamilton* v. *McClaughry*, 136 F 445 (Cir. Ct, Dist. Kan., 1904), at 450. On the Boxer intervention generally, see Grob, *Relativity*, at 64–79.

[111] Technically, it continued to be part of the Ottoman Empire. In 1914, after Turkey joined the Central powers in the Great War, Britain at last formally declared Egypt to be a protectorate.

[112] See Brown, 'Armed Occupation'.   [113] Root, 'Basis of Protection', at 521.

Hot pursuit and punitive expeditions

The hot pursuit by military forces of criminals or attackers into the territory of foreign states was another form that the protean principle of necessity took. In temporal terms, it fell between self-defence and reprisals but decidedly nearer to self-defence. It differed from self-defence in consisting of action not in the *very* face of an attack, but in the aftermath. If it occurred in the immediate aftermath of an attack, before the attacker had time to return to his home territory, then it would be an instance of hot pursuit. So close was the connection between hot pursuit and self-defence that early commentators tended to treat them in much the same light. Grotius, for example, had effectively elided the two by holding, somewhat cautiously, that 'no one... will censure' a traveller who, when attacked by a highwayman, went beyond strict self-defence by taking his assailant captive.[114] Another way in which punitive action resembled self-defence (in the narrow sense) lay in the fact that it involved action against the *very* parties who had committed the wrong, thereby differing from reprisals in which the particular parties affected were often not themselves guilty of misconduct.

Hot pursuit could take place *in* the territory of a foreign state without being regarded as an act of hostility *against* that state, although it was arguable that a violation of sovereignty would be involved, in the form of an act of trespass (as it might be termed).[115] An example of a claim to a right of hot pursuit was the claim made by the United States in the 1830s, of a right to pursue marauding Indian bands into Mexico. In so doing, the American government carefully distinguished hot pursuit from war, characterising hot pursuit as an exercise of 'the immutable principles of self-defence'. That principle, in the American view, entailed a right to take 'decisive measures of precaution to prevent irreparable evil to our own or to a neighboring people'.[116] In 1853, the United States contended that, if Mexico was remiss in restraining Indians on its side of the border, then the task could be taken in hand, on a self-help basis, by American forces operating across the border.[117]

---

[114] Grotius, *Commentary*, at 327–8.

[115] See, however, Halleck, *International Law*, at 94–6, who held hot-pursuit expeditions to be belligerent in nature, by virtue of the fact that they involved armed action outside the state's territory.

[116] Forsyth to Ellis (Minister in Mexico), 10 Dec. 1836; quoted in Hershey, 'Incursions', at 559.

[117] J. B. Scott, 'Punitive Expedition', at 339. See also Hershey, 'Incursions'.

Punitive action differed from hot pursuit in taking place at some temporal remove from the precipitating incident. In practice, however, distinctions were often not so sharp as they were in theory. The lines between self-defence, reprisal and punishment could be very hazy, particularly when private (or ostensibly private) wrongdoers were in some fashion allied with a state – say, by using a state's territory as a base of operation or as a sanctuary. In such a case, there could be a sort of composite action: defensive or punitive operations against the wrong-doers themselves, combined with reprisal action against the state harbouring them.

An illustration was the response of the United States to attacks on its shipping by North African corsairs in the early nineteenth century. In 1802, the Congress, stating that Tripoli had embarked on 'a predatory warfare against the United States', authorised President Jefferson to employ armed vessels 'for protecting effectually the commerce and sea-men' of the country.[118] This was accomplished not in a passive manner by, say, escorting ships to prevent attacks, but in a rather more active fashion by mounting a blockade of Tripoli itself. It may be noted, though, that this congressional authorisation did not purport to be a declaration of war. In 1815, similar action was authorised against Algerian predators.[119] It too did not purport, on its face at least, to be a declaration of war.[120]

Sometimes, punitive action was taken against private parties not allied with any state. The classic illustration consisted of military operations against pirate bases. In 1809 and again in 1819, for example, British forces attacked pirates based on the island of Ras al-Khayma in the Persian Gulf.[121] In 1817, the United States Navy similarly attacked a pirate base on Amelia Island, off the coast of Florida.[122] So long as these operations were directed against what may be called free-standing or independent pirate groups, they were regarded simply as law-enforcement actions, albeit of an extraterritorial character. Sometimes, it was difficult to discern whether a pirate group was connected with a state or not. An instructively close case occurred in 1832, when the United States Navy took action against a settlement on the Falkland Islands, from which

---

[118] Act of 6 Feb. 1802, 2 Stat 129. [119] Act of 3 Mar. 1815, 3 Stat 230.

[120] On American action against the Barbary pirate states of North Africa, see generally Sofaer, *War*, at 208–24.

[121] See generally Charles E. Davies, *The Blood-red Arab Flag: An Investigation into Qasimi Piracy, 1797–1820* (Exeter: University of Exeter Press, 1997).

[122] See Sofaer, *War*, at 337–41.

attacks on shipping had been launched. There was some reason to believe that these activities were carried on under the auspices, or at least with the approval, of the government of Buenos Aires. If that had been the case, then the normal procedure would have been to lodge a formal protest with that government and then to consider war measures if satisfaction was not forthcoming.[123] Against mere criminals, however, the general view was that direct action could be taken without the niceties of prior warning or negotiation.[124]

The most famous of all punitive expeditions was directed not against aboriginal peoples but rather against a privately organised army in the wake of a terrorist attack. This was an American expedition into Mexico in 1916–17, which was even officially designated as *the* Punitive Expedition. Its goal was the capture and punishment of Francisco ('Pancho') Villa for the commission of two outrages in early 1916. First was the cold-blooded summary shooting of sixteen Americans taken from a train in northern Mexico. Second was Villa's spectacular raid into American territory in March 1916, which culminated in the burning of Columbus, New Mexico, with the deaths of some nineteen Americans. The day after that incident, President Wilson announced the dispatching of an expedition into Mexico to apprehend and punish him. The expedition was punitive rather than belligerent in nature (i.e., it was directed against individual wrongdoers rather than against any nation-state). Initially, the expedition even had the permission of the Mexican government. When that consent was withdrawn, however, the two countries drifted dangerously close to war. In the event, the operation ended on President Wilson's orders in January 1917, though without having succeeded in apprehending its main quarry.[125]

Punitive expeditions, like reprisals, sometimes had effects that went well beyond their original goals of punishing wrongdoers. A notable instance was the launching by the United States of a punitive expedition (under the redoubtable Andrew Jackson) into Florida against marauding Indians in 1818 . This action led to the permanent acquisition of Florida by the United States.[126] Another case was the action taken by

---

[123] On the uncertainty regarding the need for a declaration of war, see Chapter 5 above.

[124] On the Falklands incident, see Cox, *War*, at 57–62.

[125] On this incident, see Calhoun, *Power and Principle*, at 51–67; John S. D. Eisenhower, *Intervention! The United States and the Mexican Revolution 1913–1917* (New York: W. W. Norton, 1993), at 214–40; and J. B Scott, 'Punitive Expedition'.

[126] See Sofaer, *War*, at 341–55. For the cession of Florida by Spain, see Spain-USA, Adams-Onís Treaty, 22 Feb. 1819, 70 CTS 1.

Britain against the Mahdist movement in the Sudan in 1898. This action was stimulated by a rich mix of motives. One, clearly, was the desire to avenge the death of General Charles Gordon, who had been killed in the Mahdi's capture of Khartoum in 1885 (while in the service, incidentally, of the Ottoman sultan rather than of Britain). There was also, however, a desire to forestall imminent French expansion in the upper Nile Valley, as well as (rather more remotely) to protect British interests in Egypt, especially the Suez Canal. In all events, the British troops achieved a spectacular victory over the Mahdist forces at the Battle of Omdurman in 1898. As a result, the Sudan was brought under British control (technically in the form of an Anglo-Egyptian 'condominium', which endured until 1956).

In sum, it was deeply ironic that the whole area of measures short of war – interventions, reprisals and necessity measures – would be, at the same time, so strongly reminiscent of the just-war outlook from the Middle Ages, and yet so ineluctably tied to action by major powers against lesser ones. Law enforcement, peacekeeping, the rescue of victims of aggression, the punishment of criminality – all of these were widely agreed to be worthy goals. But it is hard to deny that they became – or at least appeared to be – somewhat less worthy when they were pursued in too restrictive a fashion, for the overwhelming benefit of a small subgroup of the world's population. A full history of measures short of war would relate these actions to broader trends such as imperialist and social Darwinist thought, as well as the development of a global economy in the light of free trade and other ideas of classical political economy. Until such a fuller account appears, this all-too-cursory survey of the subject will have to suffice.

7

Civil strife

Civil war breaks the bonds of society and of government ...; it gives rise, within the Nation, to two independent parties, who regard each other as enemies and acknowledge no common judge.

Emmerich de Vattel[1]

[A]n insurrection is transformed into a war between two belligerent parties regularly organised, when it is conducted by both sides by veritable governments, by armies that respect the laws and usages of international wars; such a civil war takes the character of an international war.

Frederic de Martens[2]

Even further beneath the positivist war horizon than intervention, reprisals and other measures short of war, in nineteenth-century legal doctrine, were civil wars. In Western thought, there was a long tradition of regarding civil conflict as fundamentally distinct from true war. To Plato, for example, the terms 'war' and 'civil strife' referred to 'two different realities'.[3] Similarly, in Roman law, the distinction between *latrociniae* (bandits, pirates and the like) and true enemies, or *hostes*, had been fundamental. Cicero stressed that enemies were bodies of people with whom a peace treaty could be concluded, thereby excluding brigands and such persons.[4] Concretely, this meant that none of the rituals associated with war-making and war-waging was applicable to struggles against mere lawbreakers. Nor did the rules on the conduct of war apply. In particular, faith did not have to be kept with bandits, as it did with true foreign enemies. In the medieval just-war period, the position was little different, at least in doctrinal writings, which required of a just war that there be *auctoritas* on both sides. The result was a clear dichotomy between domestic law

---

[1] Vattel, *Law of Nations*, at 338.   [2] 3 F. de Martens, *Traité*, at 185.
[3] Plato, *Republic*, at 229.   [4] Cicero, *On Duties*, at 141.

enforcement and true war. Within a state, as between sovereign and subject, there was the enforcement of the *civil* law by magistrates. Between independent polities, there was enforcement of *natural*-law rules by means of war. This distinction between civil law and natural law was mirrored by a corresponding distinction in the nature of the powers wielded by a government in the two situations. Domestic law enforcement involved the exercise of *sovereign* rights and powers, while the enforcement of natural law against a foreign power entailed the exercise of *belligerent* rights and powers.

Before civil conflicts could be considered as true wars, a crucial conceptual step was necessary: of somehow placing insurgents on a legal par with the government that they were rebelling against, at least in matters relating to the conflict itself. It has been observed that Islamic law took a long step in that direction in the Middle Ages, with its distinction between *bughat* and 'ordinary' criminals – with *bughat* referring to persons who fought for some kind of doctrine or higher cause than mere personal enrichment. Only in the nineteenth century did comparable ideas emerge in European law and practice. In this area, perhaps more than in any other in the legal history of war, state practice took the leading role, with doctrine following demurely in its wake. The crucial step was the recognition that insurgent groups could, and should, be treated as independent bodies on a de facto basis, provided that they met certain criteria such as the control of territory and the discharging of governmental functions.

As so often, the most important factor in the Western experience was the position of third states – specifically, the question of whether or not the law of neutrality could or should be applied to cases of civil strife. The conclusion was that, in certain circumstances at least, neutrality law would apply – with the result that civil conflicts could be treated fully on a par with true interstate wars. The means by which this state of affairs would be brought about came to be known as 'recognition of belligerency' – one of the major legal innovations (from the European standpoint at least) of the nineteenth century. But recognition of belligerency turned out to be, in a manner of speaking, all *too* powerful a device. States began, first in practice and then gradually in theory, to craft a sort of trimmed-down version of it, known as 'recognition of insurgency'. This innovation would have a long career ahead of it, so it is well to take due note of its origins in the present period.

From rebellion to belligerency

In the Middle Ages, just-war doctrine closely followed the lead of Roman law in excluding civil strife from the category of war, specifically by requiring *auctoritas* to be present on both sides, not simply on the just one. The result was a clear and sharp distinction between the two categories of conflict. As John of Legnano crisply put it, 'it is not war when a robber is hanged or any one else is brought to justice'.[5] In the words of Pierino Belli (a legal adviser on military matters to the Spanish government in the sixteenth century), "enemy" and "rebel" are two very different things'.[6] In the sixteenth century, Vitoria, in words that could have come from Cicero, expressed this point by averring that only a 'perfect' commonwealth could wage a just war – i.e., only a polity which 'has its own laws, its own independent policy, and its own magistrates'.[7] Gentili, ever in thrall to Roman-law ways of thinking, was of a like mind, insisting that a true enemy must possess 'a treasury, united and harmonious citizens, and some basis for a treaty of peace'.[8]

On occasion, to be sure, it was recognised that certain outbreaks of lawlessness were serious enough to require suppression by armed forces, without a scrupulous determination of guilt and innocence of individual participants, as was required in ordinary law enforcement. The great peasant revolt in France in the mid fourteenth century, known as the *jacquerie*, was an example. Froissart characterised the rebels as an anarchic rabble – 'evil men, who had come together without leaders or arms, [who] pillaged and burned everything and violated and killed all the ladies without mercy, like mad dogs'.[9] To them, no mercy was shown by the knights who restored order. Rebels were hunted down and slaughtered or hanged on the spot. Froissart reported that, in one day alone, some 7,000 of them were killed like cattle. The marshals of France considered the question of whether this conflict constituted a war and concluded that it did not.[10]

Some medieval insurgents, on the other hand, far from being a murderous and starving rabble as portrayed by Froissart, consisted of organised and well-armed companies of knights in the employ of ambitious feudal magnates. Prominent examples included the forces fielded by the German noble Henry the Lion against various Holy Roman Emperors in the twelfth century. Rebels of this more exalted social calibre were commonly treated more in the manner of the Muslim *bughat* than of mad dogs. It became common for various attributes of war, such as the rights relating to spoil and ransom, to be applied,

---

[5] John of Legnano, *Tractatus*, at 246. [6] Belli, *Military Matters*, at 9.
[7] Vitoria, *Law of War*, at 301. [8] Gentili, *Law of War*, at 25.
[9] Froissart, *Chronicles*, at 151. [10] Keen, *Laws of War*, at 63–4.

de facto, in such contests.[11] Sometimes, a distinction was made between what were called 'open' and 'covered' wars. 'Open' wars were true wars, against foreign powers. 'Covered' wars were wars of the feudal variety – either enforcement actions by feudal superiors against recalcitrant vassals or revolts by restive vassals against oppressive lords. The *justa causa*, in such a case, might lie on either side depending on the merits of the particular dispute in question.[12] A feudal inferior, however, was generally seen as being allowed to wage *offensive* war against a superior only if he was executing the ruling of a judge.[13] Some of the rules on the conduct of hostilities differed as between the two types of conflict. For example, in a 'covered' war, property could not be taken as a spoil of war; nor was burning permitted.

The greatest rebellion of the late Middle Ages was the Dutch war of independence from Spain in the late sixteenth and early seventeenth centuries. This was no quarrel between feudal magnates but instead was, to borrow a later expression, a war of national liberation, supported by the merchant and urban classes. These various interests gradually assembled themselves into a nation through a series of contractual arrangements, culminating in a Treaty of Union in 1579, in which the rebels formed a purportedly independent polity known as the United Provinces of the Netherlands.[14] Two years later, the Estates-General of the emerging nation pronounced the forfeiture by the Spanish King Philip II of his sovereign rights over the country.[15] The new state then proceeded to enter into foreign relations with other powers, particularly England and France, and to conduct the independence struggle as if it were fully an interstate war.

Only gradually, however, could legal scholars bring themselves to concede that insurgents could be on a legal par with the rulers whom they were struggling to overthrow or separate from. Even Hugo Grotius, a loyal Dutchman who lived during his country's independence struggles, denied that a conflict between a ruler and his subjects could be a true war. Even if the rebellious subjects had good cause for their discontent – for example, if their ruler was a wicked oppressor of innocent folk – their subordinate status deprived them, in his opinion, of any legal right, or

---

[11] *Ibid.* at 80–1.   [12] *Ibid.* at 104.
[13] F. H. Russell, *Just War*, at 143–5.
[14] Pacification of Ghent, 8 Nov. 1576, 5(1) Dumont 278; and Treaty of Union, 23 Jan. 1579, *ibid.* at 322.
[15] Declaration of the Estates-General, 26 July 1581, *ibid.* at 413.

ability, to wage war.[16] A foreign sovereign might resort to war on their behalf (i.e., to what would later be called humanitarian intervention). But they themselves were required to bear their fate with as much fortitude as could be mustered.[17] The furthest that he went in bringing civil wars into the general framework of the law of war was to characterise them as 'mixed wars' – meaning conflicts pitting a government on one side against a private party on the other.[18]

In this area, as in so many others, Thomas Hobbes was an important innovator. He posited that a subject's loyalty to a sovereign persisted only so long as the sovereign actually functioned as such. When a ruler ceased to perform the functions of a sovereign – most particularly, when he turned from a protector of his subjects into an oppressor – he thereby forfeited his sovereign status *vis-à-vis* his erstwhile subjects. The effect was automatically to release the subjects from any duty of loyalty, by operation of law.[19] This idea passed into the general stream of natural-law thought in the following years. The French natural-law writer Jean Jacques Burlamaqui, for example, writing in the middle of the eighteenth century, echoed Hobbes by holding that a civil war was a true war because, in such a situation, the parties were no longer in the relation of sovereign and subject but instead were 'in a state of nature and equality, trying to obtain justice by their own proper strength, which constitutes what we understand properly by the term *war*'.[20] At about the same time, Christian Wolff took up the theme. He distinguished between rebellion and civil war properly speaking, the difference being the presence or absence (as the case may be) of a *justa causa*. A civil war properly speaking was a justified struggle by subjects against an oppressive sovereign, while mere rebellion was an unjustified revolt.[21]

Vattel then introduced a somewhat more elaborate refinement yet, which became the basis for the further consideration of the question in the nineteenth century. He made a three-fold classification: between rebellion, insurrection and civil war properly speaking. Echoing Wolff,

---

[16] Grotius, *War and Peace*, at 138–56. Grotius made a number of potentially important qualifications to his position. The general principle, though, was as stated.

[17] *Ibid.* at 472–5, 583–4.

[18] *Ibid.* at 91. See also, to this effect, Wolff, *Law of Nations*, at 311–12.

[19] Hobbes, *Leviathan*, at 144–5. It is an error, though a common one, to interpret this process as a breach by the sovereign of a contract with his subjects. The true position is that Hobbes presented it as a forfeiture of sovereign *status* on the part of the ruler.

[20] Burlamaqui, *Principles*, at 263. (Emphasis in the original.) His general discussion of the subject is at 302–5.

[21] Wolff, *Law of Nature*, at 513–14.

he held rebellion to be an unlawful revolt against authority, i.e., a revolt lacking a just cause. As such, it was mere criminality. Insurrection, in contrast, referred to cases of insurgency in which the rebels had at least 'some cause' for taking up arms, such as oppressive treatment by their sovereign – but in which they did not contest their sovereign's right, in principle, to reign over them. Insurrection, in other words, was a resort to violent self-help for the redressing of genuine grievances; but it was limited in nature in that it involved a challenge only to the ruler's conduct, not to his sovereign status as such. Insurrectionists were therefore, in Vattel's words, only 'wanting in patience rather than in loyalty'. A true civil war was a situation in which the rebellious subjects went further and wholly rejected their ruler's right to govern them. Their goal was either to overthrow and supplant their government, or else to secede and form a separate state. In this third case of true civil war, the two parties were deemed to constitute, de facto, two distinct nations. Consequently, the conflict between them was equivalent to a war between fully independent states.[22]

A notable early illustration of a rebellion being treated on a par with an interstate war was the American independence struggle of 1775–83, which, from the outset, was invested with the trappings of a true war. The insurgent colonial side issued a Declaration of the Causes and Necessity of Taking Up Arms in July 1775.[23] As a statement of the grievances which had sparked the conflict, it amounted, in essence, to a declaration of war. (It is not to be confused with the better known Declaration of Independence a year later.) The rebels prosecuted the struggle in a distinctly state-like manner, with organised, uniformed and (more or less) disciplined armies. A similar approach to the conflict came from the British side, in the form of a statute adopted by the parliament in 1777, holding the rebellious colonists to be the equivalent of foreign enemies.[24] Significantly, the statute invoked the law of neutrality by cautioning foreign states to refrain from providing aid to the insurgents. Further legislation that same year dealt with the question of treatment of American privateers who were captured on the high seas and brought to Britain. While asserting that 'acts of treason and piracy' had been committed by the American rebels, the statute delphically

---

[22] Vattel, *Law of Nations*, at 336–7.
[23] For the text of which, see Richard L. Perry (ed.), *Sources of Our Liberties* (New York: McGraw-Hill, 1959), at 295–300.
[24] 17 Geo 3 c. 9.

noted that 'it may be inconvenient . . . to proceed forthwith to the trial of such criminals'. Instead, the British policy would be to detain the persons 'in safe custody'. In the event, all of the captured persons were eventually exchanged or released, rather than prosecuted as criminals.[25]

In the Latin American independence struggles of the early nineteenth century, the position was broadly similar. In most cases, the rebels, like their North American predecessors, were organised more or less in the manner of regular European armed forces. And they were generally treated as such by their Spanish foes. For example, in 1820, Spain concluded a written agreement with insurgents in Colombia, committing both sides to abiding by the laws of war.[26] This agreement, incidentally, described the conflict as a 'war'. Governments sometimes entered into armistice agreements with rebels. Again, the Latin American independence struggles provide several examples. Spain concluded armistice agreements with rebels in Colombia (in 1820) and Peru (in 1821).[27] In both cases, the conflict was expressly referred to as a 'war', although it is difficult to be certain that the term was intended to have a technical legal meaning.

The Lieber Code of 1863 followed along the broad lines of Vattel, with a three-fold taxonomy of internal armed conflicts. The lowest-level category, which Lieber labelled 'insurrection', actually combined Vattel's two situations of rebellion and insurrection. It consisted of law-enforcement activity carried out by the state's armed forces instead of by local magistrates, a situation not uncommon in the nineteenth century. In such cases, the insurrectionists would typically have little in the way of internal organisation or discipline. Lieber's middle category, which he termed 'rebellion', was defined as 'a war between the legitimate government of a country and portions or provinces of the same who seek to throw off their allegiance to it and set up a government of their own'. It was therefore a conflict between existing political units within a state.[28] Rebellions might well have many of the outer trappings of a true interstate war, since the rebels might well possess a high degree of organisation. But they were still in the category of domestic disturbances, rather than of true wars, because the conflict was still one between a sovereign and subject.

---

[25] 2 J. B. Moore, *Digest*, at 1076.
[26] Colombia-Spain, Convention of Truxillo, 26 Nov. 1820, 71 CTS 291.
[27] Colombia-Spain, Armistice Agreement, 25 Nov. 1820, 71 CTS 281; and Peru-Spain, Armistice Agreement, 23 May 1821, 71 CTS 447. See also Buenos Aires-Spain, Armistice, 15 July 1821, 72 CTS 75; Buenos Aires-Spain, Preliminary Convention, 4 July 1823, 73 CTS 261; and Brazil-Portugal, Treaty of Armistice, 18 Nov. 1823, 73 CTS 465.
[28] Lieber Code, Art. 151.

Finally, there was civil war in the true sense. This was defined by Lieber as 'war between two or more portions of a country or state, each contending for the mastery of the whole, and each claiming to be the legitimate government'.[29] It was therefore a struggle between factions for *possession* of the sovereignty of the state, as distinct from rebellion, which was a struggle by a faction or region to *escape* from that sovereignty. In this case of true civil war, as contrasted with that of rebellion, the two sides did not face one another as sovereign and subject, but rather as co-equal contestants for the 'prize' of sovereignty.[30]

Some care needs to be taken over terminology. In the loose popular parlance, the expression 'civil war' is commonly used to refer to any situation of major strife within a country. Indeed, the Lieber Code itself noted that the term 'civil war' was commonly applied to the middle category of rebellion as well as to civil war properly speaking. In its proper legal sense, though, as expounded by lawyers like Vattel and Lieber, the term referred to internal disturbances which merited treatment on a par with interstate wars. In other words, a civil war, in this proper legal sense, was, by *definition*, a conflict that was fully the equal of an interstate war and hence was a war in the true sense.

Another way of stating the point is to say that, in dealing with lesser disturbances such as mob violence or insurrections (in Lieber's sense), states would employ their ordinary *sovereign* powers, i.e., their national laws, by bringing criminal prosecutions against individual miscreants. In cases of true civil war, however, governments would employ the *belligerent* powers which they possessed under the international law of war. This meant that captured opponents were entitled to be treated as prisoners of war, so that they could only be subjected to a *non-punitive* detention, to prevent them from rejoining and augmenting their forces. They could not be prosecuted as criminals (except in the marginal case in which they were accused of having committed breaches of the international rules on the conduct of war itself). This non-punitive approach to civil-war opponents had another interesting effect that should be noted. It entitled the government side (and the opposition as well) to capture and detain persons *merely* for being members of the opposing armed force – again, precisely as in an interstate war, when members of the enemy armed force are subject to capture and detention simply on the basis of their status. It was generally conceded, however, that these constraints on the government's conduct only applied during the struggle

[29] *Ibid.* Art. 150.   [30] See Halleck, *International Law*, at 332–3.

itself. After the disturbances had ended, the government could proceed to prosecute the rebels as criminals if it wished.[31]

If these broad principles were tolerably clear, there still remained a number of exceedingly knotty practical questions that caused much difficulty in the nineteenth century. Two issues in particular caused problems. One was how the members of the middle category of dissidents – 'insurgents' in Vattel's terminology and 'rebels' in Lieber's – were to be treated. Were they to be accorded the status of belligerents, on a par with fighters in a true civil war? Or could the government treat them as criminals, in the manner of ordinary rioters? Or did the government have a right to select either of these options at its own choice? The second issue was how, in a precise and practical manner, a true civil war was to be distinguished from the lesser forms of disturbance. This second question affected not only the government (and its internal foes) but also the world at large. The reason was that a true civil war, being fully tantamount to an interstate war, automatically activated the law of neutrality, affecting *all* foreign countries.[32] The question of the legal status of internal conflicts, in other words, had a double aspect: an external one, concerning the application of the law of neutrality to foreign states; and an internal one, concerning the kind of treatment that the dissident forces were entitled to. With little to go on in the way of doctrine, lawyers and statesmen in the nineteenth century hammered out pragmatic responses in each of these areas, in the form of two practices that became known as 'recognition of belligerency', dealing chiefly with the external question, and 'recognition of insurgency', dealing mainly with the internal one. They were amongst the most notable international legal innovations of the period.

Recognising belligerency

In broad, if somewhat abstract, terms, the position concerning the effect of internal conflicts on foreign states was simple enough. If the struggle consisted of a contest for the possession of political power, then it was a true civil war, to which the full international law of war applied – including, crucially, the law of neutrality. If, on the other hand, the conflict was merely a protest against the manner in which power was exercised, or was an attempt at secession, then the situation was in the lesser category of

---

[31] 2 Oppenheim, *International Law*, at 65–6.
[32] Vattel, *Law of Nations*, at 338–40; and 3 F. de Martens, *Traité*, at 184–5.

rebellion or insurgency. It will immediately be seen, though, that this was not a very satisfactory distinction. It is entirely possible that a quite small band of conspirators might attempt to seize governmental power, and it would seem odd to say that they could not be treated as criminals. At the other extreme, it may be observed that the best known of all 'civil wars' of the nineteenth century, the one in the United States in 1861–5, clearly did not qualify as a true civil war by this definition, although the hostilities were on a gigantic scale and the insurgent side was organised in the most elaborate manner imaginable.

Indeed, the Americans, during this crisis, fully lived up to their reputation as the most legalistic of people. One sign of this was that the term 'civil war' was carefully eschewed by the government side, which consistently referred to the struggle as 'the rebellion'. The Confederates, ironically, agreed that the conflict was not a civil war. They regarded themselves as a fully independent state and the contest, therefore, as an interstate war in the most literal sense.[33] During the thick of the struggle itself, the American Supreme Court had occasion to consider its legal character. It implied that what really made an internal conflict tantamount to an interstate war was not the goal for which the dissidents were struggling, but rather the material scale on which the hostilities were taking place. A civil war, in the true legal sense, the Court pronounced

> becomes such by its accidents – the number, power, and organization of the persons who originate it and carry it on. When the party in rebellion occupy and hold in a hostile manner a certain portion of territory; have declared their independence; have cast off their allegiance; have organized armies; have commenced hostilities against their former sovereign, the world acknowledges them as belligerents, and the contest as a *war*.[34]

For foreign countries, the chief significance of the issue concerned the effect on neutrality. If the struggle was merely a case of internal enforcement of criminal laws against unruly dissidents, then the law of neutrality would be inapplicable. Foreign states would be permitted to assist the government side, if requested to do so, but forbidden to aid the insurgents. Providing aid to the government side was permissible on the simple ground that there was nothing unlawful about providing assistance to a

---

[33] After the conflict, Southerners preferred the label 'War Between the States' to describe the crisis. 'Civil War' gradually emerged as the standard term, as a sort of rough compromise.

[34] Prize Cases, 67 US (2 Black) 635 (1863), at 666–7.

state which requested it.[35] A notable example of a state seeking foreign assistance in the subduing of a rebellion occurred in 1849, when the government of Austria requested, and received, Russian assistance in subduing a revolt in Hungary.[36] Supplying assistance to insurgents, however, was prohibited because it would constitute an act of hostility towards the government – or, stated in alternative terms, a violation of the general duty of non-interference in the domestic affairs of other countries. This was expressly confirmed in 1900 by a resolution of the Institute of International Law.[37] If a breach of this rule occurred, the government could take reprisals against the foreign country, or even declare war against it.[38]

The prohibition against aiding insurgents was never codified into an international treaty during the nineteenth century. It may be noted, however, that, in 1928, the Western Hemisphere states adopted the Habana Convention on the Duties and Rights of States in the Event of Civil Strife, which expressly prohibited states parties from providing various kinds of assistance to insurgent forces.[39] But this general legal bias in favour of governments against insurgents – in the absence of recognition of belligerency – was already widely accepted in state practice in the nineteenth century.

If, on the other hand, the conflict was a civil war in the strict sense of the term, then the law of neutrality would apply, with the result that foreign states would be prohibited from providing official assistance to *either* the insurgent *or* the government side. By the same token, foreign countries would be obligated to accede to the exercise by *both* sides of the standard belligerents' rights. This meant that both the insurgents and the government would have the right to visit and search neutral merchant ships on the high seas, to capture and condemn any contraband of war that was being carried to the other side, and also to enforce blockades against shipping from all countries. At the same time, though, foreign countries would be entitled to the full range of the *rights* of

---

[35] See, for example, Bluntschli, *Droit international*, at 254–5. This was subject to the key proviso, however, that the government side must actually be in a position to represent the state.

[36] See Austria-Russia, Convention Respecting the Reception of Russian Troops in Austrian Territory, 10 June 1849, 103 CTS 93.

[37] 'Rights and Duties of Foreign Powers and Their *Ressortissants* towards Established and Recognized Governments in Case of Insurrection', 8 Sept. 1900, in J. B. Scott (ed.), *Resolutions*, at 157–9, Art. 2. (Hereinafter 'Civil War Res. of 1900'.)

[38] See Wheaton, *Elements*, at 34.

[39] Habana Convention on the Duties and Rights of States in the Event of Civil Strife, 20 Feb. 1928, 134 LNTS 45.

neutrals. Most importantly, they would have the right to trade freely with both sides (subject, of course, to the two major exceptions of trading in contraband goods and trading with blockaded ports). The only way that the government could stop foreign states from trading with the insurgents (in non-contraband goods) would be to mount a blockade in accordance with the rules of international law.

On the thesis that the distinction between a true civil war and the lesser condition of insurgency (as it will be termed) was an objective one, as appeared to be the case in the formulations of Vattel and Lieber, the law of neutrality would *automatically* become applicable to foreign states once the line between insurgency and true civil war had been crossed.[40] Foreign states would then be violating international law if they refused to accede to the exercise of belligerents' rights by the insurgents. (In practical terms, this would mean that the insurgents would be entitled to take reprisal actions against such countries.) Conversely, if foreign states treated the insurgents as full belligerents *without* that line having been crossed, then they would be violating the law and would thereby become liable to the government side for any injury caused.

In practice, however, logic was not strictly adhered to. The practice of states, arrived at rather haltingly, was to allow foreign countries a fairly large measure of discretion in this delicate area. They were allowed to exercise their own independent assessment of the status of internal conflicts in other countries, on a case-by-case basis. The decision by a given country to treat a case of civil strife as a war in the true sense of the term became known as recognition of belligerency. Recognition of belligerency meant that, in the eyes of the recognising state, the conflict was a civil war in the true sense – i.e., was equivalent to an interstate war – and that the recognising state was now, as a consequence of its own voluntary act, bound by the law of neutrality. It may be observed that this position involved a certain reversal of logic. Logically, the fact that a conflict was a true civil war (as opposed to a mere insurgency) should automatically activate the law of neutrality for foreign states (i.e., for *all* foreign states). In practice, however, causation ran in the opposite direction. It was the application of the law of neutrality – by the voluntary action of *individual* states independently – that converted a struggle from a rebellion into a true civil war. Instead of civil war

---

[40] In support of this thesis, see Hall, *Treatise*, at 290–1.

'causing' neutrality (so to speak), neutrality would 'cause' a civil war (i.e., would convert a mere insurgency into a civil war).[41]

The leading role in the development of recognition of belligerency was taken by Britain. Its earliest important initiative occurred in the 1820s, with the recognition of the Greek independence struggle against the Ottoman Empire as a war.[42] The key indicator was the invocation by Britain of its newly enacted neutrality legislation, to prohibit its nationals from participating in the conflict on either side.[43] Britain also announced that it would respect blockades proclaimed by the Greek forces.[44] France and Russia soon followed suit. In 1828, Britain effectively recognised a civil conflict in Portugal as a civil war in the true sense, again by announcing that it would recognise blockades of Oporto and the Azores proclaimed by the rebel forces. This step, incidentally, was taken pursuant to legal advice.[45] In 1848, when seaborne rebels against Habsburg rule in the Austrian Empire invested Trieste, the British government recognised the action as a lawful blockade, on the ground that the situation amounted, in the words of the chief legal adviser, to 'a *De Facto* War'.[46] The practice reached maturity in 1861, when Britain and France issued proclamations of neutrality in the American Civil War.[47] Other states, including the Netherlands, Spain and even Hawaii followed the British and French leads.[48]

Several points should be made about recognition of belligerency for the avoidance of confusion. For one thing, it should be noted that it did *not* amount to recognition of the insurgents as an independent state,

---

[41] On recognition of belligerency, see generally Féraud-Giraud, 'Reconnaissance'; and Garner, 'Recognition'.

[42] The case of France in the American Independence War might be proffered as an earlier instance. In that case, however, France recognised the full independence of the United States, not merely the belligerent status of the colonists.

[43] Proclamation for Putting in Execution the Foreign Enlistment Act, 6 June 1823, 10 BFSP 648.

[44] See 1 H. A. Smith (ed.), *Britain and the Law of Nations*, at 281–98.

[45] H. A. Smith, 'Problems', at 19.   [46] *Ibid.*

[47] See Proclamation by the Queen [of Great Britain], 13 May 1861, in Deák and Jessup, *Collection*, at 61–2; and the French Declaration of Neutrality, 10 June 1861, in *ibid.* at 590–2. On the British action, see 1 H. A. Smith (ed.), *Britain and the Law of Nations*, at 302–12.

[48] Netherlands, Proclamation Regarding Observance of Neutral Duties by Dutch Commerce in the American Civil War, 15 June 1861, in Deák and Jessup, *Collection*, at 815. Royal Decree [of Spain] of 17 June 1861, in *ibid.* at 933; and Proclamation of the King of the Hawaiian Islands, 26 Aug. 1861, in *ibid.* at 688.

fully equal in all respects to the government side. It therefore did not entail the receipt of ambassadors from the insurgent side on an official basis. Nor did it mean that the insurgents had sufficient legal status to enter into treaty relations with the recognising country. These results could only flow from a recognition of the insurgent faction as a fully independent state. Recognition of belligerency was a lesser measure, holding the rebels to be the equals of the government *only* for purposes of conducting the armed struggle itself. This point was illustrated in the case of the American Civil War, when Britain and France (along with other countries recognising belligerency) carefully refrained from recognising the Confederacy as an independent country, pointedly declining to enter into formal diplomatic relations with it.

In addition, it should be appreciated that the expression 'recognition of belligerency' is actually somewhat misleading, in that it might be misunderstood to constitute *merely* a recognition of the insurgents as lawful belligerents, with the full rights of war, rather than as mere criminals. Recognition of belligerency did have that effect. But the full significance of it was that it referred to the over-all status of the conflict as such, not merely to the character of the rebel faction alone. In the absence of a recognition of belligerency, *neither* side could lawfully exercise rights of war *vis-à-vis* the recognising country, such as visiting and searching its ships on the high seas to ferret out arms shipments.[49] It was even doubted whether, in a situation of mere domestic unrest, the government side was entitled to place mines in its own territorial waters, on the ground that that would infringe the established right of foreign-state ships to innocent passage through the territorial waters of other states.[50]

The point is well illustrated by an instructive incident that occurred during the South African War of 1899–1902. Britain at first sought to make a legal distinction between its two enemies, Transvaal and the Orange Free State. The British conceded that the struggle against the Orange Free State was a true war, since it was an independent country. Therefore, captured Free State troops would be accorded prisoner-of-war status. Britain, however, contended that the Transvaal was a protectorate (by virtue of a treaty of 1881 establishing British 'suzerainty' there) and that, consequently, the hostilities against it were law-enforcement operations against

---

[49] See Sadoul, *Guerre civile*, at 69–70. See also Opinion of R. Palmer, R. Collier and R. Phillimore, 22 Nov. 1864, in 1 McNair, *Opinions*, at 141–3.
[50] H. A. Smith, 'Problems', at 23–4.

'domestic' rebels.[51] Captured Transvaal forces therefore would be
regarded as ordinary criminals. Britain soon found this stance to be
contrary to its own real interest, however, when it stopped and searched
a French merchant ship on the high seas, with a view to determining
whether it was carrying contraband of war to its foes. France protested,
noting that, if the conflict was a domestic law-enforcement operation as
Britain contended, then it could have no right to interfere with foreign
shipping on the high seas. The British, appreciating the force of the
argument, shifted ground and henceforth regarded the contest as a full
international war.[52] In all events, it should be borne in mind that the
expression 'recognition of belligerency' refers to the recognition of the
conflict *itself* as a fully fledged state of war – with all of the legal accoutrements thereof.[53]

Two crucial questions, above all, called out for resolution regarding
recognition of belligerency. First, did foreign states have an *entirely* free
choice on recognition of belligerency; or were there some constraints?
And second, how was recognition of belligerency actually to be
accorded? In due course, more through experience than through doctrine, European states managed to devise solutions to both of these
problems.

Criteria for recognition of belligerency

Some lawyers maintained that, in situations of civil strife, foreign countries had a free choice as to whether to recognise belligerency or not. The
American lawyer Henry Wheaton, for example, drily remarked that the
question seemed to belong 'rather to the science of politics than of
international law'.[54] The prevailing view, however, came to be that
a set of objective criteria for recognition of belligerency did exist – but
with the key proviso that, if they were satisfied, then foreign states
were *permitted* to recognise belligerency, but not *compelled* to do so.[55]

---

[51] See Great Britain-Transvaal, Convention of 3 Aug. 1881, 159 CTS 57.
[52] Sadoul, *Guerre civile*, at 165–70. Another factor inducing Britain's change of position was
the accession of the Transvaal to the Geneva Convention (of 1864) in October 1899. See 7
RGDIP 282–3 (1900).
[53] On the effects of recognition of belligerency, see generally Sadoul, *Guerre civile*, at 96–140.
[54] Wheaton, *Elements*, at 34.
[55] See, for example, Bonfils, *Manuel*, at 580–1; and 2 Oppenheim, *International Law*, at
65–6, 86.

W. E. Hall, one of the advocates of this approach, maintained that insurgents, no matter how well organised they were, or how clear their de facto independence was, could never have more than a reasonable expectation, or a moral entitlement, to recognition of belligerency by foreign countries.[56] Kaspar Bluntschli expressed broadly the same view, contending, rather warily, that, if the objective criteria were present, then the insurgent side would have a 'natural right' to be treated as a co-equal belligerent with the government side. But he carefully stopped short of holding that this natural right was matched by an actual legal duty of recognition by foreign states.[57]

This practical approach was given a legal seal of approval by the civil-war resolution adopted in 1900 by the Institute of International Law.[58] It made no provision for mandatory recognition of belligerency by foreign states, instead setting out two situations in which foreign states had the *option* of recognition. The first was when the government of the strife-torn state elected *itself* to recognise belligerency. Foreign countries then become automatically entitled (but not obligated) to follow suit. The second situation – considerably more important in practice – concerned the recognition of belligerency by foreign states on their own initiative. They were stated to have the option of recognising belligerency when three criteria were met. First, the insurgents must have 'a distinct territorial existence through the possession of a definite proportion of the national territory'. Second, they must have 'the elements of a regular government exercising in fact the manifest rights of sovereignty' over the portion of territory that they controlled. Finally, the rebels must carry on the struggle by means of 'organized troops, subject to military discipline and conforming to the laws and customs of war'. These criteria were comparatively uncontroversial, as they already commanded significant prior support from state practice and scholarly consensus.[59]

In principle, there should be legal liability on the part of a foreign state that recognised belligerency when the criteria were not met, although there is no record of any successful claim having actually been made to this effect.[60] In the run-up to the Geneva arbitration of 1871–2, between the United States and Great Britain, which dealt with various disputes arising from the American Civil War, the United States at first sought to

---

[56] Hall, *Treatise*, at 33–5.   [57] Bluntschli, *Droit international*, at 271–2.
[58] Civil War Res. of 1900, Art. 8.   [59] See, for example, 2 Rivier, *Principes*, at 213.
[60] See, on this point, Halleck, *International Law*, at 332–3; and Féraud-Giraud, 'Reconnaissance', at 288.

press a claim for premature recognition of belligerency. Britain, however, successfully resisted bringing this issue into the proceedings.[61]

One interestingly logical – if also somewhat bizarre – consequence flowed from this policy of individual state discretion. This concerned cases of internal conflict in which the three criteria were duly met, but in which some foreign states elected to recognise belligerency while others did not. This would lead ineluctably to the conclusion, which some would find odd, that the conflict would be a true civil war from the standpoint of the one set of countries, while being at the very same time a situation of mere insurgency from the viewpoint of the other group. Despite appearing very strange at first glance, this situation actually posed no real problem either in theory or in practice. No great theoretical difficulty was posed, since each state's recognition of belligerency affected only that one state itself (by subjecting it to the law of neutrality). So there was little or no scope for collisions between foreign states. From the practical standpoint too, the matter was of little moment, since recognition of belligerency was not particularly common in international practice, for reasons that will be explored presently.

Means of recognising belligerency

The question of how recognition of belligerency would be accorded caused few problems in practice in the nineteenth century and so may be dealt with briefly. The 1900 resolution of the Institute of International Law stated that recognition of belligerency could be accorded either explicitly by a formal announcement of some kind, or implicitly by way of 'a series of acts which leaves no doubt as to [the] intention' of the recognising state. There were various ways in which a clear signal of this kind could be sent.[62] In the case of one particular category of civil strife – an armed attempt at secession by a disaffected internal group – a foreign country could signal, by various means, its recognition of the insurgents as an independent state. An early instance occurred in 1578, when England effectively recognised the rebellious Northern Netherlands as an independent state by entering into a treaty of alliance with it.[63] France did much the same thing in 1778, when it

---

[61] 1 McNair, *Opinions*, at 143.
[62] See generally Sadoul, *Guerre civile*, at 86–91.
[63] England-Netherlands, Treaty of Alliance, 7 Jan. 1578, 5(1) Dumont 315. See also England-France-Netherlands, Treaty of Offensive and Defensive Alliance, 31 Oct. 1596, *ibid.* at 531.

recognised the independence of the rebellious American colonies by concluding treaties of military alliance and friendship with them.[64] Regarding civil conflicts in general, the most obvious method of express recognition of belligerency was the issuing of a formal proclamation of neutrality. As noted above, this was the method adopted by Britain and France during the American Civil War.

Implicit means of recognising belligerency took various forms. For example, ships flying the flags of purportedly independent countries might be admitted by foreign states into the ports of the foreign state on an equal footing with vessels flying the government flags. This policy was adopted by the United States in 1819, in favour of the rebellious Spanish American colonies, greatly to the annoyance of Spain.[65] Another standard means of recognising belligerency was by recognising blockades mounted by rebel naval forces (i.e., by acquiescing in the capture and condemnation of vessels by the insurgent forces). In the absence of recognition of belligerency, the capture of ships made outside of the territorial waters of a state would be piracy. This method of recognition was employed, as noted above, by the major European powers in the Greek independence struggle of the 1820s. It was also used by the United States in recognising belligerency during the Texas struggle for independence from Mexico. In 1836, the American attorney general held the capture by the Texans of an American ship to be a legitimate belligerent act and not an instance of piracy.[66] A similar means of recognising belligerency was to recognise the validity of transfers of legal title to captured ships effected by prize courts set up by insurgent groups. Conversely, a dramatic sign of *non*-recognition of belligerency was given by Germany in 1902 in the context of a civil war in Haïti. When an insurgent vessel attempted to exercise the belligerent right of capturing contraband from a German merchant ship, a German warship fired on it to ward it off.[67]

A final question regarding recognition of belligerency was how, and in what circumstances, a recognition of belligerency by a foreign state could be withdrawn. In theory at least, there could be concern to

---

[64] France-USA, Treaty of Amity and Commerce, 6 Feb. 1778, 46 CTS 417; and France-USA, Treaty of Alliance, 6 Feb. 1778, 46 CTS 447.

[65] Message of President Monroe, 7 Dec. 1819, in Bartlett (ed.), *Record*, at 181–3. See also *The Santissima Trinidad*, 20 US (7 Wheaton) 283 (1822).

[66] Opinion of Benjamin F. Butler, 'Piracy on the High Seas', 17 May 1836, 3 Op A-G 120. See also Sadoul, *Guerre civile*, at 143–5.

[67] Sadoul, *Guerre civile*, at 173–5.

avoid either of two undesirable situations: on the one hand, an overly hasty withdrawal of recognition while the struggle was still in earnest; or, on the other hand, an undue delay in withdrawing the recognition once a rebellion had ceased to be viable.[68] In practice, however, it appears that problems of this nature never actually arose, doubtless due to the rarity of recognition of belligerency in state practice. The 1900 resolution of the Institute of International Law simply gave entirely free rein to states in the matter. It allowed the withdrawal of recognition at any time for any reason, even in the complete absence of any change of circumstances in the strife-riven state itself, subject only to the proviso that a with-drawal would not have any retroactive effect.[69]

Recognising insurgency

Recognition of belligerency never became a common practice of states, for reasons that are not difficult to fathom. For one thing, recognition of belligerency was something of a legal blunderbuss. It caused the *entire* range of duties of the law of neutrality to fall onto the recognising state in a single, inconveniently large bundle – with a danger of legal claims being brought for any breaches. That this danger was not merely the-oretical was vividly demonstrated by the American Civil War, when Britain was held liable after the conflict for being remiss in its duty to police its territory to prevent the fitting-out of belligerent warships – and assessed substantial damages. It is not surprising that states were, in general, in no great hurry to follow this particular British lead. In addition, recognition of belligerency was likely to cause great offence to the government of the disordered state, as it notably did in the case of the American Civil War. As a result of these considerations, countries typically held back from recognising belligerency even when the relevant criteria were clearly present. For instance, in the Chilean civil conflict of the 1890s, the congressional faction did possess a regular army, as well as effective control of a portion of the territory and an organised govern-mental apparatus. But it appears that the only country in the world that accorded recognition of belligerency was neighbouring Bolivia.[70]

---

[68] Opinion of R. Palmer, R. Collier and R. Phillimore, 20 May 1865, in 1 H. A. Smith (ed.), *Britain and the Law of Nations*, at 324.

[69] Civil War Res. of 1900, Art. 9. See also Sadoul, *Guerre civile*, at 91–4.

[70] Sadoul, *Guerre civile*, at 154. It is likely that the Bolivian recognition was motivated by continuing resentment against Chile stemming from the Pacific War of 1879–82.

It proved possible to avoid some of the awkward features of recognition of belligerency by devising a sort of half-way version of it, known as recognition of insurgency. Recognition of insurgency is best seen as a geographically constricted version of recognition of belligerency, i.e., as a situation in which the insurgents are treated as belligerents *within* the territory of the strife-torn country, but not beyond its borders. The condition of insurgency, in other words, was a state of affairs in which, within the territory of the state concerned, the laws of war were substituted for the ordinary criminal law. The government donned, as it were, the armour of the warrior in place of the gown of the magistrate.

The most obvious difference between these two types of recognition was that the one triggered the application of the law of neutrality, while the other did not. More specifically, the effect was that recognition of insurgency (as opposed to belligerency) did not confer onto *either* the government *or* the insurgent side any right to interfere with foreign-state activities on the high seas. Neither side was conceded any right to visit and search foreign ships on the high seas or to confiscate contraband from foreign-state nationals. Within the territory of the afflicted country, however, insurgency and belligerency had much the same effect. The most obvious one was that captured insurgents were entitled to treatment as prisoners of war rather than as criminals, at least during the continuance of the hostilities. More generally, the effect was that the government was required to deal with the crisis through the use of *belligerent* powers rather than through the application of its normal *sovereign* powers. Another consequence was that both parties to the conflict were required to conduct their operations according to the rules governing interstate wars.[71]

From the standpoint of foreign countries, the principal significance of recognition of insurgency was to entitle nationals of foreign states to accept the validity of any government-like measures promulgated by insurgents in areas which they actually controlled. That meant, for example, that, if a ship from a foreign state paid port or customs duties to insurgent forces which happened to be in actual control of the port at the time, then that ship could not be compelled at any later time to make a second payment to the de jure government authorities. The acts of the insurgents therefore had, so to speak, a certain local validity arising *purely* from their de facto control of the area. An illustration of recognition of insurgency in action is afforded by the situation of civil

---

[71] On recognition of insurgency, see Lawrence, *Principles*, at 354–6; Castrén, 'Recognition of Insurgency'; and H. Lauterpacht, *Recognition*, at 270–328.

disturbances in Peru in the 1850s, when much of the coast of the country, including some of the major ports, was in the hands of insurgents. Some American ships called in these ports, paid the requisite duties in the apparently normal fashion and were granted licences to obtain guano from areas under insurgent control. While engaging in the guano gathering, two ships were captured by Peruvian government vessels during a raid into the insurgent-held areas and subjected to penalties for gathering guano without a valid government licence.

The American government strongly objected to this action on Peru's part and took the opportunity to set out its view of international law relating to civil strife. Secretary of State Lewis Cass insisted that insurgents were entitled to recognition by foreign countries as de facto sovereigns of areas over which they exercised effective control. In Cass's words, a civil-war situation

> confer[s] upon *de facto* rulers the right to govern such portions of the country as they [are] able to reduce to their possession. It is the duty of foreigners to avoid all interference under such circumstances, and to submit to the power which exercises such jurisdiction over the places where they resort, and while thus acting they have a right to claim protection, and also to be exempted from all vexatious interruption when the ascendency of the parties is temporarily changed by the events of the contest.[72]

The effect was that, 'while contending parties are carrying on a civil war, those portions of the country in the possession of either of them, become subject to its jurisdiction, and persons residing there owe to it temporary obedience.' The contrary position, Cass contended, would be clearly unacceptable, as it would expose foreign commerce to 'the most oppressive exactions and interruptions'.[73]

This right of foreign states to recognise insurgents' 'authority' in areas that they actually occupied had a logical counterpart in a right *not* to recognise the government's authority over those same areas. This issue arose when governments attempted to combat rebels by employing their sovereign powers to decree the closure to international trade of ports that were in insurgent hands. On a number of occasions, foreign countries refused to heed such closure decrees, on the ground that they were

---

[72] Cass to Peruvian Minister at Washington, 22 May 1858, 50 BFSP 1151.
[73] *Ibid.* For a similar position by the British government, see Opinion of H. Jenner, 29 July 1834, in 2 McNair, *Opinions*, at 395–6.

entitled to regard the rebels' de facto possession of the port as lawful and regular. Recognition of the closure decree would be tantamount to conscripting foreign countries onto the government side by compelling them, in effect, to participate in an economic boycott of the insurgent-held areas. If the government wished to close off the rebel areas from outside contact, then it should do so by exercising the *belligerent* power of blockade. That is to say, it must place a cordon of ships around the rebel-held area and effectively maintain the blockade by capturing and condemning any vessels attempting to enter. Merely proclaiming the port closed and then penalising foreign ships afterwards for having violated the closure proclamation would be tantamount to what lawyers called a 'paper blockade' (i.e., a blockade that was proclaimed on paper but not effectively enforced by naval vessels on the scene, as required by international law).

An early dispute on this subject arose in 1844, in the context of civil strife in Haïti, when British law officers advised that the closure of rebel-held ports by government decree was unlawful.[74] The United States followed suit in 1866, when the Mexican Emperor Maximilian, hard-pressed by insurrectionaries, declared the port of Matamoros closed to international shipping, for the obvious reason that it was in rebel hands at the time. The United States made it clear by public presidential proclamation that it did not recognise this closure by decree. It would only concede that trade with the port by Americans was unlawful if the Maximilian government mounted an effective blockade around it.[75] A similar incident occurred in 1891, during the civil war in Chile, when President José Manuel Balmaceda, attempting to suppress the insurgency, decreed all rebel-held ports closed to foreign trade. The United States, along with various European countries, refused to recognise the measure.[76] In a Haïtian civil war of 1902, the major powers refused to recognise a declaration by the government of the closure of ports that were under de facto rebel control.[77]

As noted above, insurgency rights did not extend beyond the territory of the strife-torn state. In particular, they did not entitle either side to visit and search foreign-state ships on the high seas, or to capture and confiscate contraband of war, or to enforce blockades outside of

---

[74] Opinion of J. Dodson, 30 Apr. 1844, in *ibid.* at 383–4.
[75] Proclamation of 17 Aug. 1866, 14 Stat 814.
[76] G. G. Wilson, 'Insurgency', at 58.   [77] Sadoul, *Guerre civile*, at 174–5.

territorial waters.[78] But recognition of insurgency nevertheless did have a certain effect on high-seas actions. It meant that sea-going rebels could not be treated as pirates, provided that they confined their depredations to the vessels of their government foes and refrained from attacking international shipping at large. The practical effect was that, unlike pirates, who were subject to capture by any state at any time, the salt-water insurgents were subject to attack *only* by the government that they were opposing. As American Secretary of State Frederick T. Frelinghuysen put it in 1883 (in the context of civil strife in Haïti): 'The rule is, simply, that a "pirate" is the natural enemy of all men, to be repressed by any, and wherever found, while a revolted vessel is the enemy only of the power against which it acts.'[79]

Means of recognising insurgency

A crucial question about recognition of insurgency was whether it took place automatically on the fulfilment of certain objective criteria or whether there was a degree of discretion on the part of foreign govern-ments (as there was with recognition of belligerency). Vattel contended that the question was an objective one. He was well aware that governments invariably stigmatised insurgents as mere rebels, but he contended that the objective circumstances of the case rather than the unilateral will of the beleaguered sovereign determined the issue. Once the insurgents 'became sufficiently strong to make a stand against [the sovereign], and to force him to make a formal war upon them', Vattel maintained, 'he [the sovereign] must necessarily submit to have the contest called a civil war'.[80]

Governments, not surprisingly, tended to resist this view. During the American Civil War, for example, there was judicial authority to the effect that the government had a free choice as to whether to wield weapons of sovereign right or of belligerent right.[81] The question pre-sented itself at the very outset of the conflict when a group of Confederate privateers was captured at sea. The question arose of whether they should be treated as pirates or as lawful belligerents. The

---

[78] Blockades could be enforced so long as any actual captures of foreign ships were effec-tuated within the limits of the state's territorial waters, since the capture could then be said to be an exercise of *sovereign*, rather than of *belligerent*, power.
[79] Frelinghuysen to minister in Haiti, 15 Dec. 1883, FRUS 1884, at 297. See also G. G. Wilson, 'Insurgency'.
[80] Vattel, *Law of Nations*, at 338.
[81] See, for example, *The Hiawatha*, 12 Fed Cas 95 (DC SD NY, 1861).

government elected to prosecute them for piracy, for which they were duly convicted.[82] For the most part, however – and without exception in the land-war aspects of the conflict – the government treated captured insurgents as prisoners of war. This policy was clearly stated, however, to be a humanitarian gesture and *not* a legal obligation. It was, in the American government view, an entirely pragmatic policy designed to minimise suffering and to facilitate eventual reconciliation (a position supported by the Lieber Code and by case-law both during and after the conflict).[83] In a similar spirit, the American government explained its decision to comply with the international law of blockade as a gratuitous act of friendship to foreign countries rather than as a legal duty.

It should be appreciated, though, that these American concerns in the 1860s were expressed with a view to ensuring that the policies in question were not taken to amount to a recognition of *belligerency* on the part of the United States. Moreover, this was before the concept of recognition of insurgency had crystallised. In practice, Vattel's view of automatic recognition of insurgency gained the upper hand over time. The views of Halleck were especially instructive on this point, since, shortly after setting them down, he became a leading general in the Union army in his country's Civil War. He distinguished, in effect, between insurgency and belligerency by holding that, *within* the territory of the state where the conflict occurred, the rebels had a legal right to treatment on a par with belligerents once they controlled a portion of territory and began acting as a de facto government within it.[84] Shortly after the American Civil War, Bluntschli took the same view.[85] These criteria were, for all practical purposes, the same as for recognition of belligerency: that the insurgents conducted their military operations in accordance with the laws of war, that they were in actual control of a portion of the territory and that, within that area, they exercised powers of a government-like character. Even to the present day, there is no definite judicial authority on the point. But there is little doubt that the automatic recognition of insurgency is the rule.[86]

Since the rights of insurgency (as they might be termed) arose automatically, by operation of law, once these objective criteria were

[82] Carl B. Swisher, *The Taney Period* (New York: Macmillan, 1974), at 866–76.

[83] Lieber Code, Arts. 52 and 53. See also *Fifield* v. *The Insurance Co. of the State of Pennsylvania*, 47 Pa 166 (1864); and *Thorington* v. *Smith*, 75 US (8 Wall) 1 (1868).

[84] Halleck, *International Law*, at 332–3.

[85] Bluntschli, *Droit international*, at 271–2.

[86] See, to this effect, Despagnet, *Cours*, at 605; and Sadoul, *Guerre civile*, at 50–1.

satisfied, there was no need for any kind of act of recognition (whether express or implied) to take place at all. Any explicit act of recognition would not create a *new* legal situation – as was the case with recognition of belligerency – but instead would only amount to an acknowledgment of an *existing* state of affairs.[87] For this reason, express recognition of insurgency has been commonly dispensed with. Nonetheless, certain actions were at least sometimes taken as signals of recognition of insurgency. One was the invoking of domestic neutrality laws. Insurgency could also be recognised by way of acquiescence by foreign states in government-like, or sovereign-like, acts performed by the insurgents in the areas that they controlled de facto. During a civil conflict in Colombia in 1885–6, for example, the United States accepted the right of insurgents, acting within Colombian territorial waters, to stop the carriage of goods to their government enemies.[88]

One general point about the nature of recognition of insurgency is worth noting. That is that, unlike recognition of belligerency, its effects were wholly beneficial to foreign states. It enabled the foreign state to avoid becoming embroiled in the conflict, while protecting its nationals from penalties and double liabilities that might otherwise have occurred when, say, territory changed hands in the course of the struggle. It involved virtually nothing in the way of onerous duties on the foreign state, as recognition of belligerency did. We will not be surprised, therefore, to find that, in practice, recognition of insurgency has found greater practical use than its more powerful and better-known counterpart, or that states have been quite happy to accept that recognition of insurgency can occur automatically.[89]

The two phenomena of recognition of belligerency and recognition of insurgency demonstrated the extent to which the law could be adapted, even if somewhat haltingly and untidily, to changing circumstances. Moreover, a solid foundation was laid for further development in the late twentieth century, when civil wars would become a matter of greater concern to lawyers than ever.[90] Little would be heard in the future of recognition of belligerency, for the reasons given above. If not actually abolished or obsolete, it certainly would grow exceedingly rusty from

---

[87] For those with a penchant for technical legal terminology, it would be said that recognition of belligerency is *constitutive* in effect, whereas recognition of insurgency is *declaratory*.

[88] Castren, 'Recognition of Insurgency', at 444.   [89] Sadoul, *Guerre civile*, at 50–1.

[90] See Chapter 10 below on this development.

disuse. Recognition of insurgency, on the other hand, would continue to exist, although quietly and little noticed.

In the early part of the twentieth century, however, the world's attention would be focussed elsewhere than on civil wars. International conflicts were foremost in that period – with grim pride of place going to the global cataclysm that erupted in 1914. That epic struggle had profound implications for almost every element of the social and moral world – including, most emphatically, legal conceptions of war.

PART IV

Just wars reborn (1919–)

The first stage in getting rid of our instruments of coercion, or reducing them to vanishing point, is . . . to transfer them from rival litigants to the law, to the community, to make of our armies and navies the common police of civilization, standing behind a commonly agreed rule. But, before that can be done, there must be created a sense of community, a sense of our interests being common interests, not inherently . . . in conflict.

Norman Angell

It is . . . very probable that we will have in the future, fewer wars, but more 'hostilities'.

Josef L. Kunz

The Great War of 1914–18 changed the world in many ways. It unleashed forces far beyond those of the cabinet wars of the nineteenth century. It proved, if proof were needed, that there were no significant legal barriers to the waging of total war – war prosecuted not merely against the armed forces in the field but also against the whole of the enemy's society, particularly its economic capacity and its civilian morale. It dramatically demonstrated the power of advanced technology to wreak death and destruction on a scale never seen before. Our concern, however, is with the impact that it had on legal ways of thinking about war. This may be summed up most briefly in the phrase that surfaced at the time: that this conflict must be made into something unique in history, 'a war to end all wars'. At the conclusion of the hostilities, an effort was duly made to devise a new international order in which war would be absent – or at least much rarer than it had been – with the rule of law prevailing in its stead. This was to be brought about, it was earnestly hoped, by the establishment of the League of Nations.

For present purposes, the chief significance of the League of Nations lay in the fact that it sought to reinstate the fundamental principle that underpins just-war strategies in the generic sense: the notion that the normal state of international relations is one of peace, with war permitted only as an exceptional act requiring affirmative justification. The intention was to liberate international affairs from the stranglehold of the Hobbesian outlook. No longer would international law be agnostic on the question of war and peace, with the choice between them at the mercy of state policy. Instead of being a mere extension or appendage of diplomacy, as in previous centuries, war would now be its antithesis. A juridical barrier would be erected between them that could not lightly be crossed.

It became apparent, however, that the League's regulatory approach was too narrowly focussed, in that it concentrated solely on war and thereby left unregulated the three alternative forms of interstate coercion which had been relegated to the sphere of measures short of war: interventions, forcible reprisals and acts of necessity (chiefly comprising situations of aggression-and-self-defence). To a very large extent, the legal history of war after 1918 would be a history of the interplay between these four categories of armed force. It sometimes appeared as if some kind of juridical conservation principle was at work. As one of these categories was regulated, or even altogether suppressed, others would correspondingly expand. In the League of Nations period, the resort to war was legally restricted, for the first time in history.[1] Hardly was the ink dry on the League Covenant, however, when states began to circumvent its restrictions by characterising their armed actions otherwise than as wars. An unintended effect of the League Covenant, therefore, was sharply to increase the significance of the distinction between wars and the various measures short of war. In particular, questions of aggression-and-self-defence, as distinct from wars, began to claim the serious attention of international lawyers and statesmen for the first time, though still only in a rather halting and tentative manner. A new era was at hand, but almost by accident.

It began to require an increasingly trained eye – not to mention flexibility of mind – to discern the differences between wars and the various other kinds of armed force. This could even, or especially, be the case when armed conflict was occurring on the largest scale. The Second World War provided the most striking illustration of the point. In certain respects, it had a decidedly traditional, even anachronistic, look – with formal declarations of war in traditional style, alliances, armistices, peace treaties, the full application of the laws of war (if not their invariable observance) and so forth. But the War also became a kind of template for the new just-war outlook, as it also had many of the trappings of aggression-and-self-defence, albeit on a mammoth scale. Most notably, the European and the Pacific aspects of it both began with acts of naked aggression (by Germany against Poland in 1939 and by Japan against the United States in 1941). As a result, the conflict always had the aura of a humanitarian crusade of the highest order against aggression and barbarism. In the course of the struggle, it was agreed by the major Allied powers that the crusade should be made permanent – that is, that the wartime United Nations alliance (as it was officially known) should be transformed, after the conflict, into a permanent United Nations *Organisation*, which would act as a perpetual guardian of world peace and suppressor of aggression. The Second World War, then, would be (it was hoped) a sort of dress rehearsal for a new world to come.

In this new era, both of the components of the generic just-war strategy would be present, enshrined in the UN Charter of 1945. First, there was a commitment to a peaceful world as the basic norm, from which departures would have to be justified. Moreover, this basic norm

---

[1] It will be recalled that the Porter Convention of 1907 had restricted the resort to armed reprisals, but not to war.

would be stronger than it had been in the League of Nations era, because it would prohibit not merely war as such, but also 'the use of force' in general in international affairs – thereby encompassing (so it was hoped) forcible reprisals as well. The second just-war feature of the post-1945 world was a careful, and narrow, specification of the conditions in which force could be used as an exception to the general rule. The principal form of lawful force would be community policing – something that the League of Nations had lacked. Law-enforcement operations would not be entrusted to individual aggrieved states on a self-help basis, as in the medieval just-war system. Instead, there would be a dedicated inter-national enforcement organ: the UN Security Council, operating (inevitably and predictably) under the aegis of the major Allied powers, which would hold permanent seats on that body – and also wield veto powers over its decisions. Police actions by the Security Council would be just wars of the purest kind, for the countering of aggression and the upholding of community values. On a sort of emergency, stop-gap basis, a second kind of resort to force was also recognised as lawful: self-defence, which was expressly confirmed in the text of the UN Charter.

Some lawyers rushed to proclaim the abolition of war – of war, that is, as an institution of international law in the nineteenth-century positivist sense. Such legal accoutrements as 'rights of war' would be a thing of the past, along with the old policy of scrupulous – and morally blind – even-handedness as between aggressors and victims. Gone too would be war's inseparable companion, neutrality. It is easy to smile at such idealism, especially since it proved so short-lived. The dress rehearsal may have been spectacular; but the main production proved to be a very damp squib, as the United Nations rapidly sank into impotence, an early and long-term victim of the Cold War between the Western powers and the Soviet bloc. The post-1945 world proved to be a very far cry indeed from being conflict-free.

There were, however, some notable features of the post-1945 world that could be a source of (very cautious) pride. If nothing else, at least some of the rituals of war such as declarations went abruptly out of style. Moreover, the post-1945 period was remarkable for its near-absence of armed conflict between major powers. This was a particularly striking achievement in light of the fact that the two foremost powers of the postwar world, the United States and the Soviet Union, were locked in a global competition known as the Cold War. There were several nerve-wracking moments when that expression risked becoming more than a metaphor – most notably over Berlin in 1959–61, in the Cuban missile crisis of 1962 and during the Middle East conflict of 1973. It would be comforting to believe that scrupulous regard for the UN Charter's prohibition against the use of force was the major factor preventing major-power conflict. There was, however, a disturbing suspicion that the brooding presence of nuclear weapons – and the threat of mutual annihilation that they majestically and ominously posed – might have been a more potent consideration. In all events, the only sustained collision between major powers occurred in Korea in 1950–3, when American forces (bolstered by some fifteen like-minded states) faced Chinese troops (who were thinly disguised as 'volunteers' in the cause of North Korea).[2]

Conflicts between regional powers were rather less rare, with South Asia and the Middle East being the prime areas of instability. India clashed with Pakistan on three occasions from 1947 to 1971 and with China once (in 1962). By 1998, both India and Pakistan had become nuclear powers, thereby sharply raising the stakes in any future confrontations that might occur. Armed conflict was a feature of the Middle East with almost monotonous regularity, with several of the clashes pitting Israel against neighbouring Arab states. The most sanguinary of all of these post-war interstate contests was the one between Iran and Iraq in 1980–8. The continuing status of Kashmir and Palestine as flashpoints made the possibility of renewed conflict in those areas omnipresent. Other regions had their outbursts. In Southeast Asia, Vietnam invaded Cambodia and reduced the country to a virtual puppet state in 1979, along the lines of Manchukuo in the 1930s. In Africa, Somalia and Ethiopia became locked in conflict in the late 1970s. And there were small clashes in Latin America, such as the 'Football War' of 1969 between El Salvador and Honduras.

When civil conflicts are brought into the picture, however, all pretence of optimism vanishes. Here lay the major change, in material terms, in armed conflict during the post-1945 period, as the destruction and suffering wrought by civil wars dwarfed those of traditional interstate conflicts. Internal disturbances sometimes had a Cold-War character, as in the case of the Greek civil war of the middle and late 1940s, as well as in later conflicts in such diverse countries as the Congo, Yemen, the Dominican Republic, Cambodia, Angola and Nicaragua. But civil conflicts could take other 'ideological' forms as well. One was

---

[2] It is actually open to dispute whether China should be regarded as a major power at that time.

anticolonialism or national liberation, as in Kenya, Algeria, Vietnam, Zimbabwe, Angola (again) or Eritrea. Religious or ethnic differences – often combined with other factors and nurtured by ruthless politicians – were another potent fuel, in countries ranging from Cyprus, Lebanon, Sri Lanka and the Philippines, to Sudan, Bosnia, Rwanda and Kosovo. The conflict in Afghanistan in 1979–89 had the highly dubious distinction of fitting into all of these categories.

From this maze of civil conflicts would emerge one of the most distinctive contributions of socialist and Third-World thought to the legal conception of war: the idea that one particular type of internal conflict – wars of national liberation (according to the common label) – ought to be 'promoted', for legal purposes, to the full equivalent of interstate wars. This viewpoint carried the day in 1977, when two additional protocols to the Geneva Conventions were concluded; but it remained a controversial proposition in principle, although one that, as of the early twenty-first century, had no great practical impact.

The post-1945 period witnessed other, and possibly even more momentous, challenges to traditional conceptions of war. One of these trends might be called, with misgivings, the 'democratisation' of war (with suitable apologies to those who prefer to regard democracy in a positive light). It was becoming possible for ever smaller groups of private parties to enter the war business (as it could be called). Mercenary groups were one striking example. In the early 1960s, one of these succeeded, for a time, in virtually detaching a province of the Congo from its rightful governmental owner. In a number of other African states, these new warriors plied their trade with varying degrees of success. Ideological and religious motivations could sometimes prove as inspirational as money – though major-power patronage could be a powerful supporting factor as well. Nowhere was this more in evidence than in Afghanistan in the 1980s. Kashmir also offered opportunities of this nature, as did Bosnia in the 1990s.

As the twentieth century wore on, another group of small-scale warriors of a self-selected character emerged: terrorist bands. They became a familiar feature of the Middle East landscape, as Palestinian resistance to Israeli occupation grew in intensity after 1967. But they operated on a larger canvas too. Traditionally, terrorist action had been dealt with as a merely criminal matter, unconnected to war. At the hands of Israel initially, and then the United States as well, action against terrorism was militarised – a trend that accelerated spectacularly and abruptly after the large-scale suicide attacks on New York and

Washington in September 2001. This new form of war promised, or threatened, to take the law relating to war into uncharted territory – specifically into a realm of law that had hitherto been the preserve of sober judges and meticulous prosecutors. The sword and the robe were coming into perilous proximity, with results that none could foresee.

8

Regulating war

[A]s the law seeks to exert control, militant States are not slow to seek the prizes of war, while evading the penalties. And to make war under another name is an easy way of evasion. The God Mars operates, as it were, in mufti.

Julius Stone[1]

In reaction to the manifold horrors of the Great War of 1914–18, the statesmen and people of the world showed a commendable determination to place legal restrictions on future resorts to war, to replace the anarchic Hobbesian world with a more regulated order. In particular, the drafters of the Covenant of the League of Nations sought to reinstate the idea, which had prevailed in the just-war era preceding the seventeenth century, that peace was the general condition of international life, and war the exception, requiring some kind of specific justification. A somewhat bolder initiative was the Pact of Paris of 1928, which purported to prohibit completely the resort to war 'as an instrument of national policy'. At the same time, however, the world remained in many respects in thrall to nineteenth-century ways of thinking. Legal thought in particular remained shackled to positivist conceptions of war inherited from the previous century. The result was that the League Covenant and the Pact of Paris attempted to reduce the *frequency* of war without altering its basic legal character. That strategy would become the source of a good deal of frustration.

The root of the problem was that the Covenant and the Pact of Paris were too narrowly targeted. They focussed exclusively on war, while leaving other forms of armed action, such as forcible reprisals, unregulated. The result was that some of the uncertainties that had been latent within legal thought about war during the nineteenth century now assumed an urgent practical importance. For example, the distinction

[1] Stone, *Legal Controls*, at 311.

between wars and reprisals, previously the preserve chiefly of pedants and obscurantists, now had an urgent practical significance. Now that the 'resort to war' was unlawful in a wide range of circumstances (as laid down by the League of Nations Covenant), there was a serious incentive to characterise a conflict in the one manner rather than the other. There was also the problem that, if states were allowed to self-label their actions, in the manner allowed by the subjective variant of positivist thought, then they would be able to circumvent the restrictions on war by the blissfully simple device of proclaiming their action to be, say, reprisal or self-defence rather than war.

The result was a sharp decrease in wars during this period – but in the perverse, and extremely restricted, sense that armed conflicts largely ceased to be *classified* as wars. That is to say, war as a legal institution, which had become so highly developed in the nineteenth century, lost a great deal of its utility. It took on some of the qualities of a mirage – ever on the minds of lawyers and statesmen, ever ready to erupt at any moment in a violent world, but at the same time never quite present at any given time, always looming but seldom ready to hand. There was accordingly something of an atmosphere of shadow boxing in the legal history of war in the interwar years, an unsettling disconnection between the world of real events and the musings of international lawyers. For all of this, however, the period was a crucial one, if in a somewhat disheart-eningly negative way. It vividly illustrated to lawyers and statesmen the hazards of taking too precise – or 'legalistic' – a view of war. The more carefully exact the definition of war, the easier it would be for states to ensure that their militant actions fell into some other category instead. It was a hard lesson, but a valuable one. And it would form the basis for further developments after 1945.

Making a new world

By degrees, the Great War of 1914–18 evolved into a 'war to end all wars', with the crucial event being the entry of the United States into the fray in 1917. American participation was motivated not by the pursuit of any political or strategic vision but rather by Germany's policy of unrestricted submarine warfare against neutral ships, which President Woodrow Wilson, in his war message to the Congress, denounced as an infringement of 'the most sacred rights of our Nation'.[2] Wilson took

---

[2] Bartlett (ed.), *Record*, at 454.

great pains to differentiate his country's role in the struggle from that of the Allied states. He refused, for example, to join the wartime Alliance, pointedly maintaining a distinct status for the United States as an 'associated' power rather than as an ally. The United States also declined to participate in many of the blockade programmes, having previously voiced strong doubts as to the lawfulness of some of them.[3] In his Fourteen Points address of January 1918, Wilson insisted that his country demanded from the war 'nothing peculiar to ourselves'. Instead, the goal was to forge a new kind of world, 'fit and safe to live in' with respect for the self-determination of all nations. 'All the peoples of the world are in effect partners in this interest', he asserted.[4]

In effect, Wilson favoured a return to older just-war ways of thought – fittingly for a statesman with so deeply religious an outlook. This resuscitation was not, however, anything like an instantaneous process. It was brought about in something of a piecemeal fashion. We shall look at three of the most important legal signs that a return to the older outlook was in the offing: the financial arrangements of the Treaty of Versailles; the chief features of the League of Nations Covenant; and the Pact of Paris of 1928.

Peace-making in Paris

At the Paris Peace Conference of 1919, a prominent role was played by one of the components of traditional just-war doctrine: the duty of the wrongdoing party to indemnify the innocent side for the expenses that it incurred in prosecuting the struggle. The victorious Allied powers were anxious to shift at least some of the staggering costs of the war onto the losing parties. In theory at least, they could have done this simply by following the various nineteenth-century precedents of imposing financial exactions onto the losing side as a fruit of their victory. The United States, however, vigorously objected to such a practice, on the ground that it would breach one of Wilson's firm principles: that there should be no arbitrary fines or penalties imposed on defeated parties, nor any policies of financially crippling the losing states merely to prevent them from becoming powerful at some future point. Moreover, the Americans pointed out that that principle had been one of the bases of

---

[3] See generally John W. Coogan, *The End of Neutrality: The United States, Britain, and Maritime Rights, 1899–1915* (Ithaca: Cornell University Press, 1981), at 148–220.
[4] Bartlett (ed.), *Record*, at 459.

Germany's agreement to the 1918 armistice. Wilson accordingly insisted that, if Germany was going to be required to make payments to the victors, these must take the form of compensation for some kind of genuine fault or legal wrongdoing on its part.[5] How best to put this principle to practical use presented an interesting legal challenge.

One possible means of implementing this policy was on what might be termed a war-crimes basis: assessing Germany for damages for unlawful acts committed *during* the conflict, such as the invasion and occupation of Belgium or the sinking of neutral ships. This option, however, had many drawbacks. For one thing, payments on this basis could not amount to anything like the full damage caused by the war, since most of the destruction had been committed within the bounds of the laws of war. Also, the payments would be very unevenly distributed as between the victorious powers. Belgium would be the chief recipient, on the thesis that the entire war against it (complete with a four-year occupation of virtually the whole country) had been unlawful, as a violation of its neutral status. France, however, would receive comparatively little under this heading, since the four-year German occupation of the northern part of its territory was permitted by the laws of war. Britain likewise would receive hardly anything on this thesis. In addition, there was the consideration that the Allied side may have been guilty of violations of the laws of war too, particularly with regard to blockade-related policies that may have infringed the rights of neutrals.[6] It would be offensive to any good moralist, such as Wilson, that one side should pay for its unlawful acts while the other one did not.

An alternative solution – and the one that was ultimately chosen – was to assess Germany's payments on a quite different basis: that it was entirely responsible for occurrence of the war as such. If Germany were to be assessed with the *sole* responsibility for the conflict, then there would be no cause for uneasiness about the Allies being left free. It may be noted that, under this approach, Germany's payment burden would be very dramatically larger than under the war-crimes option, since Germany would become liable not merely for specific violations of the laws of war but rather for the *entire* cost of the war. It may also be noted that this war-guilt thesis (as it might be termed) signalled a

---

[5] For opposition to Wilson's view on legal grounds, see 2 Mérignhac and Lémonon, *Droit des gens*, at 605–18.

[6] For a short survey of the Allied blockade measures in the light of the law of neutrality, see Neff, *Rights and Duties*, at 149–59.

reversion to the older just-war doctrine that the unjust side in a war was obligated fully to indemnify the just side for its costs in prosecuting the conflict.

The first step in the implementation of this solution was to make a formal determination of responsibility for the war. That task was entrusted, at the Paris Peace Conference, to a body called the Commission on the Responsibility of the Authors of the War and on Enforcement of Penalties.[7] Its key conclusion was that '[t]he war was premeditated by the Central Powers ... and was the result of acts deliberately committed [by them] to make it unavoidable'. Germany and Austria-Hungary, it concluded, had 'deliberately worked to defeat all the many conciliatory proposals made by the Entente Powers and their repeated efforts to avoid war'.[8] This conclusion was duly incorporated into the Versailles Treaty as the famous 'war-guilt clause', Article 231, in the following terms: 'Germany [the article stated] accepts the responsibility ... for causing all the loss and damage to which the Allied and Associated Governments and their nationals have been subjected as a consequence of the war imposed upon them by the aggression of Germany and her allies'.[9] The term 'war guilt' is a slightly unfortunate one, since, to lawyers, the term 'guilt' primarily connotes criminal liability. The responsibility of Germany envisaged in the Versailles Treaty, however, was civil in nature, comparable to the indemnity obligation of classical just-war theory. There was a provision, in a separate section of the Versailles Treaty, for the personal criminal responsibility of Kaiser William II, for the offence of infringing treaties. It was never implemented, however, because the Netherlands, to which the ex-Kaiser fled after the German Revolution of 1918, declined either to extradite or try him.

In all events, the 'war-guilt' clause formally identified Germany as the unjust side. But even the most vindictive peace-makers (of which there was no shortage) accepted that it would be impossible in reality for Germany to pay the entire cost of the war. So it was agreed, on strictly practical grounds, that Germany would actually be assessed for only a portion of that cost: specifically, for the injuries suffered by *civilians* on the Allied side, leaving the Allied states to bear the costs and losses associated with their own military operations. This sub-category of German liability came to be known by the emotive

---

[7] For the text of its report, see 14 AJIL 95–154 (1920).

[8] *Ibid.* at 107. (Both quotations entirely in italics in the original.)

[9] Treaty of Versailles, 26 June 1919, 225 CTS 188, Art. 231. See Kelsen, *Principles*, at 33–4.

word 'reparations'.[10] The assessment of the precise amount was left to a Reparation Commission, which eventually settled on the famous (or notorious) figure of 132 billion gold francs.[11]

The Covenant of the League of Nations

A second important sign of the revival of just-war ideas in the aftermath of the Great War may be found in the policies articulated in the League of Nations Covenant. The Covenant sought to reinstate the pre-Hobbesian picture of a world in which cooperation, shared values and a community spirit prevailed, in place of the relentless and often bloody quest of self-interest that characterised the positivist tradition. This new – or rather old – sense of community spirit was principally reflected in Article 11 of the Covenant, which declared any 'war or threat of war' to be automatically 'a matter of concern to the whole League'. The key to peace, in the eyes of the drafters of the Covenant, was to prevent wars from occurring. And the way to do that was rigorously to require League member states to settle all of their disputes peacefully. The specific arrangements need not occupy us in detail.[12] It will suffice to note that, in essence, two principal peaceful-settlement mechanisms were provided: a political one (through the League Council) and a judicial one (through a newly established World Court). There was no general prohibition in the Covenant against war, however. War remained a lawful option for states, once the peaceful-settlement processes had been tried and found wanting.

League members that resorted to armed force in violation of the Covenant's rules could have claims brought against them either in the World Court (if it had jurisdiction over the matter) or before the political organs of the League itself. A notable example occurred in 1925, in the wake of a border clash between Bulgaria and Greece, in which Greek armed forces entered Bulgarian territory without authorisation. The League established a commission of inquiry into the matter, which

[10] It will be recalled that the word had been used in this sense in Funck-Brentano and Sorel Précis, at 322–7.

[11] On the reparations question, see Camuzet, Indemnité, at 83–93; 2 H. W. V. Temperley (ed.), A History of the Peace Conference of Paris: The Settlement with Germany (London: Henry Frowde and Hodder and Stoughton, 1920), at 40–91; and A. Lentin, Guilt at Versailles: Lloyd George and the Pre-history of Appeasement (London: Methuen, 1984).

[12] For a description of the Covenant's dispute-settlement provisions, see Waldock, 'Regulation', at 469–86.

assessed a payment by Greece of some $210,000 in compensation (which Greece duly paid).[13]

The League Covenant also contained some concrete arrangements for collective sanctions by the member states against countries that waged wars in violation of its provisions. These sanctions came in two forms. First, and rather vaguely, was a collective 'guarantee' (as it was sometimes called). According to Article 10 of the Covenant, each member state undertook 'to respect and preserve' the territorial integrity and political independence of all other member states in cases of 'external aggression'. The Covenant, however, was studiously silent as to how this 'guarantee' was to be implemented in practice. In particular, no League organ was given an express power to order member states to take specific action pursuant to this provision.[14] The second, and more concrete, enforcement provision was Article 16, which provided for the *automatic* imposition of economic sanctions by members of the League against any member state that resorted to war without first exhausting the peaceful-settlement options. A supplementary resolution by the League Assembly in 1921 made it clear that these economic sanctions might, in 'special circumstances', entail a naval blockade of the seacoast of the law-breaking state.[15] No other form of military enforcement action was provided for.

It is important to appreciate that neither of these sanctions was considered to constitute a war. Regarding the Article 10 'guarantee', there was never a formal pronouncement by a judicial body or a League organ on its legal character. But there was scholarly opinion to the effect that any armed action taken against aggressor states pursuant to Article 10 would not be a war – or at least that no *state* of war would arise, in the sense in which that term was commonly understood, as inherited from the nineteenth century. The reason was that the purpose of the armed response would not be to overbear completely the will of the aggressor state – that essential feature of war in the still-prevalent positivist scheme. Instead, the purpose would be the more limited one of defeating the act of aggression.[16] The situation, in other words, would not be a war in the strict legal sense but instead a case of aggression-and-self-defence – or rather of aggression met by *collective* defence. For obvious

---

[13] F. P. Walters, *History*, at 311–15. See also LNOJ 1925, at 1693–1718.

[14] On Art. 10, see Brownlie, *Use of Force*, at 62–5.

[15] Resolution on the Economic Weapon, 4 Oct. 1921, LNOJ, Special Supp. No. 6, at 24; reprinted in 17 Brit YB 148–9 (1936).

[16] See, to this effect, Scelle, 'Théorie et pratique'.

reasons, the label 'collective security' is commonly used to describe this policy of global solidarity against aggressors.

The other type of collective enforcement measure, the imposing of economic sanctions, was similarly held not to constitute a war – not even in the 'special circumstances' in which the sanctions were bolstered by a naval blockade. This position was set out in a report by the Secretary-General of the League in 1927.[17] It concluded that such a naval blockade would not constitute a war. Instead, it would be a pacific blockade, carrying the consequences that had been set out in the 1887 resolution of the Institute of International Law. That meant that the ships of the blockaded state could only be sequestered, not confiscated. Also, the rights of third states – meaning, in this context, non-members of the League – could not be impeded. The report candidly conceded that this non-interference with third-state trade 'may greatly diminish the efficiency of the economic sanctions'. But it expressed a pious hope that non-member states would show a sense of community spirit and voluntarily respect such blockades. There may have been an element of wishful thinking on this point. For present purposes, however, the important point is that a blockade mounted in support of official League sanctions was seen to be fundamentally distinct, in legal terms, from a war properly speaking. It would be a police or law-enforcement measure, in the nature of a collective reprisal – that is to say, a measure short of war, along the lines of the great-power interventions of the nineteenth century. As such, it would be, in effect, a just-war measure of the old style.

The resemblance between the League of Nations and the medieval just-war ethos was noted by no less an authority than the Catholic Church itself. Pope Pius XI, marking the 600th anniversary of the canonisation of Thomas Aquinas in 1923, proudly claimed the angelic doctor's teachings as the true foundation of the League of Nations.[18] It would be an error, however, to suppose that the League Covenant really amounted to anything like a full reinstatement of the medieval just-war system, or to a complete discarding of the positivist view of war. Old ways are not shed so readily. For one thing, the League system did not

---

[17] Legal Position Arising from the Enforcement in Time of Peace of the Measures of Economic Pressure Indicated in Article 16 of the Covenant, Particularly by a Maritime Blockade, LNOJ 1927, at 834.

[18] Pius XI, *Studiorem Ducem*, 29 June 1923, in *The Papal Encyclicals in Their Historical Context*, ed. Anne Freemantle (2nd edn, New York: New American Library, 1963), at 224.

adopt the old just-war principle of *justa causa* in anything like a full-blooded way. The medieval doctrine of *justa causa* had been, so to speak, a 'positive' concept, referring to a valid *substantive* legal ground for waging war. The League approach, however, required a *justa causa* only of a 'negative' kind. That is to say, it allowed war to occur after the clearing of various *procedural* hurdles, i.e., after the exhaustion of the peaceful-settlement processes. As the American lawyer Quincy Wright put it, in perhaps slightly unfortunate phraseology, the Covenant provided 'artificial criteria' for determining the legality of a resort to war.[19] Once the procedural hurdles were passed, then the right to wage war re-emerged, in the traditional positivist fashion, as a permissible means of resolving the dispute in question – with, apparently, no questions asked as to which side had legal right on its side, nor any distinction between offensive and defensive war.[20] The thrust of the League scheme therefore was only to delay the onset of war, not to make it illegal *per se*. That more drastic step would only be taken in 1945.

The League system is therefore best seen as a war-*prevention* mechanism, buttressed by peaceful-settlement facilities and cooling-off periods. It was an attempt to reduce – and reduce drastically – the opportunities that states had to wage war. At the same time, however, it made no attempt to alter the legal conception of war as it had been inherited from the nineteenth century. War was still seen as a rule-governed resort to armed force for the settlement of disputes, i.e., as an institution of international law in the traditional positivist sense. War still existed as before – but it was to be given a narrower range in which to roam. It was to be, as it were, fenced in by procedural barriers, rather than tamed or put to death.

The Pact of Paris

The third major sign in the interwar period of a return to just-war ways of thought was the conclusion of the Pact of Paris of 1928 (sometimes known as the Kellogg-Briand Treaty after its two principal sponsors), on the joint initiative of France and the United States.[21] The basic idea behind the Pact was to go beyond the merely procedural strictures against war contained in the League Covenant by instituting an express *general* prohibition against war. This took the specific form of a

---

[19] Wright, 'Changes', at 767.
[20] On self-defence and the League Covenant, see Alexandrov, *Self-defense*, at 29–49.
[21] Pact of Paris, 27 Aug. 1928, 94 LNTS 57.

condemnation of 'recourse to war' for the solution of international disputes, combined with a renunciation of war 'as an instrument of national policy'. A French draft of the treaty had proposed a slightly expanded version of this – referring to war as 'an instrument of individual, spontaneous, and independent political action taken on [a state's] own initiative'.[22] This language was not, in the event, included in the treaty; but it indicated that the focus of the drafters' attention was on the elimination of war in the positivist sense.[23] Armed force remained lawful under the Pact of Paris, provided that it was waged for selfless actions such as the upholding of general community values, rather than in pursuit of specifically *national* policies. That is to say, just wars in the traditional sense were not encompassed within the prohibition of the Pact. In discussions of the Pact in the League of Nations, Germany made precisely this point. It contended that the Pact and the League Covenant, when seen in combination, made it necessary 'to distinguish clearly between war as an instrument of national policy and war as a means of international action which may be considered necessary for the maintenance of order in international life'.[24]

Some of the supporters of the Pact of Paris, drawing rather more upon its spirit than its letter, made grand claims as to its significance. The Pact was sometimes said to have 'outlawed' or abolished war, by stripping it of its erstwhile status as an institution of international law.[25] The prevailing view of lawyers, however, was that it did not have so sweeping an effect as that. For example, it was widely agreed that the rules relating to the conduct of war (i.e., the Hague Rules of 1907) remained in force, as did the Hague Convention on the Opening of Hostilities. It would be more accurate to say that the Pact of Paris, rather than making war as a national-policy instrument *impossible*, instead made it *unlawful*.[26] But even that more limited achievement was no mean feat – if it could be made effective.

The significance of the Pact is perhaps best summed as saying that it was intended to mark the definitive end of the *laissez-faire* approach to war that had culminated in the nineteenth century. Duel-wars were now

---

[22] Shotwell, *War as Instrument*, at 279.

[23] On the drafting of the Pact of Paris, see Robert H. Ferrell, *Peace in Their Time: The Origins of the Kellogg-Briand Pact* (New Haven: Yale University Press, 1952).

[24] Report of the Committee on the Reconciliation of the Pact of Paris and Covenant of the League of Nations, LNOJ 1930, at 368.

[25] See, for example, 2 Guggenheim, *Traité*, at 297.

[26] See Kunz, 'Chaotic Status', at 46–8.

to become a thing of the past. The American Secretary of State Henry Stimson expressed the new philosophy vividly: 'Hereafter [he exulted] when two nations engage in armed conflict either one or both of them must be wrongdoers – violators of the general treaty [i.e., the Pact of Paris]. We no longer draw a circle about them and treat them with the punctilios of the duelist's code. Instead we denounce them as lawbreakers.'[27]

The Pact went beyond the League of Nations Covenant in one important respect, by making the resort to war illegal even *after* the League's peaceful-settlement facilities had been exhausted.[28] In another notable regard, though, it was more timid than the Covenant: it had no provision for sanctions or for collective-security action as the Covenant did. That is only to say, however, that the Pact created no *special* sanctions mechanisms, as the Covenant did. There were, however, various adverse consequences in store for violators of the Pact, springing not from the text of the Pact itself but rather from the general law of treaties. In particular, three legal effects of violation of the Pact should be noted.

The first consequence of a violation of the Pact was that a state party that was the target of an aggressive war by another state party would have a legal claim for compensation against the aggressor. The aggressor state would presumably be liable for *all* of the damage resulting from its aggression, on the model of Germany's exclusive responsibility for the Great War. A second legal effect of a violation would be that *all* states parties to the Pact could institute reprisals against the wrongdoer. This would be on the theory that any violation of the Pact constituted an offence against all parties to it, and not merely against the particular state that was attacked. These reprisals could take a variety of forms, ranging from suspensions of treaty obligations all the way to armed action. But one type would be particularly relevant and appropriate: a suspension of the duties of neutrality that would normally arise in time of war. The effect would be that the other states parties to the Pact could refuse to abide by the normal duties of abstention and impartiality and proceed instead to provide official assistance to the victim country.[29]

The third legal consequence of a resort to war in violation of the Pact was an innovation that only emerged in clear form in the 1930s: a refusal

---

[27] Henry L. Stimson, 'The Pact of Paris: Three Years of Development', 11 (Special Supp.) *Foreign Affairs* i–ix (1932), at iv.

[28] On the Pact and its legal interpretation, see Brownlie, *Use of Force*, at 80–92.

[29] See the draft Convention on the Rights and Duties of States in Case of Aggression, 33 (Supp.) AJIL 827 (1939), Arts. 2, 4.

by third states to allow an aggressive war to be a source of legal rights. This position – which (it will be recalled) had been a key feature of just-war doctrine – was most memorably outlined by Secretary Stimson in 1932 in the wake of Japan's occupation of Manchuria. In identical notes sent to Japan and China, he insisted that a war waged in breach of the Pact could not 'be the source and subject of rights'. Consequently, the United States would not 'recognize any situation, treaty, or agreement' resulting from a violation of the Pact – a stance that promptly became known as the 'Stimson Doctrine'.[30] All three of these legal consequences of violation of the Pact received the express endorsement of the International Law Association (a private body of international lawyers) in 1934, when it adopted a set of interpretive articles on the Pact.[31]

In Latin America, a regional echo of the Pact of Paris took the form of the Saavedra-Lamas Treaty of 1933, named for the then foreign minister of Argentina.[32] It was more modest on the subject of war than the Pact. Instead of a renunciation of war as such, it contained a condemnation of 'wars of aggression' (with no definition provided). In some other respects, however, it went further than the Pact did. For example, in addition to war as such, it also prohibited 'intervention' whether 'diplomatic or armed'. And it expressly incorporated the Stimson Doctrine by providing that acquisitions made by force should not be recognised as legally valid.

The art of avoiding war

It is important to appreciate that the restrictions imposed by the League Covenant and the Pact of Paris on the resort to war did not amount to a wholesale discarding of the positivist legacy. On the contrary, much of the recent past remained. The changes that followed the Great War were, so to speak, perched uneasily atop a decidedly conservative view of war inherited from the nineteenth century. Specifically, the sharp dichotomy between war and measures short of war went largely untouched throughout the interwar period. Wars properly speaking continued, in the positivist vein, to be seen as attempts by states to impose their will

---

[30] Bartlett (ed.), *Record*, at 530.
[31] International Law Association, *Report of the Thirty-eighth Conference* (London: Eastern Press, 1934), at 66–8. For various initiatives in support of the Stimson Doctrine in this period, see 2 Margorie M. Whiteman, *Digest of International Law* (Washington, D. C.: GPO, 1963), at 1145–9. See also Langer, *Seizure of Territory*.
[32] Saavedra-Lamas Treaty, 10 Oct. 1933, 163 LNTS 393.

upon one another for the furtherance of their respective national interests. Measures short of war included actions such as interventions and reprisals, which continued, as in the nineteenth century, to be governed by the older just-war considerations. The drafters of the League Covenant, as the Austrian lawyer Josef Kunz commented, 'superimposed a superstructure of treaty norms on the unchanged sociological basis, including the individualistic distribution of power, of the primitive, decentralized international community'.[33] In short, the heady new wine of collective security and international organisation was poured into old bottles.

The problem was that there were other categories of armed force waiting in the wings, so to speak, to be put to use in situations in which war was no longer available. We have encountered the three principal ones before: interventions, forcible reprisals and emergency measures such as self-defence. Armed interventions found very little use in the interwar period. The League Covenant made no provision for them (as the UN Charter later would). The only provision in the League system for armed action in the cause of community policing was the possibility, referred to above, of deploying a naval blockade in support of economic sanctions against a state unlawfully resorting to war – an action which, in the event, never occurred. On only one occasion was a League of Nations armed contingent of any kind formed: an International Force for the supervision of the Saar plebiscite in 1934–5.

Forcible reprisals, however, were resorted to on occasion, as an alternative to war, thereby presenting the international community, in more immediate terms than ever before, with the problem of making the distinction between the two activities. In addition, and more innovatively, self-defence was also offered up as a contrast to war. This led to the first serious considerations of self-defence claims by international bodies. It should not be thought, though, that self-defence claims were merely devices to disguise war-making. They were much more significant than that, for they introduced the international community in a practical way, again for the first time, to the phenomenon of aggression-and-self-defence – something that, until now, had huddled on the far margins of legal theory without making any significant appearance in state practice. That now changed, with the United States playing the role of the leading experimenter – first with a policy of the 1930s known as the 'new neutrality' and then, more conspicuously, with its 'non-belligerency' programme of 1939–41. In retrospect, these would be seen as

---

[33] Kunz, 'Sanctions', at 337.

precursors of the post-1945 international system. But the future, as always, was hidden from view; and even the present showed a mixed and confusing picture. The world, in short, was groping its way uncertainly onto new paths.

Armed reprisal and war

The key to seeing how the League Covenant accentuated the distinction between war and measures short of war – and thereby undermined its own goals – lay in the text of the Covenant itself. Specifically, the provision on automatic economic sanctions stipulated that the sanctions were to be activated against a member state that resorted to 'war' – but not, significantly, to measures short of war – in violation of the Covenant (i.e., without exhausting its peaceful-settlement obligations). The problem first presented itself in concrete form early in the League's history: in a crisis that erupted between Italy and Greece in 1923. During the process of the fixing of the boundary between Greece and Albania, an Italian member of the boundary commission was murdered in Greek territory. Italy accused Greece of being at fault and delivered an ultimatum containing a range of far-reaching demands. Among the Italian demands was one for an inquiry into the incident in the presence of an Italian military attaché, with a five-day deadline for the entire procedure, capped off with the meting out of death sentences to the guilty parties. In addition, a financial reparation of some half a million pounds sterling was demanded. (Interestingly, Italy also demanded that the victim be given a lavish funeral service in the Catholic cathedral in Athens, with the entire Greek cabinet in attendance.) Greece accepted most of these demands, but it balked at Italian participation in the inquiry. It also refused to make any financial payment, except pursuant to an assessment of responsibility by an inquiry commission. Italy, in response, sent a fleet to bombard the ancient citadel on Corfu, causing some fifteen civilian casualties in the process. The otherwise undefended island was then occupied by Italian forces without incident.

When Greece brought the matter before the Council of the League, Italy maintained that its bombardment and occupation of Corfu was not a 'resort to war' within the meaning of the Covenant. The action, it insisted, was a reprisal, a taking of a gage. As such, it could not trigger the automatic application of economic sanctions. In taking this position, Italy was standing squarely on the subjective theory of war, insisting that the Corfu incident was not a war because neither party indicated an intention to that effect. Greece, however, contested the validity of the subjective thesis. It contended that the question of whether a given conflict was a reprisal situation or a war was an objective issue, to be decided by the world community as a whole (acting through the Council of the League of Nations), not unilaterally by the party carrying out the measures.[34]

In the event, a settlement was eventually reached, involving the payment of 50 million lira by Greece to Italy on the ground of an insufficiency of due diligence in bringing the murderer to justice.[35] But the issue of the status of measures short of war under the Covenant was perceived to be of such general importance that the League Council decided to seek enlightenment from a Commission of Jurists. Specifically, the Commission was asked whether the requirement of exhausting peaceful-settlement mechanisms prior to a resort to war also applied in cases in which a state resorted to 'measures of coercion which are not meant to constitute acts of war'.[36] The Commission failed to return a clear answer to the question or to lay down any general rule. Such measures of coercion, it delphically pronounced, 'may or may not' be covered by the peaceful-settlement provisions of the Covenant. Whether the peaceful-settlement obligations were applicable in any given case was a matter to be determined by the League Council on a case-by-case basis, 'having due regard to all the circumstances of the case [at hand] and the nature of the [particular coercive] measures adopted'.[37]

It is not surprising that there was some considerable dissatisfaction with this 'resolution' of the issue. It appeared to say that forcible measures short of war were sometimes permissible and sometimes not. Several states expressed unhappiness that the Commission had provided no criteria or guidelines whatsoever for distinguishing lawful 'measures of coercion' from unlawful ones. Some countries expressed a clear preference for objective criteria in this regard over subjective ones, i.e., insisting that states ought not to have an unfettered right to self-declare

---

[34] Council mtg, 1 Sept. 1923, LNOJ 1923, at 1277. See also Wright, 'Opinion of Commission'.

[35] For a detailed, and critical, account of the rather convoluted Corfu crisis, see F. P. Walters, *History*, at 244–55.

[36] Putting the issue in this form reflected the fact that, in the Corfu crisis, Greece had not requested the imposition of economic sanctions against Italy but had merely sought to establish that Italy had breached its peaceful-settlement obligations under the Covenant. For this reason, the question of the relation between forcible reprisals and war was presented in a somewhat indirect fashion.

[37] Council mtg, 13 Mar. 1924, LNOJ 1924, at 524.

the legal character of their armed actions. Other states contended that the Covenant should be interpreted so as to subject *all* armed actions to the peaceful-settlement processes, and not merely war *per se*.[38]

The question of the distinction (if any) between forcible reprisals and war also sparked some lively scholarly debate. A representative champion of the subjective viewpoint was the German writer Karl Strupp. As a self-proclaimed 'pure-blooded positivist', he forcefully insisted that 'it is the will of States and nothing but that which decides if there is a war or reprisals'.[39] Consequently, there could be no war, in the legal sense, without 'a "will to war" on the part of at least one of the States in dispute'.[40] The only way that a reprisal could be transformed into a war was for the target country to react by declaring war (in the manner of Mexico in the Pastry War). The French lawyer Georges Scelle agreed. 'There is war', he pronounced, 'when the injured governments *wish* there to be war, but it is necessary to prove the *intention*'.[41] He conceded that governments would sometimes try to conceal their real intentions, i.e., to wage war while labelling it as a reprisal action so as to avoid the League's sanctions. But he insisted that it was possible to expose such bad faith and to take at least some action against it, if only in the realm of public opinion.[42] This subjective stance was firmly endorsed by the League Secretariat in its 1927 report on the use of a naval blockade to enforce economic sanctions. '[F]rom the legal point of view', the report flatly pronounced, 'the existence of a state of war between two States depends upon their intention and not upon the nature of their acts'.[43] This stance by the League Secretariat, probably reflecting the views of the majority of international lawyers, helped to make this period the high-water mark of the subjective theory of war.

The foremost dissenter from this orthodox positivist position, and standard-bearer for the objective school of positivist thought, was the Greek lawyer (and sometime foreign minister) Nicolas Politis. His interest in the question was more than academic, since he had represented his

---

[38] For the texts of comments by various League member states on the Commission report, see LNOJ 1926, at 597–612.

[39] 38 *Annuaire* (1934), at 137.

[40] Strupp, 'Incident de Janina', at 281–2. See also, to this same effect, Strupp, *Éléments*, at 504–6. See also the remarks of de Visscher, 38 *Annuaire* (1934), at 144–56.

[41] Scelle, 'Règles générales', at 677. (Emphasis in the original.)

[42] See also, to this same general effect, Wright, 'Changes', at 756–9.

[43] Legal Position Arising from the Enforcement in Time of Peace of the Measures of Economic Pressure Indicated in Article 16 of the Covenant, Particularly by a Maritime Blockade, LNOJ 1927, at 834.

country before the League in the Corfu crisis. He argued for the existence of objective criteria to distinguish reprisals from war, based on material factors and independent of the will of the attacking party. Politis's position actually involved a slight modification of the traditional objective view of war, in that he did not contend that the mark of war was whether the target country fought back against the attack. The dividing line between reprisal and war, in his view, was crossed when more than minimal armed force was employed in the initial attack. Reprisals of the classic kind, involving sequestration of property or the (peaceful) taking of a gage, therefore would not be wars. But bombardments and forcible occupations (such as that of Corfu) would be. Nor, in Politis's opinion, was the justice of the cause of any relevance. The only pertinent factor was the quantity of violence used.[44]

In reality, *both* the objective and the subjective views of war led to very awkward consequences in the context of distinguishing between wars and measures short of war. Consider the subjective position first. Suppose that one state resorted to armed measures of coercion, such as a forcible reprisal, without intending its action to constitute a war. Since there was no 'resort to war', the sanctions provision of the League Covenant would not be activated, even if the attack lacked any legal justification. In that event, the target country would have a legal claim against the attacker for an unlawful use of force. If, however, the target country responded by declaring war, then a war would be in progress. But it would appear that the state which 'resorted to war' would be the target country, so that it, rather than the original attacker, would be subject to the sanctions – even if the original attack had been unlawful.[45]

The League Covenant also worked perversely from the standpoint of the objective theory of war, though in a somewhat different manner. Here, the position was that, if the target country elected to fight back rather than submit to the reprisal action, then a war would be in progress – but backdated to the time of the original attack. On this thesis, the state resorting to war would arguably be the original attacker. But it was pointed out that, on this analysis, a target country would have a positive incentive to respond to a reprisal action with armed force, instead of seeking more peaceful avenues of redress. The reason is easily seen. By responding with force, and thereby throwing the onus of

---

[44] Politis, 'Représailles'. See also, to much the same effect, Kunz, 'Plus de lois', at 45–7; remarks of Brière, in 38 *Annuaire* (1934), at 94–6; and remarks of Rolin, *ibid.* at 131–2.
[45] See Visscher, 'Interprétation', at 384.

resorting to war onto the reprisal-taking state, the target country could trigger the League's automatic economic sanctions against its foe. That is to say, it would be able, by answering force with force, to compel the entire League membership, purely at its own option, to take its side in the conflict, without any regard to the legal merits of the underlying dispute.[46]

It would appear that on only one occasion did a member state of the League actually issue a formal declaration of war against a fellow member, with instructive results. This occurred in May 1933, when Paraguay declared war against Bolivia in the course of an ongoing conflict over the Gran Chaco.[47] The incident afforded a vivid insight into the frame of mind brought on by the League Covenant. Paraguay insisted that its declaration could not be considered to be a 'resort to war' within the meaning of the League Covenant – and hence that it could not activate the sanctions provision – because a state of war was *already* in existence at the time of promulgation. The true resort to war, it maintained, was previous aggression on Bolivia's part. The Covenant's economic-sanctions provision, it insisted, was directed only against aggressors (meaning, in this case, Bolivia), not against states which merely provided formal confirmation of the existence of ongoing conflicts.[48]

Bolivia, not surprisingly, offered a more sinister interpretation of the Paraguayan declaration, characterising it as a Machiavellian ploy, designed to force neighbouring states into adopting stances of neutrality – which would compel them to disallow arms shipments across their territories to Bolivia. Landlocked Bolivia, its government pointed out, was critically dependent on neighbouring states for port and transit facilities, as Paraguay was not, since war materials could be taken directly to it by water. As a result, Bolivia would be bound in an 'iron ring' while its enemy continued to import arms.[49] Bolivia accordingly challenged the League to take the Paraguayan declaration at its face value, as a resort to war, and to apply the (supposedly) mandatory economic sanctions of the League Covenant against its opponent. The League, however, was not disposed to take so drastic a step. Instead, it effectively endorsed the Paraguayan interpretation of the declaration. The Secretary-General, for example, agreed with Paraguay that the declaration had not marked the commencement of the hostilities but

---

[46] For a clear articulation of this possibility, see the statement of Sweden, in LNOJ 1926, at 607.
[47] LNOJ 1933, at 752.   [48] *Ibid.* at 754–7, 763–4.   [49] *Ibid.* at 758–60.

instead had 'merely placed on record a *de facto* situation'.[50] The member states of the League Council expressed the same view.[51]

Bolivia's fear that Paraguay's declaration of war would induce neighbouring states to adopt stances of neutrality proved to be well founded. Declarations of neutrality were issued by the five neighbouring South American states (Argentina, Brazil, Chile, Peru and Uruguay).[52] In due course, though, Paraguay was identified as the wrongdoing party because of a refusal on its part to accept a League recommendation for peaceful settlement. Even then, however, the economic-sanctions provision of the Covenant was not invoked. Instead, there was a further legalistic debate over whether responsibility for *prolonging* an *existing* conflict should be considered tantamount to 'resorting to war' within the meaning of the Covenant.[53] In the event, that discussion became academic, by virtue of Paraguay's withdrawal from the League.[54]

Self-defence and war

One of the most significant, but least noticed, developments of the interwar period was to bring self-defence, in the narrow sense of warding off an attack, into the law of interstate relations in a significant way for the first time.[55] This was hardly by conscious design, since the Covenant of the League contained no reference to self-defence. Its first major appearance in international treaty practice came in 1925, in the Treaty of Locarno, which fixed the western frontiers of Germany and bolstered them with great-power guarantees.[56] A key part of the arrangement was a commitment by Germany on the one side, and by France and Belgium on the other, not to 'attack or invade each other or resort to war against each other'. At the same time, an express exception was made for '[t]he

---

[50] Statement by the Secretary-General to the Advisory Committee, 11 Mar. 1935, LNOJ, Special Supp. No. 134, at 7.

[51] LNOJ 1933, at 765–9.

[52] For the texts of these declarations, see Déak and Jessup, *Collection*, at 9–10, 92–7, 357–8, 873–5 and 1269, respectively.

[53] See Report to the Assembly by the Advisory Committee, 15 Mar. 1935, LNOJ, Special Supp. No. 134, at 57. The report drily noted that there were 'divergent views' on this rather fine point.

[54] The legal status of the conflict was also left tantalisingly unresolved by the peace treaty which the two states eventually concluded. See Bolivia-Paraguay, Treaty of Peace, Friendship and Boundaries, 21 July 1938, 142 BFSP 479.

[55] On self-defence in the early interwar years, see Bowett, *Self-defence*, at 120–31.

[56] Treaty of Locarno, 16 Oct. 1925, 54 LNTS 289.

exercise of the right of self-defence [*défense légitime*], that is to say, resistance to ... an unprovoked act of aggression'. Similar provisions for self-defence appeared in a number of bilateral non-aggression treaties concluded in the late 1920s.[57]

The seminal event in the legal history of self-defence was the role that it played in the drafting of the Pact of Paris in 1928. The Pact, like the League Covenant, contained no express reference to self-defence. But the subject arose in an important way during the negotiations, when it became clearly established that self-defence was quite distinct from war in the nineteenth-century positivist sense of the term. The issue arose when France proposed the inclusion of an express statement that there was no intention 'to infringe upon the exercise of ... rights of legitimate self-defence'.[58] The United States objected to this proposal, on the ground that self-defence, like aggression (to which it was a response), did not lend itself to precise or succinct definition. Nevertheless, the United States was strongly in agreement that self-defence in the face of an aggressive attack was permissible under the Pact. As Secretary of State Kellogg stated in a diplomatic note during the drafting stages, self-defence 'is inherent in every sovereign state and is implicitly in every treaty. Every nation is free at all times and regardless of treaty provisions to defend its territory from attack or invasion and it alone is competent to decide whether circumstances require recourse to war in self-defence.'[59] For this very reason, Kellogg maintained, there was no point in including an express reference to the subject in the treaty, since 'no treaty can add to the natural right of self-defence'.[60] Kellogg's advice prevailed, and self-defence duly went unmentioned in the final Treaty text – not because a right of self-defence did not exist, but, on the contrary, because it was *so* firmly entrenched, as an inherent right of states, that no treaty action could make it any stronger than it already was. In all events, there was no doubt that self-defence remained lawful even as war was renounced.[61]

On three notable occasions in the interwar period, claims of self-defence were considered by the international community – although none was by a judicial body – marking the first solid state practice in the area. The first occurred in the context of the China–Japan crisis of 1931,

---

[57] For details, see Ago, 'Eighth Report', at 58.
[58] Shotwell, *War as an Instrument*, at 279.
[59] American note of 23 June 1928, in *ibid.* at 286–7.   [60] *Ibid.*
[61] On self-defence and the Pact of Paris, see Bowett, *Self-defence*, at 132–8; and Alexandrov, *Self-defense*, at 51–76.

when Japan invaded and occupied Manchuria, establishing the nominally independent state of Manchukuo. There was no declaration of war by either side, nor were diplomatic relations broken. Japan did, however, apply the Hague Conventions of 1907.[62] No neutrality proclamations were issued by third states, although the Soviet Union cautiously promulgated a Declaration of Non-intervention.[63] Neither side made any strong attempt to present the conflict as a war. China described it in such terms as a 'premeditated attack', or as 'severe hostilities' or as 'Japanese military aggression'.[64] Japan referred to it as an 'incident'.[65] It justified its actions in various ways, for example as a punitive or hot-pursuit expedition against brigands ('undesirable elements'), or as a police-style measure to impose order in an otherwise anarchic situation – but not as a war against the state of China itself.[66] Its chief contention, though, was that it acted for the purpose of 'defending rights and interests on which her [Japan's] very existence depends'.[67] In putting forward this justification, Japan referred to the *Caroline* incident of the previous century and to the standard for necessity articulated by Webster.[68]

The matter was considered by a special Committee of Nineteen at the League of Nations. It agreed with Japan that the crisis was not a declared war contrary to the Covenant, referring cautiously to 'Japanese military operations' and to 'action taken by the Japanese troops'. The Committee also concluded, however, that the situation was not a mere frontier violation, since 'a large part of Chinese territory has been forcibly seized and occupied by Japanese troops'. It then considered Japan's self-defence claim. Conceding that Japanese officers on the scene may have sincerely believed that their actions constituted self-defence, the Committee nevertheless insisted on making its own assessment of the situation – and effectively rejecting Japan's self-defence claim.[69] The Committee's conclusion was

---

[62] Grob, *Relativity*, at 216–17.
[63] Declaration of Non-intervention in the Manchurian Conflict, 29 Oct. 1931, in Déak and Jessup, *Collection*, at 1074.
[64] Declaration of the National Government of the Republic of China, 20 Sept. 1932, LNOJ, Special Supp. No. 111, at 85.
[65] Special Session of the League Assembly, 9th Plenary Mtg, 6 Dec. 1932, Verbatim Record, at 7, 8.
[66] See Council mtg of 25 Jan. 1932, LNOJ 1932, at 328–32; Council mtg of 29 Jan. 1932, *ibid.* at 338–40; and Council mtg of 30 Jan. 1932, *ibid.* at 344–6.
[67] Council mtg of 25 Jan. 1932, *ibid.*, at 332.   [68] LNOJ, Special Supp. No. 111, at 105.
[69] LNOJ, Special Supp. No. 112, at 60, 72–3. The Committee stated its conclusion somewhat indirectly, by holding that Japan had 'forcibly seized and occupied' Chinese territory, coupling this with an express exoneration of China for any responsibility for the crisis.

endorsed by the League Assembly.[70] The most immediate consequence of the League's action was Japan's withdrawal from the organisation.

The second noteworthy self-defence claim arose in the Ethiopian crisis of 1935–6. This conflict, like the China–Japan one, lacked the traditional trappings of a war. There was no declaration of war by either side – nor even, in the early phases of the struggle, a rupture of diplomatic relations. Italy justified its military action as 'necessary defensive measures' and 'measures of legitimate defense' and the like, insisting that this was an inherent right of states that had not been limited by the Covenant of the League or by any other instrument.[71] The League established an ad hoc Committee of Six, which considered the Italian self-defence claim and rejected it, concluding instead that Italy had resorted to war in breach of the Covenant. In so holding, the Committee expressly stated that '[i]t is not necessary that war should have been formally declared' prior to an invocation of sanctions under Article 16 of the Covenant.[72] This conclusion was duly endorsed by the League Assembly.[73] This finding activated, for the first and only time in the League's history, the economic-sanctions provision – although to no avail in the event, since Italy went on to conquer Ethiopia. In mid-1936, the League conceded defeat and lifted the sanctions.

The third occasion on which the League considered self-defence was in 1937, in the wake of the armed conflict between Japan and China which followed a clash between the two states' forces at the Marco Polo Bridge near Beijing. Although Japan had withdrawn from the League by this time – thereby removing the dispute from the reach of the Covenant's provision on economic sanctions – the League Sub-Committee (of its Far Eastern Advisory Committee) which investigated the crisis held self-defence to be the only possible justification for that country's actions. It then proceeded, in the clearest statement made by the League on the subject prior to the Second World War, to hold that Japan's actions did not qualify as self-defence.[74] This finding was endorsed on the

---

[70] *Ibid.* at 22–3.

[71] See Council mtg of 5 Oct. 1935, LNOJ 1935, at 1209–12; and Council mtg of 7 Oct. 1935, *ibid.* at 1217–19.

[72] Report of the Committee of Six, Council mtg of 7 Oct. 1935, *ibid.* at 1223–5. The six members were: Britain, Chile, Denmark, France, Portugal and Romania. The report was approved unanimously, save for Italy's dissent. For documentation relating to the situation, see *ibid.* at 1534–1632.

[73] Assembly mtg of 10 Oct. 1935, LNOJ, Special Supp. No. 138, at 113–14.

[74] First Report of the Sub-Committee of the Far-East Advisory Committee, 5 Oct. 1937, LNOJ, Special Supp. No. 177, at 42.

following day by the League Assembly.[75] But the fighting continued, right up to 1945.

One important feature of these discouraging experiences should be noted, concerning the relative merits of reprisal and self-defence as a justification for a resort to armed force whenever there was concern about activating the sanctions provision of the League Covenant. Of these two possibilities, reprisal was certainly the more attractive choice for an attacking state, particularly if the subjective theory of war was held to be the correct one. Since, on this theory, the will of the attacking state was the decisive feature distinguishing reprisal from war, the attacker could self-characterise its action as a reprisal without fear of contradiction. Even if the attack was not justifiable as a reprisal – i.e., even if there was no prior wrongful act on the target state's part – there would still be no state of war because of the absence of the necessary intention, and the Covenant's sanctions provision would therefore still not be activated. Self-defence was the less attractive option because, on the basis of the treatment of self-defence claims in League of Nations deliberations, there was no right of self-characterisation, as there was with reprisals. Self-defence claims were objectively determinable by an impartial body, on the basis of all the circumstances of the particular case.[76]

Aggression and self-defence

It should not be supposed that characterising a resort to armed force as a reprisal or as self-defence, rather than as a war, was a strategem exclusively for the benefit of aggressors. During the 1930s, it became apparent that this taxonomic 'game' (if it may be so called) could also be played by states seeking to defeat aggression. The most striking demonstration was provided by the United States in the application of a controversial policy known as the 'new neutrality', which involved the express designation of foreign conflicts as wars – or, as the case may be, non-designation. One effect of this policy was to provide still further evidence of the malleability of the concept of a state of war. Another effect was to demonstrate, in concrete terms, for the first time, the difference between, on the one hand, war properly speaking and, on the other hand, a situation of aggression-and-self-defence.

---

[75] *Ibid.* at 34, 35.
[76] See, to this effect, remarks of Politis, Special Session of the League Assembly, mtg of 7 Dec. 1932, Verbatim Record, at 6.

The essence of the 'new neutrality' strategy may be stated very simply. It was to isolate armed conflict when it occurred, and thereby to prevent the violence from spreading. It was therefore, in a manner of speaking, a containment or quarantine policy, the centrepiece of which was the imposition of even-handed arms embargoes against both warring parties. This new version of neutrality therefore envisaged not only that the neutral state would abstain from entering the hostilities but also that it would take care not to 'feed' the conflict by supplying the contenders with weaponry. That meant, specifically, that the third state in question should refrain from exercising the traditional neutral prerogative of permitting its nationals to sell arms, in private transactions, to the belligerents.[77] The renunciation of this traditional right was the 'new' element of this innovative version of neutrality.

The principal inventor and champion of the policy was the American lawyer Charles Warren.[78] His primary concern was to ensure that, in the event of another major European conflict, there would be no repetition of the American experience of 1914–17. On that occasion, the American contacts with the Allied side had been so massive (it was argued) as to make the country a de facto, if not de jure, partner of the Allies – and, by that very token, to induce Germany to bring it formally into the war by launching unrestricted submarine warfare against it. The chief advantage of the plan was not so much the withholding of arms from belligerents, but rather the minimising of the chances that the third state would be 'sucked into' the conflict against its better judgment and true wishes, as had happened (in the eyes of Warren and his followers) to the United States. The policy was put into action by the United States with two initiatives in the mid-1930s. One was the Debt Default Act of 1934, designed to prohibit American bank lending to belligerents in the event of another European war. The method adopted was to ban lending by American banks to foreign states that were in default on loans to the American government (which covered all of the major European powers).[79] The other law was the Neutrality Act of 1935, which required the president,

---

[77] The basic neutral duty of abstention from participation in the war only meant that a neutral *government* could not supply arms to belligerents. Private parties were permitted to do so – subject, however, to the risk that their arms shipments might be captured and confiscated by the opposing side whilst in transit.

[78] See, for example, Charles Warren, 'Troubles of a Neutral', 12 *Foreign Affairs* 377–94 (1934); and Charles Warren, 'Prepare for Neutrality', 24 *Yale Review* 467–78 (1935).

[79] 18 USC s. 955. On the Debt Default Act, see J. C. Vinson, 'War Debts and Legislation: The Johnson Act of 1934', 50 *Mid-America* 206–22 (1968).

upon determining the existence of a foreign war, to order a halt to arms shipments to both sides, and also to prohibit American nationals from travelling in designated war zones.[80]

The 'new neutrality' policy was controversial for a number of reasons. Some opposed it as a policy of 'ostrich-like isolationism' (in the scornful words of Stimson), which undermined wider community goals of solidarity and collective security.[81] Others denounced it as a craven surrender of traditional neutral rights of which the United States had long been the world's most stalwart champion.[82] The first occasion for putting the policy into effect, the Italian–Ethiopian conflict of 1935–6, proved a painful lesson, providing support for the critics. President Roosevelt, following the lead of the League of Nations, determined a war to be in progress, despite the absence of any formal declaration by either side. As a result, American arms shipments to both sides were duly halted. Critics of this policy – and they were many and vocal – grumbled that the practical effect was to deprive Ethiopia of arms shipments that it might otherwise have received, and thereby to facilitate the Italian conquest.[83]

It soon became apparent, though, that the 'new neutrality' policy had sufficient flexibility to enable it to be applied, so to speak, in reverse. That is to say, the president might carefully find war *not* to exist in situations when partiality was the preferred policy. This inverse form of the 'new neutrality' was strikingly demonstrated in the context of the Far Eastern crisis, when armed conflict between Japan and China broke out in 1937, without formal declarations by either side. The dilemma was essentially the same as in the Ethiopian case: that an arms embargo that was impartial on its face would operate, in practice, against the victim state (China), because China was dependent on foreign suppliers for its weaponry while Japan possessed an adequate home-based arms industry. To avoid the prejudice to China that would result from an arms embargo, President Roosevelt, reflecting general American public opinion, pointedly refrained from pronouncing the conflict to be a war.

The effect of this policy was that the United States treated the conflict between China and Japan not as a war but rather as a case of aggression-

---

[80] Neutrality Act of 1935, 49 Stat 1081.   [81] Bartlett (ed.), *Record*, at 581.

[82] See, for example, Edwin M. Borchard and William Potter Lage, *Neutrality for the United States* (2nd edn, New Haven: Yale University Press, 1940).

[83] See, for example, Philip Marshall Brown, 'Malevolent Neutrality', 30 AJIL 88–90 (1936). On the American policy in the Ethiopian crisis, see Divine, *Illusion of Neutrality*, at 122–34.

and-self-defence – with the key distinction between the two being that situations of aggression-and-self-defence did not, or not necessarily, entail the automatic application of the 'new neutrality' policy, as a war did. It is true that what was at stake was not, strictly speaking, the actual international law of neutrality, but only the particular 'new neutrality' policy of the United States. In spirit, though, this distinction mattered little. The view was gradually gaining force that, in cases of aggression-and-self-defence, as distinct from wars, the law of neutrality was not applicable, or at least not in anything like its full form.

Some interesting parallel conclusions were emerging from the League's deliberations in Geneva. As noted above, the League of Nations held that Japan's action in this crisis was not justifiable as self-defence. But the League Assembly went a step further by expressly stating its 'moral support' for China and urging member states to do nothing to weaken that country's power of resistance.[84] In other words, it too was concluding that, in a case such as this one, third states were released from the obligations of the law of neutrality that normally applied in time of war.

Scholarly guidance for this juridical path-finding was provided by a research team at Harvard University Law School, headed by Philip C. Jessup (a professor at Columbia Law School and future World Court judge). This group concluded a draft Convention on the Rights and Duties of States in Case of Aggression in what proved to be the timely year of 1939.[85] It spelled out, in detail and for the first time, the way in which cases of aggression-and-self-defence differed from wars – in terms distinctly reminiscent of classical just-war thought. First and foremost, aggressor states were to possess *none* of the traditional rights of belligerents. They were, however, to be subject to all of the traditional *duties* of belligerents (such as the duty to conduct military operations in accordance with the laws of war). The defending state, in contrast, was accorded the normal range of rights, as well as duties, of belligerents. There was a similarly momentous difference regarding third states. They could become 'co-belligerents' with the defending country (or allies, in traditional parlance). More notably, a new category was established, of what were called 'supporting states'. These were countries which did not wish to become parties to the conflict but wished to make at least some material contribution to the defeat of aggression. Third countries could become 'supporting states' at will and thereby be permitted to suspend

---

[84] Assembly Res. of 6 Oct. 1937, LNOJ, Special Supp. No. 177, at 35.
[85] 33 (Supp.) AJIL 827 (1939).

the performance of any treaties which they had concluded with the aggressor. This would allow them, for example, to impose economic sanctions without legal liability, even if a trade agreement had been concluded with the aggressor state. More significantly, the law of neutrality was suspended, so as to excuse 'supporting states' from being subject to any of the traditional duties of neutrals *vis-à-vis* the attacking country – while continuing to be entitled to all of the benefits of neutrality. Further in this vein, 'supporting states' were entitled to discriminate against the aggressor, in various respects. They could, for example, assist the victim country by lending it money or allowing it exclusive access to their ports, without incurring legal liability to the aggressor.[86]

This draft Convention had no official status and was never adopted by countries. But it shone a powerful conceptual searchlight into a very murky and inchoate part of the law. It should not be thought, though, that the issues raised by the draft were merely theoretical. On the contrary, the world was just about to receive the most dramatic demonstration of the art of being a 'supporting state'. It fell to the United States to play this interesting pedagogical role.

'Non-belligerency'

The most spectacular occasion for treating an armed conflict, de facto if not quite de jure, as a case of aggression-and-self-defence instead of war was the Second World War. From the very outset of the struggle, with Germany's attack on Poland in September 1939, with no prior declaration of war, certain third countries, most notably the United States, found themselves in a painful dilemma. The American population was reluctant to enter the struggle, but sentiment was overwhelmingly on the side of the Allies. The United States accordingly became what the authors of the Harvard draft Convention had termed a 'supporting state' of the victims of German aggression. Policies were soon devised to reflect this state of affairs, with neutrality laws changed to allow arms flows to the Allied side. The United States made no serious effort to contend that its conduct was compatible with the law of neutrality. On the contrary, it characterised itself not as a neutral in the traditional sense but as a 'non-belligerent' – a supporter of the Allied side but from the sidelines, as a supplier of war materials. The culmination of this 'non-belligerency' policy was the programme labelled (somewhat

---

[86] Commentary to the Draft Convention, *ibid.* at 902.

cryptically) as 'lend-lease' for the open provision of assistance to the Allies on a huge scale.

Not surprisingly, there were misgivings about this policy on the part of some international lawyers who contended that the policy constituted a flagrant violation of the law of neutrality. Edwin Borchard, for example, a professor at Yale Law School and an unflinching champion of traditional neutrality policies, derided 'non-belligerency' as merely 'a name used as a modern excuse for violating the laws of neutrality'.[87] Supporters of the policy put forward two principal justifications for it. The first one was that the American actions could be seen as measures of self-defence or self-preservation – and, as such, having a higher legal status or priority than the duties imposed by the law of neutrality. On this argument, the United States's *own* security was in mortal danger; and the most reasonable and moderate way of meeting the challenge, in the particular circumstances, was not to become a belligerent but to provide assistance to Allied states on the front lines. A second justification was that the American policy was a reprisal measure against Germany for its violation of the Pact of Paris. By resorting to war in breach of the Pact, Germany (on this argument) had infringed the legal rights of *all* parties to the Pact. The United States (on this argument) was now taking a reprisal for that infringement, in the form of suspending the performance of its normal duties as a neutral, which it would otherwise concededly owe to Germany.[88]

There was some support for this policy in earlier pronouncements. For example, the League Assembly's resolution on economic sanctions of 1921 had specified that League members were entitled to commit 'acts of war' against a member state that went to war in breach of the Covenant, *without* these amounting to a state of war.[89] This reprisal theory also found favour in the 1934 resolution of the International Law Association on the Pact of Paris (noted above), and in the 1939 Harvard Research draft Convention on the Rights and Duties of States in Case of Aggression.[90]

---

[87] Borchard, 'War, Neutrality and Non-belligerency', at 624.

[88] Both arguments were eloquently put in Jackson, 'Address'. For an attack on the Jackson view, see Borchard, 'War, Neutrality and Non-belligerency'. For a defence, see Wright, 'Permissive Sanctions Against Aggression', 36 AJIL 103–6 (1942).

[89] Resolution on the Economic Weapon, 4 Oct. 1921, LNOJ, Special Supp. No. 6, at 24; reprinted in 17 Brit YB 148–9 (1936). There would, of course, be a state of war between the aggressor and its actual victim.

[90] International Law Association, *Report of the Thirty-eighth Conference* (London: Eastern Press, 1934), at 66–8; and Harvard Research draft Convention on the Rights and Duties of

If the argument based on Germany's violation of the Pact of Paris was carried to its logical conclusion, it could be contended that the Second World War (as it was already being labelled) was not really a war, but rather an instance of aggression-and-self-defence, on the most spectacular scale.[91] This argument was not advanced in this full and explicit form at the time. Indeed, it would have struck many persons as decidedly odd to suppose that this most titanic of all armed conflicts was not, from the legal standpoint, actually a war. Even today, that distinction can hardly be said to be an intuitive one to the average person. But the world was learning – painfully – to think in new ways. And the new order that was constructed after 1945 would be founded very strongly upon just such a proposition. The effect would be, at least in the eyes of some, to make *all* interstate armed conflicts into, so to speak, miniature versions of the Second World War – i.e., into cases of aggression-and-self-defence, rather than wars in the traditional positivist sense. In short, the end of war was nigh. Or so it was earnestly hoped.

States in Case of Aggression, 33 (Supp.) AJIL 827 (1939), Arts. 5, 12. See also Q. Wright, 'Lend-lease Bill'.

[91] See Borchard, '"War" and "Peace"', at 114–15. For a non-committal post-war exposition of the thesis that the Second World War was not a true war, see Q. Wright, 'Status', at 299–300.

9

Farewell to war?

War in the legal sense has been in large measure 'outlawed'; that is, . . .
international law . . . no longer recognizes that large-scale hostilities may
constitute a 'state of war' in which the belligerents are legally equal.

Quincy Wright[1]

Banished as a legal institution, war now remains an event calling for legal
regulation for the sake of humanity and the dignity of man.

Hersch Lauterpacht[2]

Never was there a more moralistic conflict than the Second World War. As
a contest between Good and Evil, it was seen to be at the furthest possible
remove from the positivist conception of war of the nineteenth century,
with its amoral focus on clashes between parochial state interests. In
1939–45, humankind itself was the cause. With the spirit of righteousness
as heavy in the air as the stench of corpses, it was hardly surprising that
just-war ideals should strongly pervade the immediate post-war era. And
this time, the task would be far more thoroughly done than in the interwar
period. The drafters of the United Nations Charter sought to go beyond the
League Covenant and the Pact of Paris, by banning *all* resorts to armed
force and thereby effacing the legal distinction between war and measures
short of war. The result was the establishment of a thoroughgoing general
norm of pacifism in international relations, directly reminiscent of the
pacifistic vision of the early Christian era which had lain at the heart of
medieval just-war doctrine.

The UN regime duplicated the earlier just-war vision in another
important way too: by spelling out the exceptional circumstances in
which resorts to armed force *would* be allowed. There were two such

---

[1] Wright, 'Outlawry', at 365.   [2] H. Lauterpacht, 'Limits', at 240.

situations. One was self-defence for cases of emergency action against aggression. But the primary situation in which armed force would be justified was community law-enforcement action, by the UN itself. In the early post-war years, a number of international lawyers expressed a warm approval of these new arrangements, sometimes making express comparisons with the older medieval just-war ethos. The Colombian lawyer J. M. Yepes, for example, openly welcomed 'a renaissance of this notion of the *bellum justum* which played a great role in the creation of international law'.[3] In the same spirit, some lawyers rushed to proclaim that, by implication if not expressly, the UN Charter brought about the abolition of war in its nineteenth-century sense, as an honoured institution of international law.

Events on the world stage failed, in substantial part, to fulfil these bracing promises. Even if war was no longer a legal institution in the nineteenth-century fashion, most – if not necessarily quite all – of the individual elements of that package managed to survive in other legal guises. What the world really witnessed after 1945 was less the abolition of war than its reconceptualisation. The pieces of the puzzle, so to speak, remained in existence; but they were assembled into somewhat different patterns or pictures. This process of reconceptualisation or reassembly came about largely as a result of two major factors, both of them so far-reaching as justly to merit the label of 'revolution'. One was the 'self-defence revolution' (as it will be termed). It marked the full emergence of self-defence to the front and centre of the international stage, as a kind of all-purpose justification for unilateral resorts to armed force. The other major factor undermining the abolition of war was what will be termed the 'humanitarian revolution'. This was a seismic shift in fundamental conceptions of the laws on the conduct of armed conflict: away from a focus on fairness and mutuality as between the warring states, to a primary concern with relieving the suffering of victims of war.

There was a certain division of labour, as it might be termed, between these two revolutions. The self-defence revolution was principally addressed to the question of justifications for resorting to armed force (the *jus ad bellum* in legal argot). The humanitarian revolution was chiefly concerned with issues relating to the *conduct* of hostilities (the *jus in bello*, in legal-ese). In all events, the ironic effect of these two changes, in combination, was to bring about a conception of armed conflict bearing a remarkable resemblance to the objective theory of war

---

[3] 47(1) *Annuaire* (1957), at 597. See also Yepes, *Philosophie*, at 44–8.

of the nineteenth century. Its thesis was that the outbreak of de facto armed conflict between two states, whatever the circumstances and whatever the legal justifications, automatically gave rise to a certain predictable range of legal consequences. As in the old objective theory, there was no urgency about attaching the specific label 'state of war' to the situation. The important point was the practical one of ensuring that the legal rules attaching to situations of armed conflict were duly applied. This seemed a pragmatic, if not very idealistic, way of stripping war of its legitimacy while continuing the effort to regulate it and to moderate its horrors. There continued to be doubts, though, as to whether the idea of a state of war could really be altogether dispensed with. Suspicions remained that the traditional state of war may have had certain potentially useful features that the pragmatic picture of war as de facto armed conflict failed adequately to capture.

A neo-just-war order

It is not possible to give anything like a detailed account of the UN system.[4] Instead, our task will be to point out the manner in which the UN Charter marked a forthright turning away from nineteenth-century positivist conceptions of war, in favour of a return to a just-war conception of international relations in general and of war and peace in particular. Very clearly present in the UN Charter system were the two fundamental elements of a generic just-war system. First was the thesis that the normal or residual condition of international relations was one of peace. This was directly contrary to the Hobbesian outlook that underlay the positivist view, in which competition and conflict were seen as the basic features of global affairs. The second element was the exposition of the conditions under which, exceptionally, armed force would be justified. These were two in number. First was armed enforcement action by the UN itself to defeat aggressors. This was, of course, war in the manner of the Second World War, when Britain and France leapt gallantly (if ineffectually) to the aid of Poland when it was attacked. The other kind of just war was of a very much lesser stature. This was self-defence, now expressly enshrined in the text of the UN Charter itself. This was designed to be merely a stop-gap measure, pending the

---

[4] Adam Roberts and Benedict Kingsbury (eds.), *United Nations, Divided World: The UN's Roles in International Relations* (2nd edn, Oxford: Clarendon Press, 1993), may be usefully consulted for this purpose.

mobilisation of community enforcement by the UN. A key point is that neither of these types of just war was a war in the nineteenth-century positivist sense because neither of them consisted of an attempt by a single state to bend another one to its will.

Banning the use of force

The basic prohibition against war in the post-1945 neo-just-war order was set out in Article 2(4) of the UN Charter, which read simply as follows: 'All Members shall refrain in their international relations from the threat or use of force against the territorial integrity or political independence of any state, or in any other manner inconsistent with the Purposes of the United Nations'.[5] In a certain sense, this provision signified a rejection of the Hobbesian view of international relations as being inherently competitive and war-riven. When compared to medieval just-war doctrine, however, Article 2(4) of the UN Charter was a thin brew indeed. It was simply a rule prohibiting force, with no indication that that rule has deep roots in any comprehensive and widely shared view of human social relations in general, as was the case in the Middle Ages. In that era, the pacifist outlook had been powerfully embedded in an elaborate and detailed corpus of natural-law thought, bolstered by an equally elaborate body of Christian doctrine. In the post-1945 world, there was no such rich and detailed doctrine underpinning the norm of world peace. This was due in large part of course to the high degree of religious and cultural heterogeneity of the global scene, as compared to that of Christian Europe in the Middle Ages. As a result, the rule on the non-use of force was something more in the nature of a pious hope, based on the recent searing experience of two world wars, than of a deep-rooted and widely shared value. The UN Charter, in short, was drafted by lawyers and statesmen, not by doctrinaire pacifists. It was an urgent response to local and immediate demands and conditions rather than an expression of eternal verities.

It is not possible to undertake any extensive analysis of the meaning of this basic UN Charter prohibition against the use of force. But a couple of its most salient features are worth noting very briefly. For one thing, it has become clear, largely as a result of a World Court case brought by Nicaragua against the United States in 1986, that 'force', as used in the

---

[5] The World Court has held that this ban on force is not simply a treaty rule binding UN member states, but also a general rule of customary law. *Nicaragua* v. *USA*, 1986 ICJ Rep. 14, para. 188 (hereinafter '*Nicaragua* v. *USA*').

Charter provision, has a broader meaning than the obvious one of mounting a direct invasion of another country. The ban on the use of force also encompassed such indirect measures as the supplying of an insurgent force in another country with weaponry, training, intelligence and the like, in conjunction with such measures as the mining of ports. It may be noted, though, that a supply of financial assistance to an insurgent group does not constitute a use of force.[6] Further elaboration in this area will be required in the future, but at least a start had been made by the end of the twentieth century.

It may also be noted that, although Article 2(4) did not expressly state that measures short of war, such as forcible reprisals, were within the scope of the ban, there was a broad consensus amongst lawyers that they were. The UN Security Council, for example, in 1964, stated forcible reprisals to be a violation of the Charter.[7] The UN General Assembly endorsed that position in 1970.[8] More importantly from the legal standpoint, judicial support was provided by the World Court in the *Nicaragua* v. *United States* case of 1986, and again in 1996, when it handed down an advisory opinion on nuclear weapons.[9] Scholarly commentary has been to the same effect.[10] If this position is the correct one, then the UN Charter succeeded, at one fell swoop, in eliminating the legal relevance of the distinction between wars and forcible reprisals, which had so bedevilled lawyers in the interwar period. It is only necessary to note, in passing, that the UN Charter tamed reprisals (so to speak); but it did not completely ban them. Reprisals – rechristened as 'countermeasures' in the post-1945 period – remained permissible so long as they took a non-forcible form, such as an economic boycott or the suspension of performance of a treaty obligation.[11]

Perhaps the most important point of all about the UN Charter's ban on the use of force, for present purposes, is the widespread, if largely tacit, agreement that a resort to force in violation of the ban does *not*

---

[6] *Nicaragua* v. *USA*, paras. 92–116.

[7] SC Res. 188 (9 Apr. 1964), 19 SCOR, Res and Dec, at 9.

[8] Declaration on the Principles of International Law Concerning Friendly Relations and Cooperation among States, GA Res. 2625, 25 UN GAOR, Supp. No. 28, UN Doc. A/8028, at 121; reprinted in 65 AJIL 243–51 (1971) (hereinafter 'Declaration on Friendly Relations').

[9] *Nicaragua* v. *USA*, paras. 188–91; and The Legality of the Threat or Use of Nuclear Weapons, 1996 ICJ Rep. 225, para. 46.

[10] See, for example, Partsch, 'Reprisals', in 4 *Encyclopaedia of Public International Law*, ed. Rudolf Bernhardt (Amsterdam: North-Holland, 2000), at 202.

[11] See Omer Yousif Elagab, *The Legality of Non-forcible Counter-measures in International Law* (Oxford: Clarendon Press, 1988).

constitute a war, but rather (in effect) an unlawful act of aggression committed in peacetime. If the country that was attacked responded by exercising its right of self-defence in the narrow sense (i.e., by fending off the attack but going no further than that), then the situation would be a case of aggression-and-self-defence – but still not a war. If the victim country responded by going further than the law of narrow self-defence allowed – by, say, repelling the attack and then carrying the conflict into the aggressor's home territory (as was done by Iran during the Iran–Iraq conflict in the 1980s), then there was room for debate as to whether the struggle would be a war, a matter that will be considered in due course. For the present, it is only necessary to take brief note of the legal consequences that would flow from a violation of the UN Charter's ban on the use of force. There were five such consequences. Three of them were familiar from the general international law of the interwar period, and two of them were new. A rapid survey will serve to fix them in mind. The three familiar consequences may be recalled initially.

The first consequence of resorting to force unlawfully was liability to pay compensation for all damage resulting from the wrongdoing.[12] On several occasions in the post-1945 period, this principle was actually applied. The first one was in the 1980s, when Nicaragua successfully claimed in the World Court that the United States' provision of large-scale assistance to insurgents based in neighbouring Honduras amounted to a violation of the ban against the use of force.[13] Nicaragua estimated its damages at $370.2 million, although, in the event, it withdrew its claim before the damages were actually assessed by the Court.[14] Where Nicaragua led, other countries followed, though not always so successfully. In 1999, the Federal Republic of Yugoslavia (FRY) brought legal actions in the World Court against ten NATO states for the bombing attacks in connection with the Kosovo crisis of that year. The Congo filed claims in the World Court against Uganda in 1999 and against Rwanda in 2002 for alleged armed interventions by those states in civil strife that was raging in the Congo. (Uganda then counterclaimed against the Congo.) At the end of 2003, these cases were still pending before the Court. In one especially striking case,

---

[12] See Q. Wright, 'Outlawry', at 372–3; Brownlie, *Use of Force*, at 147–9; and Baxter, 'Legal Consequences'.

[13] *Nicaragua v. USA*, paras. 227–8. Strictly speaking, the United States was held to have violated not the UN Charter but rather the *customary*-law rule to the same effect. In substance, though, this was fully equivalent to a violation of the Charter provision.

[14] The claim was withdrawn in the wake of the election of a pro-American government in Nicaragua, replacing the one that had instituted the suit.

compensation was actually paid for unlawful aggression, even if far from gracefully. This was by Iraq to the various victims of its takeover and occupation of Kuwait in 1990–1. In this case, compensation came about not from judicial action but rather at the hands of the UN Security Council, in the wake of the forcible expulsion of Iraq from Kuwait.[15] The assessment and distribution of the sums of money were undertaken by an administrative body called the UN Compensation Commission, with the necessary funds coming from the proceeds of Iraqi oil sales. By May 2004, some $48 billion worth of awards had been made (and nearly $18 billion actually distributed), not only to Kuwait but also to a host of other parties, including private individuals, who had suffered losses from the takeover.[16]

A second consequence of violating the general ban on the use of force was of the utmost importance: that third states might refrain, as a matter of reprisal, from applying the law of neutrality and instead give overt support to the victim country.[17] Herein lay perhaps the most significant difference between a war and a case of aggression-and-self-defence: that a war activates the law of neutrality, thereby making impartiality mandatory on the part of third parties; while aggression-and-self-defence situations allow third parties to be partial (towards the victim state, of course). Some even went so far as to hold partiality to be required rather than merely permitted.[18] Be that as it may, third parties are allowed, at a minimum, to be partial to victims of aggression, in the manner of the American 'non-belligerency' policy of 1939–41, without incurring legal liability for violation of the law of neutrality.[19] The effect is that third states can supply, say, armaments or funding to victim countries. This principle is of especial importance because, by its nature, it operates *during* the hostilities and thereby potentially makes a direct material contribution to the defeat of the aggressive enterprise.

---

[15] See SC Res. 692 (20 May 1991), 46 SCOR, Res and Dec, at 18.

[16] By 'billion' is meant 1,000 million (as in American usage). To track the activities of the UN Compensation Commission, see www.unog.ch/uncc. The discrepancy between awards made and funds distributed was chiefly the result of discrepancies in three categories of claims: oil-sector corporate claims, Kuwait government claims, and government claims for environmental damage. On the Commission, see Rattalma, 'Régime de responsabilité'.

[17] It should always be remembered that the UN Charter only banned *forcible* reprisals, leaving non-forcible countermeasures, such as the non-performance of normal legal obligations, in place.

[18] See, for example, E. Lauterpacht, 'Legal Irrelevance', at 64–5.

[19] See, to this effect, the Harvard Research draft Convention on the Rights and Duties of States in Case of Aggression, 33 (Supp.) AJIL 827 (1939), Art. 12.

A third consequence of aggression was that any gains made by means of an unlawful use of force would not be accorded recognition by the international community. This was, of course, the essence of the Stimson Doctrine of 1932. It was expressly endorsed by the UN General Assembly in 1970, which confirmed that '[n]o territorial acquisition resulting from the threat or use of force shall be recognised as legal'.[20] A notable application of this doctrine occurred in the wake of the effective takeover of Cambodia by Vietnam in 1979, with the installation of a puppet government (comparable to that of Manchukuo in the 1930s). The UN responded by refusing to accept the Vietnam-installed rulers as the true government of Cambodia. In this same vein, there was also universal agreement that any treaty brought about by means of an unlawful use of force would be, legally, a complete nullity.[21] Stated in its *most* general form – which, however, has not as yet received judicial endorsement – the principle would be that an unlawful use of force could not be the source of legal rights of any description whatever.

These three effects of an unlawful resort to force were familiar, in doctrine if not always in practice, from the interwar period and even earlier. After 1945, however, there were two further legal consequences of an unlawful use of force to be taken into account. The first one was the possibility of criminal prosecutions, before an international tribunal, of the individuals who were responsible for planning and executing the aggression.[22] In the Charter of the International Military Tribunal, which presided over the Nuremberg Trials of 1946, this offence was given the label of 'crimes against the peace'.[23] Sixteen defendants were charged with it at Nuremberg, of whom twelve were convicted (and seven sentenced to death by hanging).[24] In similar post-War trials in

---

[20] Declaration on Friendly Relations.

[21] Vienna Convention on the Law of Treaties, 23 May 1969, 1155 UNTS 331, Art. 52. On the Stimson Doctrine in UN practice, see John Dugard, *Recognition and the United Nations* (Cambridge: Grotius, 1987), at 27–35. On the non-recognition principle generally, see Brownlie, *Use of Force*, at 410–23.

[22] It will be recalled that the Versailles Treaty had provided for the prosecution of Kaiser William II of Germany after the First World War. The offence envisaged, though, was violation of treaties, rather than the breach of any *general* rule against the use of force. Such a rule did not exist at that time.

[23] Charter of the International Military Tribunal, 8 Aug. 1945, 82 UNTS 279, Art. 6.

[24] *In re Goering*, Int'l Military Tribunal, 1 Oct. 1946, 13 ILR 203. On the Nuremberg Trials, see generally Bradley F. Smith, *Reaching Judgment at Nuremberg* (London: André Deutsch, 1977); Ann Tusa and John Tusa, *The Nuremberg Trial* (London: Macmillan, 1983); and Telford Taylor, *The Anatomy of the Nuremberg Trials: A Personal Memoir* (Boston: Little, Brown, 1992).

Tokyo, twenty-two Japanese figures were found guilty of this offence (seven of whom were sentenced to death).[25] Since that time, there have been no further international prosecutions under this heading.[26] The major stumbling block to further action in this area was the inability of lawyers and statesmen to craft a definition of 'aggression' that was sufficiently precise for use in criminal prosecutions.[27] In 1998, however, provision was made for possible further trials of this kind by a newly created International Criminal Court. Aggression was one of the crimes covered by the Court's Statute, although that provision could not take effect until a definition of 'aggression' could be agreed.[28] On this point of criminal prosecutions, it only remains to note that the crime of aggression was reserved for the *planners* of aggressive war, not for the ordinary soldiers who were merely the instruments of it. A soldier fighting an aggressive war was only liable to prosecution if he committed some specific violation of the laws on the conduct of war.[29]

The final consequence of an unlawful resort to force was the possibility of armed action by the international community at large under the auspices of the UN Security Council. This was a just war in the fullest sense of that term. As such, it calls for some slightly fuller exploration.

The new just wars – UN enforcement action

The League of Nations Covenant could hardly be said to have had any conception of just wars in any true sense – meaning wars undertaken for the enforcement of community norms against wrongdoers. As observed earlier, the Covenant was, in essence, a war prevention device, employing peaceful-settlement obligations and cooling-off periods – but with

---

[25] *In re Hirota*, Int'l Military Tribunal for the Far East, 12 Nov. 1948, 15 ILR 356. In the Tokyo trials, two other defendants were found guilty of conspiring to wage aggressive war, though not of *actually* waging it. On the Tokyo trials, see generally Arnold C. Brackman, *The Other Nuremberg: The Untold Story of the Tokyo War Crimes Trials* (London: Collins, 1989).

[26] The international criminal tribunals established in the 1990s in the wake of crises in Yugoslavia and Rwanda did not have crimes against the peace (or aggression) within their jurisdiction.

[27] For a purported, but in fact largely *ersatz*, definition of aggression by the UN General Assembly in 1974, see GA Res. 3314 (XXIX), 39 GAOR, Supp. No. 31, at 142. For a thorough study of the problem, see Rifaat, *International Aggression*.

[28] Statute of the International Criminal Court (Rome Statute), 17 July 1998, UN Doc. A/CONF/183/9, Art. 5(2). Agreement on this point was still awaited at the end of 2003.

[29] *In re von Leeb* (High Command Case), US Military Tribunal at Nuremberg, 28 Oct. 1948, 15 ILR 376, at 381–3. On aggressive war as a crime, see Dinstein, *War*, at 106–34.

no change in the underlying conception of war as inherited from the nineteenth century. War, when it occurred, was still seen as a clash of rival state interests, having no higher legal or moral significance. The nearest that the Covenant came to a community policing measure was its provision for economic sanctions against states unlawfully resorting to war, fortified (as they might be in special cases) by a naval blockade.[30] The position under the UN Charter presented the starkest contrast. The Security Council, unlike the Council of the League of Nations, was entrusted with the power not only to impose mandatory economic sanctions against aggressor states but also to take up arms itself, on behalf of the global community, to subdue aggression on the field of battle. Ideally, swords would be beaten into ploughshares; but pending this happy development, the UN Security Council was to stand ever ready to play the role of the medieval church militant when the need arose.

It is unnecessary to embark upon a detailed exposition or history of UN enforcement.[31] But certain features of it that bear on the fate of war after 1945 should be pointed out. One is that UN enforcement was not regarded as war. That is to say, it was not seen as creating a *state* of war. This point was reflected in the terminology employed, with such labels as 'police action' or 'enforcement action' being common. The term 'intervention' – used in its nineteenth-century sense – might have been appropriate, although after 1945 that expression came to be regarded as a pejorative one.

The UN scheme was, however, in many ways, more reminiscent of the nineteenth-century Concert of Europe system than of medieval just wars. This was chiefly because the UN system, like the Concert of Europe, was more political than legal in nature. Where medieval just-war doctrine had stressed the need for a *justa causa* in the strict legal sense, the UN Security Council, like the Concert of Europe before it, addressed itself chiefly to dangerous or destabilising political situations. In the words of the UN Charter, the Security Council was empowered to take action against a 'threat to the peace, breach of the peace or act of aggression' rather than against violations of international law *per se*.[32] The UN Security Council was, admittedly, a somewhat more democratic arrangement than the Concert of Europe had been, in that the Council

---

[30] See Chapter 8 above.
[31] For a brief survey of the UN's experience, see Franck, *Recourse to Force*, at 20–44.
[32] UN Charter, Art. 39.

comprised not merely the five major powers (the United States, the Soviet Union, Britain, France and China) as permanent members but also ten other countries chosen by a vote of the UN General Assembly to serve two-year terms. But the major powers, with permanent membership and the power of veto, held strongly dominant positions.

In the post-1945 period, relations amongst the major powers were, however, far from harmonious. Cold-War rivalries and other political considerations prevented the UN enforcement system from functioning in anything resembling the manner originally hoped. Plans for the creation of a standing UN military capacity, for example, came to nothing, largely because of sharp differences of view between the United States and the Soviet Union over the arrangements.[33] Also, the possession of a veto power in the Security Council by each of the five permanent powers came close to preventing effective UN enforcement activity altogether. By the end of the twentieth century, there were only three major instances in which the Security Council authorised armed force. The first was the Korean conflict of 1950–3, when the Council was able to act only by virtue of the absence of the Soviet Union from the sessions in which the key decisions were made.[34] The other two instances both took place after the Cold War had ended: the liberation of Kuwait from Iraq in 1991 and the expulsion of an unconstitutional military government in Haïti in 1994.[35]

It is important to note that UN enforcement action, like medieval just wars, differed significantly from self-defence action in the narrow sense of merely fending off a blow. Indeed, there was no requirement in the UN Charter that enforcement action be defensive. The case of UN action in Korea in 1950–3 illustrates the point. In its earliest stages, the UN action was necessarily defensive, since the immediate task was to repel a massive invasion of South Korea by North Korean forces. The UN-supported side did not, however, rest content with expelling North Korean troops from the South, but went on to mount a large-scale military invasion of North Korea itself with a view to bringing about a complete resolution of the political situation in the Korean peninsula. The legal basis for this expansion of the conflict was found in the

---

[33] See 1 Evan Luard, *A History of the United Nations: The Years of Western Domination, 1945–1955* (London: Macmillan, 1982), at 98–105.

[34] See SC Res. 83, (27 June 1950), 5 SCOR, Res and Dec, at 5.

[35] See SC Res. 678 (29 Nov. 1990), 45 SCOR, Res and Dec, at 27 (on Kuwait); and SC Res. 940 (31 July 1994), 49 SCOR, Res and Dec, at 51 (on Haïti). Enforcement action against Southern Rhodesia in 1966–79 comprised only economic sanctions and not armed force.

Security Council resolution of June 1950, which had authorised UN member states not merely to repel the North Korean invasion but also 'to restore peace and security to the area'.[36] (In the event, carrying the conflict northward had the unintended and unwelcome effect of bringing China into the fray on North Korea's side.) The Gulf conflict of 1991 was different, in that the military action itself stopped after the liberation of Kuwait. It may be noted, though, that the peace arrangements, as set out in a Security Council resolution in April 1991, went beyond the bounds of narrow self-defence by imposing a number of conditions on Iraq designed to prevent future misconduct.[37] The most notable of these were disarmament obligations, with international inspection to ensure compliance. Furthest of all from self-defence in the narrow sense – or even from defensive action in any sense – was the case of Haïti in 1994, in which there was no pretence of any aggression or threat of aggression by that country against any other state. Haïti's only offence was to have a government constituted in a manner unacceptable to the world at large.

Finally, it may be noted that, in the matter of neutrality, the UN just-war scheme also echoed its medieval ancestor. Both saw neutrality as incompatible in principle with a just-war system, just as, in domestic societies, neutrality between law enforcement and crime is commonly regarded as incompatible with good citizenship and devotion to the rule of law. Indeed, the UN scheme outdid its predecessor on this count by instituting what amounted to an express prohibition against neutrality in UN enforcement operations. Article 2(5) of the Charter required UN member states to 'give the United Nations every assistance' in cases of preventive or enforcement action. In short, UN member states were obligated to adopt policies of 'non-belligerency' in cases of UN enforcement action, along the lines pioneered by the United States in 1939–41. Pursuant to this provision, a number of traditionally neutral states, such as Sweden, Austria and Ireland, indicated their support for the UN side in the Korean and Kuwait conflicts and provided various forms of non-military support, such as allowing overflight rights to the UN-supported side.[38]

---

[36] SC Res. 83 (27 June 1950), 5 SCOR, Res and Dec, at 5. On the American view of the legal position, see Goodrich, *Korea*, at 126–8.
[37] SC Res. 687 (3 Apr. 1991), 46 SCOR, Res and Dec, at 11.
[38] Neff, *Rights and Duties*, at 193.

The new just wars – self-defence

The second category of just war in the post-1945 era was self-defence. The two types of just war were not, however, of equal standing by any stretch of the imagination. Community action by the UN as a whole had a higher status than self-defence by individual states. The position here was very distinctly reminiscent of the medieval just-war outlook, which had looked upon self-help with dark suspicion, reserving its fullest approval for altruistic action on behalf of the community at large. This same ethos pervaded the UN Charter scheme. Self-defence was expressly described in the Charter in a thoroughly medieval, natural-law manner as an 'inherent right' of states, exercisable without *auctoritas* from any superior body.[39] This reference to self-defence as an inherent right clearly suggested that, as in classical natural-law doctrine, self-defence was to be understood in its narrow sense of merely warding off a blow that was in the course of being struck, a position that was confirmed by the World Court in 1986.[40]

Although, as just observed, self-defence was described as an inherent right of states, the UN Charter added two features to the traditional natural-law right: first, it added what was called a right of *collective* self-defence, thereby allowing states assisting a victim of aggression to fall into the category of 'self'-defenders; and second, it imposed a duty onto self-defending states to keep the UN Security Council informed of measures that they were taking. The limited character of self-defence was clearly apparent in the Charter's explicit treatment of it as an interim measure, permissible only 'until the Security Council has taken measures necessary to maintain international peace and security'.[41] Self-defence, therefore, qualified as a just war only in a rather limited and provisional – even quasi-apologetic – manner.[42] Nevertheless, for the first time in history, self-defence was in the charmed circle of just wars, if only with very junior status.

There was yet another respect in which self-defence may be viewed as, in effect, only a quasi-just war. That is, that the distinction between defence and offence, as in the Middle Ages, bore no necessary relation to

---

[39] On the drafting history of this Charter provision, see Alexandrov, *Self-defense*, at 77–93; and Franck, *Recourse to Force*, at 45–51.

[40] *Nicaragua* v. *USA*, paras. 193–5.

[41] UN Charter, Art. 51. On Article 51, see Bowett, *Self-defence*, at 182–99; Alexandrov, *Self-defense*, at 93–105; and Gray, *Use of Force*, at 84–143.

[42] See Kelsen, *Principles*, at 63–4; and Bowett, *Self-defence*, at 19–21.

the legal merits of an underlying dispute. In the UN system, an offensive resort to force was (at least in principle) illegal *per se*, even if the state taking up the sword had an impeccable legal case for its position (such as, for example, clear legal title to territory occupied by another state). UN enforcement action, in contrast, could take an offensive form, if the Security Council held that to be necessary. Enforcement action, in other words, in contrast to self-defence, was a true sanction. That is to say, it was (at least potentially) a punitive weapon, which could be wielded offensively against wrongdoers for past misdeeds, or preventively to stop wrongdoing from occurring in the first place. Self-defence, at least in principle, was stuck resolutely in the present tense, warding off attacks as they were taking place.

There was, accordingly, a kind of division of labour between these greater and lesser types of just war (as they might be termed). Self-defence, as the lesser measure, operated only on an interim, emergency basis for the strictly limited purpose of parrying an aggressor's blow. UN enforcement action, as the greater measure, could operate open-endedly and offensively, at the sole discretion of the UN Security Council. Self-defence, as a unilateral measure, dealt with the symptoms of aggression (i.e., with the actual physical attack). UN enforcement action could deal more broadly with underlying causes of world instability.

The division of labour between the two types of just war, however, was inherently adjustable. The more prompt and effective the UN Security was, the smaller a part would self-defence naturally play. But the converse was also true. The *less* active the UN Security Council was, the *greater* would be the role left for self-defence. And in the event, the Security Council, for decades after its inception, proved to be supremely feckless, largely as a result of Cold-War rivalries between the major powers. The result was to leave a gaping vacuum in the UN system – a vacuum that was duly filled by a remorseless expansion of self-defence. Where self-defence had originally been scripted to play only the most modest of supporting roles in the great drama of just-war revival, it now moved relentlessly – one could almost say imperialistically – to centre stage, with the effect that it was transmuted from its original narrow conception into a single all-purpose justification for armed force, playing the part of the older categories of just war. This was the self-defence revolution of the post-1945 era.[43]

---

[43] For a useful general survey of state practice on self-defence after 1945, see Alexandrov, *Self-defense*, at 121–290.

To appreciate the full scope and significance of this post-1945 self-defence revolution, it is well to recall just how narrow self-defence originally was. In the canonical words of Webster in the *Caroline* affair, universally quoted by lawyers, self-defence was reserved for threats that were 'instant, overwhelming, leaving no choice of means, and no moment for deliberation'.[44] In the early UN period, even the most powerful states hesitated to make too obvious a departure from this strict standard. In the Suez crisis of 1956, for example, Britain and France carefully refrained from relying exclusively on self-defence, portraying their military action primarily as a high-minded peacekeeping intervention, to separate Israeli and Egyptian forces. R. A. Butler, the British Lord Privy Seal, described it at one point as a 'police action'.[45] (The British government tactfully refrained from informing the world that it, along with the French government, had collaborated with Israel to create the very hostilities which the intervention was designed to halt.)[46] In the Cuban missile crisis of 1962, the United States also pointedly refrained from using self-defence as the justification for its 'quarantine' policy, which entailed the halting and inspecting of foreign ships on the high seas (and their diversion from Cuba if they were carrying offensive missile equipment). The reason for this caution was that there clearly had been no *actual* armed attack on the United States (although there were palpable fears for the future). The United States therefore justified its action as an enforcement measure authorised by the Organisation of American States.[47]

With the passage of time, however, qualms about invoking self-defence were brought increasingly under control by states. Self-defence claims blossomed so luxuriantly, and expanded in so many directions as effectively to encompass *any* arguably justifiable resort to force. This expansion – one could even say explosion – of self-defence claims after 1945 took place on various levels: in time, both backwards and forwards from the actual attack; in space, to geographical locations far removed

---

[44] Webster to Fox, 24 Apr. 1841, 26 BFSP, at 1137–8.

[45] Remarks of Butler, *Hansard*, HC, vol. 558, ser. 5, col. 1726–7, 1 Nov. 1956. On views within the British government as to the lawfulness of the armed action, see Marston, 'Armed Intervention'.

[46] See Keith Kyle, *Suez* (London: Weidenfeld and Nicolson, 1991), at 314–31.

[47] For doubts as to the lawfulness of the American action in the Cuban crisis, see Quincy Wright, 'The Cuban Quarantine', 57 AJIL 546–65 (1963). For the contention that self-defence would have been a more appropriate justification, see Myres S. McDougal, 'The Soviet-Cuban Quarantine and Self-defense', *ibid.* at 597–604.

from the attack; and in subject matter, beyond the protection of the territorial integrity of the defending state.

Consider first the expansion on the temporal plane. In its original and strict sense as an inherent natural-law right, self-defence in the narrow sense had been very much a matter of (so to speak) the present tense. That is to say, it did not include a right to use force either before an attack as a preventive measure or afterwards, to counteract its consequences. There was admittedly some leeway in this regard; but it was very slight, allowing preemptive action when an aggressive blow was on the *very* brink of being struck. The most notable example of this was Israel's attack on Egypt and other neighbouring Arab states in 1967.[48] With the passage of time, however, states came to take ever more generous views of self-defence, holding preventive action to be increasingly necessary – and hence lawful – in an age in which lightning-fast delivery of nuclear weapons was all too foreseeable. The only effective defence, some argued, against such a catastrophe was a steely willingness to strike the enemy (or the enemy-to-be) in ever earlier stages of its preparations.

The most striking claim of this nature was announced by the United States in 2002, when it openly and officially adopted a preventive strategy, at least against certain kinds of threats. In a statement of the National Security Strategy of the United States of America, the American government frankly announced a policy of resorting to preventive or defensive war. The United States, it was pronounced, could not 'remain idle while dangers gather' or afford to 'let our enemies strike first'. 'The greater the threat [maintained the United States], the greater is the risk of inaction – and the more compelling the case for taking anticipatory action to defend ourselves, even if uncertainty remains as to the time and place of the enemy's attack. To forestall or prevent such hostile attacks by our adversaries, the United States will, if necessary, act preemptively.'[49] Nor was it long before the United States found the opportunity to put this principle into vigorous operation. In 2003, in conjunction with Britain and Australia, it mounted an armed invasion of Iraq, which led to the swift overthrow of its government, followed by a military occupation of the country. One of the justifications given by the

---

[48] See Franck, *Recourse to Force*, at 101–5.
[49] 'US Adoption of New Doctrine on Use of Force', 97 AJIL 203–5 (2003). On this 'Bush Doctrine', as it has been labelled, see Walter LaFeber, 'The Bush Doctrine', 26 *Diplomatic History* 543–58 (2002).

United States for the attack was the existence of a programme for the production, and possible use, of weapons of mass destruction such as chemical or biological, or even nuclear, armaments.[50] The operation, however, soon turned into a vivid lesson in the risks of preventive action, when evidence of such a programme failed to materialise. It was a dramatic demonstration of the fact that, the more remote is the danger against which action is taken, the more tentative must the assessment of the situation necessarily be – a point recognised by Grotius and his followers centuries earlier, when they earnestly condemned the waging of defensive war on the basis of merely speculative future dangers.[51]

The temporal growth of self-defence was apparent in the other direction too, as a justification for armed action *after* attacks had occurred and been completed, thereby effectively reviving the second of Grotius's classic just causes of war: the obtaining of something that was owing. The British recovery of the Falkland Islands in 1982, after their forcible occupation by Argentina, was an apt illustration. Speaking in the *very* strictest sense, it was not self-defence, since the takeover had been completed. Instead, it was a recovery operation, a reversal of a *fait accompli*. Nevertheless, Britain consistently invoked self-defence as the legal justification for its action; and this was accepted by international lawyers with little opposition.[52]

Self-defence sometimes even had a backward and forward orientation at the same time – performing the dual role of rectifying past wrongs and preventing future ones. The result was sometimes to make it very difficult to distinguish self-defence action from forcible reprisals.[53] In recognition of the fineness of the line between the two, some scholars advanced the view that 'defensive reprisals' were permissible under the UN Charter, meaning actions taken after an attack had occurred, with a view to preventing or discouraging future attacks (i.e., with a broadly defensive purpose).[54] This contention did not meet with widespread scholarly acceptance or judicial approval, but there were many instances of it in state practice. It was especially a feature of Israeli policy, which responded to guerrilla or terrorist attacks by armed action afterwards,

---

[50] Britain, in contrast to the United States, was careful to base its legal justification on the breach by Iraq of its obligations under various existing UN Security Council resolutions.

[51] On the Iraq intervention and self-defence, see Sapiro, 'Iraq'.

[52] Statement of Biffen, 20 May 1982, in 53 Brit YB 519–20 (1982).

[53] For the view that there was no fundamental difference between them, see Venezia, 'Notion de représailles'.

[54] See, notably, Dinstein, *War*, at 194–203.

with a view to discouraging future incidents.[55] The United States took a similar measure in 1986, when it launched an air attack on Libya in the wake of a terrorist bombing incident which it attributed to that country. In justifying its action to the UN, the United States invoked self-defence, stating that it was 'responding to an ongoing pattern of attacks by the Government of Libya'.[56] Its objective, it maintained, was 'to destroy facilities used to carry out Libya's hostile policy of international terrorism and to discourage Libyan terrorist attacks in the future'.[57]

Grotius's third category of just war, punitive actions, were less in evidence; but an intention to inflict punishment was sometimes present, with greater or lesser explicitness, in combination with other more presentable motivations. Behind China's attack on Vietnam in 1979, for example, was an admitted intention of 'teaching Vietnam a lesson', although the action was also labelled as a 'self-defensive counter-attack'.[58] Another notable instance of an armed operation with a punitive component was the American-led action in Afghanistan in 2001, in the wake of terrorist attacks on New York City and Washington, D.C. The objective, in part, was to remove the Afghan government from power as punishment for its harbouring of the terrorist attackers, although the purpose was also genuinely defensive (if not in the narrow sense) in that it was designed to prevent future attacks from occurring.

Another sign of the mutation of self-defence into defensive war was the expansion of the range of state interests that were brought under the ever more capacious umbrella of self-defence. Instead of being confined to action against invasions of state territory, self-defence began to be stretched to include the protection of vital interests (or perceived vital interests) in general. There had been a premonition of this development during the interwar period, at the time of the drafting of the Pact of Paris of 1928. In the exchange of notes that took place at that time on the subject of self-defence, Britain gave an ominous indication of how far the right could be extended by far-thinking statesmen, by articulating its 'distinct understanding' that self-defence rights extended well beyond the mere defence of a state's physical territory from invasion. It stated,

---

[55] For a survey of Israeli practice and the reaction to it at the UN, see O'Brien, *Law and Morality*, at 99–114. See also Venezia, 'Notion de représailles', at 477–84.

[56] Remarks of Walters, 2682nd mtg, 21 Apr. 1986, UN Doc. S/PV. 2682 (1986), at 43.

[57] Letter from US to President of the UN Security Council, 14 Apr. 1986, UN Doc. S/17990, 41 SCOR, Supp. for Apr.–June 1986, at 22; reprinted in 80 AJIL 632–3 (1986).

[58] Robert S. Ross, *The Indochina Tangle: China's Vietnam Policy 1975–1979* (New York: Columbia University Press, 1988), at 224.

somewhat opaquely, that there were 'certain regions of the world' in which the country had 'a special and vital interest' for its peace and safety – regions not necessarily confined to the British Empire itself – and that it reserved its right, under the rubric of self-defence, to act against any threats to those interests. This 'British Monroe Doctrine' (as the understanding was sometimes labelled) referred primarily to strategic areas for communication and transport such as the Suez Canal and the Strait of Gibraltar.[59] An example after 1945 of a country's willingness to take up arms on this ground was provided in 1980 by President Jimmy Carter of the United States, when he announced that the gaining of control over the Persian Gulf region by any outside power would be regarded as 'an assault on the vital interests of the United States', which would be 'repelled by use of any means necessary, including the use of military force'.[60]

States – or at least powerful states – also had little difficulty in extending this modern version of defensive war to take in actions that previously had been in the category of necessity or emergency action rather than of self-defence in the strict sense. Like the dutiful Hercules with his many labours, self-defence was ever ready to answer such calls to legal duty. The principal illustration was the use of armed force to rescue nationals in danger in foreign countries. One of the most dramatic examples was an Israeli rescue mission sent to Uganda in 1976 to rescue persons held captive after an airplane hijacking.[61] By the early twenty-first century, there had not been a definitive judicial pronouncement on the extent to which such rescue missions could be justified as self-defence. In 1980, however, the World Court gave some consideration to the point, in the context of an American attempt to rescue hostages held in Tehran.[62] The question of the lawfulness of the American action was not fully argued. The Court, however, did express

[59] British note of 19 May 1928, in Shotwell, *War as an Instrument*, at 283. On self-defence and the Pact of Paris generally, see *ibid*. at 203–13. On the British position, see Brownlie, *Use of Force*, at 243–5.

[60] 1980 *Digest of United States Practice in International Law*, at 146–7. For the view that self-defence could be justified, in 'the most exceptional circumstances', for the protection of economic interests, see Bowett, *Self-defence*, at 106–14. On self-defence for the protection of 'essential rights', see *ibid*. at 23–5. See also remarks of McDougal, 56 *Annuaire* (1975), at 76–7.

[61] See Ronzitti, *Rescuing Nationals*, at 37–40; and Franck, *Recourse to Force*, at 82–6.

[62] For the American justification as self-defence, see Letter from US to President of the UN Security Council, 25 Apr. 1980, UN Doc. S/13908, in 35 SCOR, Supp. for Apr.–June 1980, at 28.

some dismay at the operation, if only on the comparatively narrow ground that the rescue mission was incompatible with the United States' own decision to resort to judicial means to resolve the crisis.[63] The Court did not go so far as to hold that, as a general principle, rescue operations could *never* qualify as self-defence.[64]

As in the nineteenth century, there was serious – and well-founded – concern that rescue missions could be used as covers for operations which actually had quite different purposes. Perhaps the most obvious examples were several American interventions into Latin American and Caribbean states. In 1965, the United States sent troops to the Dominican Republic, ostensibly to protect American nationals, but in reality to forestall a feared Communist takeover. In 1983, the United States intervened in Grenada, again to forestall the imposition of a left-wing government, but also proffering the protection of American nationals as one legal justification for its action.[65] Protection of American nationals was also one of the justifications of the United States's intervention in Panama in 1989–90 (the lawfulness of which was also vigorously disputed by many observers).[66]

It should be stressed that these various forms of expansion of self-defence came about through the practice of states, without any judicial imprimatur. When the World Court considered self-defence, it did so in the framework of the traditional narrow conception of the subject. In the *Nicaragua* v. *United States* case of 1986, for example, the Court took a thoroughly conservative and traditional approach, stressing the necessity of an armed attack before the right of self-defence could arise.[67] At the same time, it carefully pointed out that *not* every resort

---

[63] United States Diplomatic and Consular Staff in Tehran, 1980 ICJ Rep. 3, paras. 93–4. See also Opinion of Morozov, para. 8.

[64] For support of the view that rescue missions can fall within self-defence in at least some circumstances, see Bowett, *Self-defence*, at 87–105; and Dinstein, *War*, at 203–7. For the opposite position, see Brownlie, *Use of Force*, at 298–301. For the view that rescue missions might be lawful, though on some ground other than self-defence, see Alexandrov, *Self-defense*, at 188–204.

[65] On the rescue-of-nationals element in Grenada, see William C. Gilmore, *The Grenada Intervention: Analysis and Documentation* (London: Mansell, 1984), at 55–64.

[66] In favour of the lawfulness of the Panama intervention was Abraham D. Sofaer, 'The Legality of the United States Action in Panama', 29 Columbia J Tr L 281–92 (1991). Opposed to the lawfulness was Louis Henkin, 'The Invasion of Panama under International Law: A Gross Violation', *ibid.* at 293–317. For surveys of cases of rescue of nationals abroad, see Ronzitti, *Rescuing Nationals*, at 26–49; and Franck, *Recourse to Force*, at 76–96.

[67] *Nicaragua* v. *USA*, para. 195.

to force qualified as an armed attack. That is to say, that certain relatively mild forms of resorting to force would not suffice to justify armed self-defence by the target country. For example, a supply of arms to insurgents was capable of constituting an unlawful use of force (as in the *Nicaragua* v. *United States* case itself); but it was not so grave a form of it as to amount to an armed attack, i.e., it would not trigger a right of armed self-defence on the part of the government. In such a case, the aggrieved government would have to content itself with 'proportionate counter-measures' (such as, presumably, a claim for damages) instead of resorting to armed self-defence.[68]

In 2003, the Court gave further attention to the question, considering whether two American attacks on Iranian oil platforms (which had occurred in 1987–8, during the Iran–Iraq conflict) qualified as self-defence or not. On this occasion too, the Court took a traditional and narrow view of self-defence, requiring conclusive or near-conclusive evidence of an armed attack and of responsibility for it, and strictly insisting also on necessity and proportionality in the response. The standard for necessity was especially daunting, being (in the Court's words) 'strict and objective, leaving no room for any "measure of discretion"' on the part of the self-defending state.[69]

It was difficult to avoid the conclusion that a wide chasm separated the stern strictures of the World Court from the practice of states in the everyday world. By the end of the twentieth century, self-defence had blossomed so extravagantly in the practice of states as to give rise to suspicions that it was little more than war under another label. Nowhere was this more tragically visible than in 1980–8, when Iran and Iraq engaged in the largest-scale interstate conflict of the post-1945 era (to date), with each side mounting massive invasions of the other's territory – all the time under pious claims of self-defence by, inevitably, both parties. The principal hope for a reversal of this trend resided in the UN Security Council. If it could manage to breathe life into the collective-security provisions of the UN Charter, then the need for individual self-help by states could be correspondingly reduced. As of the early twenty-first century, however, it required optimism in heroic proportions to believe that this would occur on anything more than a sporadic basis.

---

[68] *Ibid.*, paras. 195, 247–9. For a cogent critique of the Court's approach, see Hargrove, 'Nicaragua Judgment'.

[69] See Oil Platforms Case (*Iran* v. *USA*), 6 Nov. 2003, 42 ILM 1334 (2003), paras. 46–78. On necessity, see paras. 73–6.

The art of abolishing war

The case for the abolition of the legal institution of war in 1945 may be put with the utmost simplicity. The thesis was that the UN Charter had the effect of forcing *all* instances of armed conflict into one or the other of two categories – neither of which constituted a war. The two categories were the ones just discussed: UN enforcement action, and cases of aggression-and-self-defence. These were, of course, just-war situations. But neither involved a state of war in the sense in which that term had come to be used in the nineteenth century, when it meant a condition in which *both* sides in a conflict were permitted, entirely lawfully, to use armed force against one another, whether in offensive or defensive modes. That was no longer so. In cases of UN enforcement and of aggression-and-self-defence, one party to the conflict was necessarily using force unlawfully – unlawfully, that is, according to the rules of the UN Charter, which held universal sway, with no question of any suspension of the normal rules of peace to make way for a special regime of war.

That much was relatively uncontroversial. There was, however, some division of opinion amongst lawyers as to the conclusions that were to be drawn from this basic analysis. Some favoured following this line of reason, without fear or hesitation, to its fullest logical conclusion. Others were more cautious and pragmatic, holding that at least some features of the erstwhile state of war had virtues that were worth retaining. There are no accepted labels for these rival groups. Not without hesitation, the first group will be referred to as the radicals and the second as the moderates or pragmatists. We will proceed to explore some of the principal issues that divided them.

Two schools of thought

The radical school of thought shared the community-minded ethos of the medieval natural lawyers, which was manifested concretely in an intense enthusiasm for the UN programme of collective security, underpinned by a powerful strain of idealism. The most outspoken figure in this camp, the American lawyer Quincy Wright, was as loud in his praise of the UN's collective-security programme as he was fervent in his belief that war (in the positivist sense) was now legally obsolete.[70] The radical

---

[70] See Q. Wright, 'Outlawry'.

position tended to focus on the subjective picture of war, which had accorded to individual states the power to create a state of war by way of (most obviously) a declaration of war. The effect of the Charter's prohibition against force was, on the radical view, to strip states of this power which they had formerly possessed. A country might, as in days of old, declare war against another one, or attack another with the intention of inaugurating a state of war – but the international community would now give no effect to that intention. Any purported declaration of war would be, from the legal standpoint, mere empty puffery. In the words of the French lawyer Georges Scelle, a declaration of war could no longer be anything more than 'a cynical admission of the intention to perpetrate the crime of war'.[71]

It was appreciated, of course, that states might well commit hostile acts against one another. But those hostile acts must now be seen as isolated incidents, whose lawfulness was to be judged on a case-by-case basis. No longer could such hostile acts be said to create or be part of any general condition known as a state of war, in which the normal rules of peace were put into abeyance. In short, armed force must now be treated in international law like crime in domestic law – as an unfortunate, but isolated, antisocial act which caused no rending of the overall fabric of law. The Austrian-American lawyer and philosopher Hans Kelsen was one of the more emphatic on this point. Any use of force, he insisted, must now be seen, from the legal standpoint, as a 'resort to an action, not a resort to a status'. The radicals therefore resembled their medieval just-war forebears in placing no emphasis on war as a state or condition, but instead merely evincing a concern over the lawfulness or unlawfulness (as the case may be) of particular hostile acts as they occurred. In short, there might be *acts* of war in the new UN-Charter world; but there could be no *state* of war.[72]

Those of the radical persuasion, as the label implies, favoured taking this line of thought to its logical conclusion. One of its more striking implications was that *none* of the legal incidents of the erstwhile state of war existed any longer. There could be no question of belligerents' rights, i.e., of legal privileges, being accorded to states simply because they had elected to go to war. Moreover, in situations of de facto conflict, there would be no reason to suppose that the laws governing the conduct of the hostilities should be rigorously even-handed, as in the traditional state of war. On the contrary, there was every reason to think

[71] Scelle, 'Quelques réflexions', at 17.   [72] Kelsen, *Principles*, at 27.

that they should not be, for why should a violator of the law be placed on a legal par with enforcers, or a criminal with a magistrate? Some lawyers of the radical persuasion maintained, on this basis, that the traditional laws of war should not hamstring UN enforcement action.[73]

Another of the more adventurous conclusions of the radical school was that war's constant companion and foil, neutrality, must also be obsolete in the new just-war era. The reason was that neutrality was based on two premises, both of which had now (in the radical view) been discarded. One was the existence of a state of war, to which the state of neutrality was correlative. The disappearance of the one logically implied the disappearance of the other. The second premise on which neutrality was based was the principle of the legal parity of the contending parties. This too was rejected by the radicals. It has been observed that, in cases of UN enforcement action, the UN Charter expressly precluded neutrality. The radical viewpoint maintained that this principle extended to *both* categories of just war – i.e., to situations of aggression-and-self-defence as well as to cases of UN enforcement. In place of neutrality, there was now (it was contended) a two-fold set of principles directly reminiscent of the position of Hugo Grotius in the seventeenth century: that third states must refrain from taking any action that would assist the aggressor; and that any action taken in support of the victim would entail no legal liability to the aggressor.[74]

These conclusions of the radicals, together with the reasoning that led to them, were strongly contested by the members of the rival moderate (or pragmatist) school. Its most outspoken champion in the early post-war years was the Austrian lawyer, Josef Kunz, now based in the United States. If there was a strong current of idealism driving the radical school, there was an equally pronounced ethos of realism and scepticism to the moderate position. The moderates were decidedly more reserved about the advent of a new era and considerably more pessimistic than the radicals about the viability of the new system of collective security established by the UN Charter.

If the radical school centred its arguments on the subjective view of war, the moderates, just as clearly, concentrated theirs on the objective picture of war, in which war was regarded as a de facto clash of armed

---

[73] See, for example, Q. Wright, 'Outlawry', at 373–6. See also remarks of Yepes, in 47(1) *Annuaire* (1957), at 329–30, 481–2; and remarks of Rolin, in 48(2) *Annuaire* (1959), at 201–2.

[74] For Grotius's position, see Grotius, *War and Peace*, at 786–7.

forces between two states, which automatically activated the laws of war (between the contending sides) and of neutrality (between the contenders and the outside world).[75] On this view, war clearly could not, by its nature, be abolished by mere pronouncement. Any de facto armed clash – or war in the material sense, as it is sometimes called – would necessarily give rise to the application of a special corpus of law regulating the conduct of the hostilities. Support for this position was provided by the World Court in 1996, when it handed down an advisory opinion on the threat or use of nuclear weapons. In that opinion, it referred – though only cursorily – to what it called a *lex specialis* ('special law') that was applicable in armed conflict for the regulation of hostilities and which differed from the law applicable in ordinary times.[76] It will be noted that this had been one of the most outstanding features of the old legal institution of war.

An interesting point of convergence – at least superficially – between the two schools lay in the fact that both of them downplayed the idea of a state of war, though in instructively different ways. The radicals, true to the label being given them, were of the more root-and-branch persuasion. A state of war, in their view, was actually a legal impossibility after 1945 because the UN Charter had stripped states of their erstwhile power to create one. The moderates downplayed the idea of a state of war not on the grounds that the UN Charter had made a radical change, but rather simply because, in the manner of their nineteenth-century forebears of the objective school, they never assigned any great importance to the concept of a state of war to begin with. Like their nineteenth-century predecessors, they reserved their primary concern for the application of the laws of war and of neutrality to situations of de facto conflict as they arose. As Kunz explained, the expression 'state of war' was really only a shorthand way of referring to the various legal consequences that followed automatically upon the de facto outbreak of an armed conflict – such as, most outstandingly, the triggering of the laws of war and of neutrality. What was important, from the practical standpoint, was to ensure that those laws of war and neutrality were properly observed during the struggle; and it made no real difference whether the particular label 'state of war' was applied to this process or not.[77]

---

[75] See Dinstein, *War*, at 136–7.
[76] The Legality of the Threat or Use of Nuclear Weapons, 1996 ICJ Rep. 225, para. 25. An advisory opinion is a court ruling given, in effect, to the world at large, without any specific parties being in contention, as in a common lawsuit.
[77] See Kunz, 'La crise', at 65–6.

The most important practical question that divided the two approaches was whether it was either possible or desirable for the law to treat the contending sides in an armed conflict on an even-handed, nondiscriminatory basis, as had been the case since the advent of the voluntary-law approach to war in the seventeenth century. According to the logic of the radical approach, the old agnostic character of the laws of war, which scrupulously and dogmatically avoided all questions of right and wrong in the *resort* to force, must be discarded. In particular, the old just-war approach should be reinstated, in which it was recognised that, in any given armed conflict, one side would have *no* right to use force. The law could not, and should not, be neutral as between crime and law enforcement. The issue first arose in a concrete manner in the Korean conflict, when Quincy Wright, championing the radical stance, advocated granting the UN-approved side greater scope in the use of force than the traditional rules of the laws of war allowed.[78] This conclusion was endorsed, if only cautiously, by a committee of the American Society of International Law, which expressed the view that the UN-supported side 'should not feel bound by all [of the] laws of war, but should select such of the laws of war as may seem to fit its purposes ... and rejecting [*sic*] those which seem incompatible with its purposes'.[79]

Lawyers of the moderate school of thought vigorously disputed this conclusion. They favoured retention of the traditional positivist position of even-handed rights of belligerents, without regard to the underlying justice of the causes for which they fought.[80] They were wary of being led astray by a mechanical following-out of the logic of the radical position. The British-based writer (and future World Court judge) Hersch Lauterpacht, for example, warned against 'indiscriminate reliance on legal logic' when dealing with the issue, and urged the need to consider the practical difficulties standing in the way of adopting a policy of discrimination.[81] The Swiss lawyer Max Huber was of a like view. He pointed out one of the main practical difficulties that a

[78] 47(1) *Annuaire* (1957), at 333–4.
[79] Committee on the Study of the Legal Problems of the United Nations, 'Laws of War', at 217. The members of the committee were: Clyde Eagleton (chairman), W. J. Bivens, Leland M. Goodrich, Hans Kelsen, Josef L. Kunz and Louis B. Sohn.
[80] For a particularly cogent statement of this position, see remarks of Schätzel, 47(1) *Annuaire* (1957), at 448–52. See also remarks of Fitzmaurice, *ibid.* at 549–50; remarks of Gidel, *ibid.* at 556–7; remarks of Huber, *ibid.* at 417–18; remarks of Castrén, *ibid.* at 404–15; remarks of Bindschedler, 50(1) *Annuaire*, at 80–3; remarks of Kunz, *ibid.* at 86–95; and 2 Guggenheim, *Traité*, at 304–5.
[81] H. Lauterpacht, 'Limits', at 217–18.

discriminatory regime would have. The less favoured party, naturally aggrieved at being placed in an inferior legal position, would resort to the principle of reprisal to bring its conduct into line with that of its foe, thereby negating the effect of the discrimination.[82]

The resolution of this dispute will command our attention in some detail, chiefly because of the manner in which it came about – through the acceptance of an importantly different conception of the very nature of the laws of war. This revolutionary change in the character of the laws of war will here be labelled 'the humanitarian revolution'. It merits some careful scrutiny, as it is likely to shape the legal picture of armed conflict in important ways for a long time to come.

The humanitarian revolution

The humanitarian revolution marked a fundamental shift in the very nature and purpose of the rules governing the prosecution of armed conflict. This shift consisted, in essence, of seeing armed conflict not (as formerly) in terms of a collision between rival national interests, but rather as a human tragedy. This marked one of the greatest conceptual steps in the legal history of armed conflict. As a result of it, the principal task of the law of nations was not to ensure fairness and even-handedness as between the contending states, but rather to place limits on the amount of damage that could be inflicted and to relieve the sufferings of victims of war. This humanitarian approach marked the abandonment of the ethos of the duellist, in favour of the more tender outlook of the physician.[83] It is therefore deeply ironic that it had the unintended side effect of going far towards resuscitating some of the very key features of the once-venerable legal institution of war.

The body of law concerned with the protection of victims of war came to be labelled as 'international humanitarian law'. Its outstanding characteristic was that it saw the laws of war in terms of restraint rather than of privilege. This was in sharp contrast to the prevailing view of the previous centuries, where there had been concern with the *rights* of belligerents. In the humanitarian area, the primary emphasis was to be

---

[82] 47(1) *Annuaire* (1957), at 417–18. See also, to the same effect, remarks of Eustathiades, 50(1) *Annuaire* (1963), at 29–30; and of Bindshedler, *ibid.* at 82. By 'reprisal' was meant *belligerent* reprisal, which was a tit-for-tat retaliation during armed conflict. See generally F. Kalshoven, *Belligerent Reprisals* (Leyden: Sijthoff, 1971).

[83] For a strong expression of the importance of humanitarian aspects of armed conflicts, see SC Res. 1296, 19 Apr. 2000, in 55 SCOR, Res and Dec, at 124.

on the *duties* of belligerents and on the many constraints on their freedom of action during armed conflict. Humanitarian law began its career as a body of rules quite distinct from the laws of war properly speaking, sometimes called 'Geneva law' in reference to the various Geneva Conventions which provided for the relief of the victims of war, chiefly wounded and sick soldiers and sailors, plus prisoners of war. The contrast was with 'Hague law', or laws of war in the strict sense (referring to the Hague Rules of 1907). This was the law that regulated the conduct of hostilities as between the contenders (by, for instance, prohibiting certain types of weapons or certain types of tactics).

In each of these areas, there were some major developments after 1945.[84] On the Geneva-law side of the ledger, there was a general updating and re-codification in 1949, when four new Geneva Conventions were concluded to replace the previous ones.[85] The Fourth Convention was the most innovative, in that it provided for major advances in the protection of civilians in time of war (chiefly with regard to occupation of territory). On the Hague-law side, international conventions were adopted that prohibited the possession of biological and chemical weapons (in 1972 and 1993 respectively), together with, in 1980, a convention on conventional weapons, with protocols restricting the use of weapons leaving undetectable fragments, mines and booby traps, incendiary weapons and blinding laser weapons.[86] In 1997, agreement was reached on a convention banning the use of land mines.[87] Environmental modification techniques were the subject of a convention in 1977.[88] In 1994, a set of rules on war at sea was produced by the

---

[84] On developments in the laws of war after 1945, see generally Best, *War and Law*. For expositions of the substantive law of armed conflict, see Green, *Contemporary Law*; and Fleck (ed.), *Handbook*. Still very useful, although out-dated in many respects, is Greenspan, *Modern Law*.

[85] Geneva Convention I on Wounded and Sick in the Field, 12 Aug. 1949, 75 UNTS 31; Geneva Convention II on Wounded, Sick and Shipwrecked at Sea, 12 Aug. 1949, *ibid.* at 85; Geneva Convention III on Prisoners of War, 12 Aug. 1949, *ibid.* at 135; and Geneva Convention IV on Civilians, 12 Aug. 1949, *ibid.* at 287. All are reprinted in Roberts and Guelff (eds.), *Documents*, at 195–369.

[86] Convention on the Prohibition of Biological and Toxin Weapons, 10 Apr. 1972, 1015 UNTS 163; Convention on Chemical Weapons, 13 Jan. 1993, 32 ILM 800 (1993); and Convention on Prohibitions or Restrictions of Certain Conventional Weapons, 10 Oct. 1980, 1342 UNTS 137; reprinted in Roberts and Guelff (eds.), *Documents*, at 515–60.

[87] Ottawa Convention on the Prohibition and Use of Anti-personnel Mines, 18 Sept. 1997, 36 ILM 1507 (1997); reprinted in Roberts and Guelff (eds.), *Documents*, at 645–66.

[88] Convention on Hostile Use of Environmental Modification Techniques, 18 May 1977, 1108 UNTS 151; reprinted in Roberts and Guelff (eds.), *Documents*, at 407–17.

International Institute of Humanitarian Law.[89] Although this was an
unofficial codification, it commanded wide respect amongst lawyers and
governments. As always, though, progress was patchy; and technology
continued to plunge forward at a faster pace than the sedate deliberations of lawyers. Perhaps the most notable gap in the law was the lack of
any appreciable restriction on the use of nuclear weapons.[90]

The issue on which the radical and moderate camps parted company
concerned whether these two bodies of law could and should remain
separate, or whether they would be merged. This question may appear
arcane in the extreme. But it was to have some momentous ramifications
for the dispute over the discriminatory or nondiscriminatory character
of the laws of armed conflict. Certainly, even-handed treatment of
belligerents, without regard to the underlying justice of the dispute
between them, had long been a fundamental principle of humanitarian
work in war. In particular, it was a basic principle of the International
Committee of the Red Cross and a prominent feature of the Geneva
Conventions which it sponsored. Nor was the advent of the UN seen as
having changed this. This became evident in 1949, when the four new
Geneva Conventions retained the traditional principles of nondiscrimination and reciprocity which had been cornerstones of Geneva law from
its outset. The advocates of the radical approach were well aware of this
fact, and they readily acknowledged that humanitarian rules (i.e.,
Geneva law) should apply with equal force to both sides, regardless
of which one was fighting lawfully and which was not. It was only the
non-humanitarian rules (Hague law), regulating the actual conduct of
the hostilities as between the opposing armed forces, that should discriminate in favour of the UN-supported side or (as the case may be) of
clearly identified self-defenders.[91]

The lawyers of the moderate school contended that it was not possible
to make such a distinction. Kunz was notably outspoken on this point.
He insisted that any attempt to create a sharp dichotomy between
humanitarian and 'other' laws of war – between Geneva law and Hague
law – was both 'theoretically wrong' and 'practically impossible'. Either *all*
of the laws of war are humanitarian in nature, or *none* of them is.

---

[89] See International Institute of Humanitarian Law, *San Remo Manual*, reprinted in Roberts
      and Guelff (eds.), *Documents*, at 572–606.
[90] On the lack of regulation of nuclear weapons by the existing laws of war, see Legality of the
      Threat or Use of Nuclear Weapons, 1996 ICJ Rep. 225, paras. 52–63, 68–73.
[91] See, for example, 'Equality of Application of the Rules of the Law of War to Parties to an
      Armed Conflict', 59(2) *Annuaire* (1963), at 376.

'The whole law of war', Kunz insisted, 'is one and cannot be split into two parts'.[92]

The humanitarian revolution tipped the balance in favour of the moderate position of traditional even-handedness, against the radical stance of discrimination against the unjust side. That revolution could be thought of as a sort of conceptual takeover of the Hague law by the Geneva law. The essence of it was the proposition that, fundamentally, humanitarian concerns were at the root of *both* of these bodies of law, rather than of the Geneva law alone. The nature of the change in outlook was explained in clear terms in the 1990s by the International Criminal Tribunal for the Former Yugoslavia. The Hague law, regulating the conduct of armed conflict, was described by the Tribunal as having originally been state-sovereignty-oriented, geared towards protecting the interests of the warring states. In recent times, however, the sovereignty-oriented approach had been 'gradually supplanted by a human-being-oriented approach'.[93] In 1996, the World Court confirmed the integration of these two bodies of law, formerly separate, into 'one single complex system' under the label 'international humanitarian law'.[94]

This confluence of Hague and Geneva law was most apparent in practical terms in the two Additional Protocols that were concluded in 1977 to supplement the four Geneva Conventions of 1949.[95] In Protocol I especially, which concerned international conflicts, the most important rules were the ones that restricted military operations in the interest of protecting civilians (for example, by protecting important civilian infrastructure from attack) – thereby inextricably blending Hague-law and Geneva-law elements together.

The effect of this merger of the two bodies of law was to resolve the debate over whether the laws of war should be biased in favour of the just party, in favour of the moderate position. If *all* of the laws of war were humanitarian in character, then the conclusion ineluctably followed that the *whole* of the law of war must be applied strictly even-handedly,

---

[92] 50(1) *Annuaire* (1963), at 42–5. See also, to this effect, remarks of Eustathiades, *ibid.* at 28–9; remarks of Castrén, 47(1) *Annuaire* (1957), at 311–13; and remarks of Giraud, *ibid.* at 313–14.

[93] *Prosecutor* v. *Tadić* (Jurisdiction), Int'l Criminal Tribunal for the Former Yugoslavia, 2 Oct. 1995, 35 ILM 32 (1996), para. 97.

[94] Legality of the Threat or Use of Nuclear Weapons, 1996 ICJ Rep. 225, para. 75.

[95] Additional Protocol I to the Geneva Conventions of 1949, 8 June 1977, 1125 UNTS 3; and Additional Protocol II to the Geneva Conventions of 1949, 8 June, 1977, 1125 UNTS 609; reprinted in Roberts and Guelff (eds.), *Documents*, at 419–512.

to aggressors and defenders alike (or, as the case may be, to aggressors and UN enforcers alike). A scholarly consensus to this effect gradually emerged – with the only division of view remaining being the psychological one of whether this principle of nondiscrimination was to be actively applauded or passively (even begrudgingly) accepted. To the radicals, of course, it was a matter for some regret. Georges Scelle, for example, candidly confessed that he could not endorse nondiscrimination with 'gladness of heart'.[96] But the practical considerations of war, the absence in most cases of any definitive identification of the just party and the dictates of the humanitarian revolution left no real choice.

State practice – perhaps strongly bolstered by various inertial tendencies – likewise favoured the moderate over the radical position. There was early evidence to this effect in 1954, when an international conference in the Hague, charged with the task of drafting a convention on the protection of cultural property in time of armed conflict, adopted a side resolution to the effect that the UN should require its forces to abide by the terms of the Convention (even though the UN as such would not be a party to it).[97] In 1971, the Institute of International Law took the position that the entire body of humanitarian law applied to UN forces.[98] Four years later, the Institute went on to hold that *all* of the laws of armed conflict applied to UN forces.[99]

In due course, the UN itself accepted this position. This was first evidenced in 1978, when a specific order was issued to a UN peace-keeping force operating in southern Lebanon, that, in the event of involvement in hostilities, it should adhere to the laws of war. All doubt on the matter was finally removed in 1999, when UN Secretary-General Kofi Annan issued a bulletin containing a set of generally applicable guidelines on the subject.[100] Although the bulletin did not actually adopt the whole of international humanitarian law *en bloc*, it did make it clear that the fundamental principles of humanitarian law were to be adhered to by UN forces. For example, it specifically held that

---

[96] 47(1) *Annuaire* (1957), at 585.
[97] Res. 1, in Jiří Toman, *The Protection of Cultural Property in the Event of Armed Conflict* (Aldershot: Dartmouth, 1996), at 355.
[98] Conditions of Application of Humanitarian Rules of Armed Conflict to Hostilities in Which United Nations Forces May Be Engaged, in 54(2) *Annuaire* (1971), at 465–70.
[99] Conditions of Application of Rules, Other than Humanitarian Rules, of Armed Conflict to Hostilities in Which United Nations Forces May Be Engaged, 56(2) *Annuaire* (1975), at 540–5.
[100] UN Doc. ST/SGB/1999/13 (1999); reprinted in 38 ILM 1656 (1999), and in Roberts and Guelff (eds.), *Documents*, at 721–30.

prisoners taken by UN forces were to be treated in accordance with the relevant Geneva Convention.[101]

If there was a reluctance to grant special rights to UN forces beyond those provided by the laws of war, there was a similar hesitation to impose liability onto aggressor states for any belligerent acts that conformed to the laws of war. This had been the case after the Second World War, when courts held that the crime of aggression could only be imputed to the actual planners of aggressive war and not to the ordinary soldiers who carried it out. In the 1990s, in the wake of the forcible expulsion of Iraq from Kuwait, a similar stance was taken. After the conflict, a claim was presented to the UN Compensation Commission for damages for injuries suffered by members of the coalition armed forces in the ordinary course of combat. In a highly summary decision issued in 1992, the Commission's Governing Council rejected it (although it declined to provide a specific reason for this conclusion). Individual coalition soldiers were eligible for compensation, it was held, only in the special case of unlawful treatment as prisoners of war.[102]

The position on belligerents' rights and the laws of war in the post-1945 era may therefore be summed up briefly, in three propositions. First, with regard to the actual *conduct* of armed hostilities, no distinction is to be made between aggressors and self-defenders or between aggressors and UN forces. Self-defenders and UN forces have no special privileges, nor aggressors any disabilities in this regard. Both are equally subject to the general laws of war. The effect, then, is that soldiers fighting on the unjust side incur no legal liability, provided that they adhere to the laws of war in conducting their operations. To this extent, the new just-war outlook was not taken to its logical conclusion. Whether this was a matter of regret (to the radicals) or of high principle (to the moderates) was a matter largely of personal preference. In any event, this effectively meant the retention of one of the most prominent features of the nineteenth-century legal institution of war: the sharp dichotomy between the law on the *resort* to armed force (the *jus ad bellum*) and the law applying to the conducting of the hostilities (the *jus in bello*).

The second point is that there is *state* responsibility for any resort to force in violation of international law, as illustrated most vividly by the

---

[101] On UN forces and the laws of war, see generally Schindler, 'United Nations Forces'.
[102] Governing Council of the UN Compensation Commission, Decision No. 11, 26 June 1992, UN Doc. S/24589 (1992), Annex II; reprinted in 31 ILM 1009 (1992), at 1067.

Nicaragua v. *United States* case in 1986 and by the compensation arrangements that followed the Kuwait conflict of 1991. It would be expected that this would only take practical effect after the conclusion of the hostilities, in the form of some kind of legal action. The principle here is that the law-breaking state is liable, in the manner of ordinary civil liability, for all damages caused by its unlawful conduct (exclusive of damage sustained by the opposing side in the military operations themselves).

Third, there is the consideration of the position of third states and the applicability of the law of neutrality, a matter in which several different scenarios must be considered. When UN forces are fighting on one side, there is no uncertainty. Traditional neutrality is clearly excluded, by the express text of the UN Charter itself, in favour of (at a minimum) a policy of 'non-belligerency' in the manner of the American policy of 1939–41. When one side has been authoritatively identified by the UN as the just one, but without UN forces being *themselves* on the field of battle, the position is less clear. State practice, however, indicates that here too, bias by third states in favour of the just side is at least permissible, if not actually required – meaning concretely, that the unjust side would have no legal claim against third states that acted incompatibly with the traditional law of neutrality. Finally, there is the situation in which there is no authoritative identification of the aggressor and the defender. In this case, the status of the law of neutrality was still open to question in the early twenty-first century.

The objective picture of war

A notable consequence of the humanitarian revolution was that it marked, in effect, the ascendancy of the objective view of war over the subjective one. That is to say, that the *lex specialis* of humanitarian law was activated by the brute *fact* of the outbreak of armed conflict, and not by an expression of will or intention on the part of one or both of the contending states. The fact of armed conflict, in other words, gives rise, automatically and of its own force, to the application of the corpus of humanitarian law, which lies dormant during times of tranquillity. This was, for all practical purposes, the objective view of war as it had been articulated in the nineteenth century – that war was a material fact giving rise to a range of specific legal consequences. Now, as then, the conception of war was not actually fundamental to the analysis. It could just as easily be said – as it now was after 1945 – simply that the fact of armed conflict automatically activated a body of law that was specially designed to regulate the conduct of the hostilities.

The status of war after 1945 may therefore be summed up in a crisp fashion. The radical school of thought was correct to hold that war in the *subjective* sense of that term was no longer possible. That is to say, that countries no longer had the power to create, by an act of will or intention, a state of war in the full nineteenth-century sense (i.e., a state of affairs in which two countries could lawfully use armed force against one another). At the same time, the moderate school was correct to hold that war in the *objective* sense of the term continued to be possible, in the sense that, upon the eruption of a de facto armed conflict, a special body of law automatically became applicable to regulate the conduct of the hostilities. There was, however, no compelling reason to employ the emotive term 'war' to describe that situation. In fact, there were two good reasons to avoid the use of that expression. First, 'war' is too limited a conception, since the objective view of war, underpinned by the humanitarian character of the laws of war, applies not only to wars of the traditional nineteenth-century kind, but also to measures short of war such as forcible reprisals. Second, the term 'war' connotes to many persons a situation in which the contending sides are *lawfully* using force against one another. The moderate school joins the radical one in holding that, after 1945, the resort to armed force is no longer a permissible means of resolving interstate disputes, as it had been in the nineteenth century – i.e., that, at least in principle, all armed conflicts that occur must be cases of either UN enforcement action or of aggression-and-self-defence. For these two reasons, the expression 'armed conflict' is preferable to 'war'.

Unanswered questions

It would be a great error to suppose that the fate of the legal institution of war had been fully settled by the beginning of the twenty-first century, or that the two phenomena of aggression-and-self-defence and UN enforcement action had *entirely* ruled out the possibility of a state of war in the pre-1945 sense. The heavy hand of past practices and modes of thought is not to be brushed aside by a few brisk lines of treaty text, even if that treaty is the Charter of the United Nations. For one thing, the idea of a state of war was so deeply ingrained in legal thought, as well as in state practice and the popular imagination, that it tenaciously continued to survive in various contexts. In addition, there was still, early in the twenty-first century, a dearth of judicial authority to the effect that the state of war was definitively a thing of the past. In 1949, for example, in the course of litigation between Britain and Albania, the World Court noted that Greece still considered itself to be in a state of war with Albania, although it made no holding on the point itself.[103]

In 1976, an interesting case arose in which the question of the existence of a state of war was directly presented in arbitration proceedings. These arose out of the armed clash between India and Pakistan over Kashmir in 1965.[104] The concrete legal question at hand was whether a bank guarantee between an Indian client and a Pakistani bank remained in force after the outbreak of the conflict – with the answer being negative if the conflict had been a war, and positive if it had not been. The opinion dealt at considerable length with the question of whether there had been a state of war, in the international legal sense of that term. In so doing, it explicitly rejected the radical position, which was frankly stated to lack general acceptance.[105] The actual effect of the UN Charter's ban on the use of force, it held, was not to make a state of war legally impossible. Instead, it merely gave rise to a presumption that, when an armed conflict did erupt, the parties did not intend it to be war, but rather to be a conflict short of war. That presumption, however, was rebuttable. The arbitrator did not adopt the objective theory of war in its purest form, however, by looking *only* at the single question of whether there was a de facto armed clash between the two sides. (Clearly there was.) Instead, he held that it was necessary to look to all the circumstances of the case.

The arbitrator went on to note that a number of the traditional outward signs of war were present. For example, the president of Pakistan had issued an emotional broadcast to the effect that the country was now at war with India. Also, both states issued contraband lists, indicating that they intended to exercise the traditional belligerent right of confiscation of war-related materials from neutrals. In the end, however, the arbitrator held the conflict not to have been a war. One reason was the limited scope of the material hostilities. The two countries did not throw anything like their entire armed forces at one another. Instead, the hostilities were largely confined to the Kashmir region and were of short duration (some two and a half weeks).

---

[103] Corfu Channel Case (*Great Britain v. Albania*), 1949 ICJ Rep. 2, at 29.
[104] *Dalmia Cement v. National Bank of Pakistan*, Int'l Chamber of Commerce, Arbitration Tribunal, 18 Dec. 1976, 67 ILR 611.
[105] *Ibid.* at 619.

Another factor was the lack of an unequivocal intention on the part of the two sides to engage in war (or *animus belligerendi*). Specifically, India was found clearly to have lacked the intention to regard the struggle as a war, while the evidence from the Pakistan side was ambivalent. Diplomatic relations between the states had not been broken, as would be expected in a time of war. Nor did either side appear to regard treaties between them as having been terminated by the crisis. On the basis of all these considerations, the conflict was held to fall short of being a war.[106] But the idea that a state of war was impossible as a matter of principle was clearly rejected.

Further evidence of the continuing hold of traditional conceptions of war in state practice was afforded by the peace treaty that Israel concluded with Egypt in 1979, which explicitly pronounced the termination of '[t]he state of war' between the two countries.[107] A similar, though somewhat less explicit, statement was made by Jordan and Israel in their Washington Declaration of 1994 (preceding their full peace agreement), which announced the end of 'the state of belligerency' that had hitherto prevailed between them.[108] It is possible that these expressions were used in an informal rather than a technical legal sense, but the point has never been adjudicated.

Perhaps the strongest reason for suspecting that the concept of a state of war might continue to play some part in international affairs lies in the possibility – to put it no more strongly – that certain practices of states could *only* be justified by recourse to the conception of a state of war. In particular, there were two areas in which this might be so. One concerned certain questions relating to the rights of belligerents and the conduct of war, in which it was possible that self-defence considerations would be too weak to provide the necessary legal justifications. The other concerned the possible continuing relevance of the law of neutrality. We shall look briefly at each of these matters.

Self-defence and belligerents' rights

After 1945, there were some indications that self-defence, even at its broadest, might be insufficient to justify certain actions of states and

---

[106] On this conflict, see Sumit Ganguly, *Conflict Unending: India–Pakistan Tensions since 1947* (Washington, D.C.: Woodrow Wilson Center Press, 2001), at 31–50.

[107] Egypt-Israel, Treaty of Peace, 26 Mar. 1979, 1136 UNTS 100, Art. 1(1).

[108] Washington Declaration, 25 July 1994, UN Doc. S/1994/939 (1994), Annex. A full peace treaty followed later that year, which did not expressly allude to a state of war or belligerency. See Israel-Jordan, Treaty of Peace, 26 Oct. 1994, 2042 UNTS 351.

that, as a consequence, recourse would have to be made instead to the existence of a state of war – in particular to claims of a right to exercise traditional belligerents' prerogatives. The root of the problem lay in the fact that self-defence action is constrained by the fundamental principles of necessity and proportionality. There has been much dispute amongst lawyers as to the precise scope of both of these. For present purposes, however, it is only necessary to recall that the traditional rights of belligerents in a state of war were much wider, with offensive action being fully permissible. Nor were the belligerents constrained by the principle of proportionality. Instead, they were limited only by rules forbidding certain specific weapons or tactics (such as chemical weapons or policies of no quarter), plus the general principle – the *very* general principle – that purely malicious damage ('unnecessary suffering' in the legal expression) was not allowed. In other words, certain belligerent acts could be lawful in a state of war which would not be allowable as self-defence in the narrow sense.[109]

One illustration of this point came before the UN Security Council in 1951, arising out of the exercise by Egypt of various traditional belligerents' rights over shipping passing through the Suez Canal. In addition to barring the passage of Israeli vessels, it insisted on visiting and searching third-state ships calling at Israeli ports and removing contraband of war from them.[110] Several European states objected to this practice. Egypt refrained from invoking self-defence, since an armistice agreement concluded with Israel in 1949 had put a halt to material hostilities between the two countries.[111] Instead, Egypt defended its actions on the ground that it was at war with Israel. Israel's position was directly in the spirit of the radical outlook. 'There can ... be no room within the régime of the [UN] Charter', it insisted, 'for any generic doctrine of belligerency'. The UN Charter, it contended, had 'created a new world of international relations within which the traditional rights of war cannot be enthroned'.[112] After an extended debate on the matter, the Security Council rejected the Egyptian stance and pronounced a state of war not to be in force, on the ground that the armistice agreement between the two states had a 'permanent character'.

---

[109] See Dinstein, *War*, at 207–13.
[110] For a thorough account of these policies, see Thomas D. Brown, Jr, 'World War Prize Law Applied in a Limited War Situation: Egyptian Restrictions on Neutral Shipping with Israel', 50 Minnesota Law Rev 849–73 (1966).
[111] Egypt-Israel, Armistice Agreement, 24 Feb. 1949, 42 UNTS 251.
[112] SC mtg 549 (26 July 1951), UN Doc. S/PV. 549 (1951), at 11–12.

Egypt accordingly was urged to discontinue its measures.[113] It should be noted, though, that this conclusion was by a political, rather than a judicial, body. It also appeared that the whole discussion took place on the tacit assumption that a state of war *might* have been in force under some circumstances.

This issue was illustrated in rather more dramatic fashion in 1981, when Israel launched an aerial attack on a nuclear reactor in Iraq. The action was widely condemned on the ground that the reactor posed no immediate threat to Israeli security. Israel's justification in the UN Security Council debates, however, was that the operation was an act of war, not of self-defence.[114] The UN Security Council condemned the attack.[115] Similar claims of a state of war were put forward from the Arab side, as a justification for economic boycott measures against states that traded with Israel. This occurred most conspicuously in 1973–4, when an oil embargo was imposed against various Western states. The reason was that there was room for doubt whether the measures could have been justified as either ordinary sovereign measures or as self-defence actions.[116] None of these incidents ever became the subject of judicial consideration. So the question of the possible continued existence of belligerents' rights was, at the outset of the twenty-first century, still awaiting clarification.

Neutrality

As has been so frequently the case in the history of legal thought on war, considerations of neutrality served to highlight contentious issues in an especially vivid fashion. That continued to be so after 1945, when neutrality provided one of the sharpest points of contention between the radical and moderate approaches to war. The radicals, noting that the UN Charter expressly excluded neutrality in cases of UN enforcement action, held that the same principle should apply to the other

---

[113] SC Res. 95 (1 Sept. 1951), 6 SCOR, Res and Dec, at 10.

[114] Remarks of Blum, SCOR, 2280th mtg, 12 June 1981, UN Doc. S/PV. 2280 (1981), at 42. See also Dinstein, *War*, at 45, 169.

[115] SC Res. 487 (19 June 1981), 36 SCOR, Res and Dec, at 10.

[116] See, for example, Marwan Iskandar, *The Arab Boycott of Israel* (Beirut: Palestine Liberation Organization, 1966), at 17–18; Ibrahim F. I. Shihata, 'Destination Embargo of Arab Oil: Its Legality under International Law', 68 AJIL 592–627, at 608, 614–16; and Hussein A. Hassouna, *The League of Arab States and Regional Disputes: A Study of Middle East Conflicts* (Dobbs Ferry, N.Y.: Oceana, 1975), at 317–18.

category of just war as well, that of aggression-and-self-defence. At a minimum, the principle pronounced by Grotius in the seventeenth century should be reinstated: that third states must do nothing to further the cause of the aggressor or to injure that of the victim. Moreover, any action in favour of the victim – such as a supply of arms by a third-state government – should not give rise to any liability to the aggressor as it formerly would have, when the law of neutrality forbade such assistance to both sides equally. The contention, in other words, was that the new law of the UN Charter era mandated 'non-belligerency' in favour of victims against aggressors, in the manner of the American policy of 1939–41. This position had been articulated in 1939 in the Harvard draft Convention on the Rights and Duties of States in Case of Aggression, which held aggressor states to be subject to all of the duties of belligerents *vis-à-vis* neutrals, whilst being entitled to none of the rights.[117] On this view, the American Lend-lease programme may have been a violation of the traditional law of neutrality; but it was a model for the UN Charter era that was soon to come.

The moderate approach rejected this thesis on the obviously pragmatic ground that it required some kind of reliable mechanism for determining which side in a given conflict was the aggressor and which the defender. In the face of the invincible doubt that is so constant a feature of international life, such a determination is not possible, with the result that neutrality must remain, if only on strictly practical grounds, as an option for third states in cases in which the aggressor has not been authoritatively identified.[118]

That neutrality continued to exist, to at least some extent, was confirmed in 1996 by the World Court in its Advisory Opinion on Nuclear Weapons, although only in very general terms. Significantly, the Court spoke of neutrality as having 'a fundamental character similar to that of the humanitarian ... rules'.[119] In particular, the duty of belligerents to refrain from inflicting injuries onto neutral states was confirmed. This fundamental duty of belligerents towards neutral ones was very far, however, from constituting the whole of the law of neutrality as it had matured in the nineteenth century. Most notably, there was uncertainty

---

[117] Harvard draft Convention on the Rights and Duties of States in Case of Aggression, 33 (Supp.) AJIL 827 (1939), Art. 3.

[118] See Castrén, *Present Law*; Tucker, *War and Neutrality*; Kunz, 'Laws of War', at 327–8; Stone, *Legal Controls*, at 382; McDougal and Feliciano, *World Public Order*, at 398–400, 427–35; and Baxter, 'Legal Consequences', at 72–3.

[119] Legality of the Threat or Use of Nuclear Weapons, 1996 ICJ Rep. 225, para. 89.

as to the post-1945 status of the traditional *rights* of belligerents *vis-à-vis* neutral states, and also, conversely, as to the duties of neutral countries to belligerent ones. On these questions, the self-defence revolution shed some light – while also leaving some important matters unresolved.

To some extent, the traditional rights of belligerents *vis-à-vis* neutrals could be resuscitated as adjuncts of the right of self-defence. In particular, two of the most important belligerent rights could be effectively revived and repackaged in this way: blockade and contraband. It was easy to see that the enforcement of blockades against third states, as well as the halting of arms flows to the enemy, could easily be justified, at least in some circumstances, as necessary and proportionate self-defence measures. The same problem existed here, though, as in the case of the rights of belligerents *inter se*: that the principle of proportionality, which always governed self-defence, gave belligerent states less freedom of action than the classical law of neutrality did.

An indication of this point was provided in 1971-2, with the American closure of Haiphong Harbour during the Vietnam conflict. Although the measure was sometimes referred to as a blockade, the United States carefully refrained from characterising it in that way. Instead, it justified it as a self-defence action, with the American government stressing that it was conducting 'more restricted operations than those permissible under traditional principles relating to blockade'.[120] For example, the United States was careful to place the mines entirely in waters which North Vietnam claimed as its own, so as to avoid any disruption of traffic on the high seas. (The traditional law of blockade permitted operations to spill over into high-seas areas.) This stance had the virtue of consistency with the American characterisation of the over-all conflict, as a self-defence exercise on behalf of South Vietnam rather than a true war – though with the logical consequence that there were greater constraints on its freedom of action than there would be in a state of war.

A more notable instance occurred during the Iran–Iraq conflict of the 1980s, when Iran, in 1985, instituted a policy of visiting and searching neutral ships on the high seas (by means of helicopter landings). By April 1987, some 1,200 ships had been boarded and 30 cargoes confiscated.[121] This policy was justified not on the ground of self-defence but instead, in Iran's words, on 'the established rules of international law

---

[120] Office of the Legal Adviser, 6 June 1972, in 'Rights and Duties of States', 66 AJIL 836–8 (1972).
[121] Nicholas Tracy, *Attack on Maritime Trade* (Basingstoke: Macmillan, 1991), at 225.

regarding the rights and duties of neutral Powers in naval war'.[122] The reactions of various third states to this assertion were of some note. Britain's response was to acquiesce in the Iranian measures – but on the basis that they constituted an exercise of the right of self-defence on Iran's part, *not* on the ground that the law of neutrality as such was applicable.[123] Britain's position, however, was not altogether consistent, as it also expressly held itself to be neutral in the conflict – though perhaps merely meaning neutral in the somewhat informal and non-legal sense of having no preference as to the outcome of the conflict.[124]

The unresolved issue here, as in the case of belligerents' rights *vis-à-vis* one another, was whether international law, after 1945, allowed the exercise of belligerents' rights *vis-à-vis* neutrals only to the extent that they fell within the bounds of necessity and proportionality as marked out by the law of self-defence, or whether those rights could be exercised in the traditional manner, against all neutral states at all times without a specific showing of necessity in each individual case. There was uncertainty, too, as to whether third states were actually *obligated* to acquiesce in such matters as visit and search, confiscation of contraband and the like. It was arguable that the exercise of a right based on necessity could impose no such obligation on innocent third parties, i.e., that necessity entitled a state to 'step outside' the framework of law (so to speak) but did not alter the legal position of third parties. If this were so, then claims based on self-defence – rooted as it was in the principle of necessity – could not impose obligations of acquiescence onto third states. In a true state of war, however, there was no doubt of the existence of a duty of submission on the part of neutral countries to such measures. The point remains unresolved. Some lawyers contend that there is a duty to acquiesce in measures of genuine self-defence, on the ground that the collective-security ethos of the post-1945 world requires states to refrain from undermining the vital right of self-defence.[125] That

---

[122] Letter from Iran to Secretary-General, 25 Sept. 1985, UN Doc. S/17496 (1985), in 40 SCOR, Supp. for July–Sept. 1985, at 127.

[123] Parliamentary statement of 28 Jan. 1986, *Hansard*, HC, vol. 90, ser. 5. col. 426, written answers, reprinted in 57 Brit YB 583. See also Parliamentary statement of 5 Feb. 1986, *Hansard* HC, vol. 91, ser. 5, cols. 278–9, reprinted in 57 Brit YB 583–4 (1987).

[124] *Hansard*, HL, vol. 2, ser. 5, col. 435, 11 May 1981; and *Hansard*, HC, vol. 8, ser. 5, col. 94, written answers, 7 July 1981. On the British position regarding the conflict generally, see Gray, 'British Position'; and Gray, 'British Position, Part 2'. Being neutral in the legal sense means being subject to the array of legal rights and duties of neutrals as prescribed by international law.

[125] See E. Lauterpacht, 'Legal Irrelevance', at 64–5.

appears to be a sensible proposition. As of the early twenty-first century, however, judicial authority in support of it was lacking.

At the start of the twenty-first century, several possible resolutions to this problem were on offer, of which two may be briefly identified. One possible solution was to regard neutrality as an option for third states, but not as a requirement or as an *automatic* effect of the outbreak of an armed conflict. Instead, third states could elect to be neutral – with the effect that they would thereby be taking upon themselves the full panoply of rights *and* duties of neutrals. The situation here would be analogous to recognition of belligerency in civil conflicts.[126] By the same token, each third state could determine, instead, that a given conflict was a case of aggression-and-self-defence rather than a war, and then proceed to decide for itself which party was the aggressor and which the defender. Pursuant to that determination, it could then choose to provide assistance to the putative defender, as a 'non-belligerent' in the manner of the United States with regard to the Allied side in 1939–41. The third country, however, would do this at its peril. In particular, it would run two very notable risks. First of all, if it was later determined (say, by a judicial pronouncement) that its favoured side had actually been the aggressor, then the assisting state would thereby be implicated in the aggression as a sort of aider and abettor (to borrow from domestic legal parlance). In addition, during the course of the conflict a partial state would inevitably risk being drawn into the hostilities by the side against which it was providing the aid (as the United States, in effect, was in 1917).[127]

A second possible solution to the neutrality problem would be to hold that the traditional law of neutrality would apply automatically to *all* armed conflicts, but only on a sort of provisional basis. That is, that it would apply *during* the hostilities but that afterwards, third states could make claims against the aggressor party for unlawful interference with their rights – on the assumption, of course, that the aggressor was authoritatively identified at some point. By the same token, any measures that the self-defending side had taken beyond the bounds of necessity or proportionality would also give rise to a duty to compensate affected parties. The conflict, in sum, would be treated as a duel-style

---

[126] See, to this general effect, Kelsen, *Principles*, at 24; and Greenwood, 'Concept of War', at 300–1. See also McNair and Watts, *Legal Effects*, at 10.

[127] See Bowett, *Self-defence*, at 179–81.

war during the period in which it was raging but would then be treated, retrospectively in effect, as a situation of aggression-and-self-defence.

These possible solutions to the various outstanding quandaries of war and neutrality, as of the early twenty-first century, were firmly in the realm of speculation rather than of established doctrine. As of that time, there was neither judicial authority nor prominent scholarly commentary in support of them. They demonstrate (if demonstration were needed) the extent to which the legal history of war is an ongoing story, in our time as in all others. Indeed, the legal history of war may even be less complete in the present time than it has been for many centuries past, for there were many challenges afoot in the late twentieth and early twenty-first centuries besides the difficulty of reconciling *past* practices with the new demands of the modern just-war era. There was no shortage of novel challenges, promising – or threatening – to take the international law of war into radically uncharted waters.

10

New fields of battle

Support for freedom fighters is self-defense.

Ronald Reagan[1]

The war on terror is not a figure of speech. It is an inescapable calling of our generation.

George W. Bush[2]

Through much of history, lawyers have scrambled to adjust the fine points of the law to a crude and violent world. After 1945, the challenges were as severe as any that had ever been faced previously, largely because of important changes in the kinds of wars that commonly afflicted mankind. Two new kinds of challenge were especially noteworthy. The first was civil conflict, which attained unprecedented prominence, as compared to interstate conflict, in the post-1945 world. In this area, the inheritance of the nineteenth century remained very much in evidence, most notably in the retention of the traditional bias in favour of established governments and against insurgents. Recognition of belligerency and of insurgency were little in evidence, at least on the surface; but it was likely that they were merely sleeping and not dead. Most conspicuous in the way of change was the promotion of one particular category of insurgents from the humble level of rebels to fully fledged belligerents: persons carrying on what came to be called a national liberation struggle. Some regarded this as a welcome extension of just-war ideals. Others saw it as an unwelcome intrusion of ideological considerations into what should be the dispassionate realm of the rules of law. Probably more important, though, was an advance – though not

---

[1] State of the Union Address, 6 Feb. 1985, in 1985 *Public Papers of the Presidents* 140.
[2] Radio address, 20 Mar. 2004, at www.whitehouse.gov/news/releases/2004/03/20040319–3.html.

so rapid a one as many hoped – in the application of international humanitarian standards to situations of internal conflict in general.

The other major new challenge was a new sort of war – or perhaps of
'war'. This was against terrorism. Terrorism was not invented after 1945
by any means. It was in this period, however, that it began to become a
threat on a global scale. And it was only in 2001, with explosive sudden-
ness, that it leaped to the very forefront of world affairs. In the immediate wake of the terrorist attacks of that year on New York City and
Washington, D.C., the American government began a systematic programme of dealing with terrorism by martial means. That is to say, that
it deployed the traditional weapons of warfare, rather than of ordinary
criminal law, to do battle with this scourge. But questions soon began to
arise as to how suitable those weapons of war would prove to be against a
foe which, though decidedly deadly, bore little resemblance to a traditional enemy armed force on the field of battle. Throughout the whole of
human history, the soldier and the murderer have both played deadly
games. Until now, though, they had always been seen to be playing very
different deadly games, governed by very different sets of legal rules.
Now, for the first time, they were being brought face to face. As a result,
the different legal regimes that had traditionally governed them were,
perforce, being brought together as well – with results that have only
begun to become apparent.

From civil war to national liberation

One of the most significant expansions of the international law of war in
the late twentieth century was into the realm of civil conflicts.[3] This was
appropriate, given that, after 1945, a very large proportion of the armed
conflict in the world occurred in struggles *within* rather than *between*
countries. Moreover, there was an increasing view, strongly undergirded
by Cold-War considerations, that modern civil wars, much more than
those of the past, often had repercussions that extended well beyond the
boundaries of the state in question. The Greek civil war of the 1940s was
an outstanding early example. Internal conflicts in such countries as the
Congo, Yemen, Lebanon, Pakistan, Angola and Afghanistan (to name
only a few) likewise involved, or threatened to involve, the interests of
major foreign powers whether overtly or covertly. As a result, there was

---

[3] For a general survey of international law relating to civil strife, see Moir, *Internal Armed
Conflict*.

increasing doubt as to whether governments should continue to enjoy the privileged status which the law had traditionally accorded them, chiefly in the form of allowing foreign states to provide assistance to them, but not to insurgents. Other developments reinforced these doubts. The human-rights movement, most outstandingly, highlighted the fact that many governments were violators of international law on a large scale. Many felt that, in cases in which the rebels were struggling for the recognition of their fundamental rights, the law should not place them at a legal disadvantage compared to their governments.

In the event, international law moved cautiously in this area – but it did move, in two main directions. The first concerned the question of foreign intervention into civil conflicts. Broadly speaking, the direction that it took was not towards allowing greater leeway for foreign intrusion, but instead – and more modestly – towards providing some welcome clarification as to the *effects* that foreign intervention would have when it did occur. Second, a larger body of international rules was brought to bear on the regulation of the conduct of civil conflicts. That is to say, that the humanitarian revolution was extended, though only to a modest extent, to civil conflicts in addition to international ones. The greatest step in this regard, at least symbolically, was to extend the full body of international humanitarian law to one particular category of internal conflicts: wars of national liberation (as they were called in everyday parlance). At the same time, though, much of the old law remained in place alongside these new developments. Recognition of belligerency and of insurgency, as inherited from nineteenth-century practice, maintained, it is true, only a shadowy presence after 1945. But it is probable that they continued to exist, and possible that they would find new utility in the twenty-first century. In sum, international law relating to civil conflicts was, like law (and life) generally, a sometimes untidy mix of old and new.

The art of foreign intervention

After 1945, the traditional bias of international law in favour of governments and against insurgents came increasingly into question. But it proved difficult to arrive at a consensus on whether to change the traditional rules and, if so, in what manner. If governments and insurgents were to be placed on a par, there were two ways in which this could be brought about. One was to place further restrictions on foreign intervention by prohibiting foreign countries from assisting *either* side – i.e., by mandating a sort of law of neutrality or recognition of belligerency that would be automatically applicable to civil conflicts generally. Within the Institute of International Law, there was support for such a total ban on intervention in internal conflicts.[4] The Institute eventually endorsed this position in 1975, reversing the stance that it had taken in 1900 (which had allowed aid to the government side).[5] Many of its members, however, resisted the change, contending that there was no support in state practice for it.[6]

The other way of eliminating the bias in favour of governments was to remove *all* restrictions on foreign intervention by allowing foreign countries to assist either the insurgents or the government, at their option. Certainly, when Cold-War considerations were at stake, the major powers sometimes showed little hesitation in supporting rebellions against governments. The Soviet Union, for example, supported insurgents against the Greek government in the 1940s, and against the South Vietnamese government from 1954 to 1975. In 1954, the United States provided assistance to insurgents in the overthrow of a left-wing government in Guatemala which was thought to be unduly sympathetic to Communism. In the 1970s and 1980s, there was further American backing for rebel forces in Angola, Afghanistan and Nicaragua, with various degrees of openness. In the 1980s, the United States even produced a more or less explicit position, known as the Reagan Doctrine (after President Ronald Reagan), to the effect that assistance to insurgent groups was permissible if the government that they were fighting against was of a Marxist-Leninist character.[7] There was a distinct whiff of classical just-war thinking in this stance: holding that the rights of parties in an armed conflict were a function of the underlying justice of the cause for which they fought.

In addition to Cold-War considerations, the humanitarian revolution provided support for allowing foreign assistance to insurgents, in appropriate circumstances. Specifically, it was contended by some that it

---

[4] See, for example, remarks of Chaumont, in 56 *Annuaire* 136–7 (1975); of Münch, *ibid.* at 138; and of Skybiszewski, *ibid.* at 143–5.
[5] 'The Principle of Non-intervention in Civil Wars', *ibid.* at 544–9.
[6] See, for example, remarks of Castrén, *ibid.* at 134–5; of O'Connell, *ibid.* at 139–40; and of Rousseau, *ibid.* at 142–3.
[7] On the Reagan Doctrine, see Jeane Kirkpatrick, *The Reagan Doctrine and US Foreign Policy* (Washington, D.C.: Heritage Foundation, 1985); and Ted Galen Carpenter, *US Aid to Anti-Communist Rebels: The 'Reagan Doctrine' and Its Pitfalls* (Washington, D.C.: Cato Institute, 1986).

should be lawful for foreign states to assist rebels who fought for the recognition and exercise of legally recognised fundamental human rights. Some went even further and contended that, in situations of gross violations of human rights by governments, foreign states were permitted to intervene directly with armed force to compel a change of policy (usually meaning, at the same time, forcing a change of government). It has been observed that there was at least some precedent for this doctrine of humanitarian intervention in the nineteenth century. Some lawyers maintained that it continued to be permitted after 1945.[8] State practice in this area was highly equivocal (to put it mildly); but there were several cases of intervention which had at least a substantial human-rights component, even if other interests were present as well. Examples included the Indian intervention in Pakistan in 1971–2, in the face of large-scale abuses of human rights in East Bengal – an operation that led to the creation of the new state of Bangladesh. In 1979, Tanzania overthrew the notoriously brutal regime of Idi Amin in neighbouring Uganda. The best example of a humanitarian intervention to protect a civilian population against repression by its own government occurred in 1999, when a coalition of Western powers – in a manner distinctly reminiscent of the Concert of Europe actions in the nineteenth century – mounted an aerial-warfare campaign against the Federal Republic of Yugoslavia, to force it to halt atrocities in the province of Kosovo.[9]

Judicial bodies, however, declined to endorse any of these proposed changes. Most notably, the World Court, in its judgment in the case of *Nicaragua* v. *United States* in 1986, expressly reiterated the principle that intervention in civil strife was allowable at the request of the government.[10] At the same time, the Court held there to be no *general* right of intervention on behalf of insurgent groups in foreign states.[11] The Reagan Doctrine in particular was effectively (if only implicitly) rejected. 'The Court cannot contemplate', it pronounced, 'the creation of a new rule opening up a right of intervention by one State against another on the ground that the latter has opted for some particular

---

[8] For the view that humanitarian intervention was permissible, see Richard B. Lillich, 'Humanitarian Intervention: A Reply to Ian Brownlie and a Plea for Constructive Alternatives', in J. N. Moore (ed.), *Law and Civil War*, at 229–51; and Fonteyne, 'Customary Doctrine'. For a defence of humanitarian intervention rooted in philosophical ideas distinctly reminiscent of natural-law thought, see Tesón, *Humanitarian Intervention*.

[9] On this incident, see Franck, *Recourse to Force*, at 163–70.

[10] *Nicaragua* v. *USA*, para. 246.   [11] *Ibid.*, paras. 206–9.

ideology or political system'.[12] At the same time, the Court carefully declined to provide any encouragement to supporters of humanitarian intervention, although it held back from making a definitive general pronouncement on the question.[13] The question of the lawfulness of humanitarian intervention therefore remained tantalisingly unresolved by the early twenty-first century, with every prospect of continuing to be well-nigh the most controversial issue in the whole of international law.[14]

If international courts, then, declined to support any loosening of the traditional ban on intervention on behalf of insurgents, they at least provided some welcome clarification on the legal *effects* that such an intervention would have when it did occur. In particular, some important light was shed after 1945 on the question of whether, or under what conditions, the involvement of a foreign state would transform an erstwhile civil conflict into an international one. In practical terms, the importance of the question was that, if a conflict became an international one, then the full range of international humanitarian law would apply to it. The most important concrete effect was that rebels would then become entitled to treatment as prisoners of war rather than as ordinary criminals, at least during the course of the hostilities.

On this question, it became established after 1945 that there were, in effect, three gradations of foreign involvement, each with its own distinctive set of legal consequences. The lowest level was one in which the foreign state's role in the struggle was performed, so to speak, from off-stage, i.e., in which the foreign country played the part of, say, a supplier of weapons or other services to the rebels. The middle gradation was a situation in which the foreign state actually participated in the struggle, but only as a kind of auxiliary or ally of the insurgent forces. The third and highest level was one in which the foreign state not only participated in the conflict but actually played the dominant part in it, so that the insurgents were, in effect, reduced to being auxiliaries of the intervening country. At the first level, a struggle is wholly internal. The middle level is a dual situation, with a civil and an international struggle raging

---

[12] *Ibid.*, para. 263.   [13] *Ibid.*, paras. 257–62.

[14] The literature on the subject of humanitarian intervention is forbiddingly large and even more forbiddingly repetitious. For a cogent justification of the practice, see Tesón, *Humanitarian Intervention*. In opposition, see Chesterman, *Just War*. For an excellent recent picture of the debate from various standpoints, see J. L. Holzgrefe and Robert O. Keohane (eds.), *Humanitarian Intervention: Ethical, Legal, and Political Dilemmas* (Cambridge: Cambridge University Press, 2003).

alongside one another. At the third level, the conflict is wholly international.

The archetypal illustration of the first and lowest-level category of foreign involvement would be a situation in which a foreign country provided financial assistance to an insurgent force in another state. This would be an unlawful act, to be sure. Specifically, it would constitute unlawful intervention by the assisting state in the internal affairs of the strife-torn country. But this comparatively minor form of assistance would not amount to a use of force contrary to the UN Charter.[15] Nor would it alter the character of the conflict, which would remain an internal rather than an international one. The rebels could be treated by their government as ordinary criminals, unless they had effective control of part of the territory, in which case the rules on recognition of insurgency would apply and would entitle them to prisoner-of-war treatment (at least during the continuance of the hostilities). Against the foreign country, the government would have a legal claim for unlawful intervention. It could obtain damages for any injury that it suffered; or, if no tribunal had jurisdiction over the matter, it could take some kind of non-forcible reprisal (such as economic measures) against the intervening state.

The second level of foreign involvement was most vividly illustrated by the civil strife in Nicaragua in the 1980s. The United States's assistance to the insurgents (known as the 'contras') went well beyond the provision of financing – extending to the supply of arms on a large scale, as well as of intelligence information. It also provided training for the insurgents in bases located in the neighbouring country of Honduras, from which the contras would launch attacks into Nicaragua. American forces did not, however, participate in those actual operations. In its action against the United States in the World Court, Nicaragua contended that the American involvement was so substantial as to transform the conflict into an international rather than a civil one. The contras, it maintained, were mere hirelings of the United States. The World Court rejected that argument, holding instead that the conflict fell into the middle category of the three just set out: a sort of hybrid situation in which a civil and an international conflict were in progress side by side.[16] The international component of the struggle consisted of a use of force by the United States against Nicaragua, in violation of the general ban in international law against the use of

---

[15] *Nicaragua* v. *USA*, para. 228.   [16] *Ibid.*, para. 219.

force.[17] To that situation, the full body of international humanitarian law would apply. The internal component of the struggle consisted of the operations mounted by the contras themselves.[18] To that conflict, the domestic law of Nicaragua applied. (As the contras controlled no territory in the country, no question of recognition of insurgency arose here.) The United States and the contras, in other words, constituted separate forces in alliance with one another, fighting separate conflicts.

At the third level of foreign involvement, the foreign state's role was so great as to swallow up that of the insurgents altogether. This would occur, as the World Court established in the *Nicaragua v. United States* case, when the foreign power exerted 'effective control' over the rebel forces which it supported.[19] The point was most strikingly illustrated in the Bosnian civil strife of 1992–5. The legal status of that conflict became a key issue in the trial of a defendant before the International Criminal Tribunal for the Former Yugoslavia in 1997. The person was accused of violating various provisions of the Geneva Conventions which were applicable only to international conflicts, but not to civil ones. The trial panel ruled that, in its initial phases, the conflict was an international one by virtue of the controlling role played by the forces of a foreign state, the Federal Republic of Yugoslavia (FRY), in support of insurgent ethnic Serb groups. It also held, however, that the character of the struggle changed on a particular date (19 May 1992) when the FRY government announced its withdrawal from the conflict. From that point onward, the trial court held, the conflict became a civil one, to which the full body of Geneva Convention law was no longer applicable.[20]

On appeal, however, this key holding was reversed; and the conflict held to be an international one throughout its duration, even after 19 May 1992.[21] The Appeal Tribunal concluded that the FRY continued to exercise effective control over the insurgent groups even after its purported withdrawal. That supposed withdrawal actually amounted,

[17] *Ibid.*, para. 228. The situation is best described as a use of force rather than as an armed conflict, since Nicaragua did not respond militarily to the American measures. Technically, the United States was held to have infringed a *customary*-law prohibition against the use of force. The Court lacked the power to consider the question of a violation of Article 2(4) of the UN Charter as such.

[18] *Ibid.*, paras. 92–116.   [19] *Ibid.*, paras. 105–16.

[20] *Prosecutor v. Tadić* (Merits), Int'l Criminal Tribunal for the Former Yugoslavia (Trial Panel), 7 May 1997, 36 ILM 908 (1997), paras. 582–607.

[21] *Prosecutor v. Tadić* (Merits), Int'l Criminal Tribunal for the Former Yugoslavia (Appeal Panel), 15 July 1999, 38 ILM 1518 (1999), paras. 83–162.

in the Tribunal's judgment, to nothing more than 'a superficial restruc-
turing' of forces, with the FRY continuing to exercise 'overall control' of
the insurgents' military effort by 'organising, coordinating or planning
the military actions' of the ethnic Serb forces in Bosnia.[22] As a result, the
insurgent forces and the regular FRY military were, in reality, not
'separate armies in any genuine sense', but instead were functioning as
a single force under the command of the Yugoslavian military in
Belgrade, for the furthering of the political and military objectives of
the FRY.[23] The practical effect of this decision was that the full body of
rules of international humanitarian law applied throughout the Bosnian
conflict of 1992–5.[24] That is to say, that the full body of humanitarian
law applied not only to clashes between Bosnian government and FRY
forces, but also to engagements between government forces and 'insurgents' of the same nationality. The effect, therefore, is that this third and
highest level of civil conflict is not, strictly speaking, a civil conflict at all.
It is a fully international struggle. The so-called 'rebels' are therefore,
legally speaking, not true insurgents at all, but rather auxiliaries of the
foreign state, who happen to possess the nationality of the country
against which they are fighting.

A couple of final points should be noted about these three categories
of civil strife (or rather, as just explained, two levels of civil strife plus
one of international conflict containing an internal sub-component
within it). First of all, the boundaries between these three levels of
conflict were not, as of the early twenty-first century, marked out in
very great detail. Consider, for instance, the boundary between the lower
and middle levels. It was clear (from the World Court's decision in the
Nicaragua v. *United States* case) that the provision of financing to rebels
by a foreign state would not amount to a use of force, but only to the
lesser offence of unlawful intervention.[25] It remained unclear, though,
just how much assistance was required from the foreign state to the
insurgents to transform the foreign country from a mere intervener (at
the lower level) into an ally of the rebels (at the middle level). Similarly,
at the boundary between the middle and upper levels, it was clear that
the *general* test to be applied was whether the foreign state had effective
control of the conduct of the hostilities. But there remained much room
for clarification as to what 'effective control' actually entailed in specific
situations.

---

[22] *Ibid.*, paras. 137, 154. [23] *Ibid.*, paras. 151–62.
[24] See generally Gray, 'Bosnia and Herzogovina'. [25] *Nicaragua* v. *USA*, para. 228.

The humanitarian revolution at home

Although, as observed above, international courts declined to put insurgent groups on a par with governments with respect to foreign intervention, some steps nonetheless were taken to put them on something approaching an equal footing in terms of the conducting of the hostilities themselves. This was a fruit of the humanitarian revolution. It will be recalled that the essence of international humanitarian law was the proposition that the fundamental purpose of the laws of war was the relief of human suffering. On this assumption, there naturally seemed to be little justification for treating civil conflicts differently from interstate ones. This logic was articulated in 1996 by the International Criminal Tribunal for the Former Yugoslavia:

> [I]n the area of armed conflict [the tribunal maintained] the distinction between interstate wars and civil wars is losing its value as far as human beings are concerned. Why protect civilians from belligerent violence, or ban rape, torture or the wanton destruction of hospitals, churches, museums or private property, as well as proscribe weapons causing unnecessary suffering when two sovereign States are engaged in war, and yet refrain from enacting the same bans or providing the same protection when armed violence erupted 'only' within the territory of a sovereign State? If international law ... must gradually turn to the protection of human beings, it is only natural that the aforementioned dichotomy should gradually lose its weight.[26]

This humanitarian logic had been at work since the late nineteenth century. As early as 1872, the International Committee of the Red Cross became involved in the Carlist War in Spain. In 1875, it decided to provide humanitarian services in a rebellion of Christian peoples against Ottoman rule in Bosnia, Herzogovina and Bulgaria.[27] By 1914, the International Committee had become involved in some nineteen civil conflicts.[28] But doubts remained on the subject. In 1912, the International Committee of the Red Cross considered the general question of involvement in civil wars, but was unable to reach any firm position. The key step was taken in 1921, when a conference of the International Committee laid down the principle that the Red Cross

---

[26] *Prosecutor* v. *Tadić* (Jurisdiction), Int'l Criminal Tribunal for the Former Yugoslavia, 2 Oct. 1995, 35 ILM 32 (1996), para. 97.
[27] Moorehead, *Dunant's Dream*, at 125–6.   [28] *Ibid.* at 231.

would aid *all* victims of wars, including civil wars, social and revolutionary struggles.[29]

Not until 1949, however, were rules on the waging of civil strife embodied in international conventions, and even then only in a very rudimentary fashion. The four new Geneva Conventions that were drafted that year (and which remain in effect) each contained a provision on internal conflicts, which became known as 'Common Article 3' – so called because it appeared, in identical terms, as Article 3 of each of the four Conventions. It set out some extremely basic human-rights standards to be adhered to in dealing with persons held in detention. It forbade various forms of inhumane treatment, such as physical abuse or degrading treatment in general, hostage-taking and punishment for crimes without due process of law.[30] It did not, however, purport to extend or apply the concept of prisoner-of-war status to internal conflicts or to require hostilities in civil conflicts to be conducted in accordance with the laws of war. Its scope therefore was very limited.

An important further step was taken in 1977, when, at the initiative of the International Committee of the Red Cross, the two Additional Protocols were drafted to supplement the Geneva Conventions of 1949. Protocol II concerned civil conflicts and contained a number of rules restraining the kinds of violence that states were allowed to use in suppressing civil unrest.[31] For one thing, it supplemented Common Article 3 by expanding the range of protections available to persons in detention. More importantly, it placed various restrictions on the waging of the conflict, largely in the interest of protecting civilians.[32] Such assistance certainly was badly needed, as it was estimated that some 90 per cent of casualties in internal struggles after 1945 were civilians.[33] Protocol II, did not, however, cover *all* civil conflicts. It only applied to ones in which three criteria were met: first, that the anti-government side consisted of 'armed forces or other organized armed groups' which are under 'responsible command'; second, that these groups exercised

---

[29] 28 RGDIP 541–3 (1921).

[30] On Common Article 3, see Moir, *Internal Armed Conflict*, at 23–67.

[31] Additional Protocol II to the Geneva Conventions of 1949, 8 June 1977, 1125 UNTS 609; reprinted in Roberts and Guelff (eds.), *Documents*, at 481–512 (hereinafter 'Protocol II'). On human-rights aspects of civil conflicts, see generally Theodor Meron, *Human Rights in Internal Strife: Their International Protection* (Cambridge: Grotius, 1987). Additional Protocol I to the Geneva Conventions of 1949, 8 June 1977, 1125 UNTS 3, will be referred to herein after as 'Protocol I'.

[32] On Protocol II, see Moir, *Internal Armed Conflict*, at 89–119.

[33] 'The Global Menace of Local Strife', *Economist*, 24 May 2003, at 23.

'such control over part of [the] territory [of the state] as to enable them to carry out sustained and concerted military operations'; and third, that the groups be able to implement the Protocol themselves.[34] It is likely, although the matter is not free from dispute, that the Protocol applies to both the government and the insurgent sides on an equal basis.[35]

The significance of Protocol II should not be exaggerated. In particular, it should not be supposed that it placed civil conflicts onto a legal par with international ones. Far from it. It made no provision for the granting of prisoner-of-war status to captured insurgents, as the old condition of insurgency did. Instead, it merely required, in general terms, that prisoners be treated humanely.[36] In various other ways too, the standards set out fell short of those required in international conflicts. For example, the Protocol did not provide for the enlistment of third states as 'protecting powers' to oversee the observance of humanitarian rules. Nor did it contain any concept of 'grave breaches' of rules of law, allowing global jurisdiction over the offenders, as in the case of interstate conflicts. As the International Criminal Tribunal for the Former Yugoslavia carefully pointed out, modern humanitarian law had not, at least as yet, brought about 'a full and mechanical transplant' of the international laws of war into the field of civil strife. Instead, only certain rules of interstate war had been imported into the realm of civil conflicts – and even of these, only their 'general essence' was applied, without the full details.[37]

There might be some temptation to suppose that Protocol II, even if it did not place civil conflicts onto a par with international ones, at least amounted to a codification of the older law on recognition of insurgency, as that practice had evolved in the nineteenth century.[38] But any such temptation should be resisted. The reason is that recognition of insurgency was primarily a means of placing insurgent and government forces on a legal par with one another as regards the prosecution of the conflict. The purpose of Protocol II was very different. In keeping with the humanitarian thrust of the laws of war after 1945, its primary function was the protection of victims (and potential victims) of war,

---

[34] Protocol II, Art. 1. The provision is curiously worded, to refer only to the *ability* to implement the Protocol, as opposed to the *actual* implementation of it.
[35] See Cassese, 'Status of Rebels'; and Moir, *Internal Armed Conflict*, at 96–9.
[36] Protocol II, Art. 4.
[37] *Prosecutor v. Tadić* (Jurisdiction), Int'l Criminal Tribunal for the Former Yugoslavia, 2 Oct. 1995, 35 ILM 32 (1996), para. 126.
[38] See Chapter 7 above for details.

most notably of civilians. In addition, the Protocol made no provision for one of the most essential elements of the old state of insurgency – the recognition of the legal validity of 'governmental' measures adopted by insurgents in areas that they effectively controlled. It seems likely, although firm authority is lacking, that recognition of insurgency continued to exist after 1945, but only, as before, in an uncodified form, as general customary law. Protocol II is therefore best viewed as a human-rights-law counterpart of recognition of insurgency, rather than as a codification of it.[39]

Recognition of belligerency – modern-style

Explicit recognition of belligerency was very little in evidence after 1945. This was hardly surprising, since its principal legal effect was the activation of the law of neutrality – the status of which was doubtful after 1945. But it was not quite so rare as has sometimes been supposed. There were several other ways of recognising belligerency besides the classical one of issuing declarations of neutrality. Specifically, two alternate methods merit attention: first, recognition (whether explicitly or implicitly) by the government side itself; and second, recognition by an international organisation. The first of these had long been possible. The other was new after 1945.

It might be thought odd that the government side in a civil conflict would ever recognise belligerency. But there could be situations in which it would. The government might, for example, wish to hold foreign states to the obligations of neutrals or to exercise the traditional rights of belligerents vis-à-vis foreign countries. There were two arguable illustrations of this phenomenon in the post-1945 period, although in neither case was there an express recognition of belligerency. The first was in the Algerian rebellion against French rule in 1956–62. In the initial stages, France maintained that the situation was merely one of civil unrest and, as such, a matter only of domestic law. In March 1956, however, it moved away from this stance by agreeing to abide by Common Article 3 and to allow the International Committee of the Red Cross to visit persons in detention.[40] The more decisive movement in the direction of recognition of belligerency, however, emerged when

---

[39] Since 1945, recognition of insurgency has attracted little attention from international lawyers. See, however, Castrén, 'Recognition of Insurgency'.
[40] Moir, *Internal Armed Conflict*, at 68–74.

France began a systematic policy of visiting and searching foreign ships on the high seas, to prevent the delivery of arms to the Algerian insurgents from foreign sources. This was a large-scale operation. In the first year alone, over 4,700 ships were visited, and over 1,300 were searched. Only 1 was actually captured, but 182 were re-routed. When the policy was challenged in a French administrative court, the French government's justification was self-defence (although the courts did not ever rule on the point).[41] It has also been asserted that President Charles de Gaulle implicitly, but effectively, accorded recognition of belligerency in statements made in a press conference in 1958.[42]

The other notable case in which it could be contended that there was recognition of belligerency by the government side was the Biafran secession crisis in Nigeria in 1967–70. The Nigerian government voluntarily applied the full range of the Geneva Conventions – not merely Common Article 3 – to the conflict.[43] Further signs of an internationalised conflict consisted of the blockading of the insurgent-held areas which began in May 1967. This extended to operations at sea, complete with captures of ships by the government side.[44] There was even a formal surrender of a sword by the insurgent commander, in the old style, to mark the formal conclusion of the hostilities. (Some vestiges of the ceremonial spirit in war remain, it would appear, even in these rough-hewn times.) The Nigerian federal government did, however, continue to refer to the conflict as a 'rebellion' rather than as a war, in the manner of the American government in the 1860s.[45]

The second means by which recognition of belligerency was brought about after 1945 was a novelty: by action of international organisations, particularly by the UN. The best illustration occurred – though only

---

[41] The courts held that they had no jurisdiction to interfere. See *Ignazio Messina et Cie* v. *L'État (Ministre des armées 'marines')*, Adm. Tribunal of Paris, 90 JDI 1192 (1965); affirmed on other grounds by Conseil d'État, 30 Mar 1966. See 70 RGDIP 1056 (1966). See also *Cie d'Assurances la Nationale* v. *Société Purfina Française*, Court of Appeal, Montpellier, 24 Nov. 1959, GP.1959.2.328, to the effect that the Algerian independence struggle was not a mere law-enforcement operation but had risen to the level of a civil war. On the international legal status of the conflict, see generally Flory, 'Algérie algérienne'.

[42] Bedjaoui, *Law*, at 171–2.

[43] 1 A. H. M. Kirk-Greene, *Crisis and Conflict in Nigeria: A Documentary Sourcebook 1966–1969* (London: Oxford University Press, 1971), at 455–7; and Moorehead, *Dunant's Dream*, at 617.

[44] On the legal aspects of the Biafra conflict, see 'Nigérie', 72 RGDIP 228–36 (1968); 'Nigérie', 73 RGDIP 193–7 (1969); and Wodie, 'Sécession du Biafra'.

[45] Duculesco, 'Effet de la reconnaissance', at 149.

implicitly – in the context of the Namibian struggle for independence against South Africa. After the termination of South Africa's League of Nations mandate over South West Africa in 1966 by the UN General Assembly, the South West African People's Organisation (SWAPO) began an armed revolt against their South African rulers. In 1969, the UN Security Council expressly recognised 'the legitimacy of the struggle of the people of Namibia' against the South African government, urging member states to provide 'moral and material assistance' to the Namibian people.[46] In 1971, in a World Court advisory opinion concerning the status of Namibia, one of the judges, in a separate opinion, commented on the legal effect of these measures. He contended that the UN's recognition of the legitimacy of the struggle of the people of Namibia amounted to 'nothing less than a recognition of belligerency'. Consequently, the conflict must now be considered to be an international one, with the law of neutrality applicable.[47] This opinion, it should be noted, was not endorsed by the Court as a whole; and it would appear that it had no great practical effect.

A privileged category of civil strife

One of the more innovative developments after 1945 in international law as it related to civil conflicts was the special status accorded to one particular category of internal struggle: wars of national liberation (as they were commonly known). This development was rooted in the idea that the principle of self-determination of peoples had an especially exalted status in the moral scheme of things. This concept had its origins in liberal romantic ideas of the eighteenth century, most notably those of the Italian philosopher Giambattista Vico and the German writer Gottfried Herder.[48] Expressed in legal terms, the idea, most closely associated with the Italian lawyer Pasquale Mancini in the mid nineteenth century, was that national communities – defined chiefly in terms of a common language but also including factors such as a common cultural heritage or religion or historical experience – once they had

---

[46] SC Res. 269 (12 Aug. 1969), 24 UN SCOR, Res and Dec, at 2.
[47] Legal Consequences for States of the Continued Presence of South Africa in Namibia (South West Africa) Notwithstanding Security Council Resolution 276 (1970), 1971 ICJ Rep. 16, separate opinion of Judge Ammoun, at 92–3.
[48] See Giambattista Vico, *The New Science*, trans. David Marsh (3rd edn, London: Penguin, 1999), at 393–480. (1st edn, Naples, 1725.) On Herder, see R. G. Collingwood, *The Idea of History* (Oxford: Oxford University Press, 1946), at 88–93.

achieved the requisite degree of coherence and self-awareness, had a kind of higher-law right to constitute themselves into a nation-state.[49]

After the Second World War, this thesis manifested itself most concretely as a claim to a legal right of decolonisation. As such, it rapidly won substantial support, not surprisingly, from developing countries, most of which were ex-colonies, as well as from socialist countries. The first step in this process was the adoption by the UN General Assembly of a Declaration on Decolonisation in 1960.[50] More decisive, though, was the concluding of the two principal UN human-rights conventions (or covenants, as they were designated) in 1966: one on Civil and Political Rights and one on Economic, Social and Cultural Rights (both entering into force in 1976).[51] Each of these Covenants stated the right of 'peoples' to self-determination.

A 'people', in other words, now became a new kind of collectivity recognised by international law. In legal parlance, they became a new 'subject of international law', alongside traditional subjects such as states and international organisations. The question naturally arose as to whether this ill-defined entity had the same right that states did to resort to armed force, i.e., whether a people possessed the valuable right of self-defence (in all of its greatly expanded post-1945 glory). This question received the attention of the UN General Assembly in 1970, when it adopted, by consensus, a Declaration on Friendly Relations between States.[52] The Declaration, however, delicately skirted the self-defence issue. On the one hand, it expressly prohibited states from resorting to 'any forcible action' to deprive a people of their self-determination right. As for the appropriate response to repression,

---

[49] On Mancini, see Arthur Nussbaum, *A Concise History of the Law of Nations* (New York: Macmillan, 1954), at 240–2. On Italian writing in this area, see Sereni, *Italian Conception*, at 160–4; and F. von Holtzendorff, 'Le principe des nationalités et la littérature italienne du droit des gens', 2 RDILC 92–106 (1870). On the political aspects of self-determination, see generally Alfred Cobban, *The Nation-state and National Self-determination* (London: Collins, 1969). On the modern international law of self-determination, see generally Antonio Cassese, *Self-determination: A Legal Reappraisal* (Cambridge: Cambridge University Press, 1995).

[50] Declaration on Decolonisation, GA Res. 1514 (XV), 15 UN GAOR, Supp. No. 16, UN Doc. A/4684 (1960), at 66.

[51] International Covenant on Economic, Social and Cultural Rights, 16 Dec. 1966, 993 UNTS 3; and International Covenant on Civil and Political Rights, 16 Dec. 1966, 999 UNTS 171.

[52] Declaration on Principles of International Law Concerning Friendly Relations and Co-operation among States in Accordance with the Charter of the United Nations, GA Res. 2625 (XXV), 25 UN GAOR, Supp. No. 28, UN Doc. A/8028 (1970), at 121.

however, the Declaration only referred ambivalently to 'actions against and resistance to' such an unlawful use of force by a government. This was a strong hint in the direction of a right of self-defence, but it fell tantalisingly short of outright recognition. In addition, the Declaration referred, also in rather vague terms, to a right of an oppressed people 'to seek and receive support' – without explicitly indicating whether this support could take the form of armed force or the supplying of weapons.[53]

International lawyers were divided on the question of whether wars of national liberation formed a new category of armed conflict, distinct from that of civil wars or insurrections in general. A number of international lawyers approved of such a legal innovation, most notably those from socialist countries – reflecting the heritage of the socialist conception of anti-imperialist struggles as just wars.[54] In 1977, the idea received the support of states when the two Additional Protocols to the Geneva Conventions were adopted. Protocol I, which dealt with international armed conflicts, expressly extended international-conflict status to 'armed conflicts in which peoples are fighting against colonial domination and alien occupation and against racist regimes in the exercise of their right of self-determination'.[55] The body acting on behalf of the people in question could activate this provision by submitting a unilateral declaration to the government of Switzerland (the depository for the Protocol), agreeing to apply the Geneva Conventions and the Protocol. The full body of Geneva-Convention law would then apply to the conflict, in place of the far more restricted rules of Common Article 3 or Protocol II. Left unclear, however, was whether the law of neutrality would necessarily be applicable as well.

This provision of Protocol I amounted, in effect, to a recognition of either insurgency or belligerency, depending on whether it was held to have made the law of neutrality applicable to liberation struggles. If the Protocol was interpreted as importing the law of neutrality into such conflicts, then it would amount fully to a recognition of belligerency. The insurgents would become entitled to exercise the complete range of belligerents' rights, including such extraterritorial privileges as the right to visit and search foreign ships on the high seas or to capture contraband. If, on the other

---

[53] *Ibid.*
[54] See, for example, remarks of the Soviet lawyer Tunkin, 55 *Annuaire* 607–8 (1973). See also remarks of Chaumont, 56 *Annuaire* 136–7 (1975); and of Zourek, *ibid.* at 148–51. On socialist doctrine on just wars, see Anonymous, *Marxism-Leninism*, at 86–98.
[55] Protocol I of 1977, Art. 1(4).

hand, the Protocol was held to place liberation groups and governments on a par *only* with regard to the struggle *within* the territory, then it would amount to recognition of insurgency.

It should be noted that, in either event, Protocol I departed in one important respect from the recognition of belligerency *and* of insurgency: in not requiring liberation groups to possess effective control of any territory or to exercise governmental functions, as 'ordinary' belligerent or insurgent groups were required to do. Protocol I may therefore be said to have placed wars of national liberation into a privileged legal position by relaxing the normal criteria for recognition of belligerency (or insurgency). Recognition was now being conferred not, as formerly, on the basis of the material strength of the insurgents but instead by virtue of the nature of the cause for which they fought. In the manner of the law concerning the Muslim *bughat*, the fact of fighting for a certain doctrine brought in its train certain valuable legal privileges.

It has sometimes been contended that Protocol I of 1977 had the effect of conferring a legal imprimatur onto wars of national liberation as a new category of just war. In a certain sense, this may be conceded. As just pointed out, special legal privileges were being accorded to a privileged category of insurgents on the basis of the justice of their cause. This was certainly in the spirit of the just-war outlook. At the same time, though, it should be appreciated that Protocol I did not purport to create any *new* category of justifiable use of force that had not existed before. The true position is that Protocol I expanded the pool of conflicts to which the full body of Geneva-Convention law applied. It is arguable (although judicial authority is lacking) that it also implicitly granted the right of self-defence to liberation groups. If so, then liberation movements would be able to qualify as just warriors, though only on the same terms that states could: by being self-defenders rather than aggressors. Liberation groups were not accorded any inherent or automatic licence to take up arms.

In all events, in the early years following 1977, the impact of Protocol I in this regard remained stubbornly confined to the realm of theory rather than of practice. International courts did not have occasion to pronounce on the many points of law involved. There was good reason for this: that the states of South Africa and Israel, which the drafters of the Protocol had especially in mind at the time, naturally declined to become parties to the Protocol. With the attaining of majority rule and independence by Zimbabwe in 1979–80 and Namibia in 1990, followed in the later 1990s by the ending of apartheid in South Africa, the principal fields of action of this provision of the Protocol lost their relevance.[56] Nevertheless, this provision of Protocol I remains in force; and it is not impossible that, at some future point, it will have a role to play in some manner not yet foreseen.

We may therefore summarise, with the utmost brevity, the basic picture of the status of civil conflicts in international law as it had evolved by the early twenty-first century. The law recognised either four, or possibly five, categories of civil disturbance, with different bodies of law applying to each level.[57] The first and lowest level consists of situations of 'isolated and sporadic acts of violence' (in the words of Protocol II). This situation is governed by the domestic criminal law of the state – with the only applicable *international* law being the law of international human rights. The second level of violence might be termed 'ordinary internal armed conflict' (for lack of an established label). This is a situation in which the disturbances are more than merely 'isolated and sporadic'. At this level, the only applicable international law is Common Article 3 of the Geneva Conventions, which applies to *both* the government and the insurgents.[58] The third level is the situation in which the rebels have effective de facto control of part of the territory of the state. Here, Protocol II of 1977 becomes automatically applicable, with its more expanded – but still very limited – set of humanitarian rules. It is likely, but not firmly established, that, in addition, traditional recognition of insurgency continues to apply here as well.[59] The fourth level comprises the special category of national liberation struggles. Here, there would be recognition of insurgency, *plus* the full application of the Geneva Conventions *within* the territory of the state (but without any requirement that the insurgents control a portion of the territory). The possible fifth level would comprise full-blown recognition of belligerency, in which the conflict is treated entirely on a par with an interstate war – including the application of the law of neutrality to relations with foreign countries and the exercise of belligerents' rights

---

[56] On the Southern African conflicts, see Grahl-Madsen, 'Decolonization'.

[57] These four (or five) levels of civil strife refer only to the internal features of struggles. They therefore are unconnected with the three levels of involvement by foreign states discussed above.

[58] On the application of Common Article 3 in practice, see Moir, *Internal Armed Conflict*, at 67–88.

[59] Protocol II is of course applicable to states which are parties to it. It seems likely, however, that the Protocol is applicable to all states on the thesis that it represents general customary law. On the application of Protocol II in practice, see *ibid.* at 119–32.

outside the state's territory. Whether this fifth level is really distinct from the fourth one depends on whether the whole of neutrality law has been enfolded into humanitarian law or not – a question that was still unresolved in the early twenty-first century.

As of the early twenty-first century, the state of international law regarding civil conflicts could scarcely be regarded as being in settled and final form. There continued to be much scope for future change and development, most notably in the direction of applying an ever larger portion of international humanitarian law to internal conflicts. There was no shortage of proposals in that direction. In 1990, for example, the International Institute of Humanitarian Law promulgated a Declaration on the Rules of International Humanitarian Law Governing the Conduct of Hostilities in Non-international Armed Conflicts.[60] This declaration stated in substantial part that the whole body of international humanitarian law should also be applicable to civil conflicts – effectively eliminating the distinction between international wars and civil wars from the humanitarian standpoint. It characterised these rules in the preamble in cautious terms as 'emergent rules of international law'. This would be an ambitious and significant development – but it belongs to the realm of the future, rather than of history.

Striking terror

One of the most dramatic challenges to international law in the post-1945 era was the emergence of new kinds of enemy – and, in their wake, of new kinds of war. Modern terrorism in particular presented the spectre of criminality so tightly organised and disciplined, and so highly destructive, as to pose a threat approximating to that of a traditional enemy state in an 'ordinary' war. On the surface, this appeared as a radical departure from any previous conception of war, which had always made a sharp distinction between, on the one hand, action against mere criminals and, on the other hand, action against foreign enemies – a distinction extending at least as far back as Roman times. As Gentili put it in the sixteenth century, the enemy side in a proper war must possess 'a state, a senate, a treasury, united and harmonious citizens, and some basis for a treaty of peace, should matters so shape themselves'.[61] Such proper enemies were contrasted with mere brigands and pirates and the like. In the eighteenth century, Vattel took the same

---

[60] See www.umn.edu/humanrts/instree/1990a.htm.   [61] Gentili, *Law of War*, at 25.

position. Despicable persons such as the 'free companies' of the Middle Ages, or pirate bands, who were motivated only by greed, had no right to be treated as enemies (i.e., as belligerents) but only as criminals. Accordingly, there was no need to issue a formal declaration of war against them or to conduct operations against them in accord with the laws of war.[62] There was modern authority to this effect, from American courts, which pronounced that belligerent acts could only be committed by states or, at the margins, 'state-like entities', i.e., 'entities that have at least significant attributes of sovereignty', thereby effectively ruling out free-standing terrorist groups.[63]

At the same time, however, it should be appreciated that, in a number of significant ways, the idea of a war against terrorism was thoroughly in keeping with traditional just-war ways of thought – although admittedly very far from the positivist conception of war, with its emphasis on the clash of rival national interests. Historically, there had always been a deep affinity between crime-fighting and the waging of just wars. Just wars were, virtually by definition, law-enforcement operations, just as ordinary crime-fighting was. Both activities therefore comprised applications of official coercive operations against evil in the name of good, on behalf of the community at large.

If there was a strong spiritual bond (as it might be termed) between these two forms of law enforcement, there was also, undeniably, a very clear *operational* distinction between them. The one process involved action within the jurisdiction of the state concerned, carried out by civil magistrates, and police and the like, under the auspices of courts of law. The criminals were regarded as evil-doers by their own personal choice and subject, as such, to appropriate punishment as enemies of society. The other involved actions against foreign states, often carried out in foreign territory, by armed forces, and without direct judicial supervision. Enemy soldiers, so long as they fought in obedience to the laws of war, were not wrongdoers, even if the state which they served was an aggressor.[64] Ordinary soldiers were subject only to administrative detention when captured, with a right to prompt release at the close of the hostilities.

---

[62] Vattel, *Law of Nations*, at 258.
[63] *Pan-American World Airways, Inc.* v. *Aetna Casualty and Surety Co.*, 505 F 2d 989 (2nd Cir. 1974), at 1012.
[64] *In re von Leeb* (US Military Tribunal at Nuremberg, 28 Oct. 1948), 15 ILR 376, at 381–3. On aggressive war as a crime, see Dinstein, *War*, at 106–34.

The line between the two types of operation was not, however, always so easily drawn in practice as in theory. There were various instances throughout history in which bands of brigands were so well organised and armed as to require full-scale military action, instead of the ordinary efforts of magistrates, for their defeat. Pirate bands were the most obvious example. The most famous instance of military action against these 'scorners of the law of nations' (in the words of Gentili) was the suppression by the famous Roman general Pompey in the first century BC of the pirate bands based in Cilicia, in Asia Minor. In the Middle Ages, the land-based counterparts of the pirates were the 'free companies' of mercenaries, notorious for murder, plunder and rapine in their periods 'between assignments'. In the Muslim world, the famous 'assassin' group of the twelfth and thirteenth centuries wrought destruction on a more tightly targeted basis. But in their case, like that of the Cilician pirates, a military expedition was required for their suppression. For the subduing of piracy in the West Indies in the seventeenth and eighteenth centuries, naval force was often required, with admirals given special commissions allowing them to step outside the strictures of ordinary criminal law enforcement in order to deal with the nautical freebooters. On many occasions since then, naval forces were employed against pirates in various lairs, from Amelia Island off the coast of Florida, to the Falkland Islands, to the Persian Gulf and beyond. It may be noted that Bluntschli maintained that armed action against pirates could be 'a veritable war' if the pirates had the aid and protection of a state.[65]

Battling Western civilisation

In the nineteenth century, a distinctively new phenomenon appeared: criminals whose principal motivating force was not the craving of riches but rather the seductive force of ideas. It is at least sometimes the case that persons who are fired with ideas, or ideals, are willing to act more ruthlessly than those who kill 'merely' as dutiful citizens, to advance their country's national interest. The soldier may kill and destroy on a far larger scale than the terrorist. But the soldier, at least ideally, kills openly and according to rules; and he kills only his opposite number. The military mind has always had a contempt, liberally mixed with horror, for the furtive assassin, the spy operating under false pretences, the guerrilla,

---

[65] Bluntschli, *Droit international*, at 275.

the saboteur. In the civilian world, much the same attitude is present. There may be a certain bemused tolerance of duelling, or even a nobility attached to it; but the murderous skulker in the alley is loathed by all. The death of the French Revolutionary leader Jean Paul Marat at the hands of an assassin in 1793 may be taken as a convenient starting point for this new kind of ideological crime, at least in its modern Western form. In the late nineteenth century, there arose, for the first time, a relatively sizeable pool of persons who were dedicated enemies not of any specific government but rather of Western capitalist society *per se* and who were, at least sometimes, prepared to kill (and die) to advance its destruction. These were the anarchists, whose 'propaganda of the deed' – as their murderous acts were euphemistically known – claimed a number of prominent figures in Europe and the United States, including heads of state and government, as well as police officials who were particularly disliked. Victims included the presidents of France and the United States, the king of Italy and the empress of Austria. The targets of anarchist terror also included persons from humbler walks of life, selected effectively at random, as in the case of bombs placed in public places such as cafés.

Anarchism was a set of political beliefs; but, in some of its manifestations, it bore attributes of a heretical religious movement. In the two countries in Europe in which anarchism acquired deep roots in rural populations – Italy and Spain – it functioned as a kind of rival religion to Catholicism. In this regard, anarchism tapped into anti-capitalist aspects of Catholicism which had deep – if not always clearly avowed – roots in gospel teachings, with their denunciations of the wealthy and championing of the poor. The anarchist movement, on its lawless fringes, amounted, then, to a sort of homicidal humanitarian movement.[66] Violent opposition to Western liberal and capitalist ways of life was also to be found in various anticolonial movements, sometimes in combination with religious fervour. This was particularly true in the Islamic world, where the nineteenth century witnessed the revival of the old, and hitherto largely dormant, concept of *jihad*.[67] The first instances of this revival appear to have been in the context of Muslim resistance to

---

[66] On the terrorist activities of anarchist groups in the late nineteenth and early twentieth centuries, see Barbara Tuchman, *The Proud Tower: A Portrait of the World Before the War 1890–1914* (New York: Macmillan, 1966), at 71–132; and James Joll, *The Anarchists* (2nd edn, London: Methuen, 1979), at 99–129.

[67] On the modern revival of *jihad*, see Peters, *Islam and Colonialism*, at 105–50.

Russian expansion into the Caucusus in the early nineteenth century and to British expansion in western India in the 1830s.

More striking invocations of *jihad* occurred in Africa, first in the Mahdist movement in the Sudan in the 1880s, which culminated in the capture of Khartoum and the death of the British General Charles Gordon in 1885. Shortly after that, *jihad* was invoked in a revolt against British rule in Somaliland. The leader was an eccentric sufi named Muhammad bin Abdullah Hassan, who was contemptuously labelled by his British foes as the 'Mad Mullah'. Mad he may have been, but his insurrection was not finally subdued until 1920. In the 1920s, the *jihad* doctrine played at least a subsidiary role in the rebellion against Spanish rule in Morocco led by Abdel Krim. He won an impressive victory over Spanish forces in 1920 and was only defeated after France entered the contest on Spain's side in 1925. In the following decade, the call of *jihad* resurfaced in a colonial context of a rather different sort: in Palestine, in the Arab revolt of 1936 against British mandate rule – and also against the ever growing Jewish settlement in the area, which Britain was accused of permitting or even encouraging.[68]

The ending of colonialism after the Second World War may have removed the most obvious grievance of what was becoming known as the developing world. It became apparent, though, that, for certain of the most radical elements, the real enemy was Western capitalist society in general. The most highly organised and ruthless enemies of secular and material civilisation were Islamic groups which combined religious fanaticism of an eccentric nature with visceral hatred of Western liberal materialism.[69] The first large-scale field of operation for these groups was Afghanistan in 1979–89, in opposition to the Soviet Union and the socialist-style government which it supported with its armed forces. One scholar has even referred to this as the first of the wars between civilisations that might well be the dominant form of armed conflict in the twenty-first century.[70] The Afghanistan conflict certainly became a major *cause célèbre* in the world of radical Islam, comparable to the way in which the Spanish Civil War had been a magnet for leftist crusaders the world over in the 1930s. The Soviet Union, as the

---

[68] For a thorough account of *jihad* in the anticolonial cause in the late nineteenth and early twentieth centuries, see *ibid*. at 39–104.

[69] For a dispassionate analysis of the relation between the Islamic faith and terrorist methods, see Esposito, *Unholy War*. See also Charnay, *Islam et la guerre*.

[70] Huntington, *Clash of Civilizations*, at 246–7.

embodiment of a forthrightly atheistic and materialist ideology clearly at odds with traditional religious thought, was as apt a target for the foes of secularism as the Spanish nationalists had been for the enemies of fascism a half-century earlier.

Some of these *jihadists*, however, were keeping strange company. For reasons of Cold-War politics, the United States became a behind-the-scenes supplier of weapons to the Afghan insurgents, with Saudi Arabia and Pakistan playing important roles as intermediaries and paymasters in the supply chain. One of the most important effects of this conflict was the accession to power in Afghanistan, in 1996, after the Soviet departure, of a Muslim extremist group known as the Taliban (meaning 'students', reflecting its origin in Muslim-run schools). The Taliban was so completely religious rather than secular in outlook that it made no serious attempt to form a government for the country, instead leaving ministries largely vacant and 'governing' instead through informal means based on its ideas of religious morality. (Afghanistan had no diplomatic relations with any country, except Pakistan, which had provided support for the Taliban movement.)[71]

An important, and ominous, legacy of the Afghan conflict was the continued existence of bands of self-selected (and now battle-hardened) radical Muslims who, after 1989, began to look abroad for new fields of action where their co-religionists were under threat. They had little difficulty finding them, whether in Bosnia, which was torn by civil strife in 1992–5 or Kashmir. Their most challenging campaign, though, was against Western secular and materialist society on its home ground. This daunting task was shouldered most conspicuously by a largely Arab group known as al-Qaeda (meaning 'the base', with reference to the large data base with which it operated), under the leadership of a disaffected Saudi Arabian national named Osama bin Laden. Ironically, this group had previously been a de facto ally of the United States, since it was formed in Afghanistan, with the Soviet Union as its immediate target. With the departure of the Soviet Union from Afghanistan in 1989, al-Qaeda began to turn its deadly attention to its erstwhile supplier.

In the late 1990s, the al-Qaeda leadership issued statements that were effectively declarations of war against its two principal enemies, Saudi Arabia and the United States. In 1996, it promulgated a lengthy and abusive tirade entitled *Declaration of Jihad against the Americans*

---

[71] On the Taliban rule in Afghanistan, see Kepel, *Jihad*, at 228–32.

Occupying the Two Holy Places, largely directed against the Saudi Arabian ruling family. Two years later came a so-called *fatwa* (or opinion from a religious authority) against the United States, asserting that 'the killing of Americans ... is a religious duty'.[72] Words were followed in due course by action. In 1998, simultaneous terrorist attacks on two American embassies in East Africa killed over 200 persons (the overwhelming majority of whom were not Americans). In 2000, an attack on an American warship in Aden harbour in Yemen resulted in some 17 deaths. Most spectacular of all was an attack on American territory itself, in September 2001, when suicide squads from al-Qaeda hijacked four commercial airliners and crashed three of them into buildings in New York and Washington, killing over 2,500 people.

This newest form of terrorist activity combined the key features of all its various depraved predecessors – the ruthlessness of the medieval *écorcheur*, the organisation of the pirate band, the secrecy of the back-alley murderer and the quasi-religious fanaticism of the anarchist. Up against this contemptible, though deadly, foe, society would bring all of the power of the modern state to bear, in the form of weaponry, surveillance techniques and so forth. But something else, perhaps every bit as important as those material things, would also be brought to bear: the just-war mentality, in a particularly naked and pure form. This was a mentality which operated instinctively in an offensive rather than defensive mode; which was contemptuous of neutrality as weakness or cowardice (if not as outright treachery); which very readily enlisted God as an auxiliary warrior; and which was inclined to rule its actions by the elastic yardstick of necessity rather than by the rigid rule of a fixed code.

From crime-fighting to war

In fighting back against political terrorism, states had a choice – not necessarily a mutually exclusive one – of two legal strategies, governed by two quite distinct sets of legal rules. Taking each in its purest or ideal form, they may be briefly summarised and contrasted. First was a *sovereign*-right approach, in which the government acts in a law-enforcement capacity, as an enforcer of the criminal law, wielding the normal powers of a sovereign. This option will be referred to alternatively as the criminal-law strategy. The second possibility is a *belligerent*-right,

---

[72] 'Terrorist Attacks on World Trade Center and Pentagon', 96 AJIL 237 (2002), at 239.

or military, mode of operation. Here, the government acts not as a sovereign or ruler, enforcing its *own* laws, but rather as a participant in an armed conflict against a foreign foe. Action of a sovereign-right character is the normal response to the commission of a crime within the territorial jurisdiction of the state in question. Belligerent action, in contrast, is normally employed against an armed attack by a foreign state. Sovereign-right action is governed by the domestic criminal law of the state concerned. Belligerent conduct is regulated by the law of war (i.e., by international humanitarian law).

Each of the two approaches is also subject, however, to some very important – and distinctive – legal constraints. Consider sovereign-right action first. One of its fundamental principles is that only persons who are *personally* guilty of wrongdoing are subject to punishment. In the language of Hugo Grotius, this means that sovereign-right measures consist of primary action by a state.[73] There is also a crucial limitation on the jurisdiction of states: that they can only exercise their police powers within their territorial boundaries (including ships and aircraft registered in the state in question).[74] To reach persons abroad, the cooperation of foreign governments is required, generally in the cumbersome and often lengthy form of extradition proceedings. Further important restrictions are imposed by international human-rights law. For example, human-rights law permits only a very narrow latitude for the lawful use of armed force by state authorities in criminal law enforcement. This was set out in clearest form in a set of guidelines on the use of force and firearms in law-enforcement operations promulgated by the UN in 1990.[75] There is also a body of case-law from the European and Inter-American Courts of Human Rights on the restrictions on the use of armed force by ordinary law-enforcement

---

[73] Grotius, *War and Peace*, at 623. See Chapter 3 above.

[74] See The SS Lotus (*France* v. *Turkey*), PCIJ, ser. A, no. 9 (1927), at 18–19.

[75] Basic Principles on the Use of Force and Firearms by Law Enforcement Officials (1990). See also UN Code of Conduct for Law Enforcement Officials (1979), Art. 3. Both are reprinted in 1 (part 1) *A Compilation of International Instruments*, UN Doc. ST/HR/1/Rev 4 (Vol. I, Part 1) (1993), at 312–23. See also General Comment 6 of the Human Rights Committee, regarding the position under the International Covenant on Civil and Political Rights, in Manfred Nowak, *UN Covenant on Civil and Political Rights: CCPR Commentary* (Kehl: N. P. Engel, 1982), at 851–2; and Barbara Frey, The Question of the Trade, Carrying and Use of Small Arms and Light Weapons in the Context of Human Rights and Humanitarian Norms, UN Doc. E/CN.4/Sub.2/2002/39 (2002).

officials.[76] International human-rights law similarly imposes a rich body
of constraints on the treatment of persons accused of crimes, once they
are in a state's custody. These may be cursorily summarised under the
broad heading of due process of law – including such matters as a right
to counsel, a presumption of innocence, a right to confront witnesses, a
right to be tried in public within a reasonable time, and so forth. If a state
fails to adhere to these fairly demanding standards, then it may be
subjected to an international legal claim, either by the aggrieved individual in question or by another state (such as the accused persons's state of
nationality, if he is a foreign national).[77]

The belligerent-right, or military, approach to terrorism presents a
contrast on all of these fronts. Here, the state is resorting to secondary
rather than primary action – i.e., using force against persons on the basis
of their enemy *status* without any regard to actual guilty *conduct* by the
individuals targeted. No trials are required – or indeed, even permitted,
since membership of the opposing belligerent force is not, as such, a
wrongful act. Consequently, captured enemies are subject only to detention as prisoners of war. This is a non-punitive form of detention,
designed only to effect the separation of the enemy from his force for
the duration of the conflict. Prisoner-of-war status carries a number of
privileges, ranging from visitations by the International Committee of
the Red Cross to guarantees of contact with the outside world, to a right
of release at the termination of the hostilities. A prisoner of war can be
prosecuted and punished for illegal acts actually committed by him,
such as war crimes, or even ordinary crimes committed prior to the
conflict. In such an event, however, the constraints of fair trials become
applicable. The law governing the actual use of force is international
humanitarian law, rather than human-rights law. Humanitarian law
places no specific limit on the quantity of force that can be used (beyond
the prohibition against inflicting 'unnecessary suffering'). Instead, there
are prohibitions against certain types of weapons (such as biological or

---

[76] From the European Court of Human Rights, see *McCann* v. *UK*, 21 EHRR 97 (1995);
Ogur v. *Turkey*, 31 EHRR 912 (1999); and *Gül* v. *Turkey*, 34 EHRR 719 (2000). From the
Inter-American Court of Human Rights, see *Velásquez Rodriguez* v. *Honduras*, 4 Inter-Am
CHR (ser. C) (1988).

[77] A person can make a complaint against his *own* state to an international body, if his state is
a party to the Optional Protocol to the International Covenant on Civil and Political
Rights, 16 Dec. 1966, 999 UNTS 171. By the end of 2002, some 104 states were parties.

chemical weapons) and certain tactics (such as starvation or environmental destruction).[78]

The criminal-law strategy against terrorism was illustrated by the
response to the anarchist attacks of the late nineteenth and early twentieth centuries. There were, to be sure, some instances in which troops
were deployed to subdue anarchist uprisings. In 1877, for example, an
anarchist band comprising some twenty-six members rose against the
Italian state near Benevento, going from village to village for several days
burning tax records (and purporting to depose King Victor Emmanuel
from power). A battalion and a half of infantry and two squadrons of
cavalry were mobilised against them, capturing the entire group with
little effort. Anarchists were not, however, actually treated as belligerents
but strictly as ordinary criminals. There was even a reluctance to regard
membership of an anarchist group as a criminal offence *per se*. Italian
courts, for example, declined to treat the anarchist International
Brotherhood as a criminal organisation, insisting instead on actual
proof of criminal conduct in individual prosecutions.[79] The position
was much the same in other countries. It might be noted that this
criminal-law action against the anarchist menace had a multilateral
component, in the form of an international agreement in 1904, for the
coordination of police measures and the extradition of suspects, to
which ten states were parties.[80] But this was still squarely in the criminal-
law, rather than belligerent, mode of operation.

That the two strategies could be employed alongside one another was
demonstrated by the case of 'Pancho' Villa. After his terroristic raid into
American territory in 1916 – the first foreign incursion into American
territory since the War of 1812 – the response took a military form even
if the situation was not regarded as a war. A reward (of $5,000) for Villa's
capture was offered, and a military expedition was dispatched into
Mexican territory to apprehend him, equipped with the latest technology, in the form of motorised vehicles and aeroplanes. Individual members of the Villa band who were captured, however, were tried criminally

---

[78] For an extended comparison of these two strategies, though largely from the standpoint of
American domestic law, see Feldman, 'Choices'.
[79] George Woodcock, *Anarchism: A History of Libertarian Ideas and Movements*
(Harmondsworth: Penguin, 1962), at 320–2.
[80] Protocol Respecting Measures to Be Taken Against the Anarchist Movement, 14 Mar.
1904, 195 CTS 118. A thorough history of police action against anarchists in this period
remains to be written.

for murder and not treated as prisoners of war.[81] The leader managed to elude capture. But the Americans could take satisfaction in the fact that no further attacks were made on its territory by Villa, who was eventually murdered in circumstances unconnected with the American raid.

Against the terrorist threat of the late twentieth and early twenty-first centuries, countries again operated in both modes, sometimes simultaneously. At times, the distinction between the two was not easy to discern. This was most notably the case with certain practices employed by Israel. Its response to the murders of its athletes at the Munich Olympics of 1972 was particularly instructive. Instead of seeking the extradition of the culprits in the orthodox manner of law enforcement, Israel resorted to more direct, and deadly, methods. Its security forces undertook the systematic killing or kidnapping of the persons held responsible for the crime, in whatever part of the world they happened to be in.[82] Here was armed action by security forces against enemies of the state in foreign territory, without any of the niceties of due process – all this was in the manner of belligerent activity. But the careful targeting of the specific individuals alleged to have committed the offences was, at the same time, reminiscent of ordinary law enforcement. In the disturbances that began in earnest in the Occupied Territories in 2000, something of the same hybrid approach was evident, as Israel adopted a policy of crowd control by means of the targeted killing by security forces of identified individuals. Israel also succeeded in assassinating two of the leaders of the radical opposition group Hamas in short succession in 2004. Some civil-liberties advocates objected that this policy smacked of extrajudicial murder and, as such, an egregious violation of basic human rights. Others held it to be a regrettable, but necessary, adaptation of belligerent operations to new conditions.[83] By the end of 2003, there had yet to be a judicial consideration of the practice.

The United States was soon to follow Israel's lead in the militarisation of the fight against terrorism. Until 2001, the sovereign-right, or criminal-law, approach was the prevailing (but not exclusive) one. In 1996, it consciously elected against taking advantage of an opportunity to capture bin Laden, on the ground that there was an insufficient likelihood of obtaining his conviction in criminal proceedings.[84] Two years later,

---

[81] Clarence C. Clendenen, *Blood on the Border: The United States Army and the Mexican Irregulars* (London: Macmillan, 1969), at 210.

[82] Nasr, *Terrorism*, at 65–75.

[83] On these controversial practices, see Ben-Neftali and Michaeli, 'Scarecrow of the Law'.

[84] Ruth Wedgwood, 'The Law of War: How Osama Slipped Away', *National Interest*, Winter 2001–2, at 69–73.

however, an indictment was issued against him in American courts for the part that he had allegedly played in training anti-American elements in Somalia – efforts which culminated in 1993 in the destruction of a military helicopter and the deaths of eighteen American servicemen at the hands of a mob. Following the attack on an American warship in Aden harbour in Yemen in 2000, further indictments against individual al-Qaeda members were handed down (with bin Laden this time taking the part of an unindicted co-conspirator). There were also occasions, though, in which the United States acted in a military mode against terrorism. The most notable instance occurred in 1986, in the form of an aerial attack against Libya. This was justified as self-defence, in response to the bombing of an entertainment establishment in Berlin that was frequented by American service personnel, for which the United States accused Libya of responsibility.[85]

The sovereign-right and belligerent-right strategies were sometimes pursued more or less in tandem, as in the case of the American response to the bombings of its embassy complexes in Kenya and Tanzania in 1998, an atrocity attributed to al-Qaeda. On this occasion, the immediate response was military, in the form of missile attacks against Sudan and Afghanistan, which had offered sanctuary to bin Laden. As in the case of the Libyan bombing of 1986, self-defence was given as the legal justification.[86] In addition, however, criminal proceedings were launched, with indictments of bin Laden and sixteen others for the atrocity. Of this group, four were actually put on trial and convicted in 2001 (although bin Laden himself was not one of them).

After the terrorist attacks against New York and Washington in September 2001 – causing a loss of life comparable in magnitude to the Japanese strike against Pearl Harbor in 1941 – the United States shifted abruptly into a predominantly (but still not exclusively) military mode of action. To the American Congress, President George W. Bush announced that 'the enemies of freedom' had committed 'an act of war' against the United States.[87] The Congress proceeded to grant the president the right 'to use all necessary and appropriate force' against the perpetrators of the attacks or any one who harboured them.[88] This was,

---

[85] Letter from US to President of the UN Security Council, 14 Apr. 1986, UN Doc. S/17990 (1986); reprinted in 80 AJIL 632–3 (1986).
[86] Letter from US to President of the UN Security Council, 20 Aug. 1998, UN Doc. S/1998/ 780. See also 'Missile Attacks on Afghanistan and Sudan', 93 AJIL 161–7 (1999).
[87] 'Terrorist Attacks on World Trade Center and Pentagon', 96 AJIL 237 (2002), at 242.
[88] PL 107–40, 115 Stat 224.

for all practical purposes, a declaration of war against persons responsible for the attacks. In November 2001, President Bush issued a military
order confirming that the various terrorist attacks of recent years against
the United States had gone beyond the sphere of mere criminal activity,
creating 'a state of armed conflict' that required the use of the American
armed forces instead of the normal domestic law-enforcement agen-
cies.[89] The response by Great Britain was more cautious, though broadly
similar. The British foreign secretary held the terrorist attacks on the
United States of September 2001 to be 'a deliberate act of war'.[90] He later
stated flatly that Britain was 'at war with terrorism'.[91]

The first major operation in this new war was directed against
Afghanistan, which had played host to al-Qaeda in the period prior to
the September 2001 attacks. The following month, the United States
issued what was in effect, if not in name, an ultimatum to the Taliban
government, ordering it to deliver the al-Qaeda operatives into
American hands.[92] (In substance, this was a repetition of an order by
the UN Security Council to that same effect made in 1999.)[93] When the
demand was not complied with, the United States launched air attacks
on Afghanistan and, in cooperation with troops from some other
Western states and with local opposition forces, drove the Taliban
government from power. At the same time, an intense military manhunt
was launched to kill or capture bin Laden. This operation bore a striking
resemblance to the punitive expedition mounted against Villa in
1916–17 (though with the difference that the Mexican government
had not been accused of collusion with Villa). As in that earlier effort,
the chief target figure eluded capture, at least for the immediate term,
although the al-Qaeda terrorist infrastructure may at least have been
seriously disrupted.

For international legal purposes, the Afghanistan campaign was justified,
inevitably, as self-defence.[94] Some misgivings were voiced on this count;
but, for the most part, the claim was accepted.[95] In the light of the scale of

---

[89] Military Order of 13 Nov. 2001, 41 ILM 252–5 (2002).
[90] Remarks of Straw, *Hansard*, HC, vol. 372, ser. 6, col. 618, 14 Sept. 2001.
[91] Remarks of Straw, *ibid.* at 693, 4 Oct. 2001.
[92] 'Terrorist Attacks on World Trade Center and Pentagon', 96 AJIL, at 243.
[93] SC Res. 1267 (15 Oct. 1999), 54 SCOR, Res and Dec, at 148.
[94] See Letter from US to President of the UN Security Council, 7 Oct. 2001, UN Doc. S/2001/
    946 (2001); reprinted in 40 ILM 1281 (2001).
[95] For scholarly support for the American position, see Franck, 'Terrorism'. For a more
    sceptical view of the action as self-defence, see Charney, 'Use of Force'.

the attacks, there appeared to be little reason to deny that the right of self-defence could be exercised against privately organised bands of criminals as well as against aggressor states. (It may be recalled, in this connection, that the *Caroline* affair, that font of official doctrine on self-defence law, had concerned action by Britain against a privately organised band of insurgents rather than against a foreign state as such.) The UN Security Council gave what could be called an implicit approval to the operation, in retrospect, by effectively endorsing the change of government.[96]

At the same time, however, it was clear that the United States was not disposed to conduct its war on terrorism on a narrowly defensive basis, simply reacting to incidents as they occurred. Fully in the spirit of classic just wars, the campaign against terrorism would be conducted in an offensive mode. In its communication to the UN justifying the Afghanistan campaign, the United States candidly stated that its intention was not merely to fend off assaults as they occurred but also 'to prevent and deter further attacks'. It also claimed the right to extend its operations, if need be, to 'other organizations and other States'.[97] To the American people, President Bush announced his determination to 'drive [terrorists] from place to place, until there is no refuge or rest'. Any state that harboured or supported terrorists would be regarded by the United States as 'a hostile regime'.[98]

In effect, the United States was asserting two of the three classic justifications for war – i.e., for *offensive* war – that had been set out by Hugo Grotius and endorsed by international lawyers for centuries afterwards: defence (in the broad sense of acting against threats and impending dangers), and punishment.[99] Indeed, seldom, if ever, was a war couched so overtly in just-war terms as this one. The most obvious sign of this was the straightforward rejection of neutrality by the United States. 'Every nation has a choice to make', Bush solemnly announced in October 2001; 'In this conflict, there is no neutral ground.'[100] It was impossible, he later emphasised, for there to be 'any neutral ground between good and evil, freedom and slavery, and life and death'.[101] Nor

---

[96] SC Res. 1378 (14 Nov. 2001), 55 SCOR, Res and Dec, at 270.
[97] Letter from US to President of the UN Security Council, 7 Oct. 2001, UN Doc. S/2001/946 (2001); reprinted in 40 ILM 1281 (2001).
[98] 'Terrorist Attacks on World Trade Center and Pentagon', 96 AJIL 237 (2002), at 244.
[99] The third justification, obtaining what was owed by a recalcitrant power, was not germane to the war on terrorism.
[100] 'Terrorist Attacks on World Trade Center and Pentagon', 96 AJIL 237 (2002), at 246.
[101] Radio address of 20 Mar. 2004, at whitehouse.gov/news/releases/2004/03/20040319-3.html.

was it envisaged that there would be a negotiated settlement in the manner of wars in the seventeenth and eighteenth centuries, with limited gains for each side, amnesties for each side, a treaty of peace restoring friendly relations and a polite and careful avoidance of imputations of fault. On the contrary, this war was fought with complete victory in mind, with a *jus victoriae* as the governing principle, in which the winning party (clearly envisaged to be the United States) would sit in stern – and probably *very* stern – judgment over the losing one.

The implications of bringing the concepts and tools of war into a realm that had previously been the domain of the criminal law were potentially many. On the national-law plane, governments began to assume increasingly draconian powers, comparable to those that were customarily exercised in times of war. At the level of international law, a number of potentially contentious questions beckoned. One of them concerned the right of states to carry the war on terrorism into the territories of foreign countries. In criminal law enforcement, this was not allowed. In war, however, if a belligerent armed force conducted operations from sanctuaries in neutral territory, then its enemy could justify attacking it there, on self-defence grounds (as in the case of the American operations against North Vietnamese forces in Cambodian territory in 1970). If the logic of war was carried to its full conclusion, then such actions as the visiting and searching of ships on the high seas for contraband (i.e., materials or equipment for terrorist attacks) could be instituted.

Taking prisoners

The importation of belligerent methods into what had previously been the sphere of law enforcement placed many strains on legal conceptions of war. The issue that most sharply illustrated the legal puzzles that could arise was the treatment of prisoners. When the sovereign-right, or criminal-law, path is taken, accused persons are captured and held on the basis of suspected personal guilt. But they are also entitled to all the due-process and fair-trial guarantees provided by national and international law – most notably the right to trial within a reasonable time, to a presumption of innocence and the assistance of legal counsel.

When the belligerent path is taken, the picture is radically different. Here, the persons captured are liable to be detained for the duration of the conflict, purely on the basis of membership in the enemy armed force, with no need for any showing of personal wrongdoing. Legal safeguards for prisoners of war find their source in the Geneva Convention on Prisoners of War of 1949, rather than in the general law of international human rights. This Convention grants a number of valuable legal privileges to prisoners of war, such as the right to communicate with the outside world, to receive relief items and to receive inspection visits from the International Committee of the Red Cross. Crucially, however, these privileges are only owed to persons who meet the definition of 'prisoners of war' set out in the Geneva Convention – meaning, effectively, persons who qualify as lawful combatants, as that term had been defined in the nineteenth century and incorporated into the Hague Rules of 1907.[102]

These seemingly arcane legal points began to assume a very great practical importance in the aftermath of the Afghanistan campaign of 2001. The United States made it clear early on that it would treat persons captured in that conflict as belligerents rather than as accused criminals. That meant that they were held as prisoners of war. It soon became apparent, though, that the detainees would not be granted the normal privileges of prisoners of war set out in the Geneva Convention. The reason was that, according to the United States, they did not meet the criteria required of lawful belligerents. Members of al-Qaeda and other terrorist groups were regarded as entirely ineligible for prisoner-of-war status in principle, on the ground that al-Qaeda was neither a state nor (perforce) a party to the Geneva Convention and that, consequently, its members had no shadow of a claim to be treated as lawful combatants.

The position of the Taliban forces was slightly different. They were conceded to be eligible, in principle, for prisoner-of-war status since they were members of the armed force of a state party to the Convention. In the particular circumstances, however, they did not qualify as lawful belligerents because they failed to meet two of the four criteria for lawful combatancy that were set out in the Hague Rules. Specifically, they did not wear a fixed sign visible at a distance, distinguishing them from civilians; and they did not conduct their operations according to the laws of war.[103]

---

[102] On the debates over combatant status in the nineteenth century, see Chapter 5 above.

[103] 'Decision Not to Regard Persons Detained in Afghanistan as POWs', 96 AJIL 475–82 (2002). Taliban forces were conceded to have met the other two criteria: organisation as an armed force, and the carrying of arms openly. The American position on this point was not free of doubt. For the view that the Taliban detainees should have had prisoner-of-war status, see Aldrich, 'Taliban'.

This determination placed the detainees in an awkward middle position. As combatants, they were liable, like any prisoners of war, to be detained indefinitely, i.e., until the termination of the hostilities. As this was a non-criminal form of detention, there was no need to accuse any particular detainee of committing any particular criminal offence. Detention was justified entirely by the *status* of the persons, i.e., by their membership in the enemy force. This meant, in turn, that there was no right to a speedy trial (or indeed to any trial at all), no right of access to legal counsel or to any of the normal human-rights protections available to persons accused of crimes. At the same time, however, the detainees' status as *unlawful* combatants meant they were also denied the full range of privileges provided for by the Geneva Conventions. They were, in short, outside the protective ambit of *both* international human rights law (for criminal defendants) *and* the Geneva Convention (for prisoners of war).[104] The effect of this American policy was that the only international legal standard governing the treatment of the detainees was the notably vague 'Martens Clause' that had been devised in 1899 for persons who failed to qualify as lawful belligerents: that such persons 'remain[ed] under the protection ... of the law of nations' deriving from 'the laws of humanity' and 'the dictates of the public conscience'.[105] The public conscience, as represented by the American government, was not in a generous mood.

Objections to this American policy were advanced from several perspectives. From the narrowest viewpoint, some pointed out that the United States was obligated, under the Geneva Convention on Prisoners of War, to have the question of entitlement to prisoner-of-war status determined by an impartial tribunal rather than by unilateral fiat.[106] This position was taken by the Inter-American Commission on Human Rights (an arm of the Organization of American States), which, in 2002, expressly requested the United States to institute hearings on the status of the detainees from the Afghanistan conflict on a case-by-case basis.[107] The American response was that the Convention required such a hearing only in cases of actual doubt as to entitlement – and that there was no such doubt in the cases at hand. In addition, the United States invoked

---

[104] See White House Fact Sheet, 7 Feb. 2002.
[105] Hague Convention IV Respecting the Laws and Customs of War on Land, 18 Oct. 1907, 205 CTS 277, preamble. On the origin of the Martens Clause, see Chapter 5 above.
[106] Geneva Convention III on Prisoners of War, 12 Aug. 1949, 75 UNTS 135, Art. 5.
[107] Inter-American Commission on Human Rights, Request for Precautionary Measures (Detainees at Guantanamo Bay, Cuba), 12 Mar. 2002, 41 ILM 532 (2002).

the 1996 ruling of the World Court on nuclear weapons, maintaining that international humanitarian law was a *lex specialis* which, in the context of the conflict against terrorism, displaced the ordinary international law of human rights.[108] On that basis, the United States declined to comply with the Commission's request.

A second, and broader, line of criticism was to the effect that the very conception of 'unlawful combatant' was not a meaningful legal category. On this thesis, all persons must be *either* lawful combatants (as defined by the Geneva Convention) or civilians. If they were civilians, then they could only be tried in civilian criminal courts for acts of individual wrongdoing committed in the past. On this thesis, the United States would be required either to treat the detainees as prisoners of war, or to charge them on individual bases with criminal offences, or to release them. The American position was that the detainees, by engaging in combat against the United States, had forfeited any right to be treated as ordinary criminals. This fact, combined with their failure to qualify as lawful combatants, inevitably meant that they fell into the middle category as described. If a detainee had committed a specific crime, then he could be put on trial. But the trial would be before a military commission rather than a civilian court, in keeping with the longstanding practice that offences committed by enemy combatants against a state's armed forces could be tried by military commissions or courts-martial of that state.[109] There were indications from the American government of possible military trials of at least some of the detainees, but none had taken place by the end of 2003. One of the more urgent tasks of international law, at the beginning of the twenty-first century, was to shed some much-needed light on this important subject.[110]

The third and broadest ground of opposition to the American policy was the contention that a belligerent strategy against terrorism was, in priniciple, inappropriate and that a criminal-law approach should be pursued instead.[111] On this point, the American government's position was that the terrorist threat was of such a magnitude as to justify a

---

[108] United States Response to the Request for Precautionary Measures of the Inter-American Commission on Human Rights, 15 Apr. 2002, *ibid.* at 1015.

[109] For authority to this effect from the US Supreme Court, see *Ex p. Quirin*, 317 US 1 (1942); and *In re Yamashita*, 327 US 1 (1946).

[110] On unlawful combatancy and war criminality, see Baxter, 'Unprivileged Belligerency'; and Dinstein, 'Distinction'.

[111] See, for example, Fitzpatrick, 'Jurisdiction'.

belligerent strategy.[112] It was plainly going to be a war like no other. For one thing, there was a conspicuous lack of chivalric spirit in this contest. On the one side, terrorist groups were devoted to the mass murder of innocent civilians as a routine mode of operation. On the other, there was no disposition to regard the opposing forces as belligerents with all of the ancillary legal privileges. 'There is no moral equivalence', the British foreign secretary pronounced, 'between us and our enemy'.[113]

What was at stake on this point were issues of the highest importance and the broadest magnitude. In a nutshell, the issue was whether the war on terrorism would be conducted within the constraints of the general international law of human rights, or whether it would be conducted instead under the umbrella of international humanitarian law. What was perhaps most likely was that, as so often in the past, state practice, with all of its murkiness, would play the leading role over legal doctrine, with all of its logical tidiness. It appeared possible that that would entail the evolution, perhaps in a decidedly rough-and-ready way, of some kind of hybrid approach, borrowing elements from both of these bodies of law. If this were so, then the result might be some sort of quasi-permanent condition of juridical twilight, a state of neither peace nor war. The dark night of war would not prevail; and to that extent, there could be some cause for satisfaction. But neither would the dazzling sunshine of peace be present. The world might find itself gradually adjusting to a long-term abridgement of civil liberties in a manner reminiscent of wartime – but with wartime, in this case, being of permanent or quasi-permanent duration – to an open-ended period of nervous vigilance, punctuated by occasional lightning-flashes of mass murder. Perhaps the result will be a kind of modern version of the medieval Islamic *ghazi* style of warfare, with all of us playing the role of frontiersmen in a never-ending battle against an ever-present enemy – and with no prospect of either lasting peace or decisive victory. If this state of affairs were to prevail on an indefinite basis, then it is likely that significant adjustments in legal conceptions of war must lie in store, and that new – but possibly very depressing – chapters in our story await us.

---

[112] In support of the position that the struggle against terrorism was of a military character, see Wedgwood, 'Al Qaeda'; and Jinks, 'September 11'.
[113] Remarks of Straw, *Hansard*, HC, vol. 372, ser. 6, col. 1057, 16 Oct. 2001.

CONCLUSION

Our journey has been a long one – from the age of the chariot and the hoplite to that of the hydrogen bomb and the cruise missile. It may be wondered whether there can be said to have been any kind of unified theme or thread to the story. In this light, some might be inclined to look for a progressivist theme – a relatively stately progression from ignorance to wisdom, from evil to good, from passion to reason, from selfishness to altruism, from darkness to light. Those searching for such a tale will have read the preceding pages with dismay. It is not easy to say whether fundamental ideas about war are today significantly more advanced than they were in the age of Cicero. It may even be contended that the post-1945 version of just-war doctrine is greatly inferior to that of the ancient stoics and the medieval Christians, in that it has no deep grounding in a rich body of ideas about the conduct of human social and political relations in general, in the manner of ancient and medieval natural law.

A more sophisticated variant of the progressivist theme might see in this history a slightly different grand theme: one of fall and redemption. On this view, there was an early state of grace or (in more secular terminology) of enlightenment, from which humankind tragically strayed, but to which it eventually returned. The original state of enlightenment was the early just-war doctrine of the ancient and medieval periods, when war was seen as the servant of justice rather than as an instrument of policy, vanity or oppression. The seventeenth century marked the beginning of a descent into a Dark Age, when a separate body of 'voluntary' law was accorded express recognition and welcomed into the very heart of the law of nations. The nadir came in the nineteenth century, with the dominance of the positivist view of war. Then, finally, in the twentieth century, and especially after 1945, came a return to the enlightened idea of war in the service of peace and justice, coupled with the laying down of appropriate penalties for the resort to armed force for egoistical ends. It might even be contended, or hoped, that the present era of redemption has been, or will be, superior to the original state of grace because there is now a more effective (or potentially more effective) mechanism for instituting just-war ideas, in the form of the UN Security Council. Be that as it may, this perspective would see the legal history of war as a grand cycle.

It may be suggested, necessarily tentatively and provisionally, that there is another way of seeing this progressive or cyclical picture: in terms of the extent to which lawyers have tried to see war as a distinct phenomenon, walled off (so to speak) from other aspects of social, political and legal life. From this perspective, as from so many others, the highest contrast is presented between, on the one hand, the Middle Ages and, on the other hand, the nineteenth century. In the Middle Ages, when natural law was the reigning legal paradigm, war can hardly be said to have been a distinct department of life from the juridical standpoint. In material terms, of course, war contrasted with peace every bit as strongly as it has before or since. But war was not seen as a distinctive *legal* or *moral* phenomenon, in the sense of being governed by principles fundamentally different from those prevailing in times of peace. The same rules prevailed whether in war or in peace, although naturally the context in which and to which those rules were applied differed markedly as between the two situations. We see this most vividly in the agonising doubts that afflicted persons (or some persons) in the medieval period over whether killing even in a just war might not be homicide.

There could scarcely be a greater contrast with the nineteenth century, when war became a quite distinct institution of international law, differing in practically every possible way from a state of peace. States of war and of peace became inversions, mirror images of one another. What was laudable in the one was apt to be reprehensible in the other. To kill in peacetime was of course a crime. But to refuse to kill in war was insubordination or shirking of patriotic duty, if not actually criminal. To the medieval mind, war was one part of the single grand symphony of social life which, for all of the cacophony, was nevertheless played always in the same key – that of the eternal and immutable law of nature. To the nineteenth-century positivist mind, war was the very negation of ordinary life, a world entirely to itself, walled off from ordinary existence, even hermetically sealed – or as much so as lawyers could make it.

Other periods of history – including our own – have been less pure than these two archetypes just identified. The present age, for example, has elements of both of these approaches. We flatter ourselves – if with little actual illusion – that we have done away with that moral and legal monstrosity known as the state of war, contenting ourselves instead with situations of aggression-and-self-defence, in which the general rule of law is not suspended, as it was in the older state of war. At the same time, however, it is admitted that, in this situation, a *lex specialis* is applied that differs from the ordinary law of peace.

On a more general level – a *very* general level, to be sure – it may be wondered which of these two strategies is preferable, or what kind of combination of them. Is it better that war be sharply cut off in a legal sense from peace, and ruled by principles that are, as it were, tailor-made for it? Or is it preferable to dissolve all barriers between war and peace to the greatest extent possible, to live in a single, undifferentiated legal and moral world at all times? In other words, it may be wondered whether war should be a distinct legal institution, as in the nineteenth century; or whether it should be seen as an aberration in a monolithic state of peace. The moralist and the idealist will instinctively incline in favour of the second of these choices, and against the idea of a special legal institution of war. The reason is easily seen. War as a legal institution smacks too strongly of a matter-of-fact acceptance of the most monstrous social evil known to the human race. It looks too much like a craven surrender of morality to the harsh demands of *Realpolitik*, too much like a legal seal of approval of large-scale psychopathy.

There is much truth in all of that. But there are grave dangers too in the effacing of all barriers between war and peace. It should be remembered that when war is not confined to an institution, so to speak, it may roam widely and infect much or all of social life in general. There was a vivid illustration of this point in the Cold War, when Western–socialist rivalry and the militaristic ethos to which it gave rise insinuated itself deeply into all walks of social, intellectual, cultural, economic and spiritual life on both sides of the Iron Curtain.[1] It is entirely possible that something of the same will occur during the war on terrorism, the first of (no doubt many) major international crises of the twenty-first century. Mars, like Yahweh, has always been a jealous god, ever ready to subsume the whole of social life to his ends.

It is entirely possible, of course, that humans, in the early twenty-first century, have no real choice in this matter, that the turbulent tides of history will throw us in unpredictable directions and leave us to make the best of our lot. As a short account of the present human predicament, that may be a more accurate summation than many would wish. But even if we cannot control the present to the extent that we would like – or, even less, foresee the future – it is at least within our power, however imperfectly, to look at the past and to see how our predecessors attempted to cope with the dilemmas that faced them. In the case of war, we have seen

---

[1] See, in this respect, David Caute, *The Dancer Defects: The Struggle for Cultural Supremacy during the Cold War* (Oxford: Oxford University Press, 2003).

the manifold ways in which lawyers have responded to it – either by trying simply to understand it or, more ambitiously, to control or regulate it, to sit in judgment on warring states, to fit it into some kind of larger intellectual framework, to devise gentler alternatives to it or even to abolish it. It is likely enough that the challenges and dilemmas that are looming will be every bit as forbidding and puzzling as those of the past. So it may be of some modest value to ponder, as we have cursorily done, the experiences of our predecessors.

BIBLIOGRAPHY

Primary sources

Ambrose of Milan. *De Officiis*. Trans. Ivor J. Davidson. Oxford: Oxford University Press, 2001. (1st published *c.* 390.)

Anonymous. *The Laws of Manu*. Trans. Wendy Doniger and Brian K. Smith. New Delhi: Penguin, 1991. (From *c.* first century BC.)

Aquinas, Thomas. *On Law, Morality, and Politics*. Ed. William P. Baumgarth and Richard J. Regan. Indianapolis: Hackett, 1988.

The Treatise on Law. Ed. and trans. R. J. Henle. Notre Dame: University of Notre Dame Press, 1993.

Aristotle. *The Nicomachean Ethics*. Trans. David Ross. Oxford: Oxford University Press, 1980. (1st edn *c.* 350 BC.)

The Politics. Trans. T. A. Sinclair. London: Penguin, 1962. (1st edn *c.* 330 BC.)

Augustine of Hippo. *The Political Writings of St Augustine*. Ed. Henry Paolucci. Washington, D.C.: Regnery Gateway, 1962.

Concerning the City of God Against the Pagans. Trans. Henry Bettenson. Harmondsworth: Penguin, 1972. (1st edn AD 414–26.)

Ayala, Balthasar. *De jure et officiis bellicis et disciplina militari*. Trans. John P. Bate. Washington, D.C.: Carnegie Institution, 1912. (1st edn 1582.)

Belli, Pierino. *A Treatise on Military Matters and Warfare*. Trans. Herbert C. Nutting. Oxford: Clarendon Press, 1936. (1st edn 1563.)

Bonet, Honoré de. *The Tree of Battles of Honoré Bonet*. Trans. G. W. Coopland. Liverpool: Liverpool University Press, 1949. (1st edn *c.* 1386.)

Burlamaqui, J.-J. *The Principles of Politic Law*. Trans. Thomas Nugent. London: J. Nourse, 1752. (1st edn 1751.)

Bynkershoek, Cornelius van. *Questions of Public Law*. Trans. Tenney Frank. Oxford: Clarendon Press, 1930. (1st edn 1737.)

Cicero, Marcus Tullius. *The Republic and the Laws*. Trans. Niall Rudd. Oxford: Oxford University Press, 1998. (Written *c.* 51 BC.)

On Duties. Ed. and trans. E. M. Atkins and M. T. Griffin. Cambridge: Cambridge University Press, 1991. (1st edn 44 BC.)

Philippics. Ed. and trans. D. R. Shackleton Bailey. Chapel Hill: University of North Carolina Prress, 1986. (1st edn 44 BC.)

Clausewitz, Carl von. *On War*. Ed. and trans. Michael Howard and Peter Paret. Princeton: Princeton University Press, 1976. (1st edn 1832.)

Froissart, Jean. *Chronicles*. Ed. and trans. Geoffrey Brereton. London: Penguin, 1968. (1st edn *c.* 1369–1400.)

Gentili, Alberico. *On the Law of War.* Trans. John C. Rolfe. Oxford: Clarendon Press, 1933. (1st edn 1598.)
De armis Romanis et iniustitia bellica Romanorum. Hanau: 1599.
Gratian. *Gratianus in Jurisprudence.* Ed. James William Somerville. Washington, D.C.: Law Reporter Printing, 1934. (1st edn *c.* 1140.)
Grotius, Hugo. *On the Law of War and Peace.* Trans. Francis W. Kelsey. Oxford: Oxford University Press, 1925. (1st edn 1625.)
Commentary on the Law of Prize and Booty. Trans. Gwladys L. Williams and Walter H. Zeydel. Oxford: Clarendon Press, 1950. (Orig. manuscript 1604.)
Herodotus. *The Histories.* Trans. Aubrey de Sélincourt. London: Penguin, 1954. (1st edn *c* 440 BC.)
Hobbes, Thomas. *De Cive; or The Citizen.* New York: Appleton-Century-Crofts, 1949. (1st edn 1642.)
Elements of Law Natural and Politic. Oxford: Oxford University Press, 1994. (1st edn 1650.)
Leviathan; or The Matter, Forme and Power of a Commonwealth Ecclesiasticall and Civil. Oxford: Basil Blackwell, 1957. (1st edn 1651.)
Hübner, Martin. *De la saisie des bâtiments neutres; ou, Le droit qu'ont les nations belligérantes d'arrêter les navires des peuples amis.* 2 vols. The Hague: 1759.
Justinian. *The Digest of Justinian.* Trans. Alan Watson. 2 vols. Philadelphia: University of Pennsylvania Press, 1985. (1st edn 533.)
Kant, Immanuel. *Political Writings.* Ed. Hans Reiss. Trans. H. B. Nisbet. 2nd edn. Cambridge: Cambridge University Press, 1991.
Kautilya. *Arthaśāstra.* Trans. R. Shamasanstry. 3rd edn. Mysore: Wesleyan Mission Press, 1929. (1st edn, third century BC.)
Legnano, John of. *Tractatus de Bello, de Represaliis et de Duello.* Ed. T. E. Holland. Trans. J. L. Brierly. Oxford: Oxford University Press, 1917. (1st edn 1360.)
Livy (Titus Livius). *The Early History of Rome.* Trans. Aubrey de Sélincourt. Harmondsworth: Penguin, 1960. (1st edn *c.* 25 BC.)
Plato. *The Republic.* Trans. H. D. P. Lee. Harmondsworth: Penguin, 1955. (1st edn *c.* 380 BC.)
The Laws. Trans. Trevor J. Saunders. Harmondsworth: Penguin, 1970. (1st edn *c.* 347 BC.)
Polybius. *The Rise of the Roman Empire.* Trans. Ian Scott-Kilvert. Harmondsworth: Penguin, 1979. (1st edn *c.* 120 BC.)
Pufendorf, Samuel. *On the Law of Nature and Nations.* Trans. C. H. Oldfather and W. A. Oldfather. Oxford: Clarendon Press, 1934. (1st edn 1672.)
On the Duty of Man and Citizen According to Natural Law. Ed. James Tully. Trans. Michael Silverthorne. Cambridge: Cambridge University Press, 1991. (1st edn 1673.)
Rayneval, Gérard de. *Institutions du droit de la nature et des gens.* 2 vols. 2nd edn. Paris: Rey et Gravier, 1832. (1st edn 1803.)

Rousseau, Jean-Jacques. *The Social Contract*. Trans. Maurice Cranston. Harmondsworth: Penguin, 1968. (1st edn 1762.)

Rutherforth, T. *Institutes of Natural Law*. 2 vols. Cambridge: J. Bentham, 1754.

Spinoza, Benedict de. *A Treatise on Politics*. In *The Political Works*, ed. and trans. A. G. Wernham, at 256–445. Oxford: Clarendon Press, 1958. (1st edn 1677.)

Suárez, Francisco. *A Work on the Three Theological Virtues: Faith, Hope and Charity*. Trans. Gwladys L. Williams. Oxford: Clarendon Press, 1944. (1st edn 1612.)

Sun Tzu. *The Art of War*. Trans. Lionel Giles. In *Roots of Strategy*, ed. Thomas R. Phillips, at 21–63. Harrisburg, Pa.: Stackpole, 1985. (1st edn c. 450–250 BC.)

Thucydides. *The Peloponnesian War*. Trans. Rex Warner. Harmondsworth: Penguin, 1954. (1st edn c. 405 BC.)

Vattel, Emmerich de. *The Law of Nations; or, The Principles of Natural Law Applied to the Conduct and to the Affairs of Nations and Sovereigns*. Trans. Charles G. Fenwick. Washington, D.C.: Carnegie Institution, 1916. (1st edn 1758.)

Vegetius, Flavius Renatus. *The Military Institutions of the Romans*. Trans. John Clarke. In *Roots of Strategy*, ed. Thomas R. Phillips, at 73–175. Harrisburg, Pa.: Stackpole, 1985. (1st edn 390.)

Vitoria, Francisco de. *On the Law of War*. In *Political Writings*, ed. Anthony Pagden and Jeremy Lawrance, at 293–327. Cambridge: Cambridge University Press, 1991. (1st edn 1557.)

Wolff, Christian. *The Law of Nations Treated According to a Scientific Method*. Trans. Joseph H. Drake. Oxford: Clarendon Press, 1934. (1st edn 1749.)

Secondary sources

Abi-Saab, Georges S. 'Wars of National Liberation and the Laws of War'. *Recueil des Cours* (Academy of International Law) (1979), **165**: 353–445.

Abi-Saab, Rosemary. *Droit humanitaire et conflits internes: Origines et évolution de la réglementation internationale*. Geneva: Institut Henri Dunant, 1986.

Ago, Roberto. 'Eighth Report on State Responsibility'. *Year Book of the International Law Commission 1980*, vol. 2 (pt 1), at 13–86. UN Doc. A/CN.4/SER.A/1980/Add.1 (part 1).

Aldrich, George H. 'The Taliban, Al Qaeda, and the Determination of Illegal Combatants'. *American Journal of International Law* (2002), **96**: 891–8.

Alexandrov, Stanmir A. *Self-defense Against the Use of Force in International Law*. The Hague: Kluwer, 1996.

Alphandéry, Paul. *La chrétienté et l'idée de croisade*. 2 vols. Ed. Alphonse Dupront. Paris: A. Michel, 1954–9.

Anderson, M. S. *War and Society in Europe of the Old Regime 1618–1789*. London: Fontana, 1988.

Anonymous. *Marxism-Leninism on War and Army*. Trans. Donald Donemanis. Moscow: Progress, 1972.

Armour, W. S. 'Customs of War in Ancient India'. *Transactions of the Grotius Society* (1922), **8**: 71–87.

Bacot, Guillaume. *La doctrine de la guerre juste*. Paris: Economica, 1989.

Bailey, Sydney D. *How Wars End: The United Nations and the Termination of Armed Conflict 1946–1964*. 2 vols. Oxford: Clarendon Press, 1982.

Bainton, Ronald. 'The Early Church and War'. *Harvard Theological Review* (1946), **39**: 189–212.

Christian Attitudes toward War and Peace: A Historical Survey and Critical Re-examination. Nashville, Tenn.: Abingdon Press, 1960.

Ballis, William. *The Legal Position of War: Changes in Its Practice and Theory from Plato to Vattel*. London: Garland, 1973.

Barès, Charles. *Le blocus pacifique*. Toulouse: G. Berthoumien, 1898.

Barnes, Jonathon. 'The Just War'. In *The Cambridge History of Later Medieval Philosophy*, ed. N. Kretzmann, A. Kenny and J. Pinborg, at 771–84. Cambridge: Cambridge University Press, 1982.

Basdevant, Jules. 'Étude sur quelques pratiques du droit des gens à la fin du XVIe siècle et au commencement du XVIIe siècle, d'après les "Annales" et "Histoires" de Grotius'. *Revue Générale de Droit International Public* (1903), **10**: 619–50.

'L'action coercitive Anglo-German-Italienne contre le Vénézuéla'. *Revue Générale de Droit International Public* (1904), **11**: 362–458.

Basham, A. L. *The Wonder That Was India: A Survey of the History and Culture of the Indian Sub-continent before the Coming of the Muslims*. 3rd edn. London: Sidgwick and Jackson, 1967.

Baxter, R. R. 'So-called "Unprivileged Belligerency": Spies, Guerrillas and Saboteurs'. *British Year Book of International Law* (1951), **28**: 323–45.

'The Legal Consequences of the Unlawful Use of Force in the Charter'. *Proceedings of the American Society of International Law* (1968), **62**: 68–75.

Bederman, David J. *International Law in Antiquity*. Cambridge: Cambridge University Press, 2001.

Bedjaoui, Mohammed. *Law and the Algerian Revolution*. Brussels: International Association of Democratic Lawyers, 1961.

Ben-Neftali, Orna, and Keren R. Michaeli. '"We Must Not Make a Scarecrow of the Law": A Legal Analysis of the Israeli Policy of Targeted Killings'. *Cornell International Law Journal* (2003), **36**: 233–92.

Best, Geoffrey. *Humanity in Warfare: The Modern History of the International Law of Armed Conflict*. London: Methuen, 1980.

War and Law since 1945. Oxford: Clarendon Press, 1994.

Bhatia, H. S., ed. *International Law and Practice in Ancient India*. New Delhi: Deep and Deep, 1977.

Blanning, T. C. W. *The Origins of the French Revolutionary Wars*. London: Longman, 1986.

Bluntschli, Kaspar. *Le droit international codifié*. Trans. M. C. Lardy. Paris: Guillaumin, 1870.

Bobbitt, Philip. *The Shield of Achilles: War, Peace and the Course of History*. London: Allen Lane, 2002.

Bohannan, Paul, ed. *Law and Warfare: Studies in the Anthropology of Conflict*. Garden City, N.Y.: Natural History Press, 1967.

Bonfils, Henry. *Manuel de droit international public (Droit des gens)*. Paris: A. Rousseau, 1894.

Borchard, Edwin E. '"War" and "Peace"'. *American Journal of International Law* (1933), **27**: 114–17.

'War, Neutrality and Non-belligerency'. *American Journal of International Law* (1941), **35**: 618–25.

'When Did the War Begin?' *Columbia Law Review* (1947), **47**: 742–8.

Bordwell, Percy. *The Law of War between Belligerents: A History and Commentary*. Chicago: Callaghan, 1908.

Bower, Graham. 'The Nation in Arms: Combatants and Non-combatants'. *Transactions of the Grotius Society* (1918), **4**: 71–86.

Bowett, Derek W. *Self-defence in International Law*. Manchester: Manchester University Press, 1958.

'Reprisals Involving Recourse to Armed Force'. *American Journal of International Law* (1972), **66**: 1–36.

Bozeman, Adda B. *Politics and Culture in International History*. Princeton: Princeton University Press, 1960.

Conflict in Africa: Concepts and Realities. Princeton: Princeton University Press, 1976.

Brière, P. Yves de la. 'Les droits de la juste victoire selon la tradition des théologiens catholiques'. *Revue Générale de Droit International Public* (1925), **32**: 366–87.

'Évolution de la doctrine et de la pratique en matière de représailles'. *Recueil des Cours* (Academy of International Law) (1928), **22**: 237–94.

'La conception de la paix et de la guerre chez Saint Augustine'. *Revue de Philosophie* (1930), **30**: 557–72.

'Les étapes de la tradition théologique concernant le droit de juste guerre: Notes d'histoires des doctrines'. *Revue Générale de Droit International Public* (1937), **44**: 129–61.

Le droit de juste guerre: Tradition théologique, adaptations contemporaines. Paris: Pedone, 1938.

Brierly, J. L. 'International Law and Resort to Armed Force'. *Cambridge Law Journal* (1932), **4**: 308–19.

Brown, Philip Marshall. 'The Armed Occupation of Santo Domingo'. *American Journal of International Law* (1917), **11**: 394–9.

Brownlie, Ian. *International Law and the Use of Force by States*. Oxford: Clarendon Press, 1963.

Brundage, James A. *Medieval Canon Law and the Crusader*. Madison, Wis.: University of Wisconsin Press, 1969.

Cadoux, C. John. *The Early Christian Attitude to War: A Contribution to the History of Christian Ethics*. London: George Allen and Unwin, 1919.

Calhoun, Frederick S. *Power and Principle: Armed Intervention in Wilsonian Foreign Policy*. Kent, Ohio: Kent State University Press, 1986.

Calvo, Carlos. *Le droit international théorique et pratique*. 2 vols. 2nd edn. Paris: A. Durand and Pedone-Lauriel, 1870–2.

Camuzet, Luce. *L'indemnité de guerre en droit international*. Paris: Réveil, 1928.

Canard, Marius. 'La guerre sainte dans le monde islamique et dans le monde chrétien'. *Revue Africaine* (1936), **79**: 605–23.

Cassese, A. 'The Status of Rebels under the 1977 Geneva Protocol on Non-international Armed Conflicts'. *International and Comparative Law Quarterly* (1981), **30**: 416–39.

Castrén, Erik. *The Present Law of War and Neutrality*. Helsinki: Annals of the Finnish Academy of Sciences, 1954.

'Recognition of Insurgency'. *Indian Journal of International Law* (1965), **5**: 443–54.

Chadwick, Elizabeth. *Self-determination, Terrorism and the International Humanitarian Law of Armed Conflict*. The Hague: Martinus Nijhoff, 1996.

Chaliand, Gerard, ed. *The Art of War in World History: From Antiquity to the Nuclear Age*. Berkeley: California University Press, 1994.

Charnay, Jean-Paul. *L'Islam et la guerre: De la guerre juste à la révolution sainte*. Paris: Fayard, 1986.

Charney, Jonathan. 'The Use of Force Against Terrorism and International Law'. *American Journal of International Law* (2001), **95**: 835–9.

Chesterman, Simon. *Just War or Just Peace? Humanitarian Intervention and International Law*. Oxford: Oxford University Press, 2001.

Chevalier, Jean-Jacques. 'Sainte-Alliance et Société des Nations'. *Revue de Droit International* (1927), **1**: 9–40.

Childress, James F. 'Moral Discourse about War in the Early Church'. *Journal of Religious Ethics* (1984), **12**(1): 2–18.

Cole, Darrell. 'Thomas Aquinas on Virtuous Warfare'. *Journal of Religious Ethics* (1999), **27**: 57–80.

Committee on the Study of the Legal Problems of the United Nations. 'Should the Laws of War Apply to United Nations Enforcement Action?' *Proceedings of the American Society of International Law* (1952), **46**: 216–20.

Contamine, Philippe. *War in the Middle Ages*. Trans. Michael Jones. Oxford: Basil Blackwell, 1984.

Cox, Henry Bartholomew. *War, Foreign Affairs and Constitutional Power: 1829–1901*. Cambridge, Mass: Ballinger, 1984.

Craigie, Peter C. *The Problem of War in the Old Testament*. Grand Rapids, Mich.: Eerdmans, 1978.

Davie, Maurice R. *The Evolution of War: A Study of Its Role in Early Societies*. Port Washington, N.Y.: Kennikat Press, 1929.

Dawson, Doyne. *The Origins of Western Warfare: Militarism and Morality in the Ancient World*. Boulder, Col.: Westview, 1996.

Delbez, Louis. 'La notion juridique de la guerre (Le criterium de la guerre)'. *Revue Générale de Droit International Public* (1953), **57**: 177–209.

Delivanis, J. *La légitime défense en droit international public moderne: Le droit international face à ses limites*. Paris: Librairie Générale de Droit et de Jurisprudence, 1971.

Descamps, Baron. 'L'influence de la condamnation de la guerre sur l'évolution juridique internationale'. *Recueil des Cours* (Academy of International Law) (1930), **31**: 393–559.

Despagnet, Frantz. *Cours de droit international public*. 3rd edn. Paris: L. Larose et Forcel, 1905.

Detter Delupis, Ingrid. *The Law of War*. 2nd edn. Cambridge: Cambridge University Press, 2000.

Dinstein, Yoram. 'The Distinction between Unlawful Combatants and War Criminals'. In *International Law at a Time of Perplexity: Essays in Honour of Shabtai Rosenne*, ed. Yoram Dinstein and Mala Tabory, at 103–16. Dordrecht: Martinus Nijhoff, 1989.

War, Aggression and Self-defence. 3rd edn. Cambridge: Cambridge University Press, 2001.

Divine, Robert A. *The Illusion of Neutrality: Franklin D. Roosevelt and the Struggle over the Arms Embargo*. Chicago: Quadrangle, 1962.

Donner, Fred M. 'The Sources of Islamic Conceptions of War'. In *Just War and Jihad: Historical and Theoretical Perspectives on War and Peace in Western and Islamic Traditions*, ed. John Kelsay and James Turner Johnson, at 31–69. New York: Greenwood Press, 1991.

Duculesco, V. 'Effet de la reconnaissance de l'état de belligérance, par les tiers, y compris les organisations internationales, sur le statut juridique des conflits armés à caractère non international'. *Revue Générale de Droit International Public* (1975), **79**: 125–51.

Dupuis, Charles. 'Les théories anglaises sur le droit de la guerre en général'. *Revue Générale du Droit International Public* (1898), **5**: 35–56.

Le droit de la guerre maritime d'après les doctrines anglaises contemporaines. Paris: A. Pedone, 1899.

'La déclaration de guerre: Est-elle requise par le droit positif? Devrait-elle être?' *Revue Générale de Droit International Public* (1906), **13**: 725–35.

Le principe d'équilibre et le concert européen de la Paix de Westphalie à l'Acte d'Algésiras. Paris: Perrin, 1909.

Eagleton, Clyde. *The Attempt to Define War*. Worcester, Mass.: Carnegie Endowment for International Peace, 1933.

'The Form and Function of the Declaration of War'. *American Journal of International Law* (1938), **32**: 19–36.

Ebren, E. 'Obligation juridique de la déclaration de guerre'. *Revue Générale de Droit International Public* (1904), **11**: 133–48.

Elbe, Joachim von. 'The Evolution of the Concept of the Just War in International Law'. *American Journal of International Law* (1939), **33**: 665–88.

Esposito, John L. *Unholy War: Terror in the Name of Islam*. Oxford: Oxford University Press, 2002.

Fadl, Khaled Abou El. *Rebellion and Violence in Islamic Law*. Cambridge: Cambridge University Press, 2001.

Farer, Tom. 'Humanitarian Law and Armed Conflicts: Toward the Definition of "Internal Armed Conflict"'. *Columbia Law Review* (1971), **71**: 37–72.

Faust, August. *Das Bild des Krieges im deutschen Denken*. Stuttgart: W. Kohlhammer, 1941.

Feinberg, Nathan. *The Legality of a 'State of War' after the Cessation of Hostilities, under the Charter of the United Nations and the Covenant of the League of Nations*. Jerusalem: Magnes Press, 1961.

Feldman, Noah. 'Choices of Law, Choices of War'. *Harvard Journal of Law and Public Policy* (2002), **25**: 457–85.

Féraud-Giraud, L.-J.-D. 'De la reconnaissance de la qualité de belligérants dans les guerres civiles'. *Revue Générale de Droit International Public* (1896), **3**: 277–91.

Ferguson, John. *War and Peace in the World's Religions*. London: Sheldon Press, 1977.

Ferrill, Arther. *The Origins of War: From the Stone Age to Alexander the Great*. Boulder, Col.: Westview, 1997.

Fiore, Pasquale. *Nouveau droit international public suivant les besoins de la civilisation moderne*. Trans. Charles Antoine. 3 vols. 2nd edn. Paris: A. Durand et Pedone, 1885–6.

Firestone, Reuven. *Jihād: The Origin of Holy War in Islam*. New York: Oxford University Press, 1999.

Fitzpatrick, Joan. 'Jurisdiction of Military Commissions and the Ambiguous War on Terrorism'. *American Journal of International Law* (2002), **96**: 345–54.

Fleck, Dieter, ed. *The Handbook of Humanitarian Law in Armed Conflicts*. Oxford: Oxford University Press, 1995.

Flory, M. 'Algérie algérienne et droit international'. *Annuaire Francais de Droit International* (1960), **6**: 973–98.

Fonteyne, Jean-Pierre L. 'The Customary International Law Doctrine of Humanitarian Intervention: Its Current Validity under the UN Charter'. *California Western International Law Journal* (1974), **4**: 203–70.

Forsythe, David P. 'Legal Management of Internal War: The 1977 Protocol on Non-international Armed Conflicts'. *American Journal of International Law* (1978), **72**: 272–95.

Franck, Thomas M. 'Terrorism and the Right of Self-defense'. *American Journal of International Law* (2001), **95**: 839–43.

Recourse to Force: State Action against Threats and Armed Attacks. Cambridge: Cambridge University Press, 2002.

Funck-Brentano, Théophile, and Albert Sorel. *Précis du droit des gens.* 2nd edn. Paris: E. Plon, 1887.

Furet, Marie-Françoise, Jean-Claude Martinez and Henri Dorandeu. *La guerre et le droit.* Paris: A. Pedone, 1979.

Gardam, Judith Gail. 'Proportionality and Force in International Law'. *American Journal of International Law* (1993), **87**: 391–413.

Garlan, Yvon. *War in the Ancient World: A Social History.* Trans. Janet Lloyd. London: Chatto and Windus, 1976.

Garner, James W. 'Recognition of Belligerency'. *American Journal of International Law* (1938), **32**: 106–13.

Ginsburgs, George G. '"Wars of National Liberation" and the Modern Law of Nations: The Soviet Thesis'. *Law and Contemporary Problems* (1964), **29**: 910–42.

Gmür, Harry. *Thomas von Aquino und der Krieg.* Leipzig: B. G. Teubner, 1933.

Goldstein, Eric. *Wars and Peace Treaties: 1816 to 1991.* London: Routledge, 1992.

Good, Robert M. 'The Just War in Ancient Israel'. *Journal of Biblical Literature* (1985), **104**: 385–400.

Goodrich, Leland M. *Korea: A Study of US Policy in the United Nations.* New York: Council on Foreign Relations, 1956.

Graham-Yooll, Andrew. *Imperial Skirmishes: War and Gunboat Diplomacy in Latin America.* Oxford: Signal, 2002.

Grahl-Madsen, Atle. 'Decolonization: The Modern Version of a "Just War"'. *German Year Book of International Law* (1979), **22**: 255–73.

Gray, Christine D. 'The British Position in Regard to the Gulf Conflict'. *International and Comparative Law Quarterly* (1988), **37**: 420–8.

'The British Position with Regard to the Gulf Conflict (Iran–Iraq): Part 2'. *International and Comparative Law Quarterly* (1991), **40**: 463–73.

'Bosnia and Herzegovina: Civil War or Inter-state Conflict?' *British Year Book of International Law* (1996), **67**: 155–97.

International Law and the Use of Force. Oxford: Oxford University Press, 2001.

Green, L. C. 'The Nature of the "War" in Korea'. *International and Comparative Law Quarterly* (1951), **4**: 462–8.

The Contemporary Law of Armed Conflict. Manchester: Manchester University Press, 1993.

Greenspan, Morris. *The Modern Law of Land Warfare.* Berkeley: University of California Press, 1959.

Greenwood, Christopher. 'The Concept of War in Modern International Law'. *International and Comparative Law Quarterly* (1987), **36**: 283–306.

'Self-defence and the Conduct of International Armed Conflict.' In *International Law at a Time of Perplexity: Essays in Honour of Shabtai Rosenne*, ed. Yoram Dinstein and Mala Tabory, at 273–88. Dordrecht: Martinus Nijhoff, 1989.

Grewe, Wilhelm. *Epochs of International Law*. Trans. Michael Byers. Berlin: Walter de Gruyter, 2000.

Grob, Fritz. *The Relativity of War and Peace: A Study of Law, History and Politics*. New Haven: Yale University Press, 1949.

Guggenheim, Paul. *Traité de droit international public*. 2 vols. Geneva: Georg, 1954.

Haggenmacher, Peter. *Grotius et la doctrine de la guerre juste*. Paris: Presses universitaires de France, 1983.

Haines, K. 'Attitudes and Impediments to Pacifism in Medieval Europe'. *Journal of Medieval History* (1981), 7: 369–88.

Haleem, Harfiyah Abdel, ed. *The Crescent and the Cross: Muslim and Christian Approaches to War and Peace*. Basingstoke: Macmillan, 1998.

Hall, William Edward. *A Treatise on International Law*. 3rd edn. Oxford: Clarendon Press, 1890.

Halleck, H. W. *International Law; or, Rules Regulating the Intercourse of States in Peace and War*. New York: D. van Nostrand, 1861.

Hallett, Brien. *The Lost Art of Declaring War*. Urbana, Ill.: University of Illinois Press, 1998.

Hargrove, John Lawrence. 'The *Nicaragua* Judgment and the Future of the Law of Force and Self-defense'. *American Journal of International Law* (1987), 81: 135–43.

Harnack, Adolf von. *Militia Christi*. Philadelphia: Fortress Press, 1981.

Harris, W. V. *War and Imperialism in Republican Rome 327–70 BC*. Oxford: Clarendon Press, 1979.

Hartigan, Richard Shelly. 'Saint Augustine on War and Killing: The Problem of the Innocent'. *Journal of the History of Ideas* (1966), 27: 195–204.

Lieber's Code and the Law of War. Chicago: Precedent, 1983.

Hautefeuille, L.-B. *Des droits et des devoirs des nations neutres en temps de guerre maritime*. 3 vols. 3rd edn. Paris: Guillaumin, 1868.

Heffter, A. W. *Le droit international de l'Europe*. Trans. Jules Bergson. 3rd French edn. Berlin: E.-H. Schroeder, 1873.

Helgeland, John, Robert J. Daly and J. Patout Burns. *Christians and the Military: The Early Experience*. London: SCM Press, 1985.

Hershey, Amos S. *The International Law and Diplomacy of the Russo-Japanese War*. New York: Macmillan, 1906.

'The Calvo and Drago Doctrines'. *American Journal of International Law* (1907), 1: 26–45.

'Incursions into Mexico and the Doctrine of Hot Pursuit'. *American Journal of International Law* (1919), 13: 557–69.

Hillenbrand, Carole. *The Crusades: Islamic Perspectives*. Cambridge: Cambridge University Press, 1999.

Hogan, Albert E. *Pacific Blockade*. Oxford: Clarendon Press, 1908.

Holbraad, C. *The Concert of Europe: A Study in German and British International Theory, 1815–1914*. Harlow: Longmans, 1970.

Holland, Thomas Erskine. *The Elements of Jurisprudence*. Oxford: Clarendon Press, 1916.

Holsti, Kalevi J. *Peace and War: Armed Conflicts and International Order 1648–1989*. Cambridge: Cambridge University Press, 1991.

Hsü, Immanuel Chung-yueh. *China's Entrance into the Family of Nations: The Diplomatic Phase, 1858–1880*. Cambridge, Mass.: Harvard University Press, 1960.

Huntington, Samuel P. *The Clash of Civilizations and the Remaking of World Order*. New York: Touchstone, 1996.

Jackson, Robert H. 'Address to the Inter-American Bar Association'. *American Journal of International Law* (1941), **35**: 348–59.

James, William. 'The Moral Equivalent of War'. In *Nonviolence in America: A Documentary History*, ed. Staughton Lynd and Alice Lynd, at 65–75. Maryknoll, N.Y.: Orbis, 1995. (1st edn. 1910.)

Jessup, Philip C. 'Should International Law Recognize an Intermediate Status between Peace and War?' *American Journal of International Law* (1954), **48**: 98–103.

Jinks, David. 'September 11 and the Laws of War'. *Yale Journal of International Law* (2003), **28**: 1–49.

Jochnick, Chris, and Roger Normand. 'The Legitimation of Violence: A Critical History of the Laws of War'. *Harvard International Law Journal* (1994), **35**: 49–95.

Johnson, James Turner. *Ideology, Reason and the Limitation of War: Religious and Secular Concepts 1200–1740*. Princeton: Princeton University Press, 1975.

Just War Tradition and the Restraint of War: A Moral and Historical Inquiry. Princeton: Princeton University Press, 1981.

The Holy War in Western and Islamic Traditions. University Park, Pa.: Pennsylvania State University Press, 1997.

Johnson, James Turner, and John Kelsay, eds. *Cross, Crescent, and Sword: The Justification and Limitation of War in Western and Islamic Tradition*. New York: Greenwood Press, 1990.

Kaeuper, Richard W. *Chivalry and Violence in Medieval Europe*. Oxford: Oxford University Press, 1999.

Kaikobad, Kaiyam Homi. 'Self-defence, Enforcement Action and the Gulf Wars, 1980–88 and 1990–91'. *British Year Book of International Law* (1992), **63**: 299–366.

Keeley, Lawrence H. *War Before Civilization*. New York: Oxford University Press, 1996.

Keen, Maurice. *The Laws of War in the Late Middle Ages*. London: Routledge and Son, 1965.

Chivalry. New Haven: Yale University Press, 1984.

Kelsay, John. 'Religion, Morality, and the Governance of War: The Case of Classical Islam'. *Journal of Religious Ethics* (1990), **18**(2): 123–39.

Kelsay, John, and James Turner Johnson, eds. *Just War and Jihad: Historical and Theoretical Perspectives on War and Peace in Western and Islamic Traditions*. New York: Greenwood Press, 1991.

Kelsen, Hans. *Principles of International Law*. 2nd edn. New York: Holt, Rinehart and Winston, 1966.

Kent, James. *Commentaries on International Law*. Ed. J. T. Abdy. Cambridge, Mass.: Deighton, Bell, 1866.

Kepel, Gilles. *Jihad: The Trail of Political Islam*. Trans. Anthony F. Roberts. Cambridge, Mass.: Harvard University Press, 2002.

Khadduri, M. *War and Peace in the Law of Islam*. Baltimore: Johns Hopkins University Press, 1955.

Klafkowski, Alfons. 'Les formes de cessation de l'état de guerre en droit international (les formes classiques et non classiques)'. *Recueil des Cours* (Academy of International Law) (1976), **149**: 217–86.

Kohlberg, Etan. 'The Development of the Imami Shi'i Doctrine of Jihad'. *Zeitschrift der Deutschen Morgenlandischen Gesellschaft* (1976), **126**: 69–78.

Kotzsch, Lothar. 'Die Blockade gegen Venezuela vom Jahre 1902 als Präzedenzfall für das moderne Kriegsrecht'. *Archiv des Völkerrechts* (1955/6), **5**: 410–25.

The Concept of War in Contemporary History and International Law. Geneva: E. Droz, 1956.

Kunz, Josef L. 'Plus de lois de la guerre?' *Revue Générale de Droit International Public* (1934), **41**: 22–57.

'The Chaotic Status of the Laws of War and the Urgent Necessity for Their Revision'. *American Journal of International Law* (1951), **45**: 37–61.

'Bellum justum and bellum legale'. *American Journal of International Law* (1951), **45**: 528–34.

'La crise et les transformations du droit des gens'. *Recueil des cours* (Academy of International Law) (1956), **88**: 1–104.

'The Laws of War'. *American Journal of International Law* (1956), **50**: 313–37.

'Sanctions in International Law'. *American Journal of International Law* (1960), **54**: 324–47.

Langan, John. 'The Elements of St Augustine's Just War Theory'. *Journal of Religious Ethics* (1984), **12**(1): 19–38.

Lange, Christian L. 'Histoire de la doctrine pacifique et de son influence sur le développement du droit international'. *Recueil des Cours* (Academy of International Law) (1926), **13**: 171–426.

Langer, Robert. *Seizure of Territory: The Stimson Doctrine and Related Principles in Legal Theory and Diplomatic Practice*. Princeton: Princeton University Press, 1947.

Lauterpacht, Elihu. 'The Legal Irrelevance of the "State of War"'. *Proceedings of the American Society of International Law* (1968), **62**: 58–68.

Lauterpacht, Hersch. *Recognition in International Law*. Cambridge: Cambridge University Press, 1948.

'The Limits of the Operation of the Law of War'. *British Year Book of International Law* (1953), **30**: 206–43.

Lawrence, T. J. *The Principles of International Law*. 4th edn. London: Macmillan, 1913.

Le Fur, Louis. 'Guerre juste et juste paix'. *Revue Générale de Droit International Public* (1919), **26**: 9–73, 268–309 and 349–405.

Levenfeld, Barry. 'Israel's Counter-*Fedeyeen* Tactics in Lebanon: Self-defense and Reprisal under Modern International Law'. *Columbia Journal of Transnational Law* (1982), **21**: 1–48.

Lewis, Bernard. *Islam from the Prophet Muhammad to the Capture of Constantinople* vol. 1: *Politics and War*. New York: Harper and Row, 1974.

'Politics and War'. In *The Legacy of Islam*, ed. Joseph Schacht with C.E. Bosworth, at 156–209. 2nd edn. Oxford: Oxford University Press, 1974.

The Political Language of Islam. Chicago: University of Chicago Press, 1988.

Lewis, Mark Edward. *Sanctioned Violence in Early China*. Albany, N.Y.: State University of New York Press, 1990.

Liska, George. 'The Reagan Doctrine: Monroe and Dulles Reincarnate?' *SAIS Review* (1986), **6**: 83–98.

Løkkegaard, Frede. 'The Concepts of War and Peace in Islam'. In *War and Peace in the Middle Ages*, ed. Brian Patrick McGuire, at 263–81. Copenhagen: C. A. Reitzels, 1987.

Lorimer, James. *The Institutes of the Law of Nations: A Treatise of the Jural Relations of Separate Political Communities*. 2 vols. Edinburgh: William Blackwood and Sons, 1884.

Lotter, Friedrich. 'The Crusading Idea and the Conquest of the Region East of the Elbe'. In *Medieval Frontier Studies*, ed. Robert Bartlett and Angus Mackay, at 267–306. Oxford: Clarendon Press, 1989.

Lucas, Charles. 'La civilisation de la guerre'. *Revue de Droit International et de Législation Comparée* (1877), **9**: 114–18.

Mallison, W. Thomas, and Sally V. Mallison. 'The Juridical Status of Irregular Combatants under the International Humanitarian Law of Armed Conflict'. *Case Western Reserve Journal of International Law* (1977), **9**: 39–78.

Mansfield, Sue. *The Rites of War: An Analysis of Institutionalized Warfare*. London: Bellew, 1992.

Markus, R. A. 'Saint Augustine's Views of the "Just War"'. In *The Church and War*, ed. W. J. Sheils, at 1–13. Oxford: Blackwell, 1983.

Marston, Geoffrey. 'Armed Intervention in the 1956 Suez Canal Crisis: The Legal Advice Tendered to the British Government'. *International and Comparative Law Quarterly* (1988), **37**: 773–817.

Martens, Charles de, ed. *Causes célèbres du droit des gens.* 5 vols. 2nd edn. Leipzig: F. A. Brockhaus, 1858.

Martens, Frederic de. *Traité de droit international.* 3 vols. Paris: Maresq Ainé, 1887.

'Les hostilités sans déclaration de guerre à propos de la guerre russo-japonaise'. *Revue Générale de Droit International Public* (1904), **11**: 148–50.

Martens, G. F. von. *A Compendium of the Law of Nations, Founded on the Treaties and Custom of the Modern Nations of Europe.* Trans. William Cobbett. London: Cobbett and Morgan, 1802. 1st edn 1785.

Mas Latrie, René de. *Du droit de marque, ou droit de représailles au Moyen-Âge.* Paris: A. Franck, 1866.

Maurice, J. F. *Hostilities without Declaration of War: From 1700 to 1870.* London: HMSO, 1883.

McDougal, Myres S. 'Peace and War: Factual Continuum with Multiple Legal Consequences'. *American Journal of International Law* (1955), **49**: 63–8.

McDougal, Myres S., and Florentino Feliciano. *Law and Minimum World Public Order: The Legal Regulation of International Coercion.* New Haven: Yale University Press, 1961.

McKay, Derek, and H. M. Scott. *The Rise of the Great Powers 1648–1815.* London: Longman, 1983.

McNair, Arnold. 'The Legal Meaning of War and the Relation of War to Reprisals'. *Transactions of the Grotius Society* (1926), **11**: 29–51.

McNair, Arnold, and A. Watts. *The Legal Effects of War.* 4th edn. Cambridge: Cambridge University Press, 1966.

Meeker, Leonard C. 'The Legality of United States Participation in the Defense of Viet-Nam'. *Department of State Bulletin* (1966), **54**: 474–89.

Melzer, Yehuda. *Concepts of Just War.* Leyden: A. W. Sijthoff, 1975.

Meng, Werner. 'War'. In 4 *Encyclopedia of Public International Law*, ed. Rudolf Bernhardt, at 1334–42. Amsterdam: North-Holland, 2000.

Mérignhac, Alexandre. *Les lois et coutumes de la guerre sur terre d'après le droit international moderne et la codification de la Conférence de la Haye de 1899.* Paris: A. Chevalier-Marescq, 1903.

Mérignhac, Alexandre and E. Lémonon. *Le droit des gens et la guerre de 1914–1918.* 2 vols. Paris: Recueil Sirey, 1921.

Meron, Theodor. *Bloody Constraint: War and Chivalry in Shakespeare.* New York: Oxford University Press, 1998.

Meyrowitz, Henri. *Le principe de l'égalité des belligérants devant le droit de la guerre.* Paris: A. Pedone, 1971.

Moir, Lindsay. 'The Historical Development of the Application of Humanitarian Law in Non-international Armed Conflicts to 1949'. *International and Comparative Law Quarterly* (1998), **47**: 337–61.

The Law of Internal Armed Conflict. Cambridge: Cambridge University Press, 2002.

Moncharville, M. 'Le conflit franco-turc de 1901'. *Revue Générale de Droit International Public* (1902) **9**: 677–700.

Moore, John Bassett. *A Digest of International Law*. 8 vols. Washington, D.C.: GPO, 1906.

Moore, John Norton, ed. *Law and Civil War in the Modern World*. Baltimore: Johns Hopkins University Press, 1974.

Moorehead, Caroline. *Dunant's Dream: War, Switzerland and the History of the Red Cross*. London: HarperCollins, 1998.

Morabia, Alfred, Roger Arnaldez and Ariel Morabia. *Le gihâd dans l'Islam médiéval: Le 'combat sacré' des origines au XIIe siècle*. Paris: A. Michel, 1993.

Morley, Jeremy D. 'Approaches to the Law of Armed Conflicts'. *Canadian Year Book of International Law* (1971), **9**: 269–75.

Murphy, Thomas P., ed. *Holy War*. Columbus, Ohio: Ohio State University Press, 1976.

Nagaoka, N. 'Étude sur la guerre russo-japonaise au point de vue du droit international'. *Revue Générale de Droit International Public* (1905), **12**: 603–36.

Nasr, Kameel B. *Arab and Israeli Terrorism: The Causes and Effects of Political Violence, 1936–1993*. Jefferson, N.C.: McFarland, 1997.

Neff, Stephen C. 'The Prerogatives of Violence – In Search of the Conceptual Foundations of Belligerents' Rights'. *German Yearbook of International Law* (1995), **38**: 41–72.

'Towards a Law of Unarmed Conflict: A Proposal for a New International Law of Hostility'. *Cornell International Law Journal* (1995), **28**: 1–28.

The Rights and Duties of Neutrals: A General History. Manchester: Manchester University Press, 2000.

Niditch, Susan. *War in the Hebrew Bible: A Study in the Ethics of Violence*. New York: Oxford University Press, 1995.

Norton, Patrick M. 'Between the Ideology and the Reality: The Shadow of the Law of Neutrality'. *Harvard International Law Journal* (1976), **17**: 249–311.

Nurick, Lester, and Roger W. Barrett. 'Legality of Guerrilla Forces under the Laws of War'. *American Journal of International Law* (1946), **40**: 563–83.

Nys, Ernest. *Le droit de la guerre et les précurseurs de Grotius*. Brussels: Librairie Européenne, 1882.

Le droit international: Les principes, les théories, les faits. 3 vols. 1st edn. Brussels: A. Castaigne, 1904–6.

O'Brien, William V. *Law and Morality in Israel's War with the PLO*. New York: Routledge, 1991.

O'Connell, Robert L. *Ride of the Second Horseman: The Birth and Death of War*. New York: Oxford University Press, 1995.

Onuma, Yasuaki, ed. *A Normative Approach to War: Peace, War, and Justice in Hugo Grotius*. Oxford: Clarendon Press, 1993.

Oppenheim, L. *International Law: A Treatise*. 2 vols. 1st edn. London: Longmans, Greens, 1906.

Ostwald, Martin. 'Peace and War in Plato and Aristotle'. *Scripta Classica Israelica* (1996), **15**: 102–18.

Padelford, Norman J. *International Law and Diplomacy in the Spanish Civil Strife.* New York: Macmillan, 1939.

Palwankar, Umesh. 'Applicability of International Humanitarian Law to United Nations Peacekeeping Forces'. *International Review of the Red Cross* (1993), **294:** 227–40.

Partner, Peter. *God of Battles: Holy Wars of Christianity and Islam.* Princeton: Princeton University Press, 1997.

Perels, Ludwig.'Droit de blocus en temps de paix'. *Annuaire* (1887), **2:** 463–74.

Peters, Rudolph F. *Jihad in Medieval and Modern Islam.* Leiden: Brill, 1977.

Islam and Colonialism: The Doctrine of Jihad in Modern History. The Hague: Mouton, 1979.

'Jihad'. In 2 *Oxford Encyclopedia of the Modern Islamic World,* ed. John L. Esposito, at 369–73. New York: Oxford University Press, 1995.

Phillimore, G. G. 'What Is a State of War in Law?' *Journal of the Society of Comparative Legislation* (1902), **4** (2nd ser.): 128–34.

Phillimore, Robert. *Commentaries upon International Law.* 4 vols. 3rd edn. London: Butterworths, 1879–89.

Phillipson, Coleman. *The International Law and Customs of Ancient Greece and Rome.* 2 vols. London: Macmillan, 1911.

Termination of War and Treaties of Peace. London: T. Fisher Unwin, 1916.

Pillet, Antoine. *Le droit de la guerre.* Paris: A. Rousseau, 1893.

Les lois actuelles de la guerre. 2nd edn. Paris: A. Rousseau, 1901.

Pissard, Hippolyte. *La guerre sainte en pays chrétien: Essai sur l'origine et le développement des théories canoniques.* Paris: A. Picard, 1912.

Pistoye, A. de, and Charles Duverdy. *Traité des prises maritimes.* 2 vols. Paris: Auguste Durand, 1855.

Politis, Nicolas. 'Effets de la guerre sur les obligations internationales'. *Annuaire de l'Institut de Droit International* (1911), **24:** 200–19.

'Les représailles entre États membres de la Société des Nations'. *Revue Générale de Droit International Public* (1924), **31:** 5–16.

Pradier-Fodéré, P. *Traité de droit international public: Européen et américain.* 8 vols. Paris: G. Pedone-Lauriel, 1885–1906.

Price, Jonathan J. *Thucydides and Internal War.* Cambridge: Cambridge University Press, 2001.

Przetacznik, Frank. *The Philosophical and Legal Concept of War.* Lewiston, N.Y.: Edwin Melle Press, 1994.

Rad, Gerhard von. *Holy War in Ancient Israel.* Ed. and Trans. Marva J. Dawn. Grand Rapids, Mich.: Eerdmans, 1991.

Rattalma, Marco Frigessi di. 'Le régime de responsabilité internationale institué par le conseil d'administration de la Commission de Compensation des Nations Unies'. *Revue Générale de Droit International Public* (1997), **101:** 45–90.

Rayneval, Gérard de. *Institutions du droit de la nature et des gens.* 2 vols. Paris: Auguste Durand, 1851.

Redslob, Robert. *Histoire des grandes principes du droit des gens depuis l'antiquité jusqu'à la veille de la Grande Guerre.* Paris: Rousseau, 1923.

Regout, Robert. *La doctrine de la guerre juste de Saint Augustin à nos jours, d'après les théologiens et les canonistes catholiques.* Paris: A. Pedone, 1935.

Renault, Louis. 'La guerre et le droit des gens au vingtième siècle'. *Revue Générale de Droit International Public* (1914), **21**: 468–81.

Rich, J. W. *Declaring War in the Roman Republic in the Period of Transmarine Expansion.* Brussels: Latomus, 1976.

Rich, John, and Graham Shipley, eds. *War and Society in the Roman World.* London: Routledge, 1993.

Rifaat, Ahmed M. *International Aggression: A Study of the Legal Concept, Its Development and Definition in International Law.* Stockholm: Almqvist and Wiksell, 1979.

Rivier, Alphonse. *Principes du droit des gens.* 2 vols. Paris: A. Rousseau, 1896.

Rolin, Albéric. *Le droit moderne de la guerre: Les principes, les conventions, les usages et les abus.* 2 vols. Brussels: A. Dewit, 1920–1.

Ronzitti, Natalino. *Rescuing Nationals Abroad through Military Coercion and Intervention on Grounds of Humanity.* Dordrecht: Martinus Nijhoff, 1985.

Root, Elihu. 'The Basis of Protection to Citizens Residing Abroad'. *American Journal of International Law* (1910), **4**: 517–28.

Roucounas, Emmanuel. 'Los acuerdos de paz como documentos para la resolución de conflictos intraestatales'. *Anuario de Derecho Internacional* (1998), **14**: 561–88.

Rougier, Antoine. *Les guerres civiles et le droit des gens.* Paris: Librairie de Société du Recueil Général des Lois et des Arrêts, 1902.

'La théorie de l'intervention d'humanité'. *Revue Générale de Droit International Public* (1910), **17**: 468–526.

Rousseau, Charles. *La non-intervention en Espagne.* Paris: A. Pedone, 1939.

Le droit des conflits armés. Paris: A. Pedone, 1983.

Rumpf, Helmut. 'Der Unterschied zwischen Krieg und Frieden'. *Archiv des Völkerrechts* (1950), **2**: 40–50.

Russell, Frederick H. *The Just War in the Middle Ages.* Cambridge: Cambridge University Press, 1975.

Russell, Ruth B. *A History of the United Nations Charter: The Role of the United States, 1940–1945.* Washington, D.C.: Brookings Institution, 1958.

Rutgers, V. H. 'La mise en harmonie du Pacte de la Société des Nations avec le Pacte de Paris'. *Recueil des Cours* (Academy of International Law) (1931), **38**: 1–123.

Ruzié, David. 'Jurisprudence comparée sur la notion d'état de guerre'. *Annuaire Français de Droit International* (1959), **5**: 396–410.

Sadoul, Paul. *De la guerre civile en droit des gens: Reconnaissance de belligérance.* Nancy: P. Scheffer, 1905.

Sapiro, Miriam. 'Iraq: The Shifting Sands of Preemptive Self-defense'. *American Journal of International Law* (2003), **97**: 599–607.

Scelle, Georges. 'Règles générales du droit de la paix'. *Recueil des Cours* (Academy of International Law) (1933), **46**: 327–703.

'Théorie et pratique de la function exécutive en droit international'. *Recueil des Cours* (Academy of International Law) (1936), **55**: 87–202.

'La guerre civile espagnole et le droit des gens'. *Revue Générale de Droit International Public* (1938), **45**: 265–301.

'Quelques réflexions sur l'abolition de la compétence de la guerre'. *Revue Générale de Droit International Public* (1954), **58**: 5–22.

Schindler, Dietrich. 'State of War, Belligerency, Armed Conflict'. In *The New Humanitarian Law of Armed Conflict*, ed. Antonio Cassese, at 3–20. Naples: Editoriale Scientifica, 1979.

'United Nations Forces and International Humanitarian Law'. In *Studies and Essays on International Humanitarian Law and Red Cross Principles in Honour of Jean Pictet*, ed. Christoph Swinarski, at 521–30. Geneva: Martinus Nijhoff, 1984.

Schwarzenberger, Georg. *International Law as Applied by International Courts and Tribunals.* 4 vols. London: Stevens and Sons, 1957–86.

Scott, George Winfield. 'Hague Convention Restricting the Use of Force to Recover on Contract Claims'. *American Journal of International Law* (1908), **2**: 78–94.

Scott, James Brown. 'The American Punitive Expedition into Mexico'. *American Journal of International Law* (1916), **10**: 337–40.

Sereni, Angelo Piero. *The Italian Conception of International Law.* New York: Columbia University Press, 1943.

Shaw, Stanford J. 1 *History of the Ottoman Empire and Modern Turkey.* Cambridge: Cambridge University Press, 1976.

Shaw, Stanford J., and Ezel Kural Shaw. 2 *History of the Ottoman Empire and Modern Turkey.* Cambridge: Cambridge University Press, 1977.

Sheehan, Michael. *The Balance of Power: History and Theory.* London: Routledge, 1995.

Shipley, Graham. 'Introduction: The Limits of War'. In *War and Society in the Greek World*, ed. by John Rich and Graham Shipley, at 1–24. London: Routledge, 1993.

Shotwell, James T. *War as an Instrument of National Policy and Its Renunciation in the Pact of Paris.* London: Constable, 1929.

Sicilianos, Linos-Alexandre. *Les réactions décentralisées à l'illicité: Des contre-mesures à la légitime défense.* Paris: Librairie Générale de Droit et de Jurisprudence, 1990.

Smith, H. A. 'Some Problems of the Spanish Civil War'. *British Year Book of International Law* (1937), **18**: 17–31.

Smith, Robert S. *Warfare and Diplomacy in Pre-colonial West Africa*. London: Methuen, 1976.

Sofaer, Abraham D. *War, Foreign Affairs and Constitutional Power: The Beginnings*. Cambridge, Mass.: Ballinger, 1976.

Sorrell, Tom, ed. *The Cambridge Companion to Hobbes*. Cambridge: Cambridge University Press, 1996.

Soustelle, Jacques. *Daily Life of the Aztecs on the Eve of the Spanish Conquest*. Trans. Patrick O'Brien. Stanford: Stanford University Press, 1961.

Speier, Hans. 'Militarism in the Eighteenth Century'. *Social Research* (1936), **3**: 304–36.

Stockton, Charles H. *Outlines of International Law*. New York: Charles Scribner's Sons, 1914.

Stone, Julius. *The Legal Controls of International Conflict: A Treatise on the Dynamics of Disputes and War-law*. 2nd edn. Sydney: Maitland, 1959.

Stowell, Ellery C. 'Convention Relative to the Opening of Hostilities'. *American Journal of International Law* (1908), **2**: 50–62.

Intervention in International Law. Washington, D.C.: Byrne, 1921.

Strupp, Karl. 'L'incident de Janina entre la Grèce et l'Italie'. *Revue Générale de Droit International Public* (1924), **31**: 255–84.

Éléments du droit international public universel, européen et américain. 2nd edn. Paris: Éditions Internationales, 1930.

Stuart, Reginald C. *War and American Thought: From the Revolution to the Monroe Doctrine*. Kent, Ohio: Kent State University Press, 1982.

Sturzo, Luigi. *The International Community and the Right of War*. Trans. Barbara Barclay Carter. London: Allen and Unwin, 1929.

Tesón, Fernando R. *Humanitarian Intervention: An Inquiry into Law and Morality*. 2nd edn. Irvington-on-Hudson, N.Y.: Transnational, 1997.

Thouzellier, Christine. 'Ecclesia militans'. In 2 *Études d'histoire du droit canonique*, ed. Gabriel le Bras, at 1407–23. Paris: Sirey, 1965.

Tooke, Joan Doreen. *The Just War in Aquinas and Grotius*. London: SPCK, 1965.

Townshend, Charles, ed. *The Oxford History of Modern War*. Oxford: Oxford University Press, 2000.

Trainin, I. P. 'Questions of Guerrilla Warfare in the Law of War'. *American Journal of International Law* (1946), **40**: 534–62.

Tuck, Richard. *The Rights of War and Peace: Political Thought and the International Order from Grotius to Kant*. Oxford: Oxford University Press, 1999.

Tucker, Robert W. 'The Interpretation of War under Present International Law'. *International Law Quarterly* (1951), **4**: 11–33.

The Law of War and Neutrality at Sea. Washington, D.C.: GPO, 1957.

The Just War: A Study in Contemporary American Doctrine. Baltimore: Johns Hopkins University Press, 1960.

'Reprisals and Self-defence: The Customary Law'. *American Journal of International Law* (1972), **66**: 586–96.

Turney-High, Harry Holbert. *Primitive War: Its Practices and Concepts*. 2nd edn. Columbia, S.C:: University of South Carolina Press, 1971.

Twiss, Travers. *The Law of Nations Considered as Independent Political Communities: On the Rights and Duties of Nations in Time of War*. 2nd edn. Oxford: Clarendon Press, 1875.

Tyerman, Christopher. *The Invention of the Crusades*. Basingstoke: Macmillan, 1998.

Vagts, Alfred, and Detlev F. Vagts. 'The Balance of Power in International Law: A History of an Idea'. *American Journal of International Law* (1979), **73**: 555–80.

Vanderpol, Alfred. *Le droit de la guerre juste d'après les théologiens catholiques et les canonistes du Moyen-Âge*. Paris: A. Tralin, 1911.

   La doctrine scolastique du droit de guerre. Paris: A. Pedone, 1919.

Venezia, Jean-Claude. 'La notion de représailles en droit international public'. *Revue Générale de Droit International Public* (1960), **64**: 465–98.

Verkamp, Bernard J. 'Moral Treatment of Returning Warriors in the Early Middle Ages'. *Journal of Religious Ethics* (1988), **16**: 223–49.

Vigor, P. H. *The Soviet View of War, Peace and Neutrality*. London: Routledge and Kegan Paul, 1975.

Villey, Michel. *La croisade: Essai sur la formation d'une théorie juridique*. Paris: J. Vrin, 1942.

Visscher, Charles de. 'L'interprétation du Pacte au lendemain du différend italo-grec'. *Revue de Droit International et de Législation Comparée* (1924), **5** (3rd ser.): 213–30, 377–96.

Viswanatha, S. V. *International Law in Ancient India*. Bombay: Longmans, Green, 1925.

Waldock, C. H. M. 'The Regulation of the Use of Force by Individual States in International Law'. *Recueil des Cours* (Academy of International Law) (1952), **81**: 451–515.

Wallace-Hadrill, J. M. 'War and Peace in the Early Middle Ages'. *Transactions of the Royal Historical Society* (1975), **25** (5th ser.): 157–74.

Walters, F. P. *A History of the League of Nations*. London: Oxford University Press, 1952.

Walters, LeRoy Brandt, Jr. 'The Just War and the Crusade: Antitheses or Analogies?' *Monist* (1973), **57**: 584–94.

Walzer, Michael. *Just and Unjust Wars: A Moral Argument with Historical Illustrations*. 2nd edn. New York: Basic, 1992.

Watson, Alan. *International Law in Archaic Rome: War and Religion*. Baltimore: Johns Hopkins University Press, 1993.

Watters, William E. *An International Affair: Non-intervention in the Spanish Civil War, 1936–1939*. New York: Exposition Press, 1971.

Wedgwood, Ruth. 'Responding to Terrorism: The Strikes Against Bin Laden'. *Yale Journal of International Law* (1999), **24**: 559–76.

'Al Qaeda, Terrorism, and Military Commissions'. *American Journal of International Law* (2002), **96**: 328–37.

Wehberg, Hans. *The Outlawry of War*. Washington: Carnegie Endowment for International Peace, 1931.

Welch, David A. *Justice and the Genesis of War*. Cambridge: Cambridge University Press, 1993.

Westlake, John. 'Reprisals and War'. *Law Quarterly Review* (1909), **25**: 127–37.

International Law. 2 vols. 2nd edn. Cambridge: Cambridge University Press, 1913.

Wheaton, Henry. *Elements of International Law*. 5th edn (of 1866), by Richard Henry Dana. Oxford: Clarendon Press, 1936. (1st edn 1836.)

Wiedemann, Thomas. 'The *Fetiales*: A Reconsideration'. *Classical Quarterly* (1986), **36**: 478–90.

Wiesse, Carlos. *Le droit international appliqué aux guerres civiles*. Lausanne: B. Benda, 1898.

Wilson, George Grafton. 'Insurgency and International Maritime Law'. *American Journal of International Law* (1907), **1**: 46–60.

Wilson, Heather A. *International Law and the Use of Force by National Liberation Movements*. Oxford: Clarendon Press, 1988.

Winfield, P. H. 'The History of Intervention in International Law'. *British Year Book of International Law* (1922–3), **3**: 130–49.

'The Grounds of Intervention in International Law'. *British Year Book of International Law* (1924), **5**: 149–62.

Wodie, Francis. 'La sécession du Biafra et le droit international public'. *Revue Générale de Droit International Public* (1969), **73**: 1018–60.

Woolsey, L. H. 'Closure of Ports by the Chinese Nationalist Government'. *American Journal of International Law* (1950), **44**: 350–6.

Woolsey, Theodore Dwight. *Introduction to the Study of International Law*. 6th edn. New York: Charles Scribner's Sons, 1891.

Wright, N. A. R. 'The *Tree of Battles* of Honoré Bouvet and the Laws of War'. In *War, Literature, and Politics in the Late Middle Ages*, ed. by C. T. Allmand, at 12–31. Liverpool: Liverpool University Press, 1976.

Wright, Quincy. 'Opinion of Commission of Jurists on Janina-Corfu Affair'. *American Journal of International Law* (1924), **18**: 536–44.

'Changes in the Conception of War'. *American Journal of International Law* (1924), **18**: 755–67.

'When Does War Exist?' *American Journal of International Law* (1932), **26**: 362–8.

'The Lend-lease Bill and International Law'. *American Journal of International Law* (1941), **35**: 305–14.

'The Status of Germany and the Peace Proclamation'. *American Journal of International Law* (1952), **46**: 299–308.

'The Outlawry of War and the Law of War'. *American Journal of International Law* (1953), **47**: 365–76.

A Study of War. 2nd edn. Chicago: University of Chicago Press, 1965.

Yepes, J. M. *Philosophie du panaméricanisme et organisation de la paix: Le droit panaméricain.* Neuchâtel: Éditions de la Baconnière, 1945.

Yin, John. *The Soviet Views on the Use of Force in International Law.* Hong Kong: Asian Research Service, 1980.

Zampaglione, Gerardo. *The Idea of Peace in Antiquity.* Notre Dame, Ind.: University of Notre Dame Press, 1973.

Ziegler, Karl-Heinz. 'Friedensverträge im römischen Altertum'. *Archiv des Völkerrechts* (1989), **27**: 45–61.

Documents and records

Albrecht-Carrié, René, ed. *The Concert of Europe.* London: Macmillan, 1968.

Anonymous. *A General Collection of Treatys, Declarations of War, Manifestos, and Other Publick Papers, Relating to Peace and War.* 4 vols. 2nd edn. London: J. J. and P. Knapton, 1732.

Bartlett, Ruhl J., ed. *The Record of American Diplomacy: Documents and Readings in the History of American Foreign Relations.* 4th edn. New York: Alfred A. Knopf, 1964.

Deák, Francis, and Philip C. Jessup. *A Collection of Neutrality Laws, Regulations and Treaties of Various Countries.* Washington, D.C.: Carnegie Endowment for International Peace, 1939.

Dumont, Jean, ed. *Corps universel diplomatique du droit des gens.* 8 vols. Amsterdam: P. Brunel et al., 1726–31.

Housley, Norman, ed. and trans. *Documents on the Later Crusades, 1274–1580.* Basingstoke: Macmillan, 1996.

Institute of International Law. *Tableau général des résolutions (1873–1956).* Ed. Hans Wehberg. Basle: Éditions juridiques et sociologiques, 1957.

Tableau des résolutions adoptées (1957–1991). Paris: A. Pedone, 1992.

International Institute of Humanitarian Law. *San Remo Manual on International Law Applicable to Armed Conflicts at Sea.* Ed. Louise Doswald-Beck. Cambridge: Cambridge University Press, 1995.

Lapradelle, Albert Geouffre de, and Nicolas Politis, eds. *Recueil des arbitrages internationaux.* 3 vols. 2nd edn. Paris: Éditions internationales, 1957.

League of Nations. *League of Nations Treaty Series.* 205 vols. Geneva: League of Nations, 1920–46.

McNair, Arnold. *International Law Opinions.* 3 vols. Cambridge: Cambridge University Press, 1956.

Parry, Clive, ed. *Consolidated Treaty Series*. 231 vols. Dobbs Ferry, N.Y.: Oceana, 1969–81.

Roberts, Adam, and Richard Guelff, eds. *Documents on the Laws of War*. 3rd edn. Oxford: Oxford University Press, 2000.

Scott, James Brown, ed. *Resolutions of the Institute of International Law Dealing with the Law of Nations*. New York: Oxford University Press, 1916.

The Controversy over Neutral Rights between the United States and France 1797–1800: A Collection of American State Papers and Judicial Decisions. New York: Oxford University Press, 1917.

The Reports to the Hague Conferences of 1899 and 1907. Oxford: Clarendon Press, 1917.

The Armed Neutralities of 1780 and 1800: A Collection of Official Documents Preceded by the Views of Representative Publicists. New York: Oxford University Press, 1918.

The Proceedings of the Hague Peace Conferences. 4 vols. New York: Oxford University Press, 1920–1.

Smith, Herbert Arthur, ed. *Great Britain and the Law of Nations: A Selection of Documents Illustrating the Views of the Government in the United Kingdom upon Matters of International Law*. 2 vols. London: P. S. King and Son, 1932–5.

Tanner, Norman P., ed. *Decrees of the Ecumenical Councils*. 2 vols. London: Sheed and Ward, 1990.

United Nations. *United Nations Treaty Series*. New York: United Nations, 1947– .

TABLE OF CASES

TABLE OF TREATIES

INDEX